CULTIVATING FAITH

A 365-DAY DEVOTIONAL

J. Betteridge

New Harbor Press

RAPID CITY, SD

Copyright © 2023 by J. Betteridge

All rights reserved. No part of this publication may be reproduced, distributed or transmitted in any form or by any means, without prior written permission.

Betteridge/New Harbor Press
1601 Mt.Rushmore Rd, Ste 3288
Rapid City, SD 57701
www.newharborpress.com

Cultivating Faith / J. Betteridge. -- 1st ed.

ISBN 978-1-63357-274-4

Scripture quotations marked AMPC are taken from the Amplified® Bible, Copyright © 1954, 1958, 1962, 1964, 1965, 1987 by The Lockman Foundation
Used by permission. lockman.org

Scripture quotations marked "CSB" are taken from the Christian Standard Bible, Copyright © 2017 by Holman Bible Publishers. Used by permission. Christian Standard Bible®, and CSB® are federally registered trademarks of Holman Bible Publishers, all rights reserved.

Scripture quotations marked "MSG" are taken from The Message. Copyright 1993, 1994, 1995, 1996, 2000, 2001, 2002. Used by permission of NavPress Publishing Group.

Scripture quotations marked "NASB" are taken from the New American Standard Bible®, Copyright © 1960, 1962, 1963, 1968, 1971, 1972, 1973, 1975, 1977, 1995, 2020 by The Lockman Foundation. Used by permission. All rights reserved.

Scriptures taken from the Holy Bible, New International Version®, NIV®. Copyright © 1973, 1978, 1984, 2011 by Biblica, Inc.™ Used by permission of Zondervan. All rights reserved worldwide. www.zondervan.com The "NIV" and "New International Version" are trademarks registered in the United States Patent and Trademark Office by Biblica, Inc.™

Scripture quotations marked NKJV are taken from the New King James Version®. Copyright 1982 by Thomas Nelson, Inc. Used by permission. All rights reserved.

Scripture quotations marked (NLT) are taken from the Holy Bible, New Living Translation, copyright ©1996, 2004, 2015 by Tyndale House Foundation. Used by permission of Tyndale House Publishers, Carol Stream, Illinois 60188. All rights reserved.

Scripture quotations marked TPT are from The Passion Translation®. Copyright © 2017, 2018 by Passion & Fire Ministries, Inc. Used by permission. All rights reserved. ThePassionTranslation.com.

CREATED WITH PURPOSE

Then the of the Lord came to me, saying: "Before I formed you in the womb I knew you; Before you were born I sanctified you;" (Jeremiah 1:4–5 NKJV)

"Before I formed you in the womb I knew [and] approved of you [as my chosen instrument], and before you were born I separated and set you apart consecrating you; [and] I appointed you as a prophet to the nations." (Jeremiah 1:5 AMPC)

I truly believe that we were all created with a plan and purpose before our parents could even dream of us! My mother talked of the day I was born as a miracle, because during her pregnancy, her doctor told her that something was wrong with me and she should consider an abortion. Imagine that, going to your doctor and the doctor telling you that the life growing inside of you isn't worth saving! I know that is a reality that has happened to many women, and I am so thankful that my mother had a faith that I was going to be well and worth carrying full-term. But more than that, as a daughter of the King, I am thankful that my Abba Father had a plan for my life even before the beginning. I want you to know that no matter where you come from, or who your parents are . . . whether you felt wanted by them or not. The Father of heaven knows who you are and He created you! You are not a mistake, or a chance happening. You were perfectly formed by the One who calls you His child. Stop looking at your past and who you thought you were, as defined by your parents and your history, and start looking at who God says you are. He says you were worth dying for! (John 3:16)

Thank you, Abba Father, that You have a plan for my life, a plan perfected by You and destined to bless me. You are so good. Thank you, the promise that I am not who others say I am, but I am who You say I am—beloved and worth dying for! Help me to let go of the past and see my identity in You. I love You! Amen.

OBEDIENCE IN THE UNKNOWN

Then Mary said, "Behold the maidservant of the Lord! Let it be to me according to your word." And the angel departed from her. (Luke 1:38 NKJV)

Being a child of God requires obedience even though we cannot see the outcome. When the angel came to Mary and told her she would carry the Son of God, she was engaged to be married to a Jewish man, Joseph. Being pregnant before they were married was not part of Mary's original plans. And, in accepting God's plan for her, Mary could be cast out and be faced with ridicule and shame for her condition. Not knowing that God would send an angel to Joseph to speak on her behalf, she accepted the call of God and to carry His Son. It was a brave choice and one of incredible faith! What is God calling you to do today? Is fear of the outcome holding you back? Faith is a process, but we have to step out in obedience to see God at work in our lives. His Word says, "Truly I tell you, if you have faith like a grain of mustard seed, you can say to this mountain, 'Move from here to there,' and it will move. Nothing will be impossible for you." (Matthew 17:20)

Father God, I thank You for Your Word and examples of how others demonstrated faith and obedience at Your calling. Please forgive me for the times I have doubted or allowed fear to hold me back. Thank you for reminding me that faith and obedience grow with each opportunity You give me. I receive Your strength and grace to face the next opportunity to walk in obedience to Your voice. Amen.

FEEDING ON THE WORD

I will meditate on your precepts, and contemplate your ways. I will delight myself in Your statutes; I will not forget Your Word. (Psalm 119:15–16 NKJV)

Have you ever had a really hard day at work and at the end of the night fall exhausted into bed only to dream about work all night long? In the morning, you don't feel refreshed at all, but just as weary! This can happen when we let our thoughts consume us. We are called to take our thoughts captive (2 Corinthians 10:5) But how do we take our thoughts captive? Well, it starts with what we are filling our minds with daily. If we are only filling our minds with things of this world (work, finances, stresses, fears, selfish pleasures), then our mind will always be on these things. However, if we meditate on God's word and educate ourselves in His wisdom and knowledge, we fill our minds with things that are refreshing to our body, heart, mind, and spirit. Reading the Bible and spending time in prayer are critical elements to understanding who God is and what He wants for His children. His Word tells us what we should be thinking about, "Whatever things are true, noble, pure, lovely, things of good report, virtuous and praiseworthy things, meditate on these things" (Philippians 4:8).

Lord, help my thoughts to line up according to Your word. I thank You for the reminder that I have the mind of Christ and I can remain in You through Your very word. Holy Spirit, thank you for Your intercession on my behalf, when I have felt too weary to even know the words to pray. As You refresh and restore me, I declare that Your powerful word will quicken to me in all circumstances that I may always meditate on Your promises and blessings. Father, You are good all the time, I rejoice in Your Truth!

CHRIST-LIKE LOVE

Therefore, be imitators of God [copy Him and follow His example], as well-beloved children [imitate their father]. And walk in love, [esteeming and delighting in one another] as Christ loved us and gave Himself up for us, a slain offering and sacrifice to God [for you, so that it became] a sweet fragrance. (Ephesians 5:1–2 AMPC)

Once we give our hearts to God, we begin to see the real wrestling of flesh against spirit. For when we didn't know God, it was easy to do as we pleased all day long and selfishly seek our own purpose, plans, and desires. But, once we surrender to God and recognize the sacrifice He made with the blood of Son, Jesus Christ, we begin to realize that our hardened hearts need to change. That means loving others. Loving others who hurt you, stepped on you, forgot you, despised you, abandoned you, and, yes, even those who hate and persecute you. I am not going to act like it isn't hard, but it is exactly what Jesus did. And don't for one minute think that you don't owe Him that . . . even if Jesus died on the cross for us it was enough of a gift, but it didn't stop there. No, Jesus' crucifixion, death, and resurrection ensured us a place in heaven, but also guaranteed us every promise from the Father, including the Holy Spirit, to be joint heirs with Christ in heaven (and so much more). God's whole plan from the time sin separated us from Him has been about redeeming us to Himself. He has always offered love, mercy, and grace. How can we do any less?

Examine my heart, God, and take out any bitterness, anger, hurt, and pride, and replace it with a love like Yours. Yes, a love that can be offered even to my enemies. You, Father, sent Jesus so that not one person would have to be separated from You. I was lost once until You found me . . . help me to point toward You always. In Jesus' name. Amen.

BOLD BECAUSE OF FAITH

David said to King Saul, "Your servant has killed both lion and bear; and this uncircumcised Philistine will be like one of them, seeing he has defied the living God. The Lord, who delivered me from the paw of the lion and the bear will deliver me from the hand of this Philistine." (1 Samuel 17:36–37NKJV, summarized)

Before David became king, he was a shepherd minding his father's flock in the fields. Sheep left unattended often became prey for wild animals looking for an easy meal. David fought to protect what his father had entrusted to him. He knew that if he didn't defend the sheep against wild animals, it could place his father and family in jeopardy (as many people relied on farming and raising animals for food and provision). But I also believe that David's fierceness, his boldness, came from faith in God. He says, "The Lord who delivered me . . . will deliver me." David had already walked with God and seen God rise to provide and protect him. We can be confident that God will do the same! God promises that He will always be with us. (Joshua 1:9)

There are many battles I am facing today, Lord, but I don't have to fear because I know that You go with me. So, I proclaim a spirit of boldness right now in any circumstance and You will equip me with the mighty word to cut down every stronghold that tries to rise against Your sons and daughters! Hallelujah! Amen.

HE REJOICES OVER YOU

The Lord your God in your midst, The Mighty One, will save; He will rejoice over you with gladness, He will quiet you with His love, He will rejoice over you with singing. (Zephaniah 3:17 NKJV)

This is one of my favorite verses and such a beautiful promise from our Heavenly Father! The New American Standard Bible says it this way, "The Lord your God is in your midst, a victorious warrior. He will exalt over you with joy, He will quiet you with His love, He will rejoice over you with shouts of joy." I just love that image of our God and Father dancing and shouting for joy as we enter His presence! Maybe it's been a while since you felt loved or like you even matter. I want you to read this verse over again . . . it is about you. God adores you and you are more valuable to Him than anything else He created. He created you to have fellowship with Him. He waits for you to come to Him, and when you do . . . He's not standing there tapping His foot with arms crossed. No! He is there with a huge smile, and arms held wide! And, as you draw close, He is singing and dancing. He has been waiting to celebrate this time with you!

Father, I thank You for the Spirit-filled and breathed word You gave to us so that we could know You more! Thank You for this beautiful picture of how You love and value each one of us. I declare over all who are reading this right now that they will have knowledge of who they are in You! And that they will always feel the love of the Mighty One. You will center them and quiet them and remind them of Your great love all the days of their life! Amen.

HONORING THE LORD

But now the Lord says: 'Far be it from Me; for those who honor Me I will honor, and those who despise Me shall be lightly esteemed.' (1 Samuel 2:30 NKJV)

To honor something or someone means that it is distinct; it is highly valued or regarded. My friend, what is holding a place of honor in your life? As Christians, we have to spend time examining ourselves and keeping track of what is most important to us in our daily lives. If we don't do this, we become complacent and stagnant, and we can feel separated from God. I am not saying that we have to spend hours every day reading, studying, and praying to show honor to God. But have we made time for Him lately? Have we made time for Him today? We all have very busy lives, and lots of demands on our time—we have to choose to make our relationship with God important. We honor Him when we make time for Him. His Word promises that He will reward those who diligently seek Him. (Hebrews 11:6)

Father, forgive me for not honoring You with my time. I thank You that You are merciful and not only promises to forgive me, but also forget my mistakes. As I make time for You, I proclaim Your promise to meet all my needs. Show me and teach me to manage my time more productively. Guide me and reveal to me which commitments and activities honor You and my family. I thank You that You equip me with every good thing! Amen.

STAYING CONNECTED

Jesus said, "I am the vine, you are the branches. He who abides in Me and I in him, bears much fruit; for without Me you can do nothing." (John 15:5 NKJV)

I have never grown grapes, but I have planted other vegetables and plants. If a branch is broken off from the main stem it dies. It can no longer get the nourishment it needs from the main source of the plant, so it dries out, withers, and dies. The same thing happens to us when we isolate ourselves from God. We become dry and brittle, and we lose our ability to live the life God wants for us. Many things can cause this breaking away, but the bottom line generally is . . . we have chosen to separate ourselves from our one true source. Whether it is anger, bitterness, unforgiveness, offense, or just sin . . . we will be like a withered branch if we chose to turn away from God. The beautiful thing is that it is never too late to call out to your Father for forgiveness and come home to His loving arms. He is in the business of restoring life!

Lord God, I thank You for the reminder that I need to stay attached to You in order to grow and thrive. You promise life-sustaining bread and water that I may never hunger or thirst! Forgive me for the things I allow to take root and become a barrier to drawing closer to You. I cast out all things that are not of You and surrender once again to Your will. Thank you for Your never-failing love and mercy. May You use me to touch the hearts of many that You may be glorified. In Jesus' name. Amen.

MY SOUL WILL SING

Sing to the Lord a new song; sing to the Lord, all the earth. (Psalm 96:1 NASB)

I'm down on my knees again;
for You Lord are my faithful friend.
Even though the darkness seems so long; I lift my
voice and sing songs of praise to You.
For You cover me; Your favor surrounds me. You are my shield.

Yours are the arms I run into.
Oh God, Yours are the arms I run into.

Your Word fills me; my dry bones are made new.
Father Your love has always held me;
I surrender all to You.
For You cover me; Your favor surrounds me. You are my shield.

Yours are the arms I run into.
Oh God, Yours are the arms I run into.

Oh Holy Spirit, bring Your fire again. I cry out for more of You.
For You cover me; Your favor surrounds me. You are my shield.
Deeper, deeper. Yes deeper, I fall in love with You. (J. Betteridge)

THE FAMILY

His intention was the perfecting and the full equipping of the saints (His consecrated people), [that they should do] the work of ministering toward the building up Christ's body (the church), [that is might develop] until we all attain oneness in the faith and in comprehension of the [full and accurate] knowledge of the Son of God, (Ephesians 4:12–13 AMPC, partial)

Brothers and sisters, we are all called as children under the sovereignty of our God to be unified. This is not from our own will, but in surrender to Him and through the love of Christ that flows from us. Scripture says that if we do not love one another then we cannot love God (1 John 4:20).

We are all members of this family. We each bring something special to the table. Just like in a potluck where each dish serves to feed the whole gathering, we each have something (a gift, a service) that we need to be willing to share with one another. We are meant to be different from one another, just as each part of the body is meant to be different yet operate together. We have to stop looking at one another, making comparisons. That breeds envy, jealousies, and strife. Why are we looking at each other when our eyes should be fixed on Christ? (Hebrews 12:2). Instead, as God places good things in our lives and grows our faith, we are called to turn outward towards others. There is strength in our unity. There is growth of the body as a whole, when we all do our part.

Father, thank you for the way You have gifted me, and that it is different from many of my sisters and brothers in Christ. Thank you that every part of our physical body works together and demonstrates how You designed Your Church to do the same. We may be different in many ways but we are unified in our salvation and our love of Christ. Forgive me for any comparisons I have made and keep my eyes firmly fixed on You. That my heart may become more like Jesus who demonstrated the greatest sacrifice. Amen.

GIVING THANKS CHANGES THINGS

In everything give thanks; for this the will of God in Christ Jesus for you. (1 Thessalonians 5:18 NKJV)

This is such a fabulous scripture and it clearly states that it is the desire of God that we give thanks in everything. According to the Merriam–Webster Dictionary, everything means "all that exists." But I will admit, there have been times in my life where I did not feel like giving thanks. Even in this year, there have been specific challenges that didn't feel good and were hard. I understand why this verse can make people shake their heads and say, "How can I be thankful when this hurts so much?"

God wants us to change our perspective and not become overwhelmed by the circumstances. That is what giving thanks allows us to do. It allows us to look at the wonder and glory of God who can do great things. And it allows us to see that whatever we are going through does not have to defeat us. When I learned to be obedient to this scripture, the situation changed because my heart has changed. I am strengthened because, during my thanksgiving and praise, the Lord sends His Holy Spirit to meet with me. He builds my spirit up during this time of communion with Him. Next time you see that trial, challenge, or storm coming your way, thank God, not necessarily for the situation, but that He will be with you every step of the journey!

Thank you, Father, for the reminder that You promise to never leave me or forsake me. You also told me that I would have trouble in this world, but that You have already overcome it. I am so thankful that I have the one true source to rely on. Help me to always see things to give thanks and praise about, change my perspective and change my heart. Amen.

FAITHFUL FRIENDSHIPS

Two are better than one, because they have good reward for their toil. For if they fall, one will lift up his fellow. But woe to him who is alone when he falls and has not another to lift him up! Again, if two lie together, they keep warm, but how can one keep warm alone? And though a man might prevail against one who is alone, two will withstand him—a threefold cord is not quickly broken. (Ecclesiastes 4:9–12 ESV)

There are many times in my life where I have failed and fallen flat on my face. It isn't our successes that God uses to teach and enrich our lives, it is the bittersweet circumstances. In those times, I have learned to run to the one who is my most faithful friend. And my Father God always lifts me up! But this scripture also reminds me of how beautiful our friendships with one another can be and how valuable they are. There are many times when at just the right moment a friend would reach out to me with an encouraging word or just let me know that they were thinking of me . . . and it was right on time!

I have also had times of life, where friendships with others have diminished, changed, or were just lacking. Although God is always my ultimate source, He created us to be a family and be together. So, when those times were thin, no matter the reason—those friendships are missed.

But God makes all things new again! (Revelations 21:5) And He has a wonderful way of bringing forth all things in due time!

Oh Lord! Thank you for the way You created us to connect with one another so that on the journey in this world we do not have to feel alone. I declare that those who are waiting on the birth of new friendships will draw close to you in the waiting. And when those friendships are manifested that they will bring strength to each member and glory to Your name! Amen.

HE CAN BRING FORTH LIFE FROM DEATH

And He said to me, "Prophesy to these bones and say to them, 'O dry bones hear the word of the Lord! Thus says the Lord God to these bones: "Surely I will cause breath to enter into you, and you shall live. I will put sinews on you and bring flesh upon you, cover you with skin and put breath in you; and you shall live. Then you shall know that I am the Lord.'" (Ezekiel 37:4–6 NKJV)

This scripture reminds me of how God can take something that is dead, resurrect it, and create life. He chose to have Ezekiel prophesy to a valley full of dry bones. Think about that . . . the bones were barren of all flesh and anything resembling life was gone from them. But once God's Word was spoken over them, they lived and, according to the Scripture, became a vast army (Ezekiel 37:10). That is why it is so important that we stay connected to God through His Word because it is "spirit and life" (John 6:63). His Word can make all things new. God's Word will always change things. It may not be immediate, and oftentimes it isn't in the way I have planned. But it is always God's purpose to make things better for us.

I experienced this firsthand this year, when our newly purchased home was damaged in a fire. Yes, there was loss, and damage, but we will have all things restored to us . . . and an opportunity to make improvements in a forty-two-year-old home that would have taken us years of planning and remodeling to attain. It wasn't what I would have imagined this past year to look like, but God saw a way to make this situation into one that demonstrates His glory and provision.

Father, thank you that You are always able to resurrect what seems lost, that even dry bones can live again. Thank you for the reminder that Your Word never fails and You are making all things new. Help me to always see how Your hand is working to restore and bless Your children. Amen.

WAKE UP

And do this, understanding the present time: the hour has already come for you to wake up from your slumber, because our salvation is nearer to us than when we first believed. (Romans 13:11 NIV)

This is the time I hear the voice of our God saying AWAKE AND ARISE! "My children the time has come for my church to be ready. The hour has come. I have been working and moving in this season. I have been sending signs and wonders, just as I declared in my word. Wipe the sleep from your eyes. See that I am sifting the wheat on the threshing floor. I need my church ready for this new season of harvest. It is time to put aside earthly distractions and look to me. Seek my face, seek the knowledge and equipping that is required in this time. Look towards my kingdom and all I will do. I always accomplish my purpose. Not one word I have spoken has returned void. It is time for you to look to My Word as the Bread of Life. Fill yourselves up with the truth. Stop convincing yourselves that the words written in My book are not for this present time. I have breathed life into every word of it. My will, My heart, My glory. Every part of it will come to be. Awake and arise. Awake and arise. I am calling My sons and daughters to the royal priesthood that I have prepared for them to operate in with the power and authority given through Christ. Listen for the Holy Spirit. Do not silence My Spirit within you, but allow it access to every area of your heart, that you may be emptied of yourselves and filled with the gifts I have imparted."

CALLED AS A PROPHET

And you, my child, will be called a prophet of the most high; for you will go on before the Lord to prepare the way for Him, to give his people the knowledge of salvation through the forgiveness of their sins. (Luke 1:76–77 NIV)

I love how God's Word is always fresh and new. I know I have read this scripture during the Christmas season before, but this morning the Lord opened my eyes to reveal new knowledge about this verse! What God quickened to my heart was not the traditional idea of Christ as our Savior (although that is true and important), but the part in the scripture that speaks about being called a prophet. True, this scripture is in reference to John the Baptist, but it is also a reminder that we as God's children are also called to show others who Christ is! It's called the Great Commission! In Matthew 28:16–20, Jesus tells His disciples that they are to go into all the world to preach the good news that Christ has come to set everyone free from their sins and that they no longer have to be separated from God. That calling is placed on every one of us who believes in the resurrection power and salvation of Jesus Christ. In this Christmas season, this scripture gives a whole new meaning to the question: "Are you ready for Christmas?" Today, after reading this scripture, it means: "Are you ready to share your knowledge of Jesus Christ?"

He is Immanuel! God with us!

UNDERSTANDING THE GIFT

Bless the Lord, O my soul, and forget not all His benefits: Who forgives all your iniquities, who heals all your diseases, who redeems your life from destruction, who crowns you with loving kindness and tender mercies . . . . (Psalm 103:2–4 NKJV)

I believe in the redeeming power of Jesus Christ. I believe it, because I have been blessed to have received His mercy and forgiveness. God helped restore things to me that I managed to destroy. You see, even though I have been a Christian since I gave my heart to Christ when I turned nineteen, I struggled with my walk of faith for many years. Although I went through years of Sunday school and through catechism, I really struggled with understanding that Christ's death and resurrection had released me from trying to live up to the Law . . . following rules to be good enough for God's love. I didn't understand or really spend time in the Word of God. I didn't recognize that the Bible was more than just stories, but the actual living Word of God. That it was truly a description of who God was and how to have the knowledge needed to help us walk each day in this life. So, for many years, I tried to control everything and I often failed. My lack of true surrender, and trying to work everything out my way, made it impossible for God to work in my life. Multiple times I ended up with my heart hurting and just not knowing how to fix the mess I had created. Through each disaster I created, I had to learn to release things into the hands of a Heavenly Father. It was then that I saw Him take my broken pieces and make something even more beautiful out of it. I had a broken life, but God restored it to me and then blessed it with abundant love. I had a heart full of hurt and bitterness, but God removed it and gave me a heart full of peace, joy, and love.

I think it is important to remember that as Christians, we pick up our cross daily and walk with God. It is a daily choice and, oftentimes, we will make mistakes. We will mess it up, because our flesh is always struggling with our spirit. But, each time we remember to surrender our lives to God, we will be able to grow in faith as we watch Him do miraculous things. He is the redeemer! There is nothing too broken that He cannot restore it. Just don't put your plans in the way. God never does anything quite the way we expect it. He does not think the way we think! (Isaiah 55:8–9)

ACTIVE WHILE STILL

Be still and know that I am God; I will be exalted among the nations, I will be exalted in the earth! (Psalm 46:10 NKJV)

The Passion Translation says it like this: "Surrender your anxiety! Be silent and stop your striving and you will see that I am God. I am the God above all the nations, and I will be exalted throughout the whole earth."

Lately, I am realizing, more and more, how my husband and I are awful at being still. First, we both enjoy projects and creating things. Second, we are overseeing the reconstruction of our house after a fire earlier this year. So often, our "downtime" has involved being there to do odd jobs, keep up with yard work, or running around to make the many choices needed about how it's going back together! Recently, I awoke in the middle of the night and couldn't go back to sleep because my mind started planning all the things I would do on an unexpected day off from work. In the morning, as I began to putter around (as my husband and I fondly call it), I heard the Spirit say "Be still." I would like to say I listened to that voice the first time I heard it but, unfortunately, I had to hear it twice before I just stopped what I was doing and listened to what the Lord wanted to say to me: "How can you refill if you cannot be still? If you are always planning, how can you know My plans for you? If you are always talking, how can you be listening to what I need you to know? I need you to rest in My presence. YOU need to find rest in my presence. The Sabbath is not just a day, but a state of your spirit, united with Me, surrendered to

Me, refilled by Me, and strengthened and restored by Me. Yes, I have called you to labor with Me, but you must make sure that you stay in balance with Me, that My work may be completed."

Maybe you, too, struggle with being still and finding rest. Listen for our Heavenly Father calling you to come sit and be still in His presence. He always has something to share during time spent with His children. Get into His presence and just breathe!

GROW YOUR FAITH

Their pleasure and passion is remaining true to the Word of "I Am," meditating day and night in his true revelation of light. (Psalm 1:2 TPT)

We are each responsible for the growing of our own faith in the Lord. The Bible specifically tells us to test the spirits (1 John 4:1 NKJV). We shouldn't rely on our pastors or spiritual leaders for all our spiritual growth. We are to look to God as our ultimate source of knowledge. His word is life and, when we read it, we become equipped for God's purpose in this life. It is great to supplement our faith through those who have studied God's Word, but we are responsible for always going back to the Word of God and making sure what we hear lines up with what is written in the Bible. People are not and never will be God. They will make mistakes, and mess things up, and get it wrong sometimes. God is not man and He cannot lie (Numbers 23:19). We can always look to God for truth and wisdom. So, if you haven't been making time to spend in God's Word, now is a great time to start! My pastor has said that the Bible is full of "love letters" that God has written to His sons and daughters. I love that thought and image! So, go pick up the most beautiful letter of love ever written to you and start learning all about our amazing and glorious God!

Oh Abba! Thank you for Your Word. It is so full of wisdom and knowledge. It is full of the fierce love You have for Your children. Your heart is that every single person on earth would know You. I declare that those who enter Your Word every day would have revelation knowledge of You. That they would be filled to overflowing with the love You have for them as displayed in the sacrifice of Your one and only son Jesus Christ. May the power of the Holy Spirit fill them, that they would overflow with Your rivers of Living Water. Your Word alone, is truth, is life, and is a glorious letter of love that fills my heart with hope, joy, peace, and strength. May it be revealed to all who search for You in Your word! Amen.

HE KNOWS YOUR SORROWS

You keep track of all my sorrows. You have collected all my tears in your bottle. You have recorded each one in your book. (Psalm 56:8 NLT)

Maybe this season has not been what you expected it to be. Your feel worn and your heart is hurting and you have cried more than you have laughed or felt joy. First, know that your Heavenly Father has His arms open wide and is waiting to provide the comfort as only He can in tough times and seasons. He has not turned His face away from you for even a second. His love is fierce and steadfast. He does not waver. But we have an enemy that seeks to separate us and to convince us that God isn't who He says He is. But that is a lie! The Bible actually calls the devil the "father of lies." King David was well-acquainted with pain, sorrow, and loss. Yet, in this song or poem that he wrote to God, David said, "You have recorded each one in your book." King David, who was overlooked by his own father (1 Samuel 16:11), had his father-in-law pursuing him to kill him (1 Samuel 19:11). One of the things that I believe helped David stay close to God in all seasons was his worship. I encourage you to keep pressing in close to your Heavenly Father. Lift up His name in praise and thanksgiving. Maybe you are not exactly where you want to be, but every day your past is further behind you! God has your future in His hands and it is secure. Lift up your eyes. He is beholding your beauty! He will not let one tear touch the ground! He will wipe them all away and we have a promised future of no more sorrow or pain (Revelations 21:4). Call on the name of Jesus in your sorrow and heartbreak. He will rescue you and help heal and restore you!

Father, I pray for whoever is reading this right now and has been experiencing a season of pain, heartbreak, or sorrow. Lord, I declare that their joy will be renewed and their strength will be renewed. I thank You that every promise for Your sons and daughters is but Yes and Amen! I declare that the Holy Spirit is interceding for them when all they have is tears to cry and cannot utter a single word. Thank you for Your Spirit that operates in and through us. It always points us towards the truth. May the power of Your Word permeate their hearts, minds, and spirits and provide the peace that they need in each and every moment. I thank You that You are working all things for their good and they will see Your Word alive and active in their situation. Father, You are good and Your glory will be revealed as You move. Amen!

PERFECT LOVE

Such love has no fear, because perfect love expels all fear. If we are afraid, it is for fear of punishment, and this shows that we have not fully experienced his perfect love. (1 John 4:18 NLT)

There is no more perfect love than that of our Heavenly Father. Some people have a concept of God that makes Him the perpetrator of every bad thing that happens on this earth. In reality, God is patient and kind. He loves us so much that He let His one and only begotten Son suffer and be crucified for all of our sins. God's plan has always been to have all of His sons and daughters reconciled to Him. Fear entered into the world only when Adam and Eve believed the lies of Satan and were disobedient to God in the Garden of Eden (Genesis 3:10). Each of us is both flesh and spirit. Once we have accepted Christ as our Savior, our spirit becomes the indwelling place for the Holy Spirit (the essence of God). Then, our flesh and spirit become in conflict with one another. Our flesh is of this world and wants to react based on what is seen, felt, and heard in nature. Our spirit recognizes the supernatural. It recognizes the power and authority of our mighty God. We begin to recognize His all-consuming love, grace, and mercy. Our faith grows and our fear diminishes. This takes action on our part, because we have to seek to find out who God really is and the only way to really do that is to look at Jesus. Jesus even says, "I and my Father are one." (John 10:30 KJV)

Jesus came so that we may overcome fear and instead have access to his perfect peace! (John 14:27)

Father, I thank You for Your tender love and mercy. I praise You for the love You have for every man, woman, and child that has been created. I declare over those who are battling with fear that, as they seek You, Your peace will flood their hearts and minds and the chains of fear will fall from them. I thank You that Christ is in us and we can access His power and authority through the Holy Spirit. May we all become more deeply aware of our victory in every situation because there is no battle where You have not already gone before us to ensure our victory. I give You all glory and honor. Amen.

CHANGING US

Taste and see that the Lord is good: blessed is the man that trusts in him. (Psalm 34:8 NKJV)

Spending time with God has the power to change things. What in your life are you looking to have changed? Stronger relationships? Better marriage? Less stress and worry? Peace for your family? Healing for your body?

God is able to do more than we could imagine or think. He cares about moving your obstacles or helping you in the details. Most of all, spending time with God has the power to change us. Change the way we think. Change our hearts. Sometimes, the change in us is the first step we need to take.

Father, I thank You for the reminder that time with You is well-spent. It changes me, and helps equip me for anything I encounter in this life. I love how You have changed me from the inside, Lord. You have changed my thinking and helped me to see that I have joy, peace, and strength because of Your indwelling. Help me keep my eyes on You, and always see how good You truly are! Amen.

THE POWER AND GLORY OF THE WORD

In the beginning was the word (Logos), and the word was with God and the word was God. He was with God in the beginning. Through Him, all things were made; without Him, nothing was made that has been made. In Him was life and that life was the light of all mankind . . . And the word became flesh, and dwelt among us, and we beheld his glory. (John 1:1–3, 14 NIV)

The power of the word that God wielded in the beginning, to create the heavens and the earth, is the same word and power that Jesus Christ used during His time on earth. Christ and God have always been one. Through Christ's death and resurrection, we as believers have access to that same power with the Word of God. We are told it is a weapon (Hebrews 4:12). We can change the world by what we say. We can speak love or hate. The power of life and death is in the tongue (Proverbs 18:21). If we want to have peace on earth, as Christians we have to start using our words to align with God's. If you have any doubt about what God would say, look at Jesus. His own words said, "I came so that they may have life and have it abundantly" (John 10:10). We cannot sit back as spectators and hope that things will change for the better. We have to activate a better world by praying and speaking the promises of God over ourselves, over our families, and over every lost soul. Jesus died to save all of them. Every single one.

Lord, help me to be conscious of my words. Let my heart, mind, and tongue be in unity and speak out life over this country, this people, and this world. Lord, may every heart be softened and clearly hear the call of Your voice. That they may know Your love and see all You have for them is meant for their good. Let people recognize that there is something more than this world and it is truly their home when they accept Jesus as their Savior. May Your Word resonate in their hearts and be what is on their lips. Amen.

SEEING HIS GLORY

When I consider your heavens, the work of your fingers, the moon and the stars, which you have set in place, what is mankind that you are mindful of them, human beings that you care for them? (Psalm 8:3–4 NIV)

When was the last time you have gone out on a warm summer night, away from all the house lights, and looked up at the sky? Whenever I look at the vast array of stars and see how they move across the sky, I am truly in awe of the majesty of God. But it's not just the stars that amaze me. It's the ocean, the mountains, the way the seasons change. All of it speaks of how wonderful and creative our Heavenly Father really is! There are animals that are uniquely designed to help each other survive. Other creatures are created to clean up the planet. How can we question that God is real? The way things work in harmony with one another clearly points to the relationship that we were designed for . . . God desires to have a relationship with us. We were created to KNOW HIM.

FIND YOUR REST

Have you not known? Have you not heard? The everlasting God the Lord, the Creator of the ends of the earth, neither faints nor is weary. His understanding is unsearchable. He gives power to the weak, and to those who have no might He increases strength. (Isaiah 40:28–29 NKJV)

There are many days when I just have felt tired even before beginning the day. Oftentimes, this has occurred during a season where there have been trials or difficulties. Usually, there are multiple areas of challenges going on at once . . . anyone else ever been there? Can I get an amen?

But if I stop and examine why I feel so exhausted, it is usually because I am striving to fix everything on my own. I don't stop and go to God for help, I just put my head down, and concentrate on taking step after step . . . all against the fierce force of the wind trying to keep me in place. I get things out of order, because I try to handle everything with my own strength. Often, during these times, I spend less time in the Word of God, because I am placing all my energy into finding external solutions to my problems.

Don't get me wrong, I believe God wants us to understand the power and authority we have within us and to be equipped for the battles of life. However, He doesn't want us to ever go into any battle without Him. He is our ultimate source for victory. If we don't stay connected to Him within the difficulties, then we are going to get weary, because we are operating within our own power and not the strength and might of our Father.

Father, keep me connected to You. I thank You that You are my source of strength and power when battles come my way. Thank you for the wisdom you give when I stay close to You. Help me return to You quickly when I get out of step with You and try to solve problems on my own. You are a good Father. Thank you for always picking me back up and restoring my strength. Amen.

LISTEN TO HIS VOICE

You have seen many things, but you have paid no attention. Your ears are open, but you have heard nothing. (Isaiah 42:20 NIV)

In these days, more than ever, I feel that God is using things to awaken us to the spiritual battle that is taking place. We as believers have a responsibility to watch for what the Holy Spirit is trying to show us. There is a true battle going on between the darkness and the light. And we cannot be complacent in shining the light and love of Jesus Christ in this world. There are lives at stake. If we believe in heaven and eternity with the Father, then we cannot be ignorant of the fact that there could be an eternity without Him for those who are lost. The Bible talks about signs in the earth (Matthew 24:6–14), including earthquakes, war, and famine. I don't believe that God causes these things, but I do believe He will attempt to reveal Himself in these times and draw hearts close to Him. We are called to be His sons and daughters and demonstrate our faith, hope, and love in the One Who Is Greater than all things of this world.

If you have been focusing more on the world than on your relationship with God, there is no better time to draw close. He is always waiting to have fellowship with you. It is how we stay equipped for spiritual battles (Jude 1:20).

Heavenly Father, help us to have eyes that truly see and ears that hear through the leading of the Holy Spirit. May the love and compassion that You poured over us, fill us and flow out of us into the world, dispelling the darkness with the light and power of Your love. It is only through You, God, that we have victory over darkness, sin, and anything that would try to become a barrier to our walk with You. I thank You for the salvation found only through Jesus Christ, and give You praise for the mercy and grace You so freely offer to all who seek You. You are an amazing Father. May everyone who calls You Father be filled again with a revitalizing fire and compassion for those who are lost, hurting, and scared. May we as Your children be fierce and bold, declaring Your love and the truth of all the promises found in Christ Jesus. Amen.

SERVE GOD FIRST

Am I now trying to win the approval of human beings, or of God? Or am I trying to please people? If I were still trying to please people, I would not be a servant of Christ. (Galatians 1:10 NIV)

This is so difficult for me in so many ways, because I abhor conflict and have always been a people pleaser. But, if I lay aside doing what is right, to keep people happy, then I am choosing people over God. The Bible clearly indicates that we cannot please the world and God at the same time (Matthew 6:24 NLT). We as Christians are called to a higher standard. We have an obligation to examine our actions and choices, and ensure that they align with God's ways. Our ways will always lead to serving ourselves or others, if we do not purposefully choose to look to God.

In his letter to the church in Galatia, Paul wants to remind them that it is important to serve God first. Yes, we are called to love others and serve them, but that does not mean that we can please all people. Oftentimes, we focus on the works rather than on pursuing the purpose and plan of God. Our first calling is to stay rooted and grounded in a right relationship with Him. Everything else flows out of that foundation.

Thank you, Lord, for the reminder that I cannot keep everyone in my life or those I meet happy. Thank you for showing me that I am not their source or their provider, but that they need to rely on You for all they need. Help me to find the balance between being called to love others and becoming a people pleaser. My heart is always to point others to You and the joy, peace, and strength that You alone can give. You alone are the way, the truth, and the life. I praise You! Amen and amen.

HIS WORDS ARE PURE

The words of the Lord are pure words, like silver refined in a furnace on the ground, purified seven times. You, O Lord, will keep them: you will guard us from this generation forever. (Psalm 12:6–7 ESV)

What are you believing in? Are you looking around at your present circumstances and believe that you have to accept what is happening in your life? It is time to look to the Heavenly Father and to speak out His promises over yourselves, your families, and this world. If you want unity and peace, then we must begin to thank God for restoring it to us. He is exceedingly and abundantly able to do all that we ask and even more! He wants to bless us simply because He loves us!

Abba, thank you for your steadfast love and kindness. We declare Your light and peace over this nation and throughout the world. Lord, we know that we have the victory because Christ already defeated death and the power of sin. We proclaim that Your kingdom reigns on earth as it is in heaven. That unity, love, and joy will flow from Your Church and be a drawing unto all that long to fill the emptiness as only You can! Lord, You said that there would be a harvest and we believe it! We are giving shouts of praise and thanks for the many lives that will be saved! In Jesus' name!

HE BRINGS LIGHT

No this is the message we have heard from Him and declare to you: God is light and there is absolutely no darkness in Him. (1 John 1:5 NLT)

I keep my eyes firmly fixed on God, my source of light and hope! He is still working all things for good for those who love Him (Romans 8:28). When I feel my peace slipping away (and there are times that we all do), I need to check on where my focus is . . . .

There are many reasons we can lose our focus. Most of us feel pulled in many directions. We feel the pull from family, work, social obligations . . . and the list can go on and on. There is one relationship that we need to make a priority, because it is the primary source of light and hope for our soul. It is the anchor in the day-to-day and in the storms. God is essential to our having peace and joy in an ever-changing world. Without Him, darkness will try to overcome and overwhelm you. Seek the One who is the source of light and life and you will find wisdom, strength, joy, and peace. You will be able to stand. Your faith will grow. You will not lose your way in the darkness, because you will carry the light within you.

OUR HOPE

God wanted to make known among the Gentiles the glorious wealth of the mystery which is Christ in you, the hope of glory. (Colossians 1:27 CSB)

I am not going to try to tell you that life isn't hard sometimes. It really is . . . full of both joy and sorrow. We love and we lose. We have successes and we have failures. We are borne and one day we each will die. But that is not the end of the story if you have asked Jesus into your heart! You have the hope of eternal glory, being part of God's family. You have the promise of heaven. Where we will know only love, joy, and peace. Not only does God offer all those things for us when we die and enter eternity, but God wants us to have all that He has promised for us as we walk this earth. We just have to hold onto our faith and trust that, even in the tough times, even in the waiting . . . He is holding onto us. He is always good. His plan is to bless us and prosper us.

Thank you, Lord, for the promise of heaven, where every tear will be wiped away. But Father, thank you for Your promises of strength, joy, and peace here on earth. You just want us to trust in Your timing. Thank you that Your peace surpasses all understanding. May our faith continue to grow in You as we see Your hand at work in all circumstances. Amen.

BOLDNESS IN EVERYDAY FAITH

The wicked flee when no one pursues, but the righteous are bold as a lion. (Proverbs 28:1 ESV)

I will be honest; this was a rough week for me. I got knocked down. I had sought the Lord, prepared with prayer, but at the end of the day, things just didn't turn out the way I thought it would. It seemed like I lost the battle I was facing and it really hurt. I cried, and I shared my pain with my husband, and let the comfort of his arms soothe my heart. Later that evening, as we prayed together, I praised the Lord. Sister and brother, no matter what it looks like here on earth , God is still at work, and He is still on the throne. If His Word says He is working all things for our good (Romans 8:28 NIV), then that is exactly what He is doing. Our responsibility is to keep walking with Him in faith.

At church, my pastor, preached on walking in faith. It's not a perfect thing, but it is a steady move forward. He referenced the faith of great saints like Daniel and David. Their faith directed them even in the midst of battle, and even though it looked like they couldn't win. During the service, I felt the Holy Spirit impress upon me that in a battle soldiers will get knocked down. The battle isn't over just because we fall . . . .

Arise and fight! Arise and fight! Arise and fight! You are equipped with the power and authority granted through Jesus Christ. Those aren't just words, but a powerful truth. I will enter this next week reminded that I can be confident of God's Word and that, no matter what it looks like, the battle belongs to God. I definitely want to be in the army of the Living God . . . it leads to victory and glory!

CHILDREN OF GOD

But now, O Jacob, listen to the Lord who created you. O Israel, the one who formed you says, "Do not be afraid, for I have ransomed you. I have called you by name; you are mine." (Isaiah 43:1 NLT)

Repeat after me: I am who the Lord says I am! I am redeemed, I am healed, I am restored, I am blessed, I am highly favored. He who created me made me to be part of His royal priesthood. I am anointed and appointed. I am strong; I am a warrior in the mighty army of the Living God. I am light; I am the beloved child of God. He calls me His precious child. He says I am worth dying for! He who has ransomed me says that I will never be taken from His hand!

I don't know what is happening in your life this very day, but our Heavenly Father sees and knows all things. He wants you to remember who you are! He wants you to remember you are never alone! All you need to do is call on His name. If that is the only thing you have strength to say, it's okay! The name of Jesus is powerful and mighty. Not one other thing that has been named can stand against it. But you will find yourself able to stand when you call on the Lord; He will strengthen you!

A VISIBLE FATHER

"I publicly proclaim bold promises. I do not whisper obscurities in some dark corner. I would not have told the people of Israel to seek me if I could not be found. I, the Lord, speak only what is true and declare only what is right." (Isaiah 45:19 NLT)

You are going to have many people trying to speak into your life. They will try to guide and direct you. Sometimes, it is with the best intentions; and, sometimes, it won't be for your benefit, but for their own personal gain. You have to be connected to the ONE. God always speaks the truth and will not guide you to things that are not for you benefit. If you are feeling lost and not sure what to do next, I encourage you to stop and talk to God about it. Ask Him for help from the Holy Spirit. God is not hiding from you, He is waiting for you to call out to Him, to trust Him, and have a daily walk with Him.

Father God, I thank You that you want to be visible, present, and active in the lives of Your children. Teach us to listen for Your voice. You promised to be our Good Shepherd. I love that it doesn't have to be complicated. I can just bring everything to You and talk to You about it. You already know everything that is happening in my life, but something changes inside me when I talk with You. I become equipped with the promise of Your peace, strength, and wisdom. You are such a good Father. Help all my brothers and sisters in Christ to hear Your voice and recognize Your promises in their lives! Amen.

A NEW THING

"For I am about to do something new. See, I have already begun! Do you not see it? I will make a pathway through the wilderness. I will create rivers in the dry wasteland." (Isaiah 43:18 NLT)

Have you ever been waiting for God to do or change something, but you are struggling to see how it's possible? I find, in these times, I begin to take control over the very thing I need the mighty hand of God to fix . . . I become a barrier. Sometimes, it is because I expect a certain outcome but, other times, it is because it doesn't happen in the time frame I had in mind. If this speaks to you as well, I want you to remember that God is not constrained by the human concept of time. Also, God's creativity and imagination is so vast, that He can do anything. Often, He will not work problems out the same way twice, because He doesn't want us to fix our eyes on the outcome, but the Way Maker . . . God Himself, who provides every good thing to us. He doesn't want us to focus and worship the blessing, but we are to worship the one who gave us the blessing.

Lord, sometimes, I get in the way of your doing a new thing. Please forgive me. I recognize that you cannot pour new wine into old wineskins. Let my heart always acknowledge You, the one who blesses; instead of focusing on the outcomes. Help me be open to the way You work in new ways. I am so thankful that I can rely on You to always make a way even when there seems to be no solution in sight. You are so wonderful and I praise You God for the hope I have found in You! Amen.

TRUE FRIENDSHIP

Iron sharpens iron; so one man sharpens another. (Proverbs 27:17 NLT)

It is very important that you surround yourself with strong and healthy relationships. This life is going to give you many moments of great joy, but it is also going to have some times of struggle. We aren't meant to go through everything alone, but it is important to have people in your life that can speak the Word of God over you and into you in those times. If you surround yourself with people who see only the bitterness, the hurt, and the disappointments, how will they help you see anything else? We need to be connected to sources that speak life, peace, hope, love, strength, and joy. It confirms what we already know from our time spent in the Word.

Lord, I thank You that You are bringing friendships into our lives that will help us grow in faith, in compassion, and in strength. I thank You that those friendships will share a deep flow of the Word and the wisdom and power given through the Holy Spirit. I don't require a great multitude of friends, but I do require the relationships that are true and will help me walk through this world that is not meant to be my home. May my friendship with them always bring love, hope, and joy in whatever season they are walking through. In Jesus' name. Amen.

NO WORD SPOKEN WITHOUT PURPOSE

"For as the rain comes down, and the snow from heaven, and do not return there, but water the earth, and make it bring forth and bud, that it may give seed to the sower and bread to the eater so shall My word be that goes forth from My mouth; it shall not return to me void, but it shall accomplish what I please, and it shall prosper in the thin for which I sent it." (Isaiah 55:10–11 NKJV)

This is the Lord, through the prophet Isaiah, telling the Israelites that they can trust in His Word. How much more so, can we who have recognized that Jesus is our Lord and Savior, recognize that God does what He says He will? We have the blessed opportunity of knowing our salvation is set, that our victory is eternal. We should see every battle as won, because the very Word of God declares it to be true. In John 1:1, it says that the Word has always been God, in Him and with Him. God is always working when His Word is spoken. We, as His children and understanding the power that is in the Word of God, need to boldly declare it over every situation.

Lord, I praise You and thank You that not a single word that You have spoken will return without fulfilling what You have proclaimed. This means that I can stand on every single promise You have made! Lord, right now I boldly proclaim that You are stirring up the hearts of Your sons and daughter to declare Your Word in every area of their lives. Lord, You are the One who rules all nations and sets Yourself as the sovereign over every kingdom and principality in the heavens and on earth. We will look to You with wonder as we watch Your kingdom grow and bring glorious light to areas that try to remain in darkness. You came that everyone held in captivity would be set free. I proclaim the victory and freedom granted by You, Lord, over every broken heart and life! To You alone, Jesus be all glory, honor, and praise! Yes, I shout for You, Lord! Victory! Victory! Victory! Amen.

A GOD OF DETAILS

"Now indeed, Elizabeth your relative has also conceived a son in her old age; and this is now the sixth month for her who was called barren. For with God nothing will be impossible." (Luke 1:36–37 NKJV)

The other day, my husband and I were at our house (it is being rebuilt after a house fire early last year) to check on the progress and do little odd jobs. We had walked out to the backyard and my husband saw something down in the woods, along the edge of our property, and went to retrieve it. He made his way back up to me and said, "I had just been thinking of how I wanted a piece of foam to go up on the roof to take the burned lights off the gable end of the house. Isn't it amazing that this rolled up foam was just lying there and it's not even wet after all the snow we've had." I replied, "God answers even our smallest needs." Our Heavenly Father is such a good God! It makes Him rejoice to be able to meet all our needs. It doesn't matter to Him if they are large needs, like healing you from sickness, or small, like giving you a piece of foam to get a job done. He loves each of us so much, and longs to fulfill the needs and desires of our hearts. The important thing is to not be afraid to bring all your needs before Him. It's not that He doesn't already know what we need, but He desires us to recognize our need for Him as our every source. Our time with Him, talking to Him and fellowshipping with Him, is what He really wants from us. Just talk to Him . . . NOTHING is impossible with God!

Father, thank you for the sweet reminder that You care about even the small things we need every day. You simply amaze me! I do need help remembering that, as my Father, You want to be my source for everything! I declare over my brothers and sisters in Christ, that they will always recognize Your willingness to help with all sizes of needs. That You are a good, good Father and that Your heart is always for us. Help us to want the source more than the provision. I give You all honor, glory, and praise. Amen.

THE PROPER ORDER

"You have sown much, and bring in little; you eat, but do not have enough; you drink, but you are not filled with drink; you clothe yourselves, but no one is warm; and he who earns wages, earns wages to put into a bag with holes." (Haggai 1:6 NKJV)

I must admit, there are Scriptures in the Bible that just hurt. They are pointed and sharp, and they don't feel good when I read them. But God uses His Word to make sure that our hearts, minds, spirits, and lives are in line with His values. And, isn't it true that most of us get wrapped up in our daily lives trying to fulfill our own needs? This scripture verse really is similar to the words of Jesus Christ in Matthew 6:33, when He says, "Seek first the kingdom of God and all these things shall be added unto you." This scripture was to remind the Israelites that, if they would work at restoring the temple of God, He would provide for their needs. We are the very temple of the living God, and we need to work on keeping our temple restored in the life-giving Word of God. We need to keep our spirits connected to the True Source. God's Word promises that, when we keep our lives connected to Him and focus on eternal things, He will work to supply everything we need. As parents, we seek to provide things that make our children feel safe and loved (a home, food, clothes). Why then would our Heavenly Father be any different?

Father God, I admit, I oftentimes become consumed with supplying all the things I think I need. Instead, I should rely and trust on You. Forgive me for the lack of faith that I demonstrate. My heart longs to stay connected to You, so that my mind will be renewed. When I fall out of step with You, I can be consumed by worry and fear. Help me to see the signs of my own striving early, so that I may lay it all down and bring it to You. You are the One who supplies all my needs. Keep the memories of the greatness of Your works in my life, fresh in eyes and mind. I thank You for this powerful word today. Amen.

A PURE LANGUAGE

"For then I shall give to the peoples the change to a pure language, in order for them to call upon the name of Jehovah, in order to serve him shoulder to shoulder." (Zephaniah 3:9 NKJV)

I am far from a biblical scholar, but I believe this is a prophetic reference in the Old Testament to a time when the Holy Spirit would fill the disciples after the death and resurrection of Jesus. As a young Christian, I didn't understand praying in tongues. It was foreign and weird. I had a very patient pastor who took the time to point out key Scriptures to help me understand the purpose of this gift offered by God to His children. "Then there appeared to them divided tongues, as of fire, and one sat upon each of them. And they were all filled with the Holy Spirit and began to speak with other tongues, as the Spirit gave them utterance." (Acts 2:3–4 NKJV) "For he who speaks in a tongue does not speak to men but to God, for no one understands him; however, in the spirit he speaks mysteries." (1 Corinthians 14:2)

Praying in the Holy Spirit (speaking in tongues) is a gift from God to us. It allows the Holy Spirit to bring our hearts and minds into alignment with the supernatural realm of God. It is a special love language from each of us individually to God. If you have been hesitant to pursue being filled with the Holy Spirit and the gifting of tongues, I encourage you to seek this gift from the Lord! It is a direct connection for your spirit and the Heavenly Father.

Lord, I thank You for the powerful gift of the Holy Spirit and the edification provided by the gift of tongues. I declare that my brothers and sisters in Christ will pursue this great gifting and be filled with the indwelling of the Holy Spirit. This will enable them to grow in their faith and connection with You. Place people in their path that will guide them according to Your Word in this pursuit! Amen.

STRENGTH OF MY HEART

My flesh and my heart may fail, but God is the strength of my heart and my portion forever (Psalm 73:26 NIV)

Let's be honest, there are times in life that just make you feel worn down and weary. That if something doesn't happen soon, the raging waters will flood over you and you will be overcome. This scripture reminds me how God's kingdom is so different from the world we live in: His Words says, "The weak will become strong, the poor will become rich, the last will be first." But, we also have an enemy who tries to overwhelm us and blind us with our present circumstances, so that we begin to doubt the very nature of our Heavenly Father. I love this verse, it is so poignant in its pain, but also in it pure faith of a good, good Father.

This past month, as we still are not in our home, ten months after a house fire, I have felt like my heart and flesh want to fail. But God gently brings sweet words of comfort to my heart and brings to mind all the times He has come through for me in the past. He renews my strength. He reminds me that He will always provide for me and make a way even when I don't see how it is possible. God will do the same for each of you!

Father God, I do not know what each of my brothers and sisters are facing in this time or season. I cannot begin to understand their hurt, or their longings of heart. But You, Lord, You see into the deepest corners of their hearts and You hear their cries. I praise You for the timeliness of Your hand, coming to their rescue and meeting all their needs. Holy Spirit, speak words of wisdom and strength to their spirits. In You, they can rest and find hope. You are a good, good Father! Amen.

CLOTHED IN CHRIST

So in Christ Jesus you are all children of God through faith, for all of you who were baptized into Christ have clothed yourselves with Christ. (Galatians 3:26–27 NKJV)

There is an awakening in the church of God in this very moment. The church is peeling the scales from their eyes, and beginning to see from an eternal perspective. There is a spiritual battle taking place. It has been growing as God's kingdom and the fallen kingdom of this world have always been in opposition to one another. The church has been complacent and worn and weary. The children of God have been deceived for too long that they are defeated. That is the opposite of the truth! God's Word declares that He is victorious. That means that we His children are victorious. The sacrifice and blood of Christ Jesus gave us power and victory. For, as Sons and Daughter of God, we have all the rights and privileges of Jesus, because we are joint heirs with Him (Romans 8:17). Rise up and start operating in the power and authority given to you! Take every stronghold captive by speaking the powerful Word of God over it! You have always been equipped for battle with the Word. It is sharper than any sword! Remember who is standing with you! You are clothed in Christ, that means you are part of His Church and anointed for this very time! We are not on our own, operating without leadership, but we are equipped by the Holy Spirit to work in all truth and righteousness to bring the glory of the Father to this world. In Matthew 16:19, Jesus stated, "I will give you the keys of the kingdom of heaven; whatever you bind on earth will be bound in heaven, and whatever you loose on earth will be loosed in heaven."

Rise up, wake up, we are called to come together to fight for the lost and the hurting. We stand against the darkness and the self-idolatry of this world. We are equipped; we are strong when we work in cooperation with each other!

TRUE LOVE

"But I say to you, love your enemies, bless those who curse you, do good to those who hate you, and pray for those who spitefully use you and persecute you, that you may be sons of your Father in heaven;" (Matthew 5:44–45 NKJV)

This verse goes on to say that if you only love the people who love you, you are no better than the average nonbeliever. This verse is digging at my heart and spirit today because it asks something that is so difficult for us. It asks us to love those that are actively hurting us . . . ouch! It goes against our flesh, which wants to rise up and shout, "You can't treat me this way, you are so wrong, and I will never forgive you!" I am pretty sure that I have said all those words, or in a variety of combinations, to someone, if not out loud, then silently in my heart. But, the word of the Lord reminds me that I have been forgiven of so much . . . I have been given so much love, grace, and mercy by my Heavenly Father. Even when I least deserved forgiveness and love, He gave it freely. God pursued me when I was at my worst.

God brought this verse to me specifically today, in a moment where I felt hurt and injustice at the hands of another imperfect person. Imperfect, just like me. God knows it is not easy to let go of hurt and pain, but He also knows it is more harmful for us to hang onto it. It becomes a bitter root. Roots that grow too deep are tough to eradicate. They come back with new growth, new sprouts. So, don't allow seeds of hurt to take root. Seek to love, bless, pray for, and forgive others.

Lord, take this word and seal it upon our hearts. That we may be more like the sons and daughters You called us to be. It may be difficult at first to let go of the hurt, but I know that You will fill me with peace and joy as I trust You and let go of the pain. Thank you, for Your kindness and mercy never fail me. I love You so much. Forgive me for when I forget the love You granted me when I least deserved it. I want to be more like You. Amen.

THE TESTING

"And I will bring the third part through the fire, and will refine them as silver is refined, and test them as gold is tested. They will call on my name, and I will answer them. I will say, This is my people; and each one will say, The Lord is my God." (Zechariah 13:9 NKJV)

In the process of refining gold, the refiner takes the gold and places it together with a flux and lead or silver. The lead helps collect pure gold, attracting it and leaving behind any alloys or metals bonded with it. The gold is heated and melted at temperatures between 1,000 and 12,000 degrees Celsius. The melted gold separates from the alloys and adheres to the lead, leaving other metals and impurities behind.

It's God's heart to draw out our impurities or things that don't align with His will. This process is ongoing for our entire lives. He continually works on one area at a time, so that we can be more like Him. Don't misunderstand me, I am not saying that God causes difficult circumstances in your life. We live in a world that is broken and that has been impacted by sin. God didn't cause that, man did. However, if we allow God to work, He takes all situations in our lives and begins to change us. Maybe we need to grow in faith. Or, maybe, we need to grow in patience. Maybe we need to let go of bitterness. Maybe we need to learn not to judge others. Maybe, we need to learn to surrender our need to know why or how God will do things, and just trust that He will because He is who He says He is! Whatever it is, God always uses every set of circumstances to work in and through our lives. We can't be more like Him if we are holding onto our right to be us!

God, there are times in life when I feel the fire, the testing of my spirit, in the storms of life. I thank You that You are using these times to refine me, to mold me more in Your image. I can't demonstrate Your perfect love if I am filled with bitterness, hurt, unforgiveness, jealousies, strife, and the need to control everything. I do want to be more like Jesus and less like me, so that You may be glorified. Amen.

ONE ACCORD

Now may the God of patience and comfort grant you to be like-minded toward one another, according to Christ Jesus, that you may with one mind and one mouth glorify the God and Father of our Lord Jesus Christ (Romans 15: 5–6 NKJV)

We were created for relationship, first with God our Father and then with other believers. We are called to be unified, each one of us working together to make the church better and to edify one another (1 Corinthians 12:12). One of the most important commandments Jesus gave the disciples was to love one another as you love yourself (Matthew 22:39). The world wants to stress our individualism, and that we should seek our own identity. The world encourages us to define ourselves and our own values. But that is dangerous ground, because our values can never measure up to the righteousness and holiness of God. As Christians, it is important that we recognize that our identity is in God. He is our Creator, He designed us for His purposes. We have to let go of the need to be an individual to compare ourselves to others. God is so amazing that He gives each of His sons and daughters different gifts, so that when we come together we operate as whole system. I am not saying that we won't ever have different ideas as Christians, we all have different backgrounds and experiences and are, often, in different levels of growth in our relationship with the Father. But, when those differences become barriers to bringing salvation to those that need it, we are allowing our personal interests to become greater than the church. We stop being unified and we definitely stop revealing God's glory. When we allow those ideas to cause churches to split and divide, we have become weapons in the enemy's arsenal. We, the Church, cannot allow our pride, our individual interests, or our needs to stand in the way of God's plan and purpose for His Church—to reach and save the lost!

Father God, I declare that Your Holy Church would be unified and come against any division or plan to separate Your children from Your calling. May they humble their hearts and submit their minds to be more like Jesus, following Him in love and compassion for one another. May they put aside their need to be first, to be right, and to be superior to others as they do Your will. Amen.

HARDENED HEARTS

Then the magicians of Egypt did so with their enchantment; and Pharaoh's heart grew hard, and he did not heed them, as the Lord had said. And Pharaoh turned and went into his house. Neither was his heart moved by this. (Exodus 7:22–23 NKJV)

This past year, I was asked to mentor someone new for the company I am employed with. This person was not only new to the job, but also a new graduate. I work in healthcare, so I don't work within a Christian-based organization. A mentorship is a great way to provide support for someone who has not had an opportunity to utilize academic skills in a real-world setting. Shortly, into the first few months, I began to realize that this person's skill set may not be best suited for the level of care our patients needed. There were some instances where patient safety was impacted. In these instances, I realized that the protocols we have in place were ignored, and this person chose to skip important steps that would have provided information to make a safer decision about the care of the patients. During a conversation regarding the issues, the mentee mentioned that they believed that the way they had been trained previously was sufficient, and that they didn't need to adjust or adapt to new clinical settings. In essence, their heart was hardened. As the months went by, it became clear with other interactions that this person did not feel like they needed to learn anything new from me. We are going to meet all sorts of people in this world, and if they aren't Christians, they might not be willing to accept the seed that you plant. That word of encouragement or wisdom that you want to sow into their life. Brother and sister, your job is to be obedient to God and do the planting He directs through the Holy Spirit. It's not up to you if the person you minister to receives it. God is capable of using that seed to grow at the right time. Moses went to Pharaoh time after time to request he let the Israelites free. He was obedient to what God wanted him to do, and he let God work out what happened to Pharaoh. Just keep shining Your light, loving God, and being obedient to His calling. He is big enough to handle the rest! Amen.

THE WELL

10 Jesus answered and said to her, "If you knew the gift of God, and who it is who says to you, 'Give Me a drink,' you would have asked Him, and He would have given you living water." 13 Jesus answered and said, "Whoever drinks of this water will thirst again, but whoever drinks of the water that I shall give him will never thirst. But the water that I shall give him will become in him a fountain of water springing up into everlasting life." (John 4:10, 13–14 NKJV)

The well in the village was central to survival. There was nothing more important than having a source of water. Jesus went to the well recognizing its importance to the people. Jesus had a way of using the essential things in everyday life to point out a deeper spiritual need in every person. When He met the Samaritan woman at the well, Jesus didn't say she needed to clean up her act first. He gave mercy and compassion; He encouraged the woman to find what would fill the hole inside her. She had been trying to find love and fill the emptiness in other ways. That is the same thing God wants for each of us. He doesn't want us to wait until we are perfect to come to Him. He is ready for us to come just as we are, whether we are broken, angry, hurting, or feeling trapped. God's purpose is to set us free. We will always be longing for more, until we accept Jesus into our heart and recognize that He is our ultimate source.

Father, thank you for bringing the life source of water found in Jesus Christ. Thank you that You accept us just as we are. I know that as I draw close to You, You will clean out the things of this world and fill me with the characteristics that are in Your Son. I want to be more like You. You are the source of all hope and life. You are the well that never runs dry. Amen.

OUR BETROTHED

I will betroth you to Me forever; Yes, I will betroth you to Me in righteousness and justice, in loving kindness and mercy; I will betroth you to Me in faithfulness and you shall know the Lord. (Hosea 2:19–20 NKJV)

What a beautiful image of God's love for each of us. The word betroth stems from English origins, the words be + truth. God is promising to be true to us forever. Just as a husband and wife promise to be faithful and true to one another. I admit that most of us have probably suffered from a broken heart at one time or another in this life. People we love have hurt us, whether accidentally or purposefully; it is bound to happen, because we are imperfect. And we all struggle with selfishness and pride. So, it's easy to see how people hurt one another. But, our Heavenly Father's love is nothing like our human capacity for love. His is deeper, and wider, than we can ever imagine. Look at some of the words our Heavenly Father uses in His love promise to us . . . in righteousness, justice, kindness, mercy, and faithfulness.

God's love for us was so great that He sent His only son, Jesus Christ, to die for us (John 3:16). So that we wouldn't have the barrier of sin keeping us from Him. He doesn't see us in our imperfection, but sees us as His beloved, because we have been made righteous through the sacrifice of Jesus. Maybe you haven't experienced a faithful love in your relationships with people, but your Father is like no other. He loves you now just as you are, in all your imperfection, with no conditions. He loves you and wants you to have all that He has to offer:

joy, peace, healing, strength, redemption, reconciliation, love, and His perfect provision. You won't know a better love. But, you have to decide it's worth the risk. Trusting God with my heart and my life, believing in the gift of salvation through Jesus Christ, is still the best decision I have ever made. And, God has always been true. His love hasn't failed me yet. It really is like no other love I have experienced before.

HIS TENDER COMPASSION

The fountain of your pleasure is found in the sacrifice of my shattered heart before you. You will not despise my tenderness as I humbly bow down at your feet. (Psalm 51:71 NKJV)

I admit it, I have had some grave errors in judgment in my past. My mistakes hurt people and it also hurt me. In my shame, I held back thinking I had gotten exactly what I deserve. I thought that God wouldn't want me or love me anymore. That was so far from the truth. It's a lie so often whispered into us, by the enemy. An enemy who wants us to believe that God only loves those who are perfect. Well, if that was true . . . goodness, no one would ever receive salvation! But, thankfully, that is the opposite of God's heart towards us when we repent. When we truly surrender to Him and say that we not only are sorry, but that we want to make a change with our lives. Listen to King David as he goes to the Lord for forgiveness. He says, "You will not despise my tenderness as I humbly bow down." King David was a man that had walked a long time with the Lord, but his own desires made him sin against God and against others. David recognized from his time with God that once he repented that God would be gracious to forgive him. God is pleased when we see our mistakes, go to Him for forgiveness, and, with a heart that longs to change, seek to become better. There is no mistake that you or I can make that God won't forgive. He forgave David for adultery and murder. He forgave the Israelites for worshipping other gods and forgetting to follow the Ten Commandments. He forgave Paul for persecuting, imprisoning, and stoning the Jewish people who became Christians. We can be forgiven for our sins and mistakes as well. Don't run away from God when you make a mistake; instead, run towards Him. He is always ready to help us when we cry out to Him.

Thank you, Father, for Your mercy and grace. I often battle my flesh and fall short of being who You called me to be. Forgive me for hurting others, and when I turn away from You in shame or selfish pride. I truly desire to be a child after Your own heart. Help me, grow me, and change me. Amen.

SEASONS OF STILLNESS

To everything there is a season, a time for purpose under heaven: A time to be born, and a time to die; a time to plant, and a time to pluck what is planted; (Ecclesiastes 3:1–2 NKJV)

Winter is not really my favorite season. Everything feels and looks barren. There aren't vibrant colors to catch the eye. The stillness makes me feel like nothing is changing or happening. As I reflect more purposefully on the way God created all things, every sunrise and sunset, and every season, all of it works together in unity. Even in winter, where things seem stagnant . . . there is something happening underneath the surface of the earth. As we watch and wait, in the early days of spring, new life bursts up from the ground!

Maybe you feel like you are going through a season that is stagnant . . . remember that God has a way of bringing forth something new to your life. However, we must also remember that during those seasons where we feel like not much change is happening, we must keep planting the Word of God in our lives. If we want God to manifest new life in us, we must be mindful of keeping close to Him regardless of our emotions and our feelings. Remember, if you do not plant seeds, then nothing will grow and you will not see a time of harvest.

Heavenly Father, thank you for reminding me today that everything You created works in perfect harmony. Without winter, seeds may not have time to take root to be ready to burst forth in springtime. Help us in the varied seasons of our lives to keep planting the seeds of life provided in Your Word into our spirits. They keep us rooted and grounded in You. Your Word never returns void and always brings forth life! I give You thanks and praise for always working things for our good when we stay close to You. Amen.

PLANTING SEEDS

"Now he who received seed among the thorns is he who hears the word, and the cares of this world and deceitfulness of riches choke the word and he becomes unfruitful. But he who received seed on the good ground is he who hears the word and understands it, who indeed bears fruit and produces: some a hundredfold, some sixty, some thirty." (Matthew 13:22–23 NKJV)

Sons and daughters of the Living God, now is the time for planting the Word! God and His Word are one. He is revealing His Word to us as we spend time reading the Bible and in time spent with God in prayer. Jesus told the disciples that they would do greater works than Jesus did during his ministry (John 14:11–13). Jesus did so many miraculous things and, when we are connected to Him through receiving salvation, we are filled with the same anointing and His power is in us! We have to begin practicing speaking out the Word of God in every area of our lives and in the lives of others. God's Word has the power to break down barriers. To change the things in this world that drastically need the hand of our wonderful Father to bring into correct alignment again. God's Word has the power to save lives! And that is the very heart of our Father: to save the soul of every man, woman, and child!

Thank you, Lord, for this illustration of how we can be fruitful as Your children! We are so thankful that You loved us so much that You sent Jesus to die for our sins that we may be reconciled to You! Help us to plant Your Word deep in our hearts and begin to speak it out boldly to break through the darkness we see all around us and reveal the light of Your love and glory! Amen.

CASTING OUR NETS

Then Jesus said to them, "Follow me and I will make you become fishers of men." They immediately left their nets and followed Him. (Mark 1:17–18 NKJV)

We all have special skills that, as we become adults, we graft into our daily lives and utilize those skills in our occupations of choice: doctors, teachers, police officers, builders, and the list goes on! I am not saying that there is anything wrong with using our talents and skills to provide for our families, but we cannot lose sight of our greater calling. As children of God we are called to become "fishers of men." God's heart is to reach the lost of this earth, and He equipped us to do it! The Great Commission was not just Jesus telling the disciples to go into all the world and preach the good news, but each one of us as well (Matthew 28:16–20).

How can we be effective at reaching others for Christ? The two easiest ways are: first, to show love to others unconditionally and, second, to proclaim the goodness of God in our lives to others. It really is that simple, but we make it difficult. We get lost in the details, and want every interaction with others to be perfect and to end in the Salvation prayer. And, if someone rejects our attempts to show the love of God to them, we tend to take it as personal rejection. We have to remember that we are not doing the saving; we are incapable of providing salvation to anyone, that comes from Jesus Christ alone. Our job is to keep talking about Him, to keep throwing our nets out into the deep waters and try to draw people closer to God.

Father, thank you for Your Word and the many gifts You give Your sons and daughters that You may use us for Your glory. Help us to remember that it is Your love and power, Your provision of salvation that changes hearts and lives. We are but one avenue that You use to reach out to lost souls. I declare that those who are willing to become part of Your Great Commission will be equipped in every opportunity to show Your love, and be given words of truth by the Holy Spirit to plant the seeds that will grow into salvation for the lost of this world. Lord, it is about You and Your plan to save every man, woman, and child that they may have eternal life. Amen.

PREPARED AT ALL TIMES

When the devil had ended every[the complete cycle of] temptation, he [temporarily] left Him[that is, stood off from Him] until a more opportune and favorable time. (Luke 4:13 AMP)

It is important that we remember that we have an enemy and that he is always in opposition to God. Satan has always tried to destroy God's plans to be united with us; he is the one that tries to separate us from the love of Christ. We need to be aware of who it is we are battling in this world. Jesus said, "When he speaks a lie, he speaks from his own resources, for he is a liar and the father of it." (John 8:44 partial) We need to remember that whenever we are going to be doing the will of God, the enemy will attempt to rise up and resist us. That is why knowing how to speak the Word of God is vital for all believers. We have been taught that prayer is going to God on our knees and begging for what we need. That is not how God said it should be! He tells us that we have all power and authority granted unto us through Christ Jesus to do mighty things! Miraculous things! We can tell our mountains to move. He said we would do it . . . not ask Him to do it for us. God wants us to know that just as there is power in the name of Jesus Christ and in the blood He shed for us on the cross, there is power in the spoken Word of God.

Thank you, Father, for helping us recognize that we have the authority to speak against situations and plans that the enemy would use to steal joy, peace, health, and strength from us. We declare that the enemy will not gain a foothold in our lives in any area. That we would be aware of any lie he tries to use that would separate us from You. I thank You, Your Word declares that nothing can separate us from Your love, once we are sealed by the Holy Spirit. We begin to operate from a place of victory and authority as granted according to Your Word. Amen.

IN THE WAY OF HIS PLANS

"For my thoughts are not your thoughts, neither are your ways my ways," declares the Lord. "As the heavens are higher than the earth, so are my ways higher than your ways and my thoughts that your thoughts." (Isaiah 55: 8–9 NIV)

Recently, I had a day off from work. I like to cook something special on my days off, because during a normal workweek meals are usually quick and easy. So, I picked out a recipe for chicken pot pie. Now it wasn't a from-scratch-type recipe, but I was still excited about the dinner because it would be different from things I had been making lately. I had this complete vision in my head about how wonderful it would be and the crust would turn out perfectly. As I began to put the pie together, my filling didn't sit nicely in the bottom crust, and the top crust pulled in half as I tried to put it over top of the filling. Instead of a perfect looking pie crust, I have one where I had to pinch it down the center to try to stick it back together. I started to feel frustrated. Then I felt in my spirit a kind of chuckle and the Lord said, "Isn't that the way with all my children, their expectations and plans for perfection get in the way of what I want to do through and for them?" As I thought about it more, I have to confess, in my own life, it has often been true. I know that God can do exceedingly above all that I could ask or need, but I have already formed my own ideas of how God should move and make things happen in my life. It was a simple reminder that we need to lay our expectations aside and just let God do what He does best. His plans are really to bless us and prosper us, so why do we get hung up on deciding what His process is going to look like?

Lord, thank you for reminding me that when I place my plans before Yours, I become the barrier. I could hinder the very movement I want to see in areas of my life. Forgive me for my constant desire to control the outcomes in my life instead of operating in the faith that You are already going before me to make a way. I praise You for the wonderful ways You restore, provide, heal, bless, and give peace in my life. I am so thankful for Your goodness! Amen.

OUR UNBELIEF

Jesus said to him, "If you can believe, all things are possible to him who believes." Immediately the father of the child cried out and said with tears, "Lord, I believe; help my unbelief!" (Mark 9:23–24 NKJV)

Let's just be honest with each other, there will be situations in this life that test our faith. I do not believe that God places bad things in our lives; those just happen because we live in a fallen world, but those challenges can enable our faith to grow. It is possible if we keep fear in check. Fear is in direct opposition to faith. Recently, I had a medical experience, and since I have had a relatively healthy life, I felt the shattering effects of what fear can do in our minds. As I waited for answers to my questions about what was happening to my body, fear tried to speak out the worst possible scenarios. I had to be purposeful about what I would speak out loud. I had to remember that life and death is in the power of the tongue (Proverbs 18:21).

Today, this scripture reminds me that we all have situations that arise. Situations that make us only see the circumstances and not the incredible love and move of God on our behalf. We all need to remember that in the battles of this life, God knows how to encourage us, keep us strong, and use people to help us hold onto our faith. I am blessed by the strong faith of my husband and a few close friends who speak the powerful Word of God to me and over me, in all of life's ups and downs. I also practice speaking the Word over myself, to prepare for all seasons of life. I can't encourage all of you enough to do the same.

Father, I thank You that we Your children are wonderfully and fearfully made. Lord, help my unbelief; I recognize that there are events in life that I cannot foresee, but You can see all things. Continue to grow and stretch my faith that I know and always trust in Your goodness in all situations. Thank you for family and friends that know You and speak Your Word into my life. Bless them and pour Your mighty favor upon them. I love You and thank You for Your perfect provision in my life. Amen.

HOPEFUL ASSURANCE

Now faith is confidence in what we hope for and assurance about what we do not see. (Hebrews 11:1 NIV)

Recently, I have been talking about faith, how it can be tested, how it can grow. I think the most important principle of faith we need to have is the basic belief and knowledge that our God is always good. His plans and purposes for our lives is always to bless us and give us a hope and future (Jeremiah 29:11). I cannot be more emphatic when I say I do not believe that anything bad that happens in our lives comes from God. We live in a fallen world with many people who do not believe in God. Those people are driven by selfishness, bitterness, and hatred, and make choices based on their own personal desires. Those choices can often lead to bad things happening to both Christians and non-Christians alike. If you need further evidence of God's basic goodness, let's look at what Jesus said about God. He stated that no one was good, except God alone (Mark 10:18 NIV). I believe that if we can first accept the goodness of God on faith, that our faith in His promises and in our daily walk with Him will have opportunity to grow. Jesus also went on to demonstrate the goodness of our Heavenly Father by having great compassion on the sick and those who were outcasts.

Next time something challenging happens, declare to yourself these basic truths about your Heavenly Father: "God, I know that You are good. There is no one who loves me like You do! You love me even through my imperfections and mistakes. You are always going before me to make a way. Your love and mercy are new every morning! Great is Your faithfulness, God! Help me when fear tries to overcome my faith. Remind me who I am in You! Amen."

GIVING IS ABOUT HEART

"I tell you the truth, this poor widow has given more that all the others who are making contribution. For they gave a tiny part of their surplus, but she, poor as she is, has given everything she had to live on." (Mark 12:43–44 NLT)

In this scripture, Jesus is talking to the disciples about giving. So many Christians don't trust God with their provisions, so they don't tithe to the church. I believe that tithing is important because it is an area that God said to "test Me"(Malachi 3:10). I confess that it took me a while after I became a Christian to grasp the importance of trusting God with my finances. However, once I did, I began to experience His perfect provision. Not only did I have all I needed, God made sure that the money I had also provided for a few nonessential items. He loves to give us good gifts! Looking more closely at this scripture, I believe that Jesus is really calling attention to the attitude of the widow's heart. She gave all that she had. The scripture doesn't say she begged others to put in money for her, or that she wailed as she gave her whole livelihood away. She gave all she had because she trusted God's goodness. When there is a deeper revelation in our hearts that we don't really own any of our possessions, that they are gifted from a God who desires to give us all that we need, we begin to have a freedom. We become less focused on money and more focused on the goodness of God. If you haven't started to trust God with your finances, give it a shot. I didn't regret it, and I bet neither will you!

Lord, thank you for the loving way You provide for us. I believe that You always want to do more than we could ever ask or think. Help me to remember the heart of the widow as she thankfully gave all that she had to honor You. Help me to have the same spirit of generosity and to be a good steward of all You have given me. Amen.

OUR FOUNDATION

"Therefore everyone who hears these words of mine and puts them into practice is like a wise man who built his house on the rock. The rain came down, the streams rose, and the winds blew and beat against that house; yet it did not fall, because it had its foundation on the rock." (Matthew 7:24–25 NIV)

This weekend, my husband began the arduous task of removing some of the concrete pad at the back of our house. He had a jackhammer, a rather large thing, to literally break of chunks of the concrete and break it away from the pad. As I watched him work at the task, it began to make me think about the way homes are built. Different areas have different codes to build to because different weather and weather events can do damage to homes that aren't built well. More specifically, houses can be damaged if they don't have a solid foundation.

That is much like our faith; if we don't work at building a firm foundation on the Word of God, when the storms of life come, we will crumble. I concede that in the early days of my Christian walk, I often felt like the slightest difficulty shook my faith. I made it a lot more difficult because, instead of running to the Father for help, comfort, and to be my source, I became prideful and even angry. I had the silly notion that because I had become a child of God that nothing would ever go wrong. This is the opposite from how it can be because the enemy wants to separate us from God at every turn. I often came back to God, when I figured out I couldn't fix anything on my own. Now, over the years, I commit to spending time in His Word, in prayer and worship. It is to keep my inner spirit centered on God, the one source for all I will ever need. I still get challenges in life, and some that could have destroyed me, except that I realize where my help comes from and I run to Him. The Holy Spirit is at work within me and assists with keeping the Word on my lips.

Look to Jesus and to God; they are the best foundation to build your life upon. Apart from them, I could do nothing!

GUARDING YOUR HEART

A good man out of the good treasure of his heart brings forth good; and an evil man out the evil treasure of his heart brings forth evil. For out of the abundance of the heart his mouth speaks. (Luke 6:45 NKJV)

Most of us have heard the phrase garbage in; garbage out. We understand that, in a physical sense, if we feed our body junk food, we will eventually have health issues. Young children have often tried this with candy only to get a terrible tummy ache! If we understand that we need to watch what we put into our physical bodies, then it shouldn't be too different to think along the same concepts relating to our minds, hearts, and spirits. For example, when I was younger, I watched scary movies. I bought into that whole concept that a scare was thrilling. Sometime later, I struggled with having nightmares and, often, if I was alone, I felt frightened. It wasn't until I heard a sermon on this very concept of "guarding our hearts" in church that I realized that I was opening myself up to fear and these bad dreams by what I spent time watching. I stopped watching scary movies from then on and I have been better for it. The nightmares stopped, and the constant fears that came when I was alone also left me. Each one of us may be dealing with different forms of "garbage," but it is very important that we are aware of what we spend time looking at and putting into our minds, hearts, and spirits.

Father, I declare over my brother or sister reading this right now, that You would give them revelation knowledge about what they are feeding their spirits. Lord God, that what they meditate on would grow them in compassion, mercy, and grace, and the anointing given to them through Christ. Lord, help them let go of the things that bring forth fear, bitterness, anger, jealousy, or strife. Grant to them Your supernatural peace to fill those spaces with more of You! Amen.

SACREDNESS

Do not give that which is holy (the sacred thing) to the dogs, and do not throw your pearls before hogs, lest the trample upon them with their feet and turn and tear you in pieces. (Matthew 7:6 AMPC).

As important as it is that we watch what we speak about the situations in our lives, it is even more important that we are cautious with what we share with others. This is especially critical with people who do not believe that the Word of God is living and active. Unfortunately, Christian churches don't always educate people on the promise and power of God that can be activated by our own praise and proclamations. I am sure that many of you have heard someone say, "If it's God's will, He will provide." This is not scriptural. Why would Jesus tell His disciples He came to heal, deliver, and set free, if it were not the will of the Father? Jesus stated that He and the Father are one (John 10:30). We need to be very careful who we decide will be in our inner circle when the tough diagnoses, or tough circumstances, happen. It needs to be people who will be in agreement with you according to God's Word. Sometimes, that means not telling your coworkers or posting it on social media. People of the world will not have the knowledge of God or His Word. Remember that I recently reminded us about the "garbage in, garbage out" theory? If you share things with everyone, even nonbelievers, you will open yourself up to their negative thoughts, emotions, and experiences. It will be in opposition to what you need to stand on, the firm foundation that is God's Word. They will speak doubt and unbelief to you, and when the storms of life happen, we need faith to stand . . . and then stand some more!

Abba, I thank You that for every storm of life, You have already prepared the perfect circle of believers to encourage and stand in agreement with me according to Your promises. I praise You for the wisdom of the Holy Spirit and His leading on when to share and when to stay silent about the things I am walking through. I declare that I will be a safe harbor for others going through the storms of life, and that I will declare Your Word over them. I thank You that when two or more people come together in agreement with Your Word—it shall be done. Amen.

EVERLASTING LIFE

For God so loved the world that He gave His only begotten Son, that whoever believes in Him should not perish but have everlasting life. (John 3:16 NKJV)

As I sit here, thinking about who might be reading this message today, I realize that this could be the most important scripture I ever share with you. I recognize that we may never meet face to face, and I may never get to hear your life story, or build a friendship with you. And, although we need friendships and relationships to walk through this life, there will be never be a more important relationship to you than the one you establish through accepting Christ as your Savior. As hard as it is for you to imagine, even though we have never met, I have been praying for you. I don't know what you look like, if you are old or young. I don't know if you like being part of a big group or like solitude. I don't know if you have it all together or if everything is falling apart. What I do know is that you are loved, and God put it on my heart to pray for you. He has been pursuing you, because you are His child and He loves you. He has always loved you. He is calling you to Him and asking you to let Him into your heart. There are no coincidences. You came across this devotion at exactly the right time. God has been working toward this moment all along. It doesn't have to be complicated, you can simply say, "Jesus, come into my heart, I know I need You. I know You came to help those who are imperfect and hurting. I have those times and so does everyone else. I am sorry for my sins, my mistakes, and I give it all to You. Thank you for loving me. Thank you for dying for me. You are my Savior."

I said a similar prayer when I was nineteen years old. Now that doesn't mean I had it all figured out at that exact moment. You don't have to have it all together the moment you accept Jesus as your Savior. Know that I have never regretted giving my heart to God. He has shown more love to me than I could write about in hundreds of books. I know He will demonstrate amazing amounts of love in your life and will always working for your good!

PRESERVING OUR DIFFERENCES

"Salt is good; but if the salt has lost its flavor, how shall it be seasoned? It is neither fit for land nor for the dunghill, but men throw it out." (Luke 14:34–35 partial NKJV)

Christians, who look like the world and act like the world, will never reach the lost. They do not fulfill their destiny in purpose in God's royal priesthood. They might be saved, but they are not changed. One of the most amazing things about our great God is that He doesn't force His will on us. He will grow us, and use us to the extent that we allow. This Scripture refers to our connection to God as our source. We cannot grow or stay steadfast in God's plan and purpose if we allow our walk with Him to grow cold. We cannot afford to grow complacent or stale in our pursuit of God. We have to want Him more than anything else.

Make no mistake, once you become a son or daughter of our Heavenly Father, you are given a mission. Just like the disciples who walked with Jesus, we are called to tell other people about the love of Christ. We have unique opportunities to share how the love of Christ changed us and changed our lives. We are given moments that become miracles as God breaks chains, heals hearts, and sets people free from sin. Those moments will only happen if we allow God to change us, to season us, grow us to be useful in His Church, in His Family.

Father, thank you for this word and the understanding that we need to remain fervent for You and Your Word. Thank you for showing us that if we become complacent, then we are like salt that loses its flavor and we become useless in reaching others who desperately need You. Holy Spirit, give us wisdom and knowledge in the moments You place before us. You will anoint our lips with the words that will allow hearts to be open to the saving grace of Jesus Christ. Thank you for the opportunity to see Your miraculous hand at work in the lives of so many. Help us to be the salt unto this earth. So many people are in need of You! Amen.

WILL YOU GIVE IT ALL?

"Again, the kingdom of heaven is like a merchant seeking beautiful pearls, who, when he had found one pearl of great price, went and sold all that he had and bought it." (Matthew 13:45–46 NKJV)

Think about something you own that is precious and dear to you. Maybe it was some china or a piece of furniture that belonged to someone you loved. Maybe it is a special piece of jewelry that has been given to you. We all have things that hold special meaning to us. Things that we value, not only because they are costly, but because they have meaning to us. That item has a special place in our home. We look after it; we protect it.

That is how God the Father wants us to feel about our relationship with Him. That we value it, that we would give all we have for it. The Lord is asking, "Are you all in? Will you give it all for me? I gave everything I had for you, my only Son. I need sons and daughters that will see Me as their greatest treasure. If you look to me first and serve me first, I will provide all that you need. Are you all in?"

Heavenly Father, thank you for Your Word and the beautiful reminder of how valuable Your kingdom is. I will give You all of me and hold nothing back from You. I thank You that You meet me in that place, and are always faithful for Your Word. I have never lacked anything when I have placed my faith in You. I desire You more than anything else. There is no rest or peace without You. Your presence is the sweetest place I have ever known. Keep my eyes fixed on You. Keep my eyes fixed on You, God. Amen.

THE KINGDOM ALIVE IN YOU

Now when He was asked by the Pharisees when the kingdom of God would come, He answered them and said, "The kingdom of God does not come with observation; nor will they say, 'See here!' or 'See there!' For indeed, the kingdom of God is within you." (Luke 17:20–21 NKJV)

Even though we still are awaiting the return of Jesus and the time when He calls all believers to join Him in heaven, we are not left powerless until His return. We understand that after Jesus' death and resurrection, He gave us the gift of the Holy Spirit which dwells within us. The Holy Spirit represents the kingdom of God and guides us in all truth. We have access to the Heavenly Father, Christ the Son, and the Holy Spirit at any given time as His children.

This concept would have been very difficult for the religious leaders of Jesus' time to understand. They had generations of traditions, and laws established by Moses which they had been taught to uphold. Even the temple was designed to keep people separate from where the holy presence of God dwelt. Now, Jesus was telling them that the kingdom of God was within them! This would have been too radical for the religious leaders of the time.

How blessed are we to be able to see that our Heavenly Father is not separated from us anymore! We have access to Him at all times. His spirit resides within us to generate knowledge, power, and gifts that will be used to glorify His name and His kingdom!

Lord, I praise You for the gift of the Holy Spirit which dwells within me. Thank you for the access to all that You are and all that You have for me. You gave more than I could ever ask or dare to dream when You gave Your Son Jesus to die for me. I declare over all my brothers and sisters, a deeper understanding of their equipping through Your anointing. That they may see the full measure of their gifts and the fruit they will bring forth as they are obedient to Your call on their lives. I give You all praise and honor and glory, for there is none like You. Amen.

AGAINST THE CURRENT

If you were to give your allegiance to the world, they would love and welcome you as one of their own. But because you won't align yourself with the values of this world, they will hate you. I have chosen you and taken you out of the world to be mine. (John 15:19 TPT)

Have you ever paddled a canoe or kayak against the current? It is hard work! If you stop paddling, the push of the current will move you quickly in the other direction. That is what being a believer is like in today's world. We have to be vigilant about our faith and relationship with God. We cannot become complacent for even a second. I am not saying that this isn't challenging, because it is, and especially for those of us who go to work every day in environments that are not Christian-based organizations.

I have had to allow God to help me stay focused on His purpose in my life. To be reminded that God purposed me in my career with a gifting. He helped me every step of the way, that I may be a blessing to those I encounter. If I take my eyes off God and focus on the happenings of the world and the injustices, I could quickly become weary and disheartened. I hold fast to Jesus' words that I have been chosen by Him and called to a higher standard. If you feel hated by the world, it's going to be okay. We can't be like the world and truly belong in the kingdom of God. You are not alone. We are all united as born-again believers. Make sure you are connecting up with a Spirit-filled church and with Spirit-filled Christians. We can persevere when we are building each other up in our faith.

Father, thank you for the reminder that I am not of this world. I am Your chosen daughter. You have called me out of the world and set me apart. I cannot be part of the world and the way it operates and be in You. I declare over my brothers and sisters, right now, that their faith is made fast and strong in Your Word and Your filling of the Holy Spirit. I declare that their eyes are fixed firmly upon You and the way You move and operate in their lives. Lord, help them see that You are always at work. That You have already had the victory. There are no battles that haven't already been won! Glory to Your name! Amen.

HOLY SPIRIT AND FIRE

"I indeed baptize you with water unto repentance, but He who is coming after me is mightier than I, whose sandals I am not worthy to carry. He will baptize you with the Holy Spirit and fire." (Matthew 3:11 NKJV)

Over the weekend, I was at our home cleaning up the yard and burning the tree limbs that have gathered over the winter months in our firepit. As I stood watching the fire, the thought about the Holy Spirit filled my mind. How being filled with the Holy Spirit is like a fire inside me that keeps my heart ablaze for God. It fills me, it never dies, even in seasons where everything seems to have grown cold there is always a burning ember. In the moment that I cry out to the Lord, the Holy Spirit is there to rekindle my heart, mind, and spirit.

Maybe you feel distant from God, like you have lost that fire or hunger for Him that you had in the beginning. Maybe some experience or hurt has left you feeling like God is far away. That He doesn't care about you. That is a lie! God never leaves us or forsakes us. I encourage you to press into Him. Spend time in God's Word, in prayer and listening to worship music. God and the Holy Spirit never leave us, but They don't force Their way into our lives if we don't make room for Them. I know it can be hard to look for God and worship Him in the middle of a heartbreak or a tough time, but He will give you the strength and grace in those moments you need it most, if you don't turn away from Him.

Father, I pray for anyone who has experienced loss or pain in this life. God, I declare that they will turn to You in the hardest of days. That they will not believe the lies of the enemy who tries to tell them that You have forgotten them or could never love them! You are the ultimate demonstration of love, and Your heart is always turned toward those that are hurting. You shower them with compassion, because Your love never fails. Father, I give You praise for meeting them in this very moment. That the Holy Spirit would breathe life on the embers in their spirit and rekindle the fire in their hearts for You. You are so good to give us the Holy Spirit who is always interceding on our behalf. I give You thanks and praise for every good provision from You, Lord. Amen.

SEEKING THE GIVER

The eyes of all look expectantly to You, and You give them their food in due time. You open Your hand and satisfy the desire of every living thing. (Psalm 145: 15–16 NKJV)

During a hike with a dear friend recently, we were catching up and discussing various things. Our conversation turned to various things that were happening in our lives and things that we knew required the hand of God to move and make miracles take place. We both have very different life experiences, but we both could clearly see the hand of God turning difficult circumstances in life and giving us the greater blessing in the end.

As we talked about this, I was reminded that it is more important to be seeking the giver of the promise, then looking for the promise itself. That is not necessarily always an easy thing to do in the waiting. Waiting for everyone is different, since God doesn't manifest in the same way or in the same amount of time for each person. The waiting can be a period of growing in faith, or growing in frustration. The choice is essentially ours. If we are looking for the promises of God, more than God Himself we will easily get frustrated and discontent in the wait. But, if we are looking to God, and recognizing how His hand has always been toward our provision, we will be faithful and steadfast. We will be able to praise Him even though we cannot see the changes He is manifesting on our behalf.

Keep your eyes fixed on our good, good Father! He is working all things for good, for those who love Him!

THE BATTLE HAS BEEN WON

So when Jesus had received the sour wine, He said, "It is finished!" And bowing His head, He gave up His spirit. (John 19:30 NKJV)

Brothers and sisters, what a blessed time we are in to be able to see this word of the Lord. We stand in this moment and recognize the victory in these words and this action of Jesus on our behalf. This action gave us the victory over sin and death once and for all! There is no greater love than this! Even when our hearts and minds were far from God, He was putting a plan into place to bring us back into His loving embrace.

I think about the men and women following Jesus at that time and how it looked, at that moment, that they had lost every hope that they were clinging to. They still did not understand that in three days' time He would be resurrected from the dead and seated at the right hand of God. He had not yet revealed Himself to the disciples or given them the Holy Spirit.

There are many times that things happen to us, and it looks like we are defeated, but that is a lie! Jesus' very words on the cross claim our victory over everything that raises its hand against the Word of God. I want you to read the words again. "It is finished!" These words mean that nothing can ever separate us from God once we accept Christ as our savior! We will have eternal life and the promises of God while we are waiting for our time to be called home to Him!

"It is finished!" My Jesus gave me the victory! He is the King of kings and Lord of lords! All my hope is in Him and He is faithful!

HE IS GENEROUS

Thus says the Lord: "Let not the wise man glory in his wisdom, let not the mighty man glory in his might, nor let the rich man glory in his riches; but let him who glories glory in this, that he understands and knows Me, that I am the Lord, exercising loving kindness, judgment and righteousness in the earth. For in these I delight," says the Lord. (Jeremiah 9:23–24 NKJV)

This generation has to be exceedingly more alert and watchful that we do not fall into self-worship. We live in a time where so many discoveries and inventions have provided access and ease to our daily lives. We have an abundance like never before. It is easy to become complacent and to begin to trust in ourselves. This can be a powerful deception.

True wisdom comes from God. God was the inventor of science. It is His very creation and how it works together that generates the provisions that we access. It was His idea to give the earth and everything in it to man. We are the caretakers of the world, but we ourselves are not its creator. We need to be thankful to the one true source of all we have, our Heavenly Father. He has always been exceedingly generous to us and provided ways that we could grow and be blessed. But we need to remember this verse, the most important thing we could ever do is to grow in our understanding of the Lord.

Father, I thank You for the wonderful blessing, inventions, and discoveries of this age. You always see before us and know the things we will need for every generation and season of life. Forgive me if these giftings have made me lose sight of the one true provider: You. You alone, God, give good gifts to Your children, because of Your tender mercies and great love for us. You gift men and women with knowledge and wisdom that allow each of us to grow and prosper. There really is none like You, and I am so thankful to be Your child. I seek You, Lord. I want to know Your ways. Amen.

LAYING IT ALL ON THE ALTAR

Then the fire of the Lord fell and consumed the burnt sacrifice, and the wood and the stones and the dust, and it licked up the water that was in the trench. (1 Kings 18:38 NKJV)

The altar of the Lord was an important part of worship for the Israelites. They were called to give an unblemished animal to offer as a sacrifice for the forgiveness of sins. In this particular Scripture, Elijah the Prophet has offered a sacrifice and drenched it with water. He was standing against the prophets of Baal, a false god. When they each had laid their sacrifice upon the altars and Elijah called on the name of Jehovah, fire fell from the heavens and consumed the bull even though it had been drenched in water.

During a time of prayer at my church recently, the Lord showed me that we need to lay our burdens, chains, anything that holds us back, and place it on the altar. We need to lay it there so that the fire of God may consume it. We cannot move into a place of authority if we keep allowing the weight of our pasts to hinder us. It is time to put aside all our past sins and shame and allow the refining fire of God to consume them so that we may be purified. We need to allow God to draw out anything that is not of Him and allow it to be burned up as chaff (Matthew 3:12). At this time, we sons and daughters need to be about the business of God and we have to let go of the things of this world. These include doubt, fear, bitterness, envy, and strife. We need to allow God to clothe us with garments of righteousness and begin seeing ourselves as members of His royal priesthood.

Lord, I declare over my brother and sister reading this right now, that they are taking their burdens, chains, and filthy rags and placing them on Your altar. Lord, I see Your fire falling and consuming them so that they are gone and can never return to try to claim them again! Lord, I proclaim that each one is clothed in a garment of praise and righteousness gifted by Your loving hand. Lord, that they may begin to have revelation of the power and authority granted to them through the Holy Spirit to move Your kingdom to the earth. Releasing Your light and love toward every man, woman, and child who is lost and needs salvation through Jesus Christ. I declare that Your Church is unified in Your work and purpose like never seen before! Amen!

THE SACRIFICE OF PRAISE

Through Him, therefore, let us constantly and at all times offer up to God a sacrifice of praise, which is the fruit of lips that thankfully acknowledge and confess and glorify His name. (Hebrews 13:15 AMPC)

Earlier I shared how the altar of the Lord was important for the Israelites because they were to offer sacrifices for the forgiveness of their sins. This, of course, we recognize as the foreshadowing of the ultimate sacrifice that Jesus would make for our sins, when He died on the cross. Here, Paul is sharing that although we are no longer bound to offer a blood sacrifice, we should offer God our worship.

There are so many examples in the Bible regarding the power of worship. I am reminded that often, when the people of God went into battle, worshippers went in advance of the army (2 Chronicles 20:21). At that moment, when the men and women began to sing and praise, the Lord went into battle for the people of Judah.

Praise and worship are an effective weapon in any spiritual warfare. Our worship, filled with the powerful words of God, allow the manifestation and movement of God; and, He enters into battle on our behalf. It builds up our faith and keeps us close to the Holy Spirit; we can receive the wisdom and guidance we need in any situation. I encourage you to enter into worship and praise often, so that it becomes a part of you. Then, when battles come, you won't have to think about what to do . . . you will just do what you already know!

BE FILLED TO OVERFLOW

A thief has only one thing in mind—he wants to steal, slaughter, and destroy. But I have come to give you everything in abundance, more than you expect—life in its fullness until you overflow! (John 10:10 TPT)

Your Heavenly Father wants you to know that He is the giver of life. He alone can fill you until you are overflowing! Nothing else on this earth will satisfy the longing of your heart the way Jesus can. There is no amount of money, no amount of earthly love, that can measure up. There is no amount of fame, and no amount of pleasure, that will give you the joy that comes from surrendering your heart to the One who created you!

He is waiting for you to stop looking everywhere and see Him waiting for you with His arms open wide. He wants to show you the real desires of your heart and how He has made you in His perfect image. You are the true treasure of His heart and He wants you to stand still in His embrace and receive the outpouring of love He has for you! I am not saying the minute you surrender to Him everything will become perfect, but He will begin to turn things for your good. He will also change you, heal you, restore you, and strengthen you. He will make you new. The old you will pass away and you will become a new creation through Christ Jesus. He will pour Himself into you through the indwelling of the Holy Spirit and you will be filled with life like never before!

Lord God, I thank You for the promise of life in its fullness until we overflow! You are so good! Thank you for the wonderful work of salvation and redemption through Jesus' death and resurrection. I give you my whole heart! You are the voice I want to hear. I trust in Your promises and Your Word alone. Thank you for strength and provision. I give You praise because You are God alone and nothing can compare to the love You pour over me! I pray that the gift of Your love and everlasting life be manifested in the lives of those reading this word today. That hearts would be softened and that they would recognize their need for You through the leading of the Holy Spirit. May You receive all glory and honor. Amen.

HIS PLAN FOR US

Then the Lord God said, "Behold, the man has become like one of Us, to know good and evil. And now, lest he put out his hand and take also of the tree of life, and eat, and live forever"—therefore the Lord God sent him out of the garden of Eden to till the ground from which he was taken. (Genesis 3:22–23 NKJV)

God's plan was always for man to have eternal life. In the beginning, when God was with Adam, He instructed Adam not to eat of the tree of knowledge (Genesis 3:17). It wasn't until after Adam disobeyed God and ate of the that tree, that the Lord placed Adam outside the Garden of Eden so that he could not eat from the tree of life. God's plan was to have an eternal relationship with us. Once man entered into sin, God began a new plan of redemption and salvation. That one day each of us would have access to the eternal life He always meant for us. In Revelation, God declares that He will give the fountain of life freely to everyone who wants to be His child (Revelation 21:6–7).

What an incredible God we have! We wanted more and created a barrier between ourselves and God when man first disobeyed God in the Garden of Eden. But God has always been working to make sure that we have a way back to the eternal life He always planned. Jesus was that plan. He was God, but became man, sacrificed all for us, and died on a cross to pay for all our sins. That is the craziest and fiercest love any of us will ever know.

Heavenly Father, thank you that Your plan for us was perfect all along. It was for us to always have a home with You. Thank you for the gift and the redemption You provided through Your Son, Jesus. His perfect work on the cross gave us the victory over death once and for all! You are worthy of all thanks and praise! There truly is no other but You, Lord! Amen.

CREATED TO CONFIRM GOD'S WORD

When outsiders who have never heard of God's law follow it more or less by instinct, they confirm its truth by their obedience. They show that God's law is not something alien, imposed on us from without, but woven into the very fabric of our creation. There is something deep within them that echoes God's yes and no, right and wrong. (Romans 2:14–16 MSG)

This scripture is amazing! It basically says that our very nature, the way we were created, has always been to coincide with God's ways. And we who have chosen to have a relationship learn that is so true. No one can satisfy and no one can understand us and the deepest desires of our hearts quite like God can. Most of us recognize that there are choices that we will make that are right and wrong, that are moral or immoral. Yet, so many people feel like following God is limiting, that it binds them from fulfilling the selfish desires of their hearts. So they reject the idea of a Holy, Heavenly God and, instead, decide to make themselves a god in their own lives. They believe that they can reconcile themselves in this life, by their works. Essentially, by being "good enough," often measuring themselves by others they see in this world. God's Word tells us that all of us fall short of His glory, and that only through grace we can be saved (Romans 3:23). Not one of us can do enough good works to measure up to the righteousness of our Heavenly Father. That is why He sent Jesus Christ to die for each one of us, as the ultimate sacrifice for our sins. We can try to deny that there is a heaven and hell, but, by our very recognition of actions that are right and wrong, we have already confirmed that God's law is true. We need to stop deceiving ourselves that we can be our own authority. There is only one true King of all of heaven and earth!

RECOGNIZING THE REAL TREASURE

"Do not lay up for yourselves treasures on earth, where moth and rust destroy and where thieves break in and steal, but lay up for yourselves treasures in heaven, where neither moth nor rust destroys and where thieves do not break in and steal. For where your treasure is, there your heart will be also." (Matthew 6:19–21 ESV)

This week we are finally seeing things come to a close on the rebuilding of our house, after our house was destroyed by fire one year ago, almost to the day. It is an exciting time, to think about moving back into our home, since we had only been living there for six months before it occurred. We have spent countless hours working out the details and choices of paint colors, fixtures, and flooring. Not to mention the hours we have spent putting in a little sweat equity of our own. I don't want to make it seem like my husband and I have been these super Christian people, with no struggles with this process for the past year. We have had our moments of sadness and frustrations during this entire process. We didn't let it destroy or tear us down because we recognized that our greatest treasure is the love God has for us. We don't make light of the tragedies or difficulties that arise in this life. I believe we have an empathy for people who have to face many different types of difficulties, because we have had difficulties of our own. However, we know that this home and this life are not all that God has for us. We are stewards of what He has provided for us. We take that responsibility seriously, and want to honor Him for the way He always looks out for us and gives us more than we could ask or expect. We loved our home when we purchased it, but like many homes built in the 1970s it needed lots of renovations. One year later, we have had all the renovations that would have taken us years to completely finish. It is not the way we would have chosen, but God has taken something tragic and turned it into a blessing. He has a way of doing that. I don't know what you are going through right now. But hear me, you are not alone. And if you don't give up, God can turn things around and bring beauty to the situation. Keep holding onto hope and faith. They are true treasures that sustain. The others are love, joy, compassion, kindness, and gentleness. Fix your eyes toward the Sustainer, the one and only Heavenly Father. He will never fail you!

HE QUALIFIES THE UNQUALIFIED

Then Moses said to the Lord, "O my Lord, I am not eloquent, neither before nor since You have spoken to your servant; but I am slow of speech and of tongue." So the Lord said to him, "Who has made man's mouth? Or who makes the mute, the deaf, the seeing or the blind? Have not I, the Lord? Now therefore, go, and I will be with your mouth and teach you what you shall say." (Exodus 4:10–12 NKJV)

When I first felt led by the Lord to begin writing this devotional, I must admit, I felt less than qualified. I am not a biblical scholar. I have not studied the Scriptures the way pastors, or other spiritual leaders have done. Then, when I realized that the Lord wanted me to write a devotional book for a whole year, I really began to doubt that I was capable. My thoughts though have been in error. Just like Moses, I was focusing on myself and my abilities. This book is not about me. It is about being obedient to God. He has things He wants to say. I am just the vessel He is using to accomplish His purpose. If I was unwilling or disobedient, God wouldn't force me to accomplish His purpose. He would just use someone else. His plan and His purpose will not be interrupted by our shortsightedness or shortcomings. It's not that I am qualified in any way to write this book, but that God is more than qualified to speak through His Word to those who need to hear it. Maybe, God has been calling you to step out and speak up to others in some way, but you feel inadequate. You are afraid of what people will say about you, or call you unqualified too. Let go and just let God do it. He is more than able. He will equip you every step of the way, just like He equipped Moses to lead the Israelites out of Egypt.

Father, forgive me for making any of this about me, when it is all about Your love for Your sons and daughters. Lord, I lay down all my doubts and fears and give You all of me. Use me to declare Your Word in a fresh and new way so that lives may be filled with hope, with salvation, with healing, and with joy. You alone are the One who can do more than we can ask or foresee. I thank You for the fresh way You are bringing Your Word to the forefront of my mind. Thank you for blessing me with an opportunity to share Your love with others, and to serve. It has never been about what I could bring, but what You can do! Amen!

THE HOPE WITHIN

But give reverent honor in your hearts to the Anointed One and treat him as the holy Master of your lives. And if anyone asks about the hope living within you, always be ready to explain your faith with gentleness and respect. (1 Peter 3:15–16 TPT)

Through thick and thin, keep your hearts at attention, in adoration before Christ, your Master. Be ready to speak up and tell anyone who asks why you're living the way you are, and always with the utmost courtesy. (1 Peter 3:15–16 MSG)

As I read this scripture, I have to be honest, I don't know the last time anyone has asked me about the hope I have within me. If you find the same thing to be true in your life, then we need to be asking why aren't they? Is it that we look just like everyone else in the world? Are we negative, talking about the darkness of the world, about how it seems hopeless? Maybe that's you . . . .

Or maybe it is more that we are so wrapped up in only showing the world how perfect everything is . . . that we are being fake and no one can relate to us, because no one can see all that God has brought us through. When is the last time you or I dared to share our testimonies? I believe Christians have begun to believe the rhetoric that we are hypocrites and, therefore, have stopped being open and honest about how our daily lives. That each day we are walking out our faith and salvation. We have bought into the social media hype to present only our best selfies . . . our perfect families, our perfect lives . . . We hide the pain, the mess, the real truth that we are all in desperate need of a living God, who helps us daily, and pours out mercy and grace over our messes. We don't trust one another because we are too busy comparing ourselves to one another. We are supposed to be keeping our eyes fixed on the One, the only One, who is perfect. Christ cleaned me up and put my feet on solid ground. Left on my own, I made a perfect mess of all of it. I broke relationships and trust; I hurt others and hurt myself. He not only restored me, but gave me a new life, filled with new relationships. Relationships that are healthy and whole. He gave me hope that I could be healed and could have a future. He placed my husband in my life and together we are building a life together, grounded in the love of God.

I challenge you to be bold and show people that you have a living hope within you from a God who loves you . . . He set you apart so that you could be a living testimony of who He is.

If you have lost your sense of hope, then you have lost your connection with Him and the way to get it back is to plug into His Word daily. Get back to basics . . . get into His Word, worship, and spend time with Him . . . He is waiting to restore your sight of who He is and what He can do in your life.

THE CHAINS OF SHAME ARE BROKEN

So now the case is closed. There remains no accusing voice of condemnation against those who are joined in life-union with Jesus, the Anointed One. For the "law" of the Spirit of life flowing through the anointing of Jesus has liberated us from the "law" of sin and death. (Romans 8:1–2 TPT)

I don't know each of you personally and can only share things based on my own experiences. However, I am willing to bet that, maybe, you at times have struggled with shame from your past mistakes. That if you were to look into the review mirror of your life, there would be images of the past that make you cringe and feel that hollow pit in your stomach. I want you to know that if you have gone to God and asked for forgiveness for your past mistakes and sin, those feelings of shame are not from the God pointing a finger at you. They are the whispers of the enemy, constantly trying to convince us that we are not good enough for God's love. That we are not worthy. And, although we recognize that when we were in our flesh and not reconciled to God through Jesus, this was true. But now, God sees us separated from our sin through the salvation and blood poured out on us through Jesus. You are no longer that person of the past. You are a new creation! (2 Corinthians 5:17)

Stop looking in the review mirror of your life and start walking forward. God has great things in store for you, but your past will hold you back if you keep returning to it! You are redeemed and set apart. You are a child of God. God no longer remembers your mistakes (Romans 4:7)

Father God, I thank You for Your grace and mercy, and how You have forgiven me of my past mistakes. I recognize that condemnation does not come from You but is a plan of the enemy to keep me isolated from Your great love. I proclaim that Satan's lies will no longer have claim on me! I am a child of God! I am brand new! Thank you for the precious gift of salvation! Amen.

DEEPLY ROOTED

As you therefore have received Christ Jesus the Lord, so walk in Him, rooted and built up in Him and established in the faith, as you have been taught, abounding in it with thanksgiving. (Colossians 2:6–7 NKJV)

My husband and I went for our first hike together this season. He selected the trail, Dragon's Tooth, along the Appalachian Trail. It is rated as difficult, and the total hike was 4.8 miles long. As we started out, I was enthusiastic and fully engaged in looking at the beauty surrounding us on the trail. The array of flowers and foliage were breathtaking along the trail. I loved the sound of the stream that wove its way along our path. We reached the summit and stopped to enjoy the amazing view. As we had to turn around and begin our descent, I felt the fatigue of my muscles and the enthusiasm of the journey began to wane. Several spots were really steep and difficult to maneuver. At times there would be a small tree in just the right spot to brace against as we climbed down. I remember looking at the trail and seeing the roots of trees come right through the path. It was amazing to see that even though many people had hiked along this path, the roots were strong and steadfast. I heard in my spirit, "Rooted in Me strengthens the weary." God wants us to stay rooted in Him. Staying connected through His Word. He and His Word are one (John 1:1). It is how when I feel worn and weak, I can be renewed and made strong. The critical piece is to press in and stay connected to the Lord. When I have been going through a hard season and isolated myself from the Lord, my situation, strength, and stress levels all increased because

I allowed myself to be separated from my source. Alternately, when I have turned to God during challenging times, He has provided me with mercy and strength for each day. I encourage you, whatever you are facing, stay connected to the One who can do more than you could ever imagine or think! Stay rooted in His Word, keep your spirit fed, and you will build up your faith and strength.

THE UNSTOPPABLE FORCE INSIDE

For since the creation of the world His invisible attributes are clearly seen, being understood by the things that are made, even His eternal power and Godhead, so that they are without excuse. (Romans 1:20 NKJV)

Last night, while at a prayer service in my church, I began to think about the power of nature. It has a force all of its own. Think about standing along the Atlantic Ocean, see the power of the waves as they crash along the shore. Hearing the distinctive roar of the movement of the water as it continuously crashes against the sandy beaches and rocks. The water has the power to erode the rocks and change their shape over time. As I continued to pray in the spirit, a realization came over me that the power of nature was purposefully chosen to represent the power of our God. As powerful as nature can be, nothing can stand against the power of our God. He is the epitome of power and strength. He, with one word, created these things we see all around us. He spoke them into existence.

We need to remember the force and power we have dwelling on the inside of us. If we are one with Christ, then we have His Spirit living in us. That means we are full of power too! It is that power that gives us strength to stand when everything around us is falling apart. We don't have to worry about what comes against us, because we have the power of God inside us, and He is always with us. His Word cannot be moved or changed. Keep your eyes open to the earth and all that is in it. See the beauty and vastness of our God. His attributes can be seen clearly in the way things were made.

Father, thank you for revelation knowledge. You make Your Word stand out in new ways at just the right time. I thank You that I can see the power of Your hand at work in the wonders You have created. Peel away the things that blind me from seeing anything but Your incredible power and strength. Continue to reveal to us the vastness of Your love through all that we see and encounter in Your creation. Just the way You created all things to work together is an incredible reminder that nothing is impossible for You! You deserve all the glory, all the honor and all the praise! Amen.

COMPLETING THE WORK

The Lord will fulfill His purpose for me. Lord, Your love is eternal; do not abandon the work of Your hands. (Psalm 138:8 HCSB)

It doesn't matter what the situation looks like, God is working all things to fulfill His purpose in your life. You were created with a purpose in mind, and given you certain gifts. God has been calling out to you the whole time. Listen for His voice and His leading. It doesn't mean the path to His purpose will be easy, but He will never fail you! Just because you fall down along the way, doesn't mean God has removed Himself from you . . . No! That is a lie from the enemy. God waits for us to get back up, set our heart, mind, and soul back into seeking Him and continue on our journey together. It is when we quit that we lose the plan and purpose that God has for us. We make everything about our inadequacies, instead of God's abilities to do the impossible! Did He not enable His Son to be resurrected from the grave? That same power lives in us! Reading His Word helps you stay connected to His truth and the power that lives inside His Word. That's why we are encouraged to keep meditating on His Word day and night (Joshua 1:8).

Thank you, Lord, for the promise of fulfilling Your purpose in my life. I yield to the Holy Spirit and allow the power and anointing granted to me to fill my heart, mind, and spirit. I want to be all You designed me to be and let my life be a magnet to others. A light, a beacon of hope, to point others to the Holy One, the Mighty God, who does the impossible. Thank you for Your goodness and Your provision. I love You, Lord.

A GENEROUS HEART

"Will a mere mortal rob God? Yet you rob me." But you ask, 'How are we robbing you?' "In tithes and offerings." (Malachi 3:8 NIV)

Now, before you roll your eyes and turn the page . . . just wait. Although, tithing is generally talking about giving back to the Lord in things that are of monetary value, that is not what I am talking about today. I want you to think about other ways you can give back to the Lord. What about through acts of service to our church or to our community or people we know? Sometimes I think it is easier to give our money than to donate our time. I get it. Many of us are juggling jobs and families. If you have children, then most likely you are taking them to their activities and events too. We quickly lose sight of the most valuable thing we can invest our time in . . . our relationship with God. That includes allotting some of our time not just attending church services, but in giving of our time in other ways. Has God given you a particular gift? Maybe you can play an instrument or sing. Maybe you love working with children. Maybe you find it easy to talk with anyone you meet. These are gifts and are much needed in any church you attend. The statistics say that of any given church, only 10% of the people attending actually serve. So, if you have a hundred people in your church, only ten people actually give of their time and serve the congregation. Remember that Jesus said the greatest among us would be the one who is a servant to others. There really is a transformation and a return (a blessing) when we give of our time and serve others. If you are not currently serving in your church, I urge you to pray about it and see where God would lead you.

HE HOLDS JUSTICE

"For the day of the Lord upon all nations is near; as you have done, it shall be done to you; your reprisal shall return upon your own head." (Obadiah 1:15 NKJV)

This is a really important word for all of us. In today's world, everyone is shouting about his or her individual rights. Many people are looking to worldly ways to seek justice for themselves. However, Christians must realize that it is God alone who may sit in judgment on every individual. We must be careful not to enter into battles with our own purposes or selfish desires. The word in Obadiah is clear that if we seek after our own justice, we will receive what we have given out.

This will be really hard for many of us to hear, because as we live out our daily lives, many of us have been hurt or wronged deeply. Ephesians 4:23 calls us to "be kind toward one another, forgiving each other, just as in Christ God forgave you." We need to be mindful of the mercy we each have received. That on our own we fall short of the glory of God because of our own sin. None of us would have salvation if not for the grace of our Heavenly Father. In response to that great love shown to us, our Father calls on us to give that same love and forgiveness to others. To not engage in any kind of worldly battle with another person. The funny thing about this challenge is that when we are able to forgive, we discover that we have set our own selves free. That we have freedom from all the damage hatred and bitterness do to our minds, our bodies, and our spirit.

Oh Father, I declare over all my brothers and sisters right now, that they will lay down any bitterness and strife in their hearts and allow Your healing to take place. That the peace and freedom You give will flow into their minds and hearts. Holy Spirit, be quick to bring remembrance of the Word declaring that we will be judged if we judge others. Help us to always come humbly before You and allow You to examine our hearts and lay anything aside on the altar that is not from You. Allow us to serve brightly with the love and compassion given so freely to each of us. That others who need You may see You in our walk. Amen.

REMAINING IN PEACE

Do not repay anyone evil for evil. Be careful to do what is right in the eyes of everybody. If it is possible, as far as it depends on you, live at peace with everyone. (Romans 12:17–18 NIV)

There are going to be times in life where you have conflict with another human being. We are in this world and, even if we do not try to hurt or offend others, it may still happen. I believe it can happen even easier, because more and more communication is sent via electronic devices and not actual conversations. However, we are responsible for our own actions. If we know that we have wronged someone, we are accountable to make it right. In Matthew 5:23, we are told to leave our gift at the altar and be reconciled to our brother first. Apologizing and attempting to make amends benefit us, because then we know we have been obedient to honor God's Word. Unfortunately, not every relationship will be reconciled. If you do what you can to correct the situation and the other person wants to hold onto anger and bitterness, then that is their choice. You will receive peace, because the Holy Spirit will bring peace to you if you fulfill the Word of the Lord.

Thank you, Father, for teaching me that I am responsible for my own actions and that I am not to attempt to take justice into my own hands. I should always try to make amends and live at peace with those around me, reflecting Your love and light. Thank you for the promise of supernatural peace, when relationships do not heal, but I have been obedient to Your Word. Holy Spirit, I trust You to guide my words to speak or to be quiet in every conversation. Help me to always treat others with compassion, and to offer the same grace and mercy I have received. Amen.

THE RETURN OF JOY

To console those who mourn in Zion, to give them beauty for ashes, the oil of joy for mourning, the garment of praise for the spirit of heaviness . . . . (Isaiah 61:3 NKJV partial)

Son and daughter of the Most High King, you will feel joy again! This is the prophetic promise of Your Heavenly Father. The current situation may seem dark and may have tried to shake your faith, but Jesus is the very light in the darkness and that darkness can never put out His light. Lift up your eyes to your Father and allow Him to wipe every tear from your eyes (Revelation). Even if the only thing you can say from your heart today is, "Abba, I need you," our Lord hears you! He is close to those who are brokenhearted. In this life, we are called to stand in our faith no matter what the situation looks like. That faith brings forth a response from our God to provide supernatural strength, supernatural peace, and so much more! Our God isn't changed or moved by circumstances. He is for you, not against you. He is always working for your good! Cling to Him. Hang on tight. He will not let you go.

Father God, I pray for my brothers and sisters reading this right now. I declare that the Holy Spirit will fill them with supernatural strength to stand in faith no matter what the circumstances look like. That through the Spirit, their mind will be renewed by Your Word and filled with the truth of Your incredible love for them. I prophecy that they will have revelation knowledge that permeates their spirit with the depth of Your love for them. That the overwhelming love fills them to overflowing and pours out of them helping them with new strength every day. Lord, I thank You for the promise that You are always working things for our good. We receive Your perfect plan and purpose in all we do every day. Thank you for the reminder that in You we will find our strength. You are a good, good Father. Thank you that I will receive beauty for ashes and joy in place of mourning! Amen.

REVELATION IN THE EARTH

The heavens declare the glory of God; and the firmament shows His handiwork. Day unto day utters speech, and night unto night reveals knowledge. (Psalm 19:1–2 NKJV)

When you gaze up into the sky, on a clear night, does it take your breath away? The vastness of space seems infinite, and yet according to scientists ours is only one of many galaxies in space. Think about space and how great it is . . . that is only a fragment of God's love for you! It is impossible to wrap our minds around a love like His. I am speechless when I think about it. Your Heavenly Father wants you to know that He sees you. You are so precious to Him. He would have sent His Son Jesus to die on the cross if you were the only one who needed Him. He longs to call you closer, deeper into His presence. He wants you to hear His voice louder than any other voice, even your own. He calls you beloved, prized, treasured, worthy of it all! I love the way our Father talks about us. He calls you son and daughter!

Look up! Look up! Raise your eyes and see the Glory of the Lord! He is speaking to you in every single part of the world He created for you! Don't doubt His love for you. Nothing can separate you from the love of God (Romans 8:31).

Abba, how great You are! I thank You for the way Your creation reveals knowledge. Thank you for the loving way You speak to our hearts and minds. Thank you for a love like no other. I declare we carry Your voice with us as we interact in this world. And the breadth of

Your love would be like a shield that aids us in the battles that we face every day. Thank you for the promise that the victory is already ours. There is no one like You! Holy, holy, holy are You, Lord. May my praises never stop! You alone deserve all the glory and honor. Amen.

THE ROOT SUPPORTS EACH ONE

For if the firstfruit is holy, the lump is also holy; and if the root is holy, so are the branches. And if some of the branches were broken off, and you being a wild olive tree, were grafted in among them, and with them became a partaker of the root and fatness of the olive tree, do not boast against the branches. But if you do boast, remember that you do not support the root, but the root supports you. (Romans 11:16–18 NKJV)

This scripture aligns with how Jesus stated, "I am the vine and you are the branches" (John 15:5). We have been adopted into the family of Christ, along with many other members. As the body of Christ, we are all at different levels of faith and growth. We are not to compare ourselves to our fellow brothers and sisters in Christ, but to fix our eyes on the one whom our salvation and redemption comes from. Not one of us is without sin. Not one of us is worthy. Thankfully, Jesus stands in the gap for each one of us. Through His sacrifice, we are now covered in His righteousness. We need to stay close to Jesus and facilitate relationships that grow and nurture each one's faith. Jesus reminds the disciples in John 15:5, "If you remain in me and I in you, you will bear much fruit; apart from me you can do nothing."

This world has people scrambling and trampling over each other. Each person is determined to look out for their own self-interests. This is in direct opposition of the kingdom of God. Christ came and served others. His ministry is the only example we should be following.

Holy Lord, thank you for Your Word. The image of us being connected to You as branches connected to a vine. We need the foundation of Your Word to be manifested in our hearts, minds, and spirits. Remove from our hearts the desire to be first and, instead, infuse our hearts with a Christlike spirit. Let us serve others with love and compassion. Help us to always see the beautiful flow of grace and mercy in our lives and offer that same gift to others. In Jesus' name. Amen.

A CALL TO SERVE

"Then the righteous will answer Him, saying, 'Lord when did we see You hungry and feed You, or thirsty and give You drink? When did we see You a stranger and take You in, or naked and clothe You? Or when did we see You sick, or in prison, and come to You?' And the King will answer and say to them, 'Assuredly, I say to you in as much as you did it to one the least of these My brethren, you did it to Me.'" (Matthew 25:38–40 NKJV)

This past week, my husband and I went with other members of our church to visit some of our veterans in a senior living facility. It was a cool day, with quite a bit of breeze. Thankfully, the sun was shining and a few of the veterans gathered in a sunny spot outside the building. Those of us attending had to pass a screening, due to current policy and restrictions for this facility. We sang a variety of songs for them, some hymns, gospel music, contemporary Christian music, and even a little Elvis. Once we were finished singing , we spread out and mingled with those that had come out to see us. The facility activities coordinator had informed us that we could only stay about an hour, due to having to have our visit outside. So we began to shake hands and say goodbye to the veterans. One gentleman said to me, "Thank you so much, I am a Christian and can't go to church anymore. I haven't been to church in three years. You just don't know what this means to me." He thanked me. He thanked me. He served our country and fought for our freedoms, and he thanked me for one hour worth of time and a few songs. We owe our veterans and our seniors, in general, so much more. It really is shameful how this world has become so self-centered and so desensitized to the needs of others with less. As Christians, we are called to see people the way Jesus did and to fight for the marginalized. Our veterans and our seniors have become that peripheral group. We are called to serve them. Provide them with food, drink, clothing, and comfort in all of their days. The Bible says that we can't say we love God but not treat our fellow brother or neighbor with love (1 John 4:20).

Thank you, Lord, for challenging me to do better and serve those who have become marginalized. Thank you for allowing my eyes to be opened to see as Jesus does, with love and compassion. Keep pushing me, Lord, to not make excuses, but to make time for others. What we plant will be grown into a harvest. Amen.

BITTERSWEET GROWTH

Then the Lord said to him, "This is the land of which I swore to give Abraham, Isaac, and Jacob, saying, 'I will give it to your descendants.' I have caused you to see it with your eyes, but you shall not cross over there." (Deuteronomy 34:4 NKJV)

I wonder how Moses felt to be leading the Israelites as they wandered in the desert for forty years? To never be able to cross into the land that was promised to them because of unbelief. It must have been bittersweet to see the land of Jericho and to know that he himself would not be able to set his own feet upon the land. I believe many of us are going to have that bittersweet moment as well. When we realize how many opportunities that God laid before us, to go and serve, or to share our hearts and our faith. How many times have I allowed fear to leave me wandering far away from God's purpose in my life? It fills my heart with heaviness to know that I have allowed myself to get in the way of God's plan.

Wisdom brings about the opportunity for growth and change! Once aware of the areas where I am weak brings chances for God to mold me, and shape me, to be more like His Son! He can take out the parts that hinder Him, and fill me with all truth and power through the Holy Spirit. I can yield to His voice and step into obedience the next time He leads me to reach out. Faith will build upon faith!

Lord, thank you for the image of the bittersweet experience of Moses, who You blessed with a glimpse of Your beautiful promise for the

Israelites. I yield any area of unbelief and declare that my heart and spirit will be filled with faith upon faith. Not because of anything that I bring into any situation, but because of what You bring, God. Through You and in You is all power, and all honor and all glory! It is You that allow Your children to be filled with the anointing power of Christ! Amen.

LOVED IN OUR BROKENNESS

However, we possess this precious treasure [the divine Light of the Gospel] in [frail, human] vessels of earth, that the grandeur and exceeding greatness of the power may be shown to be from God and not of ourselves. (2 Corinthians 4:7 AMPC)

Over the past few weeks, my husband and I have been working on settling back into our house, after its restoration from a fire. Many of our belongings were packed up and taken to a warehouse, where a fire restoration company would clean and salvage whatever they could. As we began unpacking, I realized that many items that had been listed "restored" have damage to them. Today, looking at a plaque that had been returned as restored, I saw water marks on the paint causing visible rings. I began to feel a little frustrated because I felt like quality work on the care of our items really hadn't been done. As I went over it in my mind, I heard in my spirit, "The scar or imperfection is there to remind you of all I have brought you through. You weren't perfect, when I found you." Truly an amazing and timely bit of wisdom from my Heavenly Father.

This scripture talks about vessels, other versions refer to "jars of clay." Clay can be broken if dropped or too much heat or pressure is applied to it. It can also be mended back together. Many of us are waiting to be made perfect or without blemish, thinking we can't be used by God until that very thing happens. But God loved us in our brokenness, and when we were still walking in sin. His love for us has been fervent from the beginning. It is the broken pieces of your life that He restores, that reveals His power and His glory. He didn't cause those things, but He always uses them to reveal Himself to those who witness your transformation.

Abba, how wonderful You are! To always be looking for ways to reveal Your wisdom to Your sons and daughters. I thank You that You love me enough to correct my perspective. Your wisdom is truly beautiful. I declare over all those reading this right now, that You would show Your power and glory in their lives as You continue the refining process in their hearts. That they would embrace the sweet remembrances of all the broken places that You have healed. Father God, that they would see their scars as Your beautiful handiwork in their lives. Amen.

BE STILL AND LOOK UP

My voice you shall hear in the morning O Lord; in the morning I will direct it to You and I will look up. (Psalm 5:3 NKJV)

Just the other evening, as my husband and I were heading home from our church service, I saw the most beautiful sunset. I grabbed my cell phone and got ready to take a picture. We were in my husband's truck, which is very bouncy with its stiff suspension. Several attempts to get the picture or a video of the sunset left me feeling disappointed. Quietly, in my spirit, I heard, "Sometimes it is better to just be still in the moment and enjoy what you see."

Be still. Isn't that so hard for so many of us to do? I know it is for my husband. He is a doer. He always has a list of things he wants to accomplish. They are good things. Many of them are providing the maintenance our home, vehicles, or other items need. There are times, when I cannot keep up with him. I feel in myself the need to slow down, find rest, and just sit quietly.

If we never set time aside to spend it with God, how can we possibly know what He has in store for us? All relationships take time. If you are married, you know that you have had to invest time in that relationship to make it work. If you are a parent, you have to invest time in your children (for their care and emotional well-being). Why do we think we can grow in our faith, our relationship with God, if we give Him such a small portion of our time? I used to think that I didn't have time to start my day off in the Word, or in prayer. My time in the morning was too short before work. Until I committed to getting up a half hour earlier than I used to. It was hard at first, but over time it became easier. Now I look forward to my morning time with my Father. It helps me prepare my heart, my spirit, and my attitude for the day. It really is vital to be equipped for those of us who work in the world on a daily basis. I challenge you to learn to find time, to be still, before the Lord and enjoy all He has for you. How He loves you and wants to fill your day with such joy and goodness!

THE ONE VOICE TO HEAR

But you do not believe, because you are not of My sheep, as I said to you. My sheep hear My voice, and I know them and they follow Me. (John 10:26–27 NKJV)

We have come into a time, where everyone believes their voice should be heard. Everyone has something to say, and there are more platforms than ever for someone to utilize so that their opinion may be heard. There are even people trying to shout over each other in public forums to have their viewpoints heard.

I want you to remember to listen for the small, still voice of the Lord. It is the most valuable source of truth, when everyone in this world has their own version of "truth." Jesus said, "I am the way, the truth, and the life." Brothers and sisters, our ideas and what we speak out must be filtered through the Holy Spirit. We cannot speak like the world, or sound like the world. We should speak from an eternal perspective. Our political views aren't going to turn someone to Jesus. Our belief in whether or not the gun laws and regulations violate people's First Amendment rights aren't important when people are living in darkness, fear, and are without hope. We are called to build each other up in truth (1 Thessalonians 5:11).

I am hearing more fear being spoken out by those around me than ever before. People's sources of information are not based on biblical truth, but on information produced by man via the media. They are not here to keep us informed, but to be profitable, and to "sound the alarm." That is where the whole "if it bleeds, it leads" perspective has manifested itself. Help yourself by staying plugged into the Word of God, and plug in less to the world. Spend time away from the news and social media. It quiets the outside noise and allows you to hear the still, small voice that has always been trying to get your attention.

HIS PROMISE OF JOY

Weeping may endure for a night, but joy comes in the morning. (Psalm 30:5 NKJV partial)

Lately, it seems that many people I know are going through something that is causing them heartaches. The trials of this life, the attacks of the enemy through sickness, and the losses seem to not relent. I have heard anger and bitterness in the voices of those who are trying to bear up. Feelings of confusion and not understanding why this is happening to them. My words of encouragement sound hollow in my own ears as I watch them struggle in the day-to-day. I am reminded that, apart from God, I cannot accomplish anything, even choosing the correct words of encouragement for another. It is only His truth and His promises that truly matter in our darkest hours.

Lord, I thank You for this beautiful promise, that we will have sadness and tears, but there is always the promise of new hope and joy on the other side of our experiences. We will find it if we stay connected to You. I declare over each person reading this and going through a personal heartache, that they will feel Your supernatural peace like never before. Lord God, that Your voice through Your Spirit will continuously speak truth into their minds, reminding them of Your power, Your love, Your mercy, and Your goodness. That, at just the right moment, Lord, You will provide the joy that is needed to refresh their hearts. Lord, Your promise of working all things for our good stands firm forever. You are the same yesterday, today, and forever. There is no falseness in You. I praise You as You begin to make a way for everyone to know the extent of Your love for them and Your will in their lives. Amen.

FILTER WHAT YOU PUT IN YOUR SPIRIT

Summing it all up, friends, I'd say you'll do your best by filling your minds and meditating on things true, noble, reputable, authentic, compelling, gracious—the best, not the worst; the beautiful, not the ugly; things to praise, not things to curse. (Ephesians 4:8 MSG)

We may not always have a choice of what is happening around us in this world. It is a fallen place, and we are just visitors. However, we do have a choice about how we will react to the circumstances and situations we find ourselves in. Our Heavenly Father promises that He will never leave us unprotected or unequipped in whatever we are facing (Deuteronomy 31:6). We are instructed to shed our minds and be filled with the mind of Christ. This instruction from Paul to the Ephesians gives us insight on how to do just that. If you are watching the media for hours each day, then that is what your mind will focus on. If you are filling your mind with God's Word, and with worship and praise, you will elevate your view from this earthly place to one that is eternal. You will be equipping and building yourself up in strength, truth, and knowledge that will allow you to hold fast in any set of circumstances. Faith comes by hearing and hearing by the Word of God (2 Corinthians 5:17). You must consistently work on building up your faith in God's Word. Apart from God and His truth, we lose sight of Him and His purpose for our lives. The truth is that God loves you with a fierce and mighty love. He has given you countless blessings and miracles in your life. We just need to have our hearts open and our eyes ready to see them clearly.

Father God, thank you for this truth today. I praise You for I see the countless ways You have produced miracle after miracle in my life. You have redeemed me, set me feet on a firm foundation, and poured out Your abundant grace and mercy on my life. It was something I could never earn and most definitely did not deserve. Lord, that alone would be enough, but You want me to have an abundant life filled with joy and peace. I see You everywhere I look. You made this world so beautifully! I submit my mind to things that are eternal and pleasing to You, God. Help me meditate on Your Word and goodness all day and all night! Amen.

WHAT YOU SAY MATTERS

And remind them to never tear down anyone with their words or quarrel, but instead be considerate, humble, and courteous to everyone. For it wasn't long ago that we behaved foolishly in our stubborn disobedience. We were easily led astray as slaves to worldly passions and pleasures. (Titus 3:2–3 TPT)

We are told that there is life and death in the power of the tongue (Proverbs 18:21). It is likely that we have all had people speak both words that have built us up and words that have hurt us and made us feel worthless. In his letters to the various churches, Paul revisits this concept of loving people through our actions and our words. We need to have a healthy remembrance of the grace that was given to us. Our lives are redeemed only because of the love and sacrifice of Jesus Christ, who humbled Himself and died for our sins. We have never done any deed good enough to earn our salvation. It is a gift. God's vast love is a gift. We are reminded to offer that love, compassion, and grace to others. This is not an easy task, because it is just not something we are called to do for believers, but for those still living and serving their own selfish ambitions. We don't have to accept what they stand for, or be taken advantage of, but we are to always be courteous and kind. I know that there are specific encounters I have had in this world that have made this a significant challenge.

Heavenly Father, I know that I have often failed at showing kindness to everyone I have interacted with, and it hurts You. You love them and sent Jesus for their salvation as well. Lord, I need Your help to see them with eyes of compassion and to keep a healthy remembrance of the grace and mercy I have received. May the Holy Spirit speak to me and guard my tongue that I may always have control over my words. Do not allow me to tear down those who desperately need to hear of how You love them. Let my heart and mouth always be a light to Your glory and show honor to Your name. Amen.

INNER ADORNMENT

For when they observe your pure, godly life before God, it will impact them deeply. Let your true beauty come from your inner personality, not a focus on the external. For lasting beauty comes from a gentle and peaceful spirit, which is precious in God's sight and is much more important than the outward adornment of elaborate hair, jewelry, and fine clothes. (1 Peter 3:2–4 TPT)

It took me a long time to understand that my true identity was found in Christ. This led to years of looking to worldly ways to improve myself, and left me in a constant state of comparing myself to others. The results were that I always felt undeserving of love. The concern I have in my heart for this generation and the generations to come is great. The world seems to have an even louder voice than ever. Social media has become the main stage for many to get information and to form opinions. The noise coming from the world is always opposite God's truth. Comparison is the quickest way to stir up envy, strife, and bitterness in your spirit.

I feel strongly that God wants you to know that He cares about your heart. He finds you beautiful and more precious to Him than all that He has created. His love is so deep and so wide that, oftentimes, we cannot fully understand it. You cannot do anything that will change His love for you. There is no mistake, no choice, that will ever make Him take His love away. You are enough. Right now just as you are. You are worth dying for and God sent His Son Jesus to do that very act. He says you are chosen. He says you are made new and whole in

Him. Let the power of His love wash over you. See yourself through His eyes. His arms are open wide to embrace you. He sings over you! He is so happy to spend time with you and for you to know His love and to know Him as a father.

If you feel like you have never heard these things spoken before, I encourage you to look in the Bible. These truths are written there from God for you. He wrote down His heart through the Holy Spirit, so that we would have the truth about who He is and His plan for us. He is going to bless your life. His promises are always fulfilled.

HE CAN USE YOU

What is man that You are mindful of him, and the son of man that You visit him? (Psalm 8:4 NKJV)

Have you ever missed an opportunity to do something that God was leading you to do because you doubted that He could use you? I believe that if we are all honest with ourselves, we all can recognize opportunities that we have let slip by. In this Psalm, even King David is in wonder of God's desire to love and use us. In verse 5, David goes on to state, "For You have made him a little lower that the angels, and You have crowned him with glory and honor." David recognized that God had the power to create and determine the order of things. He believed that God's plan was designed and developed to show His glory and splendor.

We need to recognize that God has the ability to use anything that He has made to carry out His plans and purposes. It is His heart to use us, because then we become a witness to His power and might. It also develops our faith in His Word and who He is as our Heavenly Father. When we doubt our usefulness to God, we are basically stating that we don't believe and trust in God's promises, His Word. We put our own abilities, our strengths and weaknesses, at the forefront, instead of the mighty power of the One who created all things. We need to remember, that we get to be vessels for the anointing of Christ, who dwells in us. We ourselves, on our own, will not accomplish anything. It is Christ in us that equips us with all strength, all power, and the anointing to manifest change in the world and in individual lives.

Father, forgive me for getting in the way of Your plans and purposes. There are so many times that I have taken my eyes off You. I have only seen my inadequacies and forgotten that I am equipped because of all You have given me. Forgive me for making myself bigger than You. Grow my faith in every area, that I may recognize the move of Your hand and be subject to Your call and direction. That I may not miss an opportunity to be useful to the One who has breathed His breath of life into my very spirit. Keep my heart tender toward those You place in my path. Amen.

RICHLY BLESSED

The blessing of the Lord makes one rich, and He adds no sorrow with it. (Proverbs 10:22 NKJV)

It is the Lord's heart to bless you. Over and over again, in His Word, He tells us that His plans for us are good. Yes, there is sorrow in this world. It comes from the world and not from God. It comes from our separation from God because of the sin Adam and Eve committed in the garden when they disobeyed God. Do not believe the lie of the enemy, that only if you are perfect and do everything correctly that God will then bless you. If we needed to be perfect before coming to God, He never would have sent His Son Jesus. Jesus is one of the greatest treasures we can ever receive from the Lord! His sacrifice makes it possible to come to God and receive His mercy and grace. We don't have to be perfect, we just have to be willing to allow God to change us from the inside out!

I look around at the world and all the sorrow that it brings people, and I want to cling to Jesus even more. He is my source for all things! Through Him I have the promise of all hope, all peace, and all joy. Not just once I join Him in eternity, but now on this earth too! But I have to focus on the blessings of the Lord. I need to recall His faithfulness and steadfast love. If I take my eyes off Jesus, then I will become like Peter and allow fear to enter into my heart, which lessens my faith (Matthew 14:30–31). Keep your eyes on the Lord; recount the ways He has blessed you. Start somewhere; thank the Lord that He woke you up this morning! That is a wonderful thing! He woke you up and is waiting to spend time in this day with you!

Lord, You are good and faithful. There is no love like Your love, God! Thank you for this day to recount Your goodness, and how You have chosen to bless me. There are many times I have missed the way You are and have been moving in my life. Forgive me for not seeing, Lord. I will keep my eyes fixed on You and my faith will grow. I love You, Lord! Amen.

READY WARRIOR

Put on the whole armor [the armor of a heavy-armed soldier which God supplies], that you may be able to stand successfully to stand up against [all] the strategies and deceits of the devil. (Ephesians 6:11 AMP)

We had a guest speaker recently at our church, ministering on the Body of Christ being encouraged by God to be strong and courageous (Joshua 1:6–7). This speaker cited this scripture and talked about the promise of God to never fail or forsake His children. During the message, I had a vision of myself clad in armor. I looked like a Viking warrior, with bold determination on my face. I looked ready for battle! I remember thinking about the armor of God and how this scripture calls us to put on God's armor. I heard the Holy Spirit's voice say to me, "You are already covered in armor, because Christ lives within in you and His power is within you." It is amazing to me how God sees us. If we could just see ourselves more through the eyes of our Heavenly Father, we would operate in the full authority He has given us. Jesus told us that if we believed in Him and the works He did, that we would do even greater things (John 14:12–14). The armor of God scripture in Ephesians talks about all the equipment God supplies us to live in this world. We have to grasp hold of the basic fact, God has already supplied us with it. He didn't just place us here and leave us. He has already made every provision for us to be victorious. His life-giving Word has the victory written down for us to see! There is no question of how our stories will end. We will be with the Father, welcomed home! Everything that tried to oppress us in this world will be removed. We will see the glorious love of our Heavenly Father and rejoice with all the angels and saints!

Lord, I thank You for the way You continue to reveal things to us. The Holy Spirit is a precious gift, so that we may be guided into all truth. I surrender my heart to You. Keep it tender to Your leading, filling me with godly wisdom and knowledge. I declare that all Your Church is having new opportunities to have a fresh falling of the Holy Spirit. All truth of who You are is in Your Word, but it is often revealed by Your Spirit. New opportunities for growth will flow over Your sons and daughters. May the recognition of their victory ring in their hearts!

OBEDIENT TO THE CALL

And He Himself gave some to be apostles, some prophets, some evangelists, and some pastors and teachers, (Ephesians 4:11 NKJV)

Let's be clear, I have never gone to Bible school. I am not a theologian in the respect that I have any formal training to be a minister. My knowledge about God has come from pastors who have always pointed me directly to the Bible. They have graciously shared insights and the revelation knowledge that has been granted to them under their anointing. Being a part of a church that is Spirit-filled is how I have grown over the past several years. I am blessed to be part of a church and under the leadership of my pastors.

My pastors have often referred to the scripture about the Great Commission. That all who follow Christ should tell others the good news of the gospel. That is where the basis of this devotional comes from. It is born of my desire to be obedient to God's calling for me to share His Word. To build up others and reveal the glorious nature of our Heavenly Father. I realize that He doesn't need me to do this, but I am so thankful that He is willing to use me.

We all need each other to grow in faith, through the Word. Fellowship with believers is important. Making sure that anyone that is speaking into your life aligns with the Bible and Word of God is vital.

Father God, I thank You for speaking into my life, and allowing me the opportunity to share the things You reveal through Your spirit to others. I declare that the Holy Spirit will guide my words and that only Your truth will permeate throughout these pages. I praise You, God, for You alone are good, and You graciously allow Your children to be utilized in Your plans. May You alone be glorified! There is no other like You and no other deserves honor or praise! Amen.

BOLD PROCLAMATIONS

He has lifted up a horn for His people [giving them power, prosperity, dignity, and preeminence], a song of praise for all His godly ones, for the people of Israel, who are near to Him. Praise the Lord! (Hallelujah!) (Psalm 148:14 AMP)

Recently, I have been meditating on why Christians, as a whole, don't recognize the anointing that God has granted them. I believe one of the reasons is we have grown to have a twisted view of humbleness. Somehow, we have grown to believe that humbleness is equated with staying silent. That we do not have a right to have a voice. That is just the opposite of what Jesus demonstrated during His years of ministry. Humbleness for Christians is about knowing where our source is! Everything we have or have been equipped with is through the Mighty One, our Creator and Heavenly Father. Humbleness is giving Him the glory and praise in everything we say or do! It is not capitulating to the world and its sway. Jesus had a way about him. People wanted to be near Him, not just because of what He could do, but also because of the way He spoke. He made people recognize that the God of the universe cared about each and every one of them. He shared that God was making a way for those who were marginalized in the world to have a seat at the table with Him! You have a place in the Kingdom of God! He has a destiny for your life, here on earth, to serve in all He has called you to do! Walk with humbleness, granting love and compassion to others, but do not mistake that for staying silent. We are equipped to speak out and declare the promises of God on our lives and in the lives of others. Our enemy, Satan, would love for all

Christians to be silent during these last days. We need to recall that we already operate from a place of victory. That if we walk in the salvation of Jesus Christ, then we are equipped with the power and authority to throw down everything that raises itself up against God, our Father! Amen!

LEADING FROM GLORY TO GLORY

And all of us, as with unveiled face, [because we] continued to behold [in the Word of God] as in a mirror the glory of the Lord, are constantly being transfigured into His very own image in ever increasing splendor and from one degree of glory to another; [for this comes] from the Lord [Who is] the Spirit. (2 Corinthians 3:18 AMPC)

"Arise Church! Look at the splendor in which I have arrayed you! You are no longer clothed in filthy rags and sackcloth. I have placed the robes of righteousness over you. I have placed a crown upon your head. I have equipped you with every heavenly weapon and tool to break forth upon the earth and declare the truth of My Word. Stop looking back at who you were and look forward to where My Mighty hand will lead you. I will part the waters for you. I will make a way in the desolate places. You never walk anywhere without My Spirit within you. Stop looking at yourself and instead look at Me, know Me. I am revealed to you through the Holy Spirit and the Word like never before. I make known to you the wonderful mysteries. I reveal wonders, signs, and miracles. I will lead you from glory to glory. Arise, Church! Arise, Church! Arise, Church. I Am the Great I Am and it will be according to My Word that all may know that I am the Living God."

Thank you, Father God, for speaking through Your Spirit to us this day. I embrace Your Word and keep my eyes fixed firmly on You.

Lead me where You will according to the Holy Spirit. I praise You for I see You at work in new and unexpected ways every day. I praise You and receive new revelation of who You are. I see Your might, power, and splendor that manifests itself from You alone, Lord. Keep my eyes fixed firmly on You and who I am because I am grafted to You as one of the body of Christ. I give You all glory, honor, and praise. In Jesus' mighty name! Amen.

OVERFLOW IN THE ANOINTING

You prepare a table before me in the presence of my enemies. You anoint my head with oil; my [brimming] cup runs over. (Psalm 23:5 NKJV)

King David definitely could identify with having enemies. He fought for the Israelites against the Philistines; defeating a giant. His own father-in-law tried to hunt him down and kill him. The Israelites were often in battles with other countries because land and resources were vital. This verse in Psalm 23 clearly declares David's confidence in the Lord God. David was saying that although he had enemies, he knew that God prepared a table for him. Envision a large banquet table laden with foods and platters of every type of delicacy. David was intimately aware of the lavish nature and provision of his God. He goes on to state that God not only prepared a feast for him, but anointed him, in essence gave His blessing and seal upon David. King David boldly proclaims that his cup runs over. He is declaring the fullness of the blessing of God on his life.

We are going to have opposition as Christians. Every person in the world who is not a born-again believer is essentially aligned with Satan (1 John 5:19). There will be times when we have to stand in resistance to things that don't align with God's Word. It is important in those times to recognize that we are connected and filled with the strength and power of God. David recognized where his every source came from. We need to have the confidence of King David as we act at Christ's disciples. If we cannot identify ourselves as grafted and joined with the invincible, omnipotent, omnipresent God then we will falter. Our strength comes from the Lord.

Father God, thank you for the words and the wisdom to recognize that, connected to You, we are anointed and have the abundance of everything needed to operate according to Your will. That our enemies are defeated and will see how You lift up Your children and place them at the head of the banquet table and pour out Your abundance on them! Thank you for Your gracious love and mercy. Thank you for gifting us with Your anointing and power. Amen!

BEYOND OUR PERCEPTIONS

Do not be conformed to this world (this age), [fashioned after and adapted to its external, superficial customs], but be transformed (changed) be the [entire] renewal of your mind [by its new ideals and its new attitude], so that you may prove [for yourselves] what is the good and acceptable and perfect will of God, even the thing which is good and acceptable and perfect [in His sight for you]. (Romans 12:2 AMP)

This is a really powerful scripture about the importance of keeping the knowledge of God at the forefront of our minds. We need to abandon our self-concepts about who God is, because when we look at Him within our human construct we tend to limit Him. "For My thoughts are not your thoughts, neither are your ways My ways" (Isaiah 55:8).

Sometimes our beliefs and thoughts are tied to what we have learned. Until I was taught differently, I believed prayer was bringing our requests before God. That was what I had learned and all I knew. It wasn't until I was taught, and shown in Scripture, that God declares that all His promises are already given to us. We just have to receive them. That changes our prayers from petitions to praise! For all of the Lord's work was manifested and completed through the death and resurrection of Jesus Christ. It's our mindset, our thoughts, that need to be changed to be shown revelation about who our amazing God is and all He is capable of. His Word says, "I will give you the keys to the kingdom of heaven; whatever you bind of earth will be bound in heaven, and whatever you loose on earth will be loosed in heaven."

(Matthew 16:19) Think about that for a minute. If God is willing to give us access to all of heaven and the ability to have power and authority over things, then why do we seem so unsure of His promises, His love, and His power that lives inside of us? We need to get plugged into His Word and make sure that what we are learning comes from His Scriptures. He already promised to make known His mysteries. We just have to ask for revelation of what He wants to reveal to us about His Word each and every day.

THE INFINITE ONE

God said to Moses, "I Am Who I Am and What I Am, and I will be What I Will BE;" and He said, "You shall say this to the Israelites, 'I Am has sent me to you.'" (Exodus 3:14 AMPC)

"I am The Way and The Truth and The Life: no one comes to the Father except by (through) Me." (John 14:6 AMPC)

Lately, I have been meditating on the things that could be barriers for me operating in the anointing given to me as a daughter of Christ. I have begun to realize that I haven't surrendered everything to God. I haven't surrendered my need to know why. The Holy Spirit is teaching me that when I ask Why? it weakens my faith. The answer to this question becomes what I seek more than trusting in the God who is faithful to keep every promise. It becomes the stumbling block that keeps me from the power grafted through Christ and the indwelling of the Holy Spirit.

We cannot see everything that God sees. He is the Alpha and Omega (Revelation 21:6). He was before the beginning of everything and He will go beyond the end of all things. Time has no impact on God. It doesn't work the same way because He is infinite. We try to squeeze God into our plans and our concepts, but that is too finite for God. We have to let go of our need to know WHY and hold onto the fact that HE IS and HE ALWAYS WILL BE!

Abba Father, please forgive me for not completely surrendering all to You. I lay down my need to know why. I recognize it is holding me back from the deeper things You have called me to. I thank You that Your love surpasses my weaknesses and continues teach me how I can deepen the strength of my faith. I want to walk in the power You have granted me, so that Your name will be glorified. You alone are the Great I Am. What You see is so vast compared to what I can see. I will not make You conform to my ideals and my concepts. Holy Spirit, grant me greater revelation of our Infinite God! Amen.

ELOHIM HAYYIM

In the beginning [before all time] was the Word (Christ), and the Word was with God, and the Word was God Himself. (John 1:1 AMP)

It can be really difficult for us to imagine God as being timeless. Everything in our lives has its rhythm and movement connected to the concept of time. We have a past we know as history. We have our present, the day-to-day life in which we move in. Most of us have a future that we are imagining (dreams, aspirations). We have an idea of these things, but they are still finite. They do not go beyond the normal life span of a human. God surpasses all of that. He has existed before anything on our earth was created (Genesis 1:1).

Elohim hayyim translates into the "the living God." God is active and always moving on our behalf. We, who are His children, need to be consciously looking for the movement of God in the day-to-day. We need to be expecting God to show up and do more than we could ever hope for! I keep feeling my spirit say, "I believe, but help my unbelief!" We have to put aside our concepts, because the living God, Elohim hayyim, lives beyond the constructs we have formed in our minds. That is why staying connected to God through His Word and through prayer is vital. It is in those two places that we can find the truth about who God is and all He is capable of. We need the knowledge so that we are less likely to form God in our own image. That is just the type of thinking that hinders God.

Lord, I praise You for being more than I can imagine, dream, or hope. Give me revelation about the vastness of You, the living God. Forgive me for the times that I have put my humanness, my frailness, upon You. Keep me connected to the truth of who You are in Your Word and through Your Spirit. Expand my thinking giving me a greater eternal perspective. I praise You for always helping me understand how wide, how deep, and how vast Your love is for each and every one of us! I declare that the same revelation You grant for me will be given to all who are seeking greater knowledge, greater connection, with You. I proclaim that they will know Your Son Jesus Christ as their Savior and acknowledge His resurrection power in their life! Amen.

UNITY IN THE COMING TIMES

And let us consider and give attentive, continuous care to watching over one another, studying how we may stir up (stimulate and incite) to love and helpful deeds and noble activities, not forsaking or neglecting to assemble together [as believers], as is the habit of some people, but admonishing (warning, urging, and encouraging) one another, and all the more faithfully as you see the day approaching. (Hebrews 10:24–25 AMP)

There has been a shifting happening. Maybe it was there all along and only recently my eyes are more open to seeing it. It is a tangible battle intensifying for the souls here on earth. I see a stirring in the hearts of God's people, but at the same time I see the growth of darkness in this world. I believe the apostles could see the same spiritual battle taking place when they were writing these very words to believers. There was a recognition of how the sons and daughters of God would need to join together, to be united.

There is something beautiful about God's people joining together and offering worship to the one true God Jehovah. The power of our words build up our spirit and release the power of heaven right here on earth. I see how connected we are strong, and it is the way God intended for His Church to operate. We need each other because, until we are face-to-face with our God and Savior, we still battle the enemy of this world: Satan. He is going to try to keep you alone and isolated, so he can convince you that God doesn't love you with an everlasting love. We have to use all the resources available to us to fight. That includes fellowship with believers. Listening to one another, praying and worshipping together.

Father, thank you for opening my eyes to see things shifting as the battle intensifies for the souls of the lost. I prophesy that Your children will hear clearly the sound of Your voice calling them to join together in unity and corporately declaring Your Word. You promise to be among us when we are joined together and it releases the power of the Holy Spirit here on earth. We want more of heaven on earth this very moment! We declare that hearts will be softened and will receive salvation through Jesus Christ all over the world today! In Jesus' mighty name! Amen.

ROOTED IN LIFE-GIVING KNOWLEDGE

All Scripture is God-breathed and is useful for teaching, rebuking, correcting, and training in righteousness, so that the servant of God may be thoroughly equipped for every good work. (2 Timothy 3:16–17 NIV)

We have the tools to operate and serve God in the capacity He has called each one of us. We have to stop deceiving ourselves and pretending that time away from His Word doesn't negatively impact our walk. I used to be very sporadic about the time I spent in the Word. I used to believe that I didn't have time to spend with God before starting my day. The evidence of my lack of relationship and time with God was that I became dry, that I no longer surrendered any aspect of my life to God. I looked a lot like every nonbeliever in the world. My life that began to unravel faster than I could ever have imagined. The enemy used my separation from God to attack my mind, and create shame and fear. I allowed his lies to keep me away from God far longer than I should have. Eventually, in desperation for help, I cried out to God and confessed my sins. I began making spending time in His Word, through devotionals and Bible reading plans, a priority. It is the first thing I do in the morning before starting my day. My time with Him has helped equip me for every day and has allowed me to see His hand in multiple moments of each day. I wouldn't have the knowledge and the tools to walk in the day-to-day if I neglected His Word and time with Him. He has become my very Source. He provides every good thing: strength, peace, joy, faith, love, redemption, healing, and victory! He has blessed me beyond all I could have ever imagined. I am just always amazed at how He meets me and spends time with me, whenever I call out to Him. He never turns away His children.

Isn't it time to move into the deeper things of God? Isn't it time to recognize that His Word is the Bread of Life? Jesus told Satan, "Man shall not live by bread alone but on every word that comes from the mouth of God." (Matthew 4:4)

God, Your Word is life-sustaining! Apart from You, and all that You have to teach me, I will be lost. I praise You for loving us enough to share who You are and equipping us to walk here in the world until we are restored with You in glory. I will meditate on the Bread of Life that You have gifted us with! Amen.

HE IS REVEALED TO THOSE WHO SEEK

"I have revealed to them who you are and I will continue to make you even more real to them, so that they may experience the same endless love that you have for me, for your love will now live in them, even as I live in them!" (John 17:26 TPT)

In this prayer, Jesus is telling us that His life and example demonstrate who God really is, because They are one. God isn't remote, He isn't hiding from us. God is loving and is always working things for our good. He wants to bless us more than we could ever hope or imagine. God is in the details. He is abundant and all around us, manifesting His majesty in everything He has created.

If you feel like God is distant, then you need to look at things that could be creating barriers between you and the Lord. He never keeps Himself from us; however, we can choose to be distant from Him. Sin, disobedience, and neglecting our pursuit of a relationship with Him are some of the primary barriers that result in us feeling separated from God.

Getting reconnected with God doesn't have to be difficult. Go to Him, confess your sins or disobedience. He promises to forgive those who are truly contrite and provide restoration. Spend time with Him in prayer and in worship. He promises to always hear the voices of His sons and daughters. He hears our voices but, oftentimes, we need to be better at listening to His. He wants us to recognize that He is real and that He has a powerful love for each of us. Nothing we do or fail to do will ever make Him love us less. He sent His only son to die for us! There is no greater love (John 15:13).

Father, thank you for showing us Your nature through the life and experiences revealed through Your Son Jesus Christ. I cannot express the how safe and loved I feel when I think about the sacrifice given that I might have a place in Your family. That You would send Jesus to be crucified and die so that I might have eternal life and forgiveness. To have a hope and future because of Your great love. My only response can be to praise You and offer You all that I am, that others may see You in my life. That my words and actions may bring You glory and honor. Thank you, Father. You are so very good! Amen.

WE ARE ALL EQUAL IN HIS EYES

My dear brothers and sisters, fellow believers in our glorious Lord Jesus Christ—how could we say that we have faith in him yet we favor one group of people above another? (James 2:2 TPT)

I look at this scripture and realize that I constantly need to be watchful of what is taking place in my heart and in my mind. If we are not aligning ourselves to the Word of God, we can quickly fall into the sway of the patterns of the world. In church, especially larger churches, it is easy to have many acquaintances but only a few friends. We can begin to set ourselves in a position of judging one another without really knowing someone. We need to be quick to recognize this air of comparison quickly. Recently, the Holy Spirit reminded me that the same everlasting love offered to me is offered to everyone who belongs to Jesus Christ and we are all equal in the eyes of our Father. I have no right to look at myself as more worthy than another. I have no right to think my time is more valuable than anyone else's. I need to remember that every interaction is an opportunity to build one another up and grow our faith. If we are more open, maybe our interactions would open opportunities to build each other up in faith. We have to wait and watch for doors that God opens and be obedient. God doesn't see the outside appearance, but looks at our hearts. I know He is not pleased with how my heart looks when I am fixing my eyes on other people instead of Him. As the kingdom of God grows, we need to be willing to look at the hearts of men and women and not at the exterior. We cannot judge the world unless we want to be judged as well.

WISDOM IN WAITING

But the wisdom that comes from above leads us to be pure, friendly, gentle, sensible, kind, helpful, genuine, and sincere. When peacemakers plant seeds of peace they will harvest justice. (James 3:17–18 CEV)

Being at peace with everyone is no easy task. We all have past hurts, ambitions, desires, and beliefs that can oftentimes clash with the instruction from God to be kind, compassionate, and at peace with those around us. It is easier than ever to read more into a text or email, than a person intended. We no longer have to be careful with our presentation or content as long as we are expedient with our communications. That often can cause misunderstanding. Recently, I received a text message that upset me. I thought that the request of the person was pushy and a little over the top. However, I chose to wait to respond and not respond quickly, especially since it bothered me more than usual. I discussed the text message with my spouse, who was able to help me see a different perspective. Although I thought there was plenty of time and no need to hurry with a response on a scheduled item four weeks from now, the administrator of that service needed to plan a month in advance. I didn't realize that what I perceived as "pushy" was that person's desire to be prepared. Thankfully, this time I waited and didn't respond in a negative way, driven by emotions.

Thank you, Father, for the reminder that we need to seek wisdom over emotions. That our responses and interactions with people matter. That we need to ensure clear communication and to operate with kindness on our lips. Help me to always see everyone through the eyes of compassion. You have given me such love, mercy, and grace. I need to remember to offer that to others as well. Amen.

HE IS OUR COMFORT

In the multitude of my anxieties within me, Your comforts delight my soul. (Psalm 94:19 NKJV)

This week it seems like there have been obstacles from every side and I felt my stress building. I got entangled with my emotions about various situations. I talked to my husband about how I was feeling but his honest response of, "The Word says we will face trials," just made me feel angry. I happened to share my anger with a friend. She instantly stated, "I really feel you need to spend time with the Lord right now." She couldn't have been more right at that moment.

God knows us; He understands that we are going to feel overwhelmed. He created us, so our flesh and emotions are no surprise to Him. He doesn't reject us just because we feel anger, or sadness, or fear. He just doesn't want us to stay in those emotions for long periods of time because they can become a powerful cycle and keep a hold over us. He wants us to come to Him in every situation and talk to Him. He wants to be our source of comfort.

I did spend time with the Lord. I cried, I prayed in the spirit, and I worshipped. God met me in the place I was at, without me having to be perfect. Feeling messy and uncertain. He is my Father, and He was waiting with open arms for me. He always is. He provided words of comfort to my heart and mind. He reminded me of other times where He never let go of my hand.

God wants you to know that He is never letting go of you either. There is nothing you can do to make God love you less. Don't believe the lie that if you are angry, or upset, that you can't go to God. Go to Him in those moments because that's when you truly need Him. He can break through those things that hurt and keep your heart tender. Run to the Father. Don't wait another moment. He is our one source of comfort.

POWER AGAINST THE ENEMY

The thief comes only to steal and kill and destroy; (John 10:10 NIV partial)

The Bible is very clear that if we are following God we have an enemy. Satan has been trying to separate us from the love of God since the beginning of Creation. We need to be knowledgeable of this fact, because the more we walk with God and serve God, the more Satan attempts to oppose us. This is just fact, but I don't want it to cause fear. As believers, we know the end of the story. We who are in Christ have the victory. Not just in our death, because we will be reunited with God for eternity. We have victory in the midst of the battles we face here and now. Jesus said we would be equipped with the same power that He had and do mightier works than He did. Why are we living a defeated life? When did we allow the power and workings of the Holy Spirit to become so stifled?

God didn't take the power away, that goes against the very nature of Him and His Word. He cannot lie. So the blame lies with mankind. We put our human perspective on His Word and brought His Word to an earthly place. We made Him small in our image instead of trying to rise ourselves up to the heavenly places He has promised us. Somewhere along the way, we believed the whispered lies that to try to be more like God was prideful. We can never be God, but we can try to be like Him. That is the whole meaning of a Christian walk. To walk in the footsteps of Jesus. That means recognizing the power manifested through the Holy Spirit, gifted and granted by our

Heavenly Father. When we operate in those gifts, giving the glory and honor to God. Not having pride in the accomplishments because they do not come from any man, but the One true Living God, Jehovah.

Father, thank you for the gift of the Holy Spirit. Help us recognize that we have every equipment to bind or lose here on this earth. That we can be victorious in our day-to-day battles because we hold You inside our spirits. We have spirit and truth and power living inside us. Let us boldly proclaim Your Word and see Your power manifested over the earth. That all may truly see the Glory of the Lord and feel Your love. Amen.

NOT OVERCOME

The light shines in the darkness, and the darkness has not overcome it. (John 1:5 NIV)

It doesn't matter what it looks like in your present circumstances. God has overcome it through the blood of Jesus Christ. Maybe it looks like a broken relationship, a negative medical diagnosis/report, an addiction, or someone struggling with mental illness. Victory over every single one of these situations has been accomplished through the death and resurrection of Jesus Christ. Satan wants you to believe the lie that God is not big enough for your situation, but we recognize that Christ defeated him over 2,000 years ago. He has no authority over anything concerning the anointed of the King of kings and Lord of lords!

Our Father God is telling you to hold fast to Him. He has not forsaken you. Just because the thing you have been waiting for God to do in your life hasn't manifested itself yet, doesn't mean God's Word isn't truth. God is not man that He should lie (Numbers 23:19). There is nothing that can separate you from the love of God. He is good all the time. Regardless of your circumstances, regardless of what it looks like. He is working all things for your good. I have been in the valley, and it looked like I would never overcome. It was not easy to hold on or to praise Him in the tough times, but I recalled His mercy and love for me in other valley experiences. Just as in those other times, when things finally began moving, I realized God was making a way the entire time. Faith is hard; it is believing regardless of what we see. But faith grows more faith.

Father, I declare over those in battle that the darkness will not overcome them. They will see evidence of Your amazing love and goodness. They will see the Light of the World piercing through the darkness and breaking forth in this moment. Lord God, I declare that they will press into the One who holds them tightly in His hand. They will hear Your voice whispering how much they are loved and treasured. That they will remember the words in the book You created for them to know You and Your very nature. I praise You and thank You for the love and tender mercy given so graciously in my life. Amen.

USE THE SPIRIT NOT EMOTION

But don't let the passion of your emotions lead you to sin! Don't let anger control you or be fuel for revenge, not for even a day. Don't give the slanderous accuser, the Devil an opportunity to manipulate you! (Ephesians 4:26–27 TPT)

It was a hot summer day, I had just left a prayer time at church and went to pick up much needed items from a local retailer. Nearing the end of my shopping, I looked up and saw someone who used to attend my church. We greeted each other and spent a few minutes catching up. Then they looked at me and said, "I expected you to be pregnant by now!" I looked at them and gently said, "God's timing is perfect." My emotions at that moment didn't feel gentle at all, but I had a choice to react harshly or gently. I have come to realize that most people don't say things to purposely hurt us, they just don't know the details of our lives. They don't know that my husband and I want to have a child, and that we have been trying to have a child. They don't recognize that the wait may not be purposeful, or that their polite inquiries could be hurtful. People are curious and sometimes less than courteous in their comments and opinions about families and children. Whatever their actions or comments, I have to let go of anger or bitterness because these are not healthy for me. Bitterness hurts the one holding onto it, not the people it is directed at.

Father, I thank You, for only with Your help and knowledge and through the power of the Holy Spirit I can forgive as I have been forgiven. I can choose to show kindness without receiving it from others.

You give me wisdom to see that walking as the world in anger and bitterness leads to my own destruction. It does not give You glory or reveal the power of Your love to others that know I follow You. I surrender my emotions to You. My spirit is what will lead me, because it is connected directly to You through the saving work of Your Son Jesus Christ! I give You praise for I know that Your promises are to bless me and give me a hope and a future! Amen.

THE VINEDRESSER

"I AM the True Vine, and My Father is the Vinedresser. Any branch in Me that does not bear fruit [that stops bearing] He cuts away (trims off, takes away); and He cleanses and repeatedly prunes ever branch that continues to bear fruit, to make it bear more and richer and more excellent fruit." (John 15:1–2 AMPC)

A vinedresser is one who cultivates vines, who watches over them daily, and who nurtures them so that they grow. If a vine is unhealthy then it will be unable to grow and sustain any fruit. When the vinedresser walks among the vines, he doesn't just make random cuts at the branches or shoots that are growing. His choices are purposeful. The vinedresser must also protect the vines from pests or things that could make it unhealthy. The vinedresser must determine that the vines are getting proper nourishment, both nutrients from the soil and moisture for steady growth.

God is doing the same with each one of us. He watches over us and provides sources for us to be nurtured and grow (His Word). He studies us and decides what inside us is counterproductive for living a healthy life and how we can sustain our spiritual growth. He goes before us and protects us from the attacks of the enemy, often using the Holy Spirit to guide us. The pruning process for some of us can be painful. It requires of us letting go of the things God has decided may not be helpful to us for bearing spiritual fruit. It could be a friendship that isn't good for us or an addiction. It could simply be staying away from social media or the news. It is important that we trust God to cultivate us into branches that grow and yield patience, kindness, love, generosity, faithfulness, and many other good spiritual fruits that others will see God through our demonstrations.

FOCUSED ON ONE THING

Jesus answered her, "Martha, Martha, you are anxious and troubled about many things, but one thing is needed." (Luke 10:41 GNT)

It is easy to get distracted, anxious, and allow the cares of our daily life to consume us. When we get consumed with our cares, we begin to take our eyes off Jesus. Martha did just that and began comparing her hard work to her sister, who chose to sit and listen to Jesus' teaching. She felt so justified in her judgment that Mary was wrong in her choice, that she brought it to Jesus' attention. Jesus' complete response was, "Martha, Martha you are anxious and troubled about many things, but one thing is needed. Mary has chosen the right thing, and it will not be taken away from her." (Luke 10:41–42) Jesus wanted to help Martha see that the business and needs of the day do not replace our ultimate need for time with our Savior. He is water for the thirsty soul, rest for the weary, healing for the brokenhearted, and health for those who are sick. We cannot operate day in and day out without connecting with Him. Remember the verse about Jesus as the vine and we are the branches? It says that apart from Him we can do nothing. I used to think that I didn't have time in my day to start with a devotion and prayer time with God. Several years ago, I was challenged after a Sunday message about personal growth. I wanted more of God. More of His power and giftings through the Holy Spirit. I recognized that I couldn't have more of God if I wasn't going to invest time in a relationship with Him. It took a bit of discipline, but I started getting up just thirty minutes earlier every day to make time to be in His Word and pray. Over time, my faith has grown. I have new-found wisdom, and a connection that I never felt before. I still have busy days, but I don't start my day without spending time with God. It renews my mind, so that when I face difficulties, I have the Truth and life-breathing Word of God to speak into those situations. I encourage you to find the time to rest in the presence of the Lord. All the things of this earth will pass away, but our relationship with Him is eternal.

THE GREAT COMMISSION

"But you shall receive power when the Holy Spirit has come upon you, and you shall be witnesses to Me in Jerusalem, and in all Judea and Samaria, and to the end of the earth." (Acts 1:8 NKJV)

We had a fantastic message about faith at church tonight. The speaker basically shared a testimony that indicated that the faithful prayers and love of a few people planted the seeds that helped him receive the salvation of Jesus Christ. It got me to thinking about how Jesus gave the Great Commission to His disciples, and that includes us, as we are adopted into His royal priesthood (1 Peter 2:9). I began to think how complicated I have made sharing the gospel over the years. I have turned something that God has equipped us all to do into something that I have to do in my own power. I have complicated it, imagining I have to follow a certain formula. I have made people's rejection of the Word shared, a personal rejection. It has never been about me, but somehow I have twisted it and made it so very difficult. How about you? Ever done the very same thing?

I imagine that we all have a certain circle of influence, people that we interact with, that God purposefully placed us in their lives. They have been watching our actions and words in the day-to-day. Our righteousness, our peace, our hope, our joy, and our strength in all situations have been speaking to their heart. Maybe you have mentioned your love of God and Christ and they know where your victory comes from. Perhaps at the right moment they will ask. We don't have to make it complicated. We just have to share how we have experienced the love of God in our lives, and how accepting Jesus as our Savior has given us this beautiful love relationship with our Creator.

Heavenly Father, forgive me for making something that is about You and Your love for every person into something it isn't. I thank You that You provide Your Spirit to give me discernment in all situations. The words will be quickened to my spirit and mouth, that I may share Your love and the joy of Salvation. Thank you for the grace and mercy poured out abundantly in my life. May my every word and action reflect that precious gift and love readily to others. You alone deserve all glory, all honor, and all praise. In Jesus' mighty name. Amen.

TRUSTING THE GIFTS OF THE HOLY SPIRIT

'And it shall come to pass in the last days, says God, That I will pour out of My Spirit on all flesh; Your sons and your daughters shall prophesy, Your young men shall see visions, Your old men shall dream dreams.' (Acts 2:17 NKJV)

During dinner with a friend recently, the conversation turned towards visions that they had been given by God regarding specific events. I love how God uses our time together as believers to cause new revelation or build up our faith! However, during the conversation, they were questioning what they saw because others had spoken words of unbelief over her. It made me think of the Book of Daniel. In Daniel, King Nebuchadnezzar has a dream that he wants interpreted. The king's prophets or divine interpreters wanted the king to share the dream with them to give the interpretation. The king wanted both the dream and the interpretation given to him to test the truth of the interpretation that would be shared. God not only revealed the interpretation to Daniel, He gave Daniel the same dream the king had!

God is our creator, and He created our brains and the magnificent way in which they work. Sometimes we dream just to process information, but other dreams and visions are God sharing something intimate with us. Sometimes those moments are just for us and at other times they reveal something that will have eternal impact. We have to start recognizing that every word in the Bible has the life-breathed power of our God. We have to stop doubting that He continues to work in us through spiritual gifts and will reveal knowledge and wisdom in a multitude of ways.

Abba, thank you for stirring up Your truth in my heart with encounters with other believers. I believe that conversations around You reveal divine truths to my heart! Lord, I prophecy that Your sons and daughters will have understanding and discernment regarding the dreams and visions You grant them. That the spirit of unbelief would be bound and cast down. May it yield power and build their faith toward You. You alone are great and You alone deserve all praise! Amen.

SALVATION FOR THE WORLD

He is the atoning sacrifice for our sins and not only for ours but also for the sins of the whole world. (1 John 2:2 NIV)

Maybe you just stumbled onto this devotional and have been reading the quoted Scriptures. You read them and you find this longing in your heart to understand this powerful God I keep mentioning and His Son, Jesus Christ. You long for a love that supersedes every mistake you ever made. That loves you and sees you as perfectly created and a treasure. You can have that kind of love. All you have to do is receive Jesus Christ as Lord and Savior over your life! Pray this prayer out loud wherever you are right now:

Lord, I long to know You and receive the love You have for me. I have made mistakes, and I have sinned. Please forgive me. I thank You that Jesus died for me and for my sins. I ask Jesus to come into my heart and make me new and whole. The past is gone and I begin again this very moment. I now have eternal life and salvation as promised by You. Thank you for Your grace and love. I surrender all of me to You. In Jesus' name. Amen.

FAITH IS THE CURE

But blessed is the one who trusts in the Lord, whose confidence is in Him. They will be like a tree planted by the water that sends out its roots by the stream. It does not fear when heat comes; its leaves are always green. It has no worries in a year of drought and never fails to bear fruit. (Jeremiah 17:7–8 NIV)

Worry is best described as a cancer. Cancer starts small, attacking cells; but if not detected and treated, it spreads attacking all systems and areas of the body. Worry is similar; it starts small and then it builds up in our mind, until we are consumed with it. It has a negative effect on our bodies as well, and can result in fatigue, illness, and changes in personality. Suddenly, we can find ourselves angry and feeling isolated. We believe no one can possibly understand what we is happening in our lives. We feel defensive about our right to feel angry and worried over the things that have taken hold of our minds.

The medicine for worry is faith. Quite simply, worry stems from fear. Faith and fear are in opposition to each other. Faith and fear cannot coexist. So, we have to purposefully plan on attacking and eradicating fear and worry by building our faith through the Word of God. In Romans 10:17, it states, "So then faith comes by hearing, and hearing by the word of God." Finding God-breathed word in the Bible and reading out loud over yourself is a powerful weapon against worry. It isn't instantaneous and the process will take repetition to wash over you. You have to change your current way of thinking, and repetition is what changes our habits and thought patterns over time. Psalm 91 is a favorite of many Christians and a great place to start combating worry and fear.

Father God, thank you for making a way to battle worry and fear that can attack our minds. Thank you for Your Word, it does breath life and strength into my mind, heart, and soul. It is where I run to when life throws something unexpected in my path. I declare that my brothers and sisters in Christ grow in operation of their faith. That they recognize their anointing and the power that resides inside them through the indwelling of the Holy Spirit. Quicken Your Word to them in all seasons. You never leave us and are always working toward our good. I love You and give You all honor and praise. Amen.

KEEP YOUR LIGHT ABLAZE

Set your gaze on the path before you. With fixed purpose, looking straight ahead, ignore life's distractions. (Proverbs 4:25 TPT)

Recently, I had a long weekend off from work. It was fabulous. My husband and I were off together. We had both needed a break. We relaxed, had a great time taking walks, sitting on our deck, and just enjoying the beauty of God's creation. We had a fabulous service on Sunday, and enjoyed our time with the Lord. Soon, the long weekend was over and I went back to work. I quickly realized that relaxing was over. Our floor was busy, and even the evening prior to going back to work, I received text messages about what to expect the next day. What I didn't expect was the level of negativity that flowed all around that day. The stresses of other people were palpable and strong. Conversations and comments filled the air with heaviness. Ever experienced something similar? If you work in the world, as I do, I am sure you have.

Later in the evening, as I had time to reflect, this scripture popped up in a Bible application I use. The realization came to me, through the Holy Spirit, that I took my eyes off my path, Jesus. He is a true light to my soul. We cannot expect to find light in the world or the people who live their lives under the sway of the world. That is why we are called to purposefully think about things that are good, pure, lovely, and praiseworthy (Philippians 4:8). That is why worship is such a vital part of our lives. So that when we don't have fellow believers around, we can think of songs or scripture verses to meditate on and keep ourselves built up.

Thank you, Lord, for this valuable reminder. How I needed it today! Thank you for the way You continue to grow me, imparting knowledge. Help me keep my mind stay on You through things that are praiseworthy. Keep Your Word fresh on my heart and on my lips. May Your voice and the leading of the Holy Spirit ring louder in my ears than anything that I hear from the world. Lord, I declare that we Your children will see Your kingdom here on earth. That we will see goodness in the land of the living. For You alone are Jehovah, the great I Am. Not one of Your promises will fail us! I love You, for You have showered me with such loving kindness. You are an amazing Father! Amen.

WRONG DIAGNOSES

Who has believed our report? And to whom has the arm of the Lord been revealed? (Isaiah 53:1 NKJV)

For the word of the Lord is right and true, and all His work is done in truth. (Psalm 33:4 NKJV)

I want to talk to you about wrong diagnoses. Recently, a colleague was talking about a medical experience they had. They had a tumor on their abdominal wall. The doctors came in and one stated, "I am 99% sure that it is cancerous." The doctor went on to state that only a biopsy would confirm his diagnosis, but that surgery for this colleague was the next step. The tumor, although abnormal where it grew, was benign. No cancer. Praise the Lord for sure! This story had me meditating on the report of man versus the report of God. Which one is the Creator of all things? Which one is the Alpha and the Omega, beginning and end? Which one speaks of life and life more abundantly in our lives? Which one prophesies to give us hope and a future? Not man, not men of wisdom or science. But our Lord God Almighty! Now, I am not saying that medicine and doctors aren't important. I am just reminding each and every one of us that the ultimate source of truth is the Lord. We have to be careful what we will allow men and women of science to speak over our lives. We have the power to let people speak into our lives. We know this to be true. Some words spoken build us up and help us grow. Other words spoken will tear us down, hurt us, or cause doubt and fear. I spoke previously about the change or shift I see happening all around us. More than ever, in every facet of our lives, we have to stand on the Word of the Lord. We decide right now whether we believe the Lord or we believe man. This is a decision no one can make for you. But don't be ignorant of the fact that there are men and women out there that have set themselves up as false idols. No man has more wisdom than God, because none other than God created man. I will stand on the report of the Lord. I will believe that He is faithful and true.

I will believe Him when He says that because of the Holy Spirit in me and the anointing that I have through salvation and carrying the resurrection power of Christ, I am healed and whole. Whose report will you believe?

THE COST OF SILENCE

For if you remain completely silent at this time, relief and deliverance will arise for the Jews from another place, but you and your father's house will perish. Yet who knows whether you have come to the kingdom for such a time as this? (Esther 4:14 NKJV)

Working this past year in a medical setting, I have seen how the loss of hope and the power of fear can overwhelm people. It is palpable and oppressive and, oftentimes, depletes the strength of the people who need it most. Even prior to the pandemic, I have treated people with the same exact illness, but the one who has hope and embraces life as a gift, heals faster and has a better rate of recovery. It creates a realization in my spirit that hope and faith are such powerful forces. It compels me to make sure that I tell others all Jesus Christ has done in my life. That His death and resurrection have set me free, and proven to be a true source of life, hope, and a beautiful promise for my future. That every Christian is part of a chosen people. A royal priesthood. We were all chosen for such a time as this.

Father God, thank you for instilling in my heart the understanding, that speaking life and hope into those around me is never without merit. It could be the very thing that changes their lives. Through me, because You live in me. Without You it wouldn't be possible. Kindle the fire in my heart, to speak, declare, and provide the prophetic words that need to be heard. Do not allow me to become silent and complacent. Keep my heart tender and my spirit ready for Your every leading. Have Your way in and through me. Let my light shine for You. In Jesus' name. Amen.

DISCOVER TRUE LIFE

All who seek to live apart from me will lose it all. But those who let go of their lives for my sake and surrender it all to me will discover true life. (Matthew 10:39 TPT)

Read this verse over again. Don't breeze past the first sentence. There is a choice every person has to make. They will either except Jesus Christ as Lord and Savior or they won't. It isn't negotiable. It isn't gray or a blurry line. It is a definitive choice. A mother cannot make it for her son or daughter. A wife cannot make the choice for her husband. A child cannot choose for his brother or sister. Every person will decide for themselves. Live apart from Jesus and lose it all. Choose Him and have life, joy, peace, hope, grace, forgiveness, and a love like no other.

SPIRIT AND TRUTH

"But the hour is coming, and now is, when the true worshipers will worship the Father in spirit and truth; for the Father is seeking such to worship Him. God is Spirit, and those who worship Him must worship in spirit and truth." (John 4:23–24 NKJV)

Many people don't like the Bible because it is often black and white. They can't change what is says to suit what they want. Here, Jesus is referring to a time when the Holy Spirit will be manifest in believers. He will equip each one with the ability to speak in a heavenly language. It's hard for people to tap into this because it isn't something that we in our minds can understand. The language is between our spirit and the Lord. It supersedes our flesh and that includes our minds. I remember that when I first asked to receive the Holy Spirit and the gift of speaking in tongues, it felt unnatural and in the beginning it felt forced. It was hard to let go of control and let the Holy Spirit guide me. It took time and repetition for it to become more natural to me. Some people believe that the gifts of speaking have passed away. But this scripture leaves no room for interpretation. If Jesus is the same, yesterday, today, and forever, then His Word remains the same. We, His followers, must worship Him in spirit and truth.

Lord, help those who are seeking a deeper relationship with You recognize the gift of the Holy Spirit. The ability to pray in tongues for the edification of their spirits. Lord, I bind the voice of the enemy that tries to hinder the Church through false teachings that the gifts of the Spirit are lost to us. Christ is alive and all that He promised us in

His Word is active and available to us today. Lord, make us a Church united in boldness. Declaring the victory and the glory of our God over this earth, now and forever! Amen.

WHEN YOU LEAST EXPECT IT

"But realize this: If a homeowner had known what time of night the burglar would come to rob his house, he would have been alert and ready, and not let his house be robbed. So always be ready, alert, and prepared, because at an hour when you're not expecting him, the Son of Man will come." (Matthew 24:43–45 TPT)

Let me ask you a personal question: Are you living like Jesus is coming back today? Are you thinking you have all the time in the world to get ready for the return of Christ? His return could be sooner than any of us expect. Time does not operate in heaven and earth in the same way. Scripture tells us that one day is as a thousand years with God (2 Peter 3:8). Every day is another day of God's amazing grace and mercy, allowing that not one should perish (2 Peter 3:9).

We cannot become complacent in our relationship with God and trying to love others, and share our faith with one another in this world. I can see the world changing, and I can sense the increasing need for people to have hope, peace, and love that can only come through our Heavenly Father and through the salvation of Jesus Christ. Christians have become weary in the waiting and are being lulled into a sense of complacency. Instead, I feel the urgency: the urgency to worship, the urgency to gather together as a corporate body, the urgency to pray, the urgency to find God's truth and put it into practice. At the time of His coming, there will be those who are gathered in that instant, and then there are those who will be left behind. Some of those will be Christians who have fallen away (2 Thessalonians 2:3). If we are not actively pursuing the things of God, then we are under the sway of the world. Faith is an action; we have to actively do the things of God: pray, worship, spend time in the word, pray in the Spirit. We are here to do battle, not just wait for God to change things. He said that He gave the earth to man. We have recognize the spiritual battle taking place for the lives that are here now.

God, help us to see the urgency of need now. Peel back the scales from our eyes, and the hardness of our hearts. Forgive us for becoming complacent in the waiting and acting like Your gift of grace and mercy is endless. Quicken our hearts with the truth of the Spirit and bring a new sense of boldness and purpose to Your Church. In Jesus' name! Amen.

LIVING IN SURRENDER

Since we are receiving our rights to an unshakeable kingdom we should be extremely thankful and offer God the purest worship that delights his heart as we lay down our lives in absolute surrender, filled with awe. For our God is a holy, devouring fire! (Hebrews 12:28–29 TPT)

I believe that although we shouldn't hold onto our past, we should all have a healthy perspective of what our God has brought us through. Ever have any unanswered prayers that you now recognize as God's incredible mercy and grace? What you thought would have brought you happiness or fulfill your desire at that moment, was only a fraction of what God had in store for you? How about the times we tried to solve our problems our own way? Did it end up a battle you were unable to overcome on your own? I know that those are some of my own experiences.

When I see God's hand on my life, guiding me, helping me, and pouring out His love and favor, I am humbled. I recognize my own shortcomings and inability to earn His love. Yet, I know without a doubt that He has never loved me more or less. It has been a steadfast love, an all-pursuing love. Even if the only thing that the Lord had done for me was to provide salvation . . . that would be enough to offer all my worship. But God doesn't stop there for His children. He equips them with access to every good gift that He has. The Holy Spirit is available to everyone of us. It is our constant guide to walk in spirit and truth. It leads us and draws ever closer to the heart of our Father. To trust Him and be filled with the peace He offers when we surrender it all to Him.

Father God, I am humbled by the graciousness of Your hand upon my life. I could not live this life without You. You are my every source. My peace, my hope, my strength, and my joy. You give us victory in all things. Your ways are perfect. Once again, I commit to surrender my life wholly into Your hand. Keep my heart tender to the voice of Your Holy Spirit. I want to stay within Your will and have discernment in all You have called me to do. I declare over Your Church that a fresh and powerful spirit of awe and holy fear of You, in all Your glory, is manifested. This manifestation will open the heavens and will allow Your Church to operate in the anointing like never before. I see the move of Your hand on the Church, the people You have called to serve like never before. They will recognize the victory in You and through You. They will operate from a heavenly perspective and release the things of heaven here on earth. All will give glory and honor Your name. King of kings and Lord of lords. Jesus Christ the Light of the World. Amen!

THROUGH HIS FAITHFULNESS

Your faithfulness endures to all generations; you have established the earth, and it stands fast. (Psalm 119:90ESV)

Maybe you have had a day like mine recently, where you know you missed the mark. You had an opportunity to shine like a light with the love of God, but instead you reacted in emotion. Instead of using wisdom, you used a worldly view to make your point to people. The instant I reacted and the words were released from my mouth, I felt shame. Shame comes quickly, the minute we recognize we chose to operate out of the will of God and His Word. I asked the people I spoke harshly to for forgiveness, and I asked God to forgive me.

Today, I am grateful for this scripture verse. It is reminding me of God's faithfulness to us in our least attractive moments. He loves us like no one else can. He even knows when we are going to make mistakes. He waits patiently for us to come back to Him and tell Him we need Him and cannot make it in this life on our own. It's not my heart to let Him down, and He is able to recognize true repentance in His children. We don't have to hide from Him when we mess it all up. He is faithful to love us, offering us mercy and grace.

Thank you, Father, for the way You love me. Your love isn't reliant on my works or require perfection in those who are Your children. You just love us, because You are a good Father. It is Your very nature to love us. Thank you that I have the wonderful intercession of Jesus to have direct access to You when I make mistakes and fall into sin. I know that I need You and that apart from You I have nothing. Thank you for Your faithfulness. I love You. I love You. You are so good, and sometimes it just goes beyond my understanding. But I feel Your love, and I am so thankful. I love You, Abba. Amen.

WHAT WILL YOU CHOOSE?

"Don't think for a moment that I came to grant peace and harmony to everyone. No, for my coming will change everything and create hostility among you. From now on, even family members will be divided over me and choose sides one against another. (Luke 12:51–52 TPT)

Lately, this scripture has been working its way around inside my mind. I can say honestly that this is not one of the Scriptures that I love meditating on, because it talks about division among our own families. If I am honest though, it is a division that many of us already recognize between members that serve the Lord and those that are going their own way. It pierces my heart that there could be animosity between myself and members of my family. But, moreover, it breaks my heart for those that could be lost for all eternity. It's a very long time. Many people believe that hell is just something that people talk about to scare people into doing the right thing. What it if is exactly what the Word of God says it is? Eternal separation from him, and a place of endless suffering? There isn't a single person I want to see in that place. We have to risk the division. We cannot be silent about the God who saves, when our families' eternal lives are at stake. Maybe they won't see eye to eye with us, but they will not be able to say we were silent about our faith and about Jesus Christ.

Lord, forgive me for wanting peace more than I have wanted to obey Your voice to tell everyone I know about You. Forgive me for staying in the safe places and avoiding the risk of tough conversations. Help me to be bolder, and to speak with the clarity of the Holy Spirit. Let there be no evidence of self-righteousness on my lips, just a heart full of gratitude for the love and mercy I have received. Let the words of my mouth reflect the goodness of Your love and who You are. I know You are already moving through Your Holy Spirit to make eyes open, ears to hear, and hearts that are tender. Thank you, Lord, for the way You love each and every one of us. In Jesus' name. Amen.

WALKING IN TRUST

Some trust in and boast of chariots and some of horses, but we will trust in and boast of the name of the Lord our God. They are bowed down and fallen, but we are risen and stand upright. (Psalm 20:7–8 AMP)

It is God who grants all men wisdom. Who can stand before the Creator of the heavens and the earth and understand all the intricate details of His design and plan? Not one of us can grasp the depths of His workings. He reveals things to each of us, but it is never the complete picture. He never reveals the end from the beginning. There are things that we are not meant to understand until we stand before Him. If we understand the very nature of man, then we recognize that God protects us from ourselves. We have a tendency to trust in the tangible and what we can see—even if that is only a part of the whole picture. We have a tendency to try to control our environment and to work things out on our own. God wants us to trust and rely on Him. There is nothing that man has created that hasn't come from the power of our God. He is the revealer of all truth. We can become our own idols. We ourselves become the barrier to walking in the will of God. When we seek to solve our own problems and situations without bringing things before Him, we block His ability to move supernaturally in our lives. Our Heavenly Father wants to be our every source, in every area of need, and in every season of our lives.

Father, thank you for showing me that I need to rely on You and You alone. I cannot rely on man or the things of men. You are the only one who sees the end from the beginning. Early I will seek You to guide my steps throughout the day. Your voice will grant me wisdom and knowledge for every season and every area of need in my life. I thank You for Your steadfast love and patience with me as I walk out my faith with You daily. Amen.

EQUIPPING IN THE WAITING

"But this kind does not go out except by prayer and fasting." (Matthew 17:21 AMP)

I have been looking for a breakthrough, for certain mountains to move in my life, so that I can receive the full manifestation of God's blessings and promises that He has for me. After worship practice last night, I felt this scripture reverberate inside me. It has been an echo in my mind and heart since its first sounding.

Let's think about this. The God who created the universe, and all of me, the One who wove me together is telling me to fast and pray. I believe that it is for my benefit that it is required. God does not need my prayers to make things happen. He is using the time together to help me grow in wisdom, in faith, and in perseverance. This life brings things to us that require a deep connection with out God so that we can stand strong and courageous. He is building us up for the battles in this life and in the spirit. He never leaves us unequipped.

Believe me, I am not great in the waiting. I have been a product of this instant gratification generation as much as anyone else. There are battles that take perseverance. They will not necessarily be changed from one instance of prayer. Fasting and prayer allow us the opportunity to seek God and to ensure that He is the source we rely on. Fasting can take many forms. Sometimes it is giving up a meal, but other times it is giving up other things that are stealing our time from God. Maybe it is sports, television, Facebook, or other social media.

Maybe it is something specific like coffee or sweets. It doesn't have to be difficult; it just has to represent a commitment between you and God as you seek Him in prayer. He is faithful to reveal all things to us.

Holy Spirit, I believe You spoke this scripture to my heart not only in my season, but to share with others. We all go through seasons in life that involve waiting and staying faithful in the seeking. Lord God, You are not slow to respond as some believe, but in all things Your timing is perfect. May I grow and be changed in the waiting, Lord, always recognizing the power and glory of Your hand. Amen.

CONDITION OF THE HEART

So rend your heart, and not your garments; return to the Lord your God, for He is gracious and merciful, slow to anger and of great kindness; (Joel 2:12 NKJV partial)

Rending, or tearing of clothing, was an act of sorrow or indignation in Hebrew customs. In this scripture, the prophet Joel is telling the people of Israel to rend their own hearts and not their clothing. Traditions and customs can become ordinary and lose the intent of their purpose. Later in the New Testament, we see Jesus point out the Pharisees and the Sadducees for this very thing. Putting on a display of righteousness, but their hearts were far from God and His will. They lacked tender hearts. They sat in judgment over the people instead of interceding for them and providing the help or comfort that they needed. God wants our hearts more than He wants our actions. Actions can become meaningless if they are not borne out of a heart of love for Him.

Abba Father, thank you that You are the one that removed my heart of stone and gave me a heart of flesh. Keep that heart tender in Your Word and in Your will. Help me to hear Your voice clearly and to keep my flesh and my will submitted to You. Forgive me for the times I have acted righteous like the Pharisees and failed to help those that needed comfort. Keep my eyes open to the ones You place before me so that I may show Your tender mercy and love. It was given so freely to me and I should give it away freely to others. Lord, You are great in kindness and I am so thankful. There truly is no one like You. I rend my heart before You. Take out anything that is displeasing to You. I want to be more like You and less like me. In Jesus' name. Amen.

HIS SPIRIT CHANGES EVERYTHING

Now the Lord is the Spirit, and where the Spirit of the Lord is, there is liberty (emancipation from bondage, freedom). (2 Corinthians 3:17 AMP)

Recently, I sustained an injury to my body. It has been both painful and at times all-consuming. My husband and I have prayed together about it, and stand in agreement that my healing is provided by the Lord according to His Word. During this time, whether in prayer or during times of worship, I have been pain-free. It is like the injury never occurred. I have begun to realize the meaning of this verse like never before. Being in the presence of God is being absent from all the things of this world. Absence from pain, absence from worry and fear, and absence from shame and brokenness. The things of this world do not coexist in His presence.

If you have never thought about the power and gifting of the Holy Spirit as tangible and real before, I encourage you to test it out. The gifting of tongues, praying or singing in the Spirit, has the power to change things. It is a direct language between you and your Heavenly Father. It has the power to break down pain, hurt, and brokenness.

Those of you, brothers and sisters, who already operate in the gifting of tongues, press in. I feel the Lord saying that we need to take our time in prayer, in worship, and engage in spiritual battle like never before. We have the weapons at hand. They are mighty and powerful. When we stand in the equipping of our God, filled with the anointing granted through Jesus Christ, nothing can stand against us. The time for oscillation between the world and living a life sold out to Jesus Christ is over. Be fierce. Be warriors in the army of our God. We are fully anointed to do battle in His name and using the sword of the Spirit (Ephesians 6:17).

BREAKING DOWN YOUR BARRIERS

And Jesus cried out again with a loud voice, and yielded up His spirit. Then, behold, the veil of the temple was torn in two from top to bottom; (Matthew 27:50–51 NKJV partial)

Jesus said, "It is finished." He did not say it was partially completed. He didn't say I will start it today and finish it later. He didn't say He would work on finishing it when it was a convenient time for Him. He went to the cross and died. At that moment. He completed the planned works of our Heavenly Father. He gave us victory over sin and gave us a direct connection to God. He released every promise of the Father to us. There is nothing in this world than has power over us if we chose life and wholeness through the saving work of Jesus Christ.

If you feel there is something keeping you from connecting with God, then that thing is you. Don't make it complicated. Call out to Him, tell Him you need Him, that you have sinned and fallen short trying to complete life on your own. Break down your own barriers and walls that you have erected around your heart and receive His grace. He will meet you in that place of submission. He has been waiting for you with open arms.

YOU ARE FAMILY

Since the One who saves and those who are saved have a common origin, Jesus doesn't hesitate to treat them as family, saying, "I'll tell my good friends, my brothers and sisters, all I know about you; I'll join them in worship and praise to you." (Hebrews 2:11–13 MSG)

Depending upon the experiences you have in your life, it can be hard to grasp the simple truth of this scripture: Jesus counts you as part of His family. Not only does He say He is our brother, but He joins us in our times of worship and praise to our Heavenly Father. I don't know about you, but the thought of Jesus always being with us during our times of worship fills me with the desire to press deeper into time with God. We always have Him as an advocate. More importantly, Jesus has felt everything we will ever feel as men and women walking on this earth. He knows exactly how we feel or will react to everything we experience. He is filled with compassion on our behalf. I love the thought of never having to walk through this world alone. Always having the One, who is seated at the right hand of God, fighting for me. It reminds me of when, as a child, if someone bigger than me was picking on me, my brother would come and intervene and protect me. We have that very same thing with Jesus! We never have to fear the things that will arise against us in these days, because we have victory through Christ.

Father God, thank you for the wonderful gift of Jesus. Not only did He die for me so that I could be with You always. He is the One who fights for me. Always with me, never leaving my side. I am always protected. What a precious gift and perfect provision You have devised for Your sons and daughters. I thank You that You always make a way. Let me boldly come to You to rejoice and praise You, knowing that I do in the presence of my Brother who joins me in giving You all the glory. Amen.

WHAT TO DO IN BATTLE

We are hard-pressed on every side, yet not crushed; we are perplexed by not in despair; persecuted, but not forsaken; struck down but not destroyed— (2 Corinthians 4:8–9 NKJV)

My brothers and sisters, the enemy hates it when we serve and worship the Lord. He will attack you any chance he gets. He will try to overwhelm you so that you feel all alone. He will attack you at work, he will attack your body, he will attack you through relationships and family. Satan will try anything to get you to take your eyes off God. Think about Peter being called out by Jesus to walk on the water. When did Peter begin to sink? When he took his eyes off the Lord (Matthew 14:28–29).

We may be under attack, but we are not abandoned! We are never alone. We have the weapons to fight. Hold fast. Have the Word of God ready to build up your faith. If you don't know what to pray at that moment, pray in the Spirit. The Holy Spirit will always intercede for us. Our faith will equip us to boldly put Satan in his place. He is defeated. Jesus made sure of that when He went to the cross. Our God is King and He will reign on the throne forever and ever!

Repeat this prayer: "Jesus is the name above every name. Through Him I have victory, I have healing, I have joy, I have peace, I have strength. There is nothing that will ever separate me from the hand of my God. My Father loves me. He is more than able to do more than I could ask or need in every situation I face. I am His and He is my God! Praise be to the One who is the beginning and the end! His promises are true. He is my portion! I am victorious because Jesus lives in me! Hallelujah!"

GOD HAS A HOME

In My Father's house are many mansions; if it were not so, I would have told you. I go to prepare a place for you. (John 14:2 NKJV)

The Father's heart for us it to be at home with Him forever. He wants all His children to be a family. His Word not only talks about a new kingdom, but also a home waiting for each one of us. Many of us have spent our whole lives struggling to feel safe and secure; many of us don't know what being home really means. Often, we not only connect it with a physical building, but with the people that we have spent our lives with. Maybe you are lacking some of those experiences. It doesn't really matter, because any home we have here on earth is only temporary. We are not from here. Heaven and eternity with our God and Father is our true home. We can never fill ourselves with anything that comes from this world. Only God can fill you, only God can give you peace, joy, hope, and rest. Rest from your longing for things that we just can't quite reach. He is a father to the fatherless. He is a shelter for those who struggle to find rest and refuge.

Father God, I thank You for reminding me that everything I experience here and now is nothing compared to what is waiting for me in eternity with You. Even the most lavish home will not compare to the heaven that awaits us. Sometimes, I don't think I can even comprehend the beauty that I will see and experience there. The most glorious sunset will pale in comparison. I praise You for Your perfect provision. Maybe I have felt the pull and struggle to feel safe and secure at times in my life, but I am always safe in Your arms, Lord. Help me to see how You are making a way when there seems to be no way. I know that there is nothing that is impossible for You. I know that You are my shelter and my hiding place. Thank you for that promise. All glory and honor belongs to You! Amen.

HE WILL OPEN A DOOR

"I know your works. Behold, I have set before you an open door, which no one is able to shut." (Revelation 3:8 NKJV)

Ever have a season in life where you feel like you just aren't moving forward or making progress? The same challenges or mountains seem to be always popping up in your path and you feel like you have failed in your walk of faith? We are going to have some failures in this life, but isn't it wonderful to know that our God never fails! Here in Revelation, He is letting the church in Philadelphia know that He is in control. They have committed their lives to following the Lord and, therefore, God is making a way for them. Nothing can stand against the power and authority of the Almighty. There is no name that is greater than the name of Jesus. We are told that one day, everything will bow down and recognize His Sovereignty. Just because we make a mistake, or take our eyes of the Lord for a moment, doesn't mean that He takes His hand off us. His Word states that He is faithful. It declares that He will never cast us off even if our own parents were to leave us (Psalm 27:10). Don't lose sight of the love and great mercy of our Heavenly Father. Your mistakes and failures cannot separate you from His great love.

Declare from your heart: "Oh Lord, thank you for Your great love. Thank you that You loved me before I even knew You and even in my sin Your heart was full of mercy towards me. I am going to make mistakes and fail in my walk in this life of faith, but You promise to put my feet back on the right path when I come back to You. Forgive me for my doubts and fears and seeing more with my human heart instead of growing in my faith. Continue to change me, grow me, and reveal to me the things that are not in alignment with Your plan for my life. I want to do it Your way, so that I can see the doors that will be opened and cannot be shut against me. Once again, I surrender control to You. You see the end from the beginning. You see the glory You want to accomplish in my life. Have Your way in me. Thank you, Abba, You are so amazing! Amen."

DON'T LOSE HEART IN THE WAITING

How long, O Lord? Will you forget me forever? How long will you hide your face from me? How long must I take counsel in my soul and have sorrow in my heart all the day? (Psalm 13:1–2 NKJV)

I'm hurting, Lord—will you forget me forever? How much longer, Lord? Will you look the other way when I'm in need? How much longer must I cling to this constant grief? I've endured this shaking of my soul. (Psalm 13: 1–2 TPT)

Let's talk about the times in life when God seems silent. The rug has been torn out from underneath us. All we expected and anticipated seems turned upside down and our hearts are hurting. We feel like we are just barely getting through the basic things required to manage the day. We cry out to God, and wait for His response, but nothing about the situation is changing. It seems contrary to all we know about our good and faithful Father, our Champion, our Redeemer. Ever been in this place? King David found himself in this place, when his own father-in-law pursued him to have him killed. I have found myself in this place, and I am sure many of you have, too. I feel the pain and anguish in David's voice as he asks, "How long will you hide your face from me?" It's important to point out that David's experiences with God and his faith in all he has seen God do in His life lead him past this moment. Later in this psalm David declares, "My enemies say that I have no Savior, but I know that I have one in you!" (vs., 6,

TPT). We have to be active by renewing our faith in God's Word, in singing praises to Him and allowing our souls to be strengthened in times of waiting. We are going to have those times in life, it is just inevitable. God doesn't cause those times, but He will use them to grow our faith, to deepen our walk with Him.

Father God, I am terrible at waiting, but I want to do better. I want to seek You in these moments. I want to draw closer to You, because I know in these times You alone can comfort me. Holy Spirit, give me words of wisdom and knowledge, or a song to refresh my spirit. You are the one who guides me in all truth. You fill my spirit again and again, keeping me refreshed. Empty me of myself, so I can see life as how You see it and have a heart like Your heart, Lord. Life without love and compassion is worthless. Amen.

BATTLE-READY

Put on God's whole armor [the armor of the heavy-armed soldier which God supplies], that you may be able to successfully stand up against [all] the strategies and deceits of the devil. (Ephesians 6:11 AMP)

Perhaps I have mentioned this before, but it is vital that we, as Christians (born-again believers), recognize that we are in a spiritual battle. As a Christian, you must be prepared for the enemy, Satan, to come against you. As a young Christian, I was not prepared for this. I spent many years struggling and losing momentum in my Christian walk. It wasn't until I became aware of how the enemy was attacking me and keeping me in a position of defeat. I wasted many years, giving Satan victories, because I often questioned God's very presence in my life. Now that I am filled with more knowledge, through entering in the Word of God, Satan now tries to attack me to keep me from moving forward in my God-given purpose. That is why it is so important that we recognize that we operate from a position of victory, because we belong to God. His Word states we can never be removed from His hand (John 10:28). Additionally, we are equipped with the very Word of God, which is described as a sword (Ephesians 6:17). When Jesus came into contact with demons or Satan, he used the power of God's Word to silence them. We must do the same. We must allow the Word of God to become a living, breathing, connection to our spirit and hearts—so that it will flow from our lips! For out of the abundance of the heart one speaks (Matthew 12:34).

Lord, I need greater knowledge of Your Word. I declare that I will have greater recall of all that I read in the Bible. I declare that my eyes will see clearly all You have for me, as I spend time gaining wisdom by reading the living word that You had Spirit-filled men write for all of us. It is part of our armor, and we will need it for battle and to enable us to stand against Satan and all his schemes. Keep it always on my lips, meditating on it day and night. It is my strength, because You and Your Word are one and the same. I thank You that I am seated in the heavenlies with You and that I never enter into any battle alone. I already have the victory, because Jesus Christ ensured it on the cross! Amen.

HIS WORD ALWAYS FULFILLED

So Sarah laughed to herself [when she heard the Lord's words], saying, "After I have become old, shall I have pleasure and delight, my lord (husband) being also old?" (Genesis 18:12 AMP)

In Genesis, the Lord has come to Abraham and just promised him that he would be a father to the nation of Israel. The Lord is promising Abraham that he will have children after he and Sarah are beyond childbearing years. This story reminds me of how we let the tangible interfere or question the supernatural hand of our God. Sarah saw her age and the age of Abraham as a barrier. It became a hindrance to her remembering the faithfulness of God in their lives and she questions His power. I love that God does not allow her lack of faith to stop His Word from being fulfilled. That is the difference between God and man. God is not man that He should lie (Numbers 23:19). His very nature is good, and His plan was to establish a covenant and build up nations through Abraham.

It's important to note that because God did not reveal His plan to them until they were much older, Sarah had taken measures in her own hand and had given her maidservant to Abraham. Abraham had a child with Hagar and that brings discord into all their lives once Sarah gives birth to Isaac. We need to be very conscientious about not running ahead of the Lord's plans in our lives. When we move too quickly with our own plans, we often can end up delaying God's promises in our lives. We often end up worse off in the situation than at the start. If we choose to operate in our power, attempting to control our own lives, God often allows us to do so. He uses our disobedience as an opportunity to display that His Word and His way is better than our own choices. Unfortunately, in my life, that has generally meant I have made a complete mess of everything; and, in my brokenness, I see clearly His perfect hand. I am so thankful He has never held back from me when I have asked for forgiveness and help.

Lord, help me to always wait on You. Let me not run ahead of Your timing and Your direction in my life. Plant my feet on the path of Your Word and do not let me depart from it. I want Your perfect way in my life. You alone know the end from the beginning. You alone are the One who always sustains me. Thank you for teaching me to wait and, even if my faith is not perfect, You cannot go against Your nature or Your Word. Glory and Honor belong to You! Amen.

THE KEYS TO LIFE

And to the angel (messenger) of the assembly (church) in Philadelphia write: These are the words of the Holy One, the True One, He Who has the key of David, Who opens and no one shall shut, Who shuts and no one shall open (Revelation 3:7 AMP)

Mighty God! Your Word alone brings life and wholeness to Your Church! Thank you for the victory in these words. I have seen You shut doors that would have led to brokenness and death in my life. You have also opened doors and made a way. You alone made a way when I could not find a way through on my own. I declare over my brothers and sisters right now that You, Father God, are opening doors in every area of their lives. Doors to promotions, wisdom, and knowledge; doors to reconciliation; and, doors to healing, health, and restoration! You are opening the storehouses of heaven and pouring it over Your children, because You are always good and always on time! You never change, Your Word is life and it will be manifested in those who love You and serve Your kingdom. Your Word builds faith in my spirit because it calls to remembrance all the doors You have opened in my life. How You have poured out mercy and grace that I don't deserve, but have given me so freely because of Your great love for me. I prophesy that Your sons and daughters will have greater understanding of Your faithfulness and power in their lives that they may boldly walk out all that You have called them to be. In Jesus' name! Amen.

KEEPING THE DIRT OUT

There is a class of people who are pure in their own eyes, and yet are not washed from their own filth. (Proverbs 30:12 AMP)

Don't imagine yourself to be quite presentable when you haven't had a bath in weeks. (Proverbs 30:12 MSG)

Most days of our lives are very full. Our feet barely hit the floor after the alarm sounds that we aren't mentally going over the list of things we have to get done that day. Before we know it, it can be days before we have spent any time with the Lord or in His Word. I particularly like the Message version of this scripture, because it gives such a vivid image of how I feel when I have walked in the world and not spent any time in my prayer closet. I begin to feel dirty. I might disguise it for a while, but the dirt begins to seep out. I start to lose the ability to operate in the fruit of the Spirit and I begin to look more like everyone else in the world. My focus becomes inward. Lots of my thoughts begin with the word "I" or "me." Has this happened to anyone else? I begin to speak words that don't represent the love of Christ to others. I react with anger instead of patience and kindness. I begin to judge instead of act with grace.

Many pastors and speakers have often talked about washing yourself in the Word. It really is a great description of the transformation that happens when we spend time with the Father. Just like standing under the head of the shower washes the dirt off our bodies. The Word of God begins to transform our minds and hearts from the inside. That is why I have to be so intentional about making sure I spend time in His Word every day, before I start anything else. It helps keep my eyes fixed on the One who loves completely and without reservation. It helps me recognize the difference between the light and glory coming from Him alone and the darkness of this world. It helps me fill my heart and mind with His goodness. It is what I need more of every day. I bathe myself in His Word so that I can keep my spirit strong and in alignment with His will. It washes me clean and helps me start fresh every day. I challenge you to join me. Find time to start your day fresh in His Word. It will restore you and change you like nothing else ever can or will.

OUTSIDE YOUR COMFORT

But Jesus said, "Someone touched me, for I perceive that power has gone out from me." And when the woman saw that she was not hidden, she came trembling, and falling down before him declared in the presence of all the people why she had touched him, and how she had been immediately healed. (Luke 8:46–47 NKJV)

Recently, during an exchange with a friend, the conversation turned to the changes that had manifested in our lives. I felt in my spirit the words, "Change rarely happens when we are in our comfort zone."

Consider the woman in this scripture with the issue of blood. The prior Scriptures tell us she had the issue for twelve years, and that she had spent every resource, but had not been healed (v. 43). The laws of this time included that she should not be out in public among people. She was supposed to keep herself separate from everyone because she would be considered unclean. She wanted something from Jesus so desperately that she went against the rules and made herself uncomfortable. Even more, she was revealed to all who were there after she touched the hem of Jesus! He was in a crowd of people and stopped. Verse 47 says, "She came trembling." An indication that she was not sure how her actions were going to be received. She could be punished for what she had done. But the change she needed in her situation would never have happened if she did not act. It was a big step of faith in many ways. She could have been called out by someone else in the crowd before she ever got to Jesus.

What are you praying for right now that you have been waiting for a move from God? Is there any step you need to take? Maybe you feel God calling you into an area or asking you to do something, but fear is holding you back? If God is calling you to it, He will prepare you and walk you through it! Don't let fear of change keep you from the promises of God!

Thank you, Father, for this reminder that we have to be ready to move and even be uncomfortable at times for change to happen. Even in the refining process, the heat that removes the dross is intense, but what remains is purified. That is what I want in my heart and in my spirit. The refinement that is pure and resembles Christ in me. May You alone be glorified in all I do. Amen.

OUR FEET PLACED UPON HIM

He drew me up out of a horrible pit [a pit of tumult and of destruction], out of the miry clay (froth and slime), and set my feet upon a rock, steadying my steps and establishing my goings. (Psalm 40:2 AMP)

There are various Scriptures that talk about how the Lord will steady our steps. That He will guide us on the path He has created for us before we were even brought into this world. I am not saying that we ourselves can't get off track, but if we are placing our trust in the Lord and maintaining a relationship with Him, He is guiding us. We just have to relinquish control. God doesn't force anything upon us. We have to trust.

I had this beautiful image of being at a celebration with my Heavenly Father. There was a banquet of food, talking and laughter and music playing sweetly all around us. Then a moment of my Lord walking toward me with a smile on His face and His hand out for me to take. The music gets louder, and I realize that my Father wants to dance with me. As we start to move to the music, I am unsure of the steps and keep moving in the opposite direction. I feel awkward and frustrated because I am ruining this precious moment with my Father. The music stops and I feel horrible and ashamed. I couldn't do it, I couldn't just dance with my Father. I didn't know how to move with Him. Suddenly, I am tenderly picked up and the Lord set my feet right on the top of His. The music begins to play again, and with my feet placed firmly on His, we were able to dance and twirl and move as one.

Brothers and sisters, this is what God wants for us, to be so connected with Him that we move as one. It means we have to let go of our plans and doing things our way. We have to just allow Him to work in our lives. It's definitely not easy and oftentimes I surrender everything over to Him, but then retake control, because God is doing it differently than I imagined He would. This walk by faith is a process; and, the moment we surrender to Him again, God in His infinite mercy and grace begins to move on our behalf.

Papa, thank you for this beautiful picture of what life with You can be like if I just place my feet over Yours so that we can move as one. Forgive me for all the times I didn't allow You to place my feet on solid ground, because I thought I was strong enough on my own. Sometimes, I am no more than a rebellious child. I thank You for the tender heart You have towards all of Your children. The mercy and grace that You have showered on us. I will keep working at this walk of faith every day, because I know You are ready to meet me in each moment. You are an amazing Father and God! Amen.

THE DOOR IS UNLOCKED

"I am the Door; anyone who enters in through Me will be saved (will live). He will come in and he will go out [freely], and will find pasture." (John 10:9 AMP)

I love the image of Jesus describing Himself as a door to all people. A door is a tangible concept that we can all understand. It is a passageway that opens and allows us access to an area we are trying to get to. The world is trying to tell people that there are multitudes of ways to love and be loved. To worship God, Jesus was explicit, He is the only way. It is exclusive, and many people struggle with the concept of exclusivity because it doesn't fit the lifestyle they want to live. It impacts their control and their need to for self-gratification. It is easier to focus on the concept of Christianity being a religion, a set of rules. All the dos and don'ts. In this scripture, Jesus does talk about the exclusivity of following Him, but He also talks about the freedom found in Him.

I spent many years looking for love and approval through man. It was an empty pursuit. I have many good, loving people in my life, but people will make mistakes. Hurt or misunderstanding often occurs in every human relationship. A relationship with Jesus, and understanding that He embodies a sacrificial love like no other, truly gives me freedom. I am free from striving to please people, and can simply live the best life I know how. A life guided by the perfect example. Christ himself. And if I mess it up (as I have often done), I don't have to worry about losing that love. I just go to the Lord, tell Him I made a mistake, and truly repent. His mercy and grace are offered freely.

Imagine going to a hike in a location you have never been before. You come to split in the path that isn't marked. That path could lead you away from the destination you are intending to go. It could lead to you being lost in unfamiliar surroundings. Why would God allow multiple paths to lead to Him? Unmarked paths lead to the possibility of getting lost and being defenseless in the wilderness. That is not God's plan for any of His children. He devised a plan for all of us. He sent His only son to die on a cross that, if we believe in Him, Jesus Christ, we would have eternal life and all the promises of God. One way, one path, that leads to surety and to freedom. Set your feet at the Door. He is waiting to open it to you that you may find security and rest. Amen.

LAYING ASIDE SELF

He sat down and summoned the Twelve. "So you want first place? Then take the last place. Be the servant of all." (Mark 9:35 MSG)

Over and over again, as Jesus teaches those following Him, we see that the values of God are not the same as the values of the world. It really makes sense that they are in opposition to each other because the world is home to our flesh and our spirits belong in heaven. There are really two different kingdoms. The one where we temporarily reside which is marked by the sin of man. The other is home our Heavenly Father is calling our eternal spirits to, a place that is pure, holy, and filled with peace and love. This scripture is just another reminder to those walking with Christ, that we cannot value the things of this earth. We must always look to the Word of God and determine if they align with His view.

One of our greatest challenges as believers is the surrender of self. To truly surrender and be ready to be obedient, and to offer our gifting and possessions freely. The world tells us to fight for what we want. That if we don't go after it, we will be walked over and we will be seen as weak. "But seek first the kingdom of God and His righteousness, and all these things will be added to you." (Matthew 6:33) Here we have a picture of God's heart and desire for us. He knows everything we need, and it is His desire to provide it for us. He wants our eyes fixed on Him. Talking with Him, deepening our faith and relationship with Him. It is how we grow stronger. How we change and become more like Him, in His image, as we were created before sin became part of our nature.

Father God, I thank You for this Word. Maybe it's just me, but I see that as the world becomes darker, and men and women draw farther away from you, I need to check my heart. I need to ensure I don't conform to the world, but pursue Your will and Your Word and ways. I need to go deeper, draw closer, and lay aside the things that don't align with Your teaching. Take out anything that isn't pleasing to Your eyes, God. I want to be more like You. Thank you for the promise that You will take away all my dirt, all my shame, all my mistakes. You will give me beauty for ashes, garments of praise, and You will clean me. I will be covered in the righteousness of Your Son, Jesus Christ. I don't want to be like this world I see around me, it is dark and full of people who have made themselves into their own idols. Help me to put myself aside and be a light for Your kingdom. I don't have to do it in my own strength because You dwell in me and I have Your power and equipping through the Holy Spirit. Thank you for the opportunity to serve You. Amen.

A ROAD MAP

Blessed (happy, fortunate, to be envied) are they who keep His testimonies, and who seek, inquired for and of Him and crave Him with the whole heart. (Psalm 119 :2 AMP)

I truly love my church and the leadership we have there. My pastor has a heart of preparation. He seeks God for the year ahead, he doesn't wait for it to start, he begins praying about it well in advance. He has done this for as long as I have attended the church, but every November I am always surprised that it is time to begin thinking of the year ahead. I wonder if this happens to anyone else? It's like I have my head down, and am just busy doing life day-to-day. The next minute I look up and the whole year has flown by. I am thankful for the people in my life, much like my pastor, who encourages me to stop and look up. To raise my eyes and to look around to see where I am going. Am I heading where God is leading me? Or am I too busy just getting through the day-to-day moments of life to really focus on what His plan is?

I like to think of the Bible like an atlas. It provides direction to where I am going. The future isn't somewhere I have been. How will I know exactly how to plan for it? That is the wonderful thing about God, His Word, and walking out this journey of faith with Him. In unknown territory, He is the perfect GPS. He goes with me and, if I pay attention to His directions, keeping my heart open, I don't have to end up going in the wrong direction. It is such a source of peace because my God has already seen the end from the beginning. He knew what was going to take place in every moment of every day of my life. It really is difficult to fully grasp because my view is so limited in comparison.

Maybe, today, you feel lost. You have looked up and suddenly realize you are very far from where you thought you would be. You don't have to try to navigate your way alone. Just stop right where you are and call out to your Heavenly Father. Say this from your heart: "Father, I feel lost right now. This is not where I thought I would be, but I know that You created me with a plan and purpose. I trust You. You, Jesus, are a light and will guide me through Your Holy Spirit to walk and become all that You have willed for me. Forgive me for getting off course and thinking I could do this one my own. I need You to be my atlas. To guide me. I will keep my eyes lifted up to see You and where You are leading me. Thank you for speaking to my heart. Amen."

SUPERNATURAL LANGUAGE

Pursue love, and earnestly desire the spiritual gifts, especially that you may prophesy. For one who speaks in a tongue speaks not to men but to God; for no one understands him, he utters mysteries in the Spirit. (1 Corinthians 14:1–2 NKJV)

During the early years of my Christian faith, I did not understand about the indwelling of the Holy Spirit and the gift of tongues. It wasn't something taught to me as I was growing up and learning about God. As an adult, it took a really great pastor explaining the purpose of it and showing me how it is biblical to use this prayer language in our lives. It isn't an easy skill that will naturally develop once you set your mind to use it. Just like all things, it is something that requires practice. Now, when there are times in my life that I don't know how to pray, praying in the Spirit is my first step. I realize that the Holy Spirit will help me say what I really need to share with my Heavenly Father. Romans 8:26–27 tells us that the Spirit intercedes for us on our behalf, with sighs and groanings too deep for words. It is a language of our spirit connecting to the Spirit of God. It is the source that each of us needs to keep our spirit filled up and connected with the source of supernatural power.

RESTORATION IS COMING

And the God of all grace, who called you to his eternal glory in Christ, after you have suffered a little while, will himself restore you and make you strong, firm, and steadfast. (1 Peter 5:10 NIV)

The suffering won't last forever. It won't be long before this generous God who has great plans for us in Christ—eternal and glorious plans they are!—will have you put together and on your feet for good. (1 Peter 5:10 MSG)

The word restore means, "to repair or return something back to its original condition or to give back to the original owner or recipient." Since we were created in the image of God and by His hand, we as His children belong to Him. We are all part of His family. He is working to bring you back to Him where you belong. Maybe you think that you are beyond His reach. That you are too lost or too broken for God to be able to help you, but nothing is impossible for God. If God is the same yesterday, today, and forever, then He is the same God who rescued the Israelites, restored sight to the blind, and helped the deaf to hear and the lame to walk. He is the same God with resurrection power. He brings the dead to life.

I don't know exactly what is going on in your life this moment, but I don't need to know. I know the One who can do the impossible. I know the Miracle Maker.

Lord, I speak over my brothers and sisters right now. Lord God, may the knowledge and recognition of Your awesome power arise in their hearts, spirits, and minds right now. Lord, I declare that You are bringing them back together. You are causing restoration to happen in their lives. Lord, reveal the evidence of Your moving on their behalf. Allow them a glimpse of Your goodness at work that they may have hope and give You all praise and glory. I see resurrection power at work in their lives: dreams long forgotten brought back to life in You, Lord! You are the wonder-working God! Amen and glory be to Your Name!

A CONSUMING FIRE

Therefore let us be grateful for receiving a kingdom that cannot be shaken, and thus let us offer to God acceptable worship, with reverence and awe, for our God is a consuming fire. (Hebrews 12:28–29 NKJV)

I have been thinking about the word consume in this scripture. One of the definitions of the word means to, "absorb all the attention and energy of (someone)." This word has its origins in Latin, from the word con—altogether and sumere—take up.

In the Old Testament, there are several passages where God describes Himself as a jealous God (Exodus 34:14). God desires our entire energy to be on Him. He longs for us to give our time and attention to Him. Why does the God of the universe need and require this from us? First, He is our Father and Creator, and He desires us to be close to Him, and to know who He is and His heart and tender love towards us. However, I also believe it is because if we give Him all our attention and energy, it will drive out the things that don't belong in us. In Isaiah 61:3, the Lord promises to give His people "beauty for ashes, oil of joy instead of mourning, and a garment of praise instead of a spirit of despair." In Matthew 11:28–30, Jesus promises that we can rest in Him. He promises that He does not give us heavy burdens.

I believe that when we allow ourselves to be consumed by all that God has for us and when we allow Him to fill us—our thoughts, our prayers, our worship, our time and service—we begin to let go of the things of the world that are stealing our joy, our peace, our strength, and our hope.

God, what a beautiful thought that You want me to spend all my attention and energy on You. Not because You need it, but because of how it benefits my soul. It allows me to lay my burdens down. Jesus told us that we weren't meant to carry the trials of this life alone. It is the very reason He went to the cross. To conquer death and every other thing trying to keep me chained up and defeated. Lord, I want to be consumed by You. You are light and when I am consumed by the light, darkness has no place in me. Holy Spirit, I welcome Your voice to keep me centered on my Shepherd. The One who leads me beside the still waters and restores my soul. Amen.

THE SOVEREIGN PLAN

The Lord brings the counsel of the nations to nothing; he frustrates the plans of the peoples. The counsel of the Lord stands forever, the plans of his heart to all generations. (Psalm 33:10–11 ESV)

The Holy Spirit led me to this scripture verse during my prayer time today. I have been feeling righteous anger towards the dark things I see happening all over the world. I have been feeling righteous anger at the fear that has been spoken into the hearts of men, women, and children from many different arenas: the media, the government, and our medical professionals. I don't need to understand motives or the perspectives of man. I know in my heart that fear is not of the Lord. It is never His intention to leave His people without a plan, a future, and hope. His Word tells us that His design for us is to renew our minds in Him, in His truth.

Maybe you are one of those people who is beginning to feel worn down by all the negativity and the fear and darkness you have been seeing in the world. I want you to read the words of this scripture King David wrote thousands of years ago. It is still true today. Man is not in control. The Lord our God is! The Holy One, the Mighty One. He created the heavens and the earth and all that is in them. He is not surprised by the events that take place. He will always have victory. We just need to keep talking to Him. Speaking out in agreement to His plan and purpose on this earth, just as it is in heaven. His Word, His truth, will stand. Nothing can come against the mighty Jehovah! He is the same yesterday, today, and forever. If He was capable of making

Pharaoh release the Israelites after years and years of slavery, then He is capable now in this season's trials.

Thank you, Lord, for the reminder that man cannot set himself against Your righteousness and power and win. The enemy who continues to attack people with fear and darkness has already been defeated. Your people are already victorious. Not even death can stop us because we already have eternal life in You! I declare that You will continue to frustrate the plans of people who come against You and Your wisdom and knowledge and righteous Word! I declare that every nation, every tongue and tribe, will bow down and declare that You alone are worthy of all praise. Glory, glory, glory and honor be to the Alpha and the Omega. You are all-powerful and amazing! I love You, Father God! Amen.

CHANGING FROM THE INSIDE OUT

For he knew all about us before we were born and he destined us from the beginning to share the likeness of His Son. This means the Son is the oldest among a vast family of brothers and sisters who will become just like him. (Romans 8:29 TPT)

There are so many things I love in this verse. First, God knew us before we were brought into the world. He already had a design and plan for each of our lives. So many of us live with the idea that we are a mistake, that we have no value. But that is just not true. We are children created with such love and care. In fact, we were created in the likeness of God's own son, Jesus Christ. That means that God's plan was for us to always be part of His own family. The next part of the scripture actually confirms that God's plan for us was to bring us into His family after His Son Jesus was crucified, died, and resurrected. Through that death and resurrection, we have been grafted into the family of God as brothers and sisters when we believe in the salvation provided by Christ.

The next part of the scripture is just as important. Not only do we have Jesus Christ as an older brother, but we are changing to become just like Him. I love the very idea of this, because it means that we have the same access to our Heavenly Father and to the life-changing power and knowledge that Christ has. It means that we don't have to be constrained to the concepts that we can only see and touch. But we can access the anointing and power that is granted through the Holy Spirit and through Christ. Power to be free, power to heal, power to restore, power to love, power to show forgiveness, mercy, and grace. Power to lift up those who are broken and need the same love that we all needed.

As those that once were outside, but now part of God's own family, how can we not share the gift we so freely received? How do we see the broken, the hopeless, those living in fear and oppression, and not offer the same opportunity at a new beginning that was offered to us?

I declare over each of us that the boldness to share the love of Christ is an overwhelming tidal wave in our spirits. That we can no longer be silent when we see the hurting. That we will be led by the Spirit of God to speak with tender mercy and grace about the transforming love of an amazing God. To tell of Jesus and His all-consuming love for each one of us. So great a love that He gave His own life as a ransom for all. We will see goodness in the land of the living, through the power of the life-transforming blood of Christ. Amen.

DEEPER UNDERSTANDING

And God gave Solomon wisdom and understanding beyond measure, and the breadth of mind like the sand on the seashore, (1 Kings 4:29 NKJV)

One of my favorite things to do on a vacation at the beach is to walk along the water's edge looking for seashells. It was a great delight to do that recently on a trip with my husband, to a beach we have never been to, with types of shells I have really never seen. I never realized how many different variety of shells there were until looking at an information board in a nature preserve around the point at Sanibel Island. The vastness of God's creativity far exceeds all that I can imagine.

During our time on the beach, as I walked along the water's edge, many of the shells that get washed up by the waves are pitted or broken. I felt in my spirit the idea to get into the water and look back at the shore where thousands upon thousands of shells were gathered. I found some beautiful shells just by changing how I was looking for them. I changed my perspective. Even some of the broken shells were quite beautiful because you could see how they looked from the inside of the shell.

I feel that is the message on the Lord's heart for today. He wants to change our perspectives and our minds. We need to look at things differently and from knowledge and wisdom granted through Him. It is an important equipping of the sons and daughters of the Living

God. One that will allow us to be prepared for the journey ahead. God is never taken by surprise. He sees the end from the beginning. Although He may not reveal everything to man, He still demonstrates how we can stay built up and prepared. Staying connected to Him through His Word and in prayer is a key component of tapping into the wisdom of God.

Thank you, Heavenly Father, for the beautiful and creative ways You speak to my heart. What an amazing and wonderful God You are! You desire us to have wisdom and understanding that is greater than we can imagine. You even equate the measure to the sand on the shore! Particles too great to even count! Thank you for showing us that You want us to be ready for the journey and path You are placing us on. I will do my part to be ready by reading Your Word and keeping it in my heart and mind daily. I give You all glory and honor and praise! You do not leave Your children without access to all we need. I declare that all Your sons and daughters will have even greater revelation of who You are and how You are preparing a way in their lives. They will see the very provision of Your hand everywhere they look! Amen.

COME AND FIND REST

Now God has offered to us the same promise of entering into his realm of resting in confident faith. So we must be extremely careful to ensure that we all embrace the fullness of that promise and not fail to experience it. (Hebrews 4:1 TPT)

In Hebrew, the word nuach means "to rest, to repose." In this verse in Hebrews, the author is encouraging Christians during trying times to remember who their God is. He is the Great I Am, the one who fulfills His promises to the Jewish people and everyone who believes in His Son, Jesus Christ.

In these days, the sons and daughters of God will also see trials. Until the return of Christ, we will see the struggle between light and darkness. We will see the battle between good and evil. This struggle will cause many to fall away. They will lose sight of who God is, and that His promises to His people will prevail. This scripture is great reminder that we can simply have confident faith in the power of our mighty God and His Word.

It is another great reminder of how important pursuing our relationship with God, and keeping our hearts, minds, and spirits renewed in His presence, really is. Although resting in God seems inactive, it is actually the opposite. Building our faith is actually a very active process. It involves purposefully choosing things that will build up our spirit in knowledge and truth. The two key components of these things include prayer and reading the Word of God. Just like any other relationship, we must spend time with God to grow that relationship.

Abba Father, I will rest in Your promises that You will never fail those whose hearts and minds are fixed on You. You alone are the picture of love, compassion, and grace. I will actively pursue a relationship with You. I will read Your Word and hold it in my mind and heart. It is what gives me hope and faith in times that seem dark. Your Word reminds me that You already have the victory. You, in such tender mercy and compassion, continue to reach out to the lost. May my knowledge of who You are bring boldness to my speech and actions, that those who see me will see Your hand. All glory and honor belong to You, Lord. Amen.

HARD TRUTHS

"For I have come to set a man against his father, and a daughter against her mother, and a daughter-in-law against her mother-in-law. And a person's enemies will be those of his own household." (Matthew 10:35–36 NKJV)

This is one of those verses that makes most Christians very uncomfortable. It is a hard truth for many believers to face: that sometimes persecution comes from within one's own family. For the most part, Westerners do not understand religious persecution to the same depths as those in Eastern cultures. There are still many places outside of North America that Christians are imprisoned or even face death for their beliefs. Jesus is not unaware of the persecution that believers face. In fact, Jesus Himself faced ridicule from within His own hometown and people that He grew up with (Matthew 13:57).

We have to recognize that there are varying levels of Christian faith and growth. Our spiritual growth is connected to our developing and growing our knowledge and understanding of God through His Word. Oftentimes, people rely on others for understanding; however, we are told in God's Word that we are to each ourselves test what is spoken against the Word of God in the Bible (1 John 4:1). We need to be wise in our relationships and who we let fill us with God's Scripture. We need to be observant of their spiritual fruit. Look at it this way, we wouldn't ask a five year old what to do with a large sum of money. We recognize that they don't understand such things. In the same way, we need to be sure that we have Christian mentors that demonstrate experience, faith, and integrity in their own lives if we are allowing them to speak or guide us in our lives. Don't get me wrong, our mothers and fathers are important, and we need to show them honor. However, if my parents believe in generational curses, and I believe that Jesus' death and resurrection breaks every generational curse, we do not have the same measure of faith on this point (2 Corinthians 5:17, Ezekiel 18:19–20). In an instance like this, I would seek another Christian believer to stand in agreement with me in prayer regarding generational health and well-being.

Father, forgive me for my fear regarding discussing hard scriptures. I should realize by now that You just want Your children to see the challenges of life with their eyes wide open. To understand that knowledge and wisdom are what help us continue to walk in faith in Your Word during difficult seasons. I thank You that I am not where I was yesterday, and that every morning is a new opportunity to be all that You have called me to be. I declare over Your children, that we would be wise concerning our counsel. That we would watch the spiritual fruit of people and that Your Holy Spirit would guide us in our relationships. Our relationships are important because they can build up or tear down. Thank you that You care about our relationships, and about equipping us for times of persecution. We are never unarmed when we carry You in our hearts!

THE REFRESHING NEEDED

He makes me lie down in green pastures, he leads me beside the quiet waters, he refreshes my soul. (Psalm 23:2–3 NIV)

This is just a small portion of Psalm 23, which is oftentimes used during funeral services for loved ones. Over the past several years, I have looked at this particular psalm with fresh eyes. Looking past where I have heard it used and what I have connected it to emotionally and really looked at what the writer was saying about the Lord. King David penned this psalm not for those who have fallen asleep, but for himself, as a reminder that God is able.

I want to look a little closer at this particular verse today. Here, David is talking about finding rest and comfort in the presence of God. Oftentimes, when trials come my way, I use avoidance techniques so I am not alone with my own thoughts. My avoidance techniques involve cleaning, baking, cooking, and crafting or a myriad other projects. This definitely helps me not to become consumed with my thoughts, but it does not provide my soul with comfort or rest. Maybe someone reading this today can relate.

Today, with this scripture, Father God is calling us to run to Him with every situation. Only in His presence will we find the refreshment we need in times of great trial. We have to set aside our previous ways of dealing with struggles and operate in faith. God is who He says He is and will do all that He has promised. I am working at getting better at resting in His presence and not running to my strategies of staying busy in the midst of crisis. I am still very much a work in progress, but my God is faithful to complete a good work in me! He can do the same in each and every one of you as well.

GOD IS TRUTH

We couldn't be more sure of what we saw and heard—God's glory, God's voice. The prophetic Word was confirmed to us. You'll do well to keep focusing on it. It's the one light you have in a dark time as you wait for daybreak and the rising of the Morning Star in your hearts. The main thing to keep in mind here is that no prophecy of scripture is a matter of private opinion. And why? Because it's not something concocted in the human heart. Prophecy resulted when the Holy Spirit prompted men and women to speak God's Word. (2 Peter 1:19–21 WEB)

We are not so far past of the recent state and local elections in the area that we live. It is a time I have come to dread because I have learned to not believe the promises of any politician. During campaign speeches, we hear grand promises about changes and making local or area problems disappear. After the election is over, many of those campaign promises never come to pass. In politics, many elected officials have their own agendas. There is a general lack of integrity that becomes even more evident during election time.

I believe that many people struggle with a human perspective when reading God's Word. They see it through the filter of human experiences. This verse reminds me that faith is not in our mind. Faith is activated in our spirit. The Word of God is designed to change our hearts and grow our faith. It's designed to connect with our spirits and not our minds. Even the parts of God's Word that I may not particularly like or understand. Every time I open the Bible, I find that God reveals something new to me. I believe it is because I understand that it is not stories written by man, but God's own words and message to me. It is a manual for living in this life, until I can be joined with Him for eternity. I believe, for years, I read the Word with my eyes covered by a filter. I was blinded by my own understanding, but when I looked at the same words with the revelation that God breathed those words onto the page and that they are alive and active, I began to see new and wonderful things in verses I had read many times before. I encourage you to lay aside your own head knowledge, and ask God to use His Word to stir up knowledge, wisdom, and hope in your heart today. When you come to the realization of God's immense love for you, His Words become precious, like the greatest love letter ever written. A love letter just for you.

A SURRENDERED WILL

Then he said to them, "My soul is very sorrowful, even to death; remain here, and watch with me." And going a little farther he fell on his face and prayed, saying, "My Father, if it be possible, let this cup pass from me; nevertheless, not as I will, but as you will." (Matthew 26:38–39 NKJV)

The Bible clearly states that Jesus and God were not only connected as father and son, but They were indivisible; They were one. This verse distinctly demonstrates that Jesus was very aware of His Father's plan and the amount of pain and suffering that He would have to endure in the coming days. There was not one part of His persecution, rejection, suffering, and death that the Lord withheld from Him. Jesus' surrender of His own will to carry out the plans of God for all mankind is a clear picture of reckless love. A love so pure and so great that Jesus was obedient even to the point of His death on a cross.

I think about Jesus' complete surrender to His Father's will, and reflect on my own life and actions. I still have so much to learn about completely surrendering my life to my God and Father. This isn't to live in complete condemnation at how I am lacking , but as a true, honest look at my walk with God and how I can grow. A stagnant Christian life is a life that is under the sway of the world. scripture clearly states that we cannot serve both God and the things of this world.

God, look at my heart and show me the things that do not please You. Show me the areas that are not completely surrendered to Your Word and Your commandments. Allow Your Word to be what is treasured in my life. Allow it to cut out the areas that have barriers to all that You desire for me to be as Your child. Teach me to walk a surrendered life as demonstrated by Christ. For, if I wish to gain life, first I must being willing to lose it. I realize how little I know about completely surrendering to You, Lord. Forgive me. I confess that I have been slow to be obedient to Your leading through the Holy Spirit. I want to do better. My act of surrender is the only response to the grace and mercy given to me when Jesus died for my salvation. Thank you for loving me enough to continue to provide discipline and direction in every area of my life. I love You, Abba Father.

WITHOUT DELAY

For the vision awaits its appointed time; it hastens to the end—it will not lie. If it seems slow, wait for it; it will surely come; it will not delay. (Habakkuk 2:3 NKJV)

Over the past several months, I have been battling with an injury in my body that has resulted in ongoing pain. Prior to this, I really have never experienced pain in any significant way, although I have observed many people I love deal with chronic pain for various medical issues. In this season, I have begun to have a greater understanding of how pain and fear work together against us. Please understand me, I am in no way suggesting that pain is not real; however, I am suggesting that pain is something that the enemy will use to get into our minds and make us question the goodness of God. He will use anything to try to destroy our faith, because then we are powerless against him (John 10:10).

In Genesis, when Adam and Eve bring sin into existence, God blocks them from access to the tree of life (Genesis 3:22–24). It is here that we see that sickness and death become part of life for mankind. However, that is not the end of the story! We have a new beginning through the death and resurrection of Jesus Christ. As believers, we become grafted into His family, and the very Word of God in 1 Peter 2:24 proclaims that "by his stripes you were healed."

I don't know each of you personally, or know your journey or how chronic pain has affected you. I do know that Jesus healed a man who has spent thirty-eight years of his life paralyzed by the pool of Bethesda (John 5:5). God wants you to know that He is never late. He is always right on time. Don't interpret God's motives because that becomes a ground to grow unbelief and bitterness. The voice of your Father is saying, "Press into me, I am with you and will never leave you. Keep your heart surrendered to me. Keep praising me in faith for the things you long for. Stay connected to me. Listen for voice. I will provide the words of hope and encouragement you need. Stay surrendered to me in the waiting. Keep your lips speaking the seeds of life I have planted in your spirit. Speak life and not death. I am yours and you are mine. It will come to completion, all that I have spoken for you." Amen, thank you, Abba, Father. We receive it!

HOLDING IT CLOSE

And all who heard it wondered at what the shepherds told them. But Mary treasured up all these things, pondering them in her heart. (Luke 2:18–19 NKJV)

They told everyone they met what the angels had said about the child. All who heard the sheepherders were impressed. Mary kept all these things to herself, holding them dear, deep within herself. (Luke 2:18–19 WEB)

Today, I am enthralled by the part of the scripture that mentions what Mary did in these moments before the birth of Jesus. She treasured them, and stored them deep in her heart. It reminds me that God did not reveal His whole plan to Mary. God sent His angel with key messages, when she or Joseph needed to know what to do next. She did not have every day of Jesus' life revealed to her in her encounter with God's messenger. But I love the wisdom that she already had as a child of God. She understood that to be strong and to walk the path that God had chosen for her, she would need to hold onto God's words, and His wondrous acts in her heart. She would not let them go, because she would need to remember them to encourage her, to retain her faith and hope in the future.

We need to mirror the actions of Mary in our own lives. God has provided salvation, broken down strongholds, healed brokenness, restored relationships, healed the sick, raised the dead, breathed His spirit into us! We need to treasure these things in our hearts, so that we will always be able to recall the mighty power of our God in every situation. Then we can praise Him in confidence, no matter what the situation looks like from our limited perception.

Lord, thank you for all the moments in my life that I can look at the mighty works of Your hands. Lord, I know that You will help me keep them stored in my heart and place them in my remembrance exactly when I need them. How great is Your faithfulness to me, my God and Father. This Christmas season brings such great revelation knowledge of how You are calling Your children to deeper understanding of the equipping You have provided. How I worship and adore You! Glory be to Your name! Amen.

A WORD UNLIKE ANY OTHER

Blessed by the God and Father of our Lord Jesus Christ! According to his great mercy, has caused us to be born again to a living hope through the resurrection of Jesus Christ from the dead, to an inheritance that is imperishable, undefiled, and unfading, kept in heaven for you, (1 Peter 1:3–4 NKJV)

Let's dive in and take a look at the words imperishable, undefiled, and unfading in this verse. The Oxford Dictionary describes imperishable as "enduring forever." It defines undefiled as "pure" and unfading means "never losing brightness, vitality, or strength."

The description the apostle Paul uses to describe the eternity waiting for us in heaven with our God and Father is in direct contrast to what we see here on this earth. There are many beautiful sites and the creation of the Lord is truly beautiful here; however, it is not everlasting. The Word of God tells us that this world is not part of our eternity. "Then I saw a new heaven and a new earth, for the first heaven and the first earth had passed away and the sea was no more." (Revelation 21:1)

More than ever, we need to be looking to God's Word to see His promises. This world is not our home, and it will always be in direct opposition to the ways of God, because it is influenced by sin and Satan. But our hope can remain steadfast, because we recognize that Jesus Christ is the final authority and through Him we have every victory over sin, fear, darkness, and Satan! We just need to stand firm in the Word of God and firm in our faith.

Keep filling your heart daily with the words of our God and His Son Jesus Christ. Say them aloud in your lives and over the lives of your family. His Word is powerful. His Word is victorious. His Word is alive and active. Keep looking ahead for our Heavenly Father has promised us an inheritance that is imperishable, undefiled, and unfading. It awaits us who persevere and finish our walk with the Lord in faith.

A DIFFERENT PLAN

Simeon went on the bless them, and said to Mary his mother, "This child marks both the failure and recovery of many in Israel, a figure misunderstood and contradicted—the pain of sword-thrust through you—but the rejection will force honesty, as God reveals who they really are." (Luke 2:34–35 MSG)

According to the Scriptures, Simeon was a righteous man who was filled with the Spirit of the Lord. He had received a vision that he would live until he has seen the coming of the Messiah with his own eyes. In this part of the Scripture, Simeon begins to prophesy about how many will reject Jesus as the Messiah.

We have the distinct advantage of having the Word of God to look at to learn about God and Jesus. This was a time when the Jewish people only had the scriptures from the Old Testament. They had been living in a state of waiting for the Messiah for a very long time. They were now occupied by the Roman Empire, and subject to the authority of a foreign king. They had preconceived ideas of what the Messiah would be and what He would do for the people of Israel. No wonder they did not see Jesus as the Savior of the world. He did not fit the constructs of a king to rule over the world. In their minds, He was no one, a man from Nazareth (John 1:46). Before we judge the blindness of the Jewish men and women of Jesus' time, we should look at our own lives. How many times have we developed our own ideas of how God should answer prayers or work on our own behalf? How many times have we made the Almighty God in our image, because we narrow His ability to work and move based on our own human understanding?

This Christmas season, as we are reminded of how Christ came to dwell among us, let us remember that God's plan was unconventional. It was the opposite of what men and women would think and expect. God's way is so vastly different from ours because He sees everything. As you think of how our Savior was born, be reminded that God designed the entry of His Son into this earth, so that we may understand the longing of God's heart to draw close to us. To be among us. God loves you. He is closer to you than you can possibly imagine. He is working on your behalf. It may just not look like you anticipated or expected, because He is not confined to the imaginings and thoughts of man.

A STAR OF HOPE

"While you have the Light, believe in the Light [have faith in it, hold to it, rely on it], that you may become sons of Light and be filled with Light." (John 12:36 AMP, partial)

This Christmas, I find myself digging deeper into the symbolism we find all around us in the decorations that adorn many of our homes. The Christmas tree, which points to the tree that would become the cross that Jesus is crucified upon. The presents, which symbolize the gifts brought by the Magi to honor the baby Jesus, the Messiah. These beautiful traditions have deep and powerful meaning and point to the celebration of the Christ. My husband and I have been in our home two years and, although this is the second year setting up our Christmas tree, we still don't have a tree topper. We don't have a tree topper because I didn't want to put something there just to have it. Especially knowing that these decorations are about honoring the birth of my Savior and King. I know many people love to place an angel on the top of their tree to represent the angelic host coming to proclaim the birth of Jesus. There are many very beautiful angels that adorn many trees around the world. My mind keeps coming back to the star that guided the wise men on their journey to find Jesus (Matthew 2:7–10).

God is a creative God. I think about how He used a star to provide light in the darkness and to guide the wise men to Jesus. At the same time, Jesus Himself is the light of the world. He is the one who will conquer death and darkness, or eternal separation from God through the sin of mankind. The symmetry of this is so beautiful. That is what a star on top of the tree reminds me of—that Jesus who would later die for me, on a tree, would be the one to provide light in my life. I still haven't found the star that I will place on my Christmas tree, but I am not in a hurry to figure it out. I am just enjoying the deeper revelation of beauty in the symbols and traditions that remind us that this season of hope and promise is about the true light of the world. The light that dwelt among us and made us realize the love and compassion of our God and Father like never before.

Lord, You never stop amazing me with the way You leave no detail unfinished. What an intricate way You weave all the pieces together to show us Your love and Your plan! May I always have a heart that is softened and open to see the beauty of works, Your creation, and the meaning of Christmas. May I always recognize Jesus as the light of the world and that His light now resides inside my spirit. Help me to shine that light outward in the darkness so that anyone living without hope may see it. May it help them know the love You have for them and lead them to salvation. Amen.

HOLD ON FOR GOD'S BEST

And they who know Your name [who have experience and acquaintance with Your mercy] will lean on and confidently put their trust in You, for You, Lord, have not forsaken those who seek (inquire of and for) You [on the authority of God's Word and the right of their necessity]. (Psalm 9:10 AMP)

Some of you have been in a long season of waiting. It could be for healing, or a desire of your heart. Whatever it is, you have been waiting for that moment of breakthrough. In these times, there are moments when it is difficult to quiet your mind from the questions on repeat: Why? What if? How long? When?

I want to ensure you that God is not silent in these moments. He is actively working and moving. God is not slow in His response. He is always on time. God's Word and wisdom are always available. I cannot count the number of times I was looking for wisdom or guidance and the Holy Spirit led me to the scripture verse that I needed. We grow in our faith in seasons of waiting and we are refined as we draw closer to the Lord. Other times, we are waiting because God is working things to bless us above all we could ask or expect. What we think we need may not be in alignment with the very best God wants to give us.

There have been times, when I have grown impatient in the waiting and have pursued my own purpose, or taken control of the situation, thinking God wasn't going to help me. I deceived myself, and ended up with less than God's plan for my life. Seeing the opportunities that

God had prepared, but missing it can be a painful lesson. I encourage you to find scriptures that will keep your eyes fixed on the promises of God and renew your strength in Him. I have listed a few below:

Psalm 25:5–9, Psalm 27:14, Psalm 37:7–9, Psalm 37:34, Psalm 62:5, Habakkuk 2:3, Isaiah 40:31

TRIUMPHANT JOY IN ALL SEASONS

And even more than that, we overflow with triumphant joy in our new relationship of living in harmony with God—all because of Jesus Christ! (Romans 5:11 TPT)

Christmas day has passed and the hustle and bustle of the world has slowed and may appear more like deafening silence to your spirit. Maybe you embraced the frenzy of the season because it was a great distraction to the heartbreak you have been feeling deep in your spirit. As you read this scripture, you might be struggling to feel the joy that others seemingly so easily embraced at this time of year. I cannot change the circumstances of your heartbreak. I cannot easily understand the struggles that you are walking through, but there is a God and Father who is more than able. When we take a moment to remember all that Jesus accomplished when He came to earth to dwell among us, and to give His life as a living sacrifice for each one of us, we can tap into that triumphant joy no matter what we are going through in the day-to-day.

Start simple, just spend a few minutes focusing on being thankful to God for the gift of salvation. I can't promise that it will change the circumstances immediately, but it will slowly begin to shift your focus from the challenges that seem so overwhelming to the overwhelming love God has for you. Once you recognize the beautiful and powerful love of God in your life, then you will be able to remember the promises of God, His faithfulness towards you. That He sees you as His child. If He sent His Son to die for you, He will fulfill His plan and purpose in your life.

Abba Father, I lift up my brothers and sisters in Christ, who are walking through a season of heartbreak. May they see the joy and the beauty in remembering the gift of Your Son Jesus sent to earth to demonstrate a love so great! May the simple act of recognizing Your love, help to spark recollection of Your wonder working power and faithfulness to Your children. May it strengthen them as they wait on You. Holy Spirit may the word pour over them, bringing them wisdom and renewing their mind daily. I give You praise for the gift of Your Son Jesus. His salvation made a way for me to connect to You directly. To be called Your daughter for all eternity. There is no greater love, no greater gift. I praise You! You are such a good, good father! Amen.

UNDERSTANDING OUR POWER

And when the Lord saw her, he had compassion on her and said to her, "Do not weep." Then he came up and touched the bier, and the bearers stood still. And He said, "Young man, I say to you, arise." And the dead man sat up and began to speak, and Jesus gave him to his mother (Luke 7:13–15 NKJV)

The more I study the Word of God, the more I realize that God is very purposeful in His Word. He uses it to teach us, to provide guidance in our daily lives and wisdom for decisions we need to make. If we recognize that God is very purposeful in His Word, then we realize that He had written accounts of ten different resurrections throughout the Old and New Testaments. Not just one, not just the resurrection of Jesus Christ, but nine other instances of resurrection.

This is just one demonstration of God's miraculous power. This power was manifested in His prophets, through Jesus, and through disciples containing the indwelling of the Holy Spirit. This is a demonstration of the power that is available to us. I do not believe that is coincidence that we have accounts prior to Jesus' presence, during His ministry and after. I think God wants us to recognize that if we have the indwelling of the Holy Spirit, then we have access to His anointing and the ability to do all that we saw Jesus do during His ministry. Jesus even tells His disciples this very truth in John 14:12, that they will be able to do the same works or greater works than what He has done, if they believe in Him.

Lord, I thank You for Your Word and how You intricately weave these accounts together to demonstrate Your power. Thank you for also using Your Word to teach me and give me knowledge about the power of the Holy Spirit living in me. I confess that I have often not recognized the anointing and authority that I carry. I have made Your works more about my inadequacies instead of Your power. Forgive me. Help me to be obedient to Your leading that I may be used to bring about glory to You and Your kingdom. That lives may be changed because I no longer allow fear to drown out the truth of who I am in You. I am the temple of the living God through the manifestation of the Holy Spirit. You are faithful to complete Your plan in me and to use me to grow Your kingdom. Help me to hear Your voice clearly above all other sounds. You are such a good and amazing Father. I am so blessed to be Your child. I praise Your name. Amen.

A COMPASSIONATE FRIEND

When he went ashore he saw the crowd, and he had compassion on them and healed their sick. (Matthew 14:14 NKJV)

Think about the number of times the words mercy and compassion are used throughout the Bible. Compassion simply means "having concern for the suffering of others." In the accounts of Jesus' ministry, we have a clear view of His deep care and concern for the things that caused others to suffer. He went from town to town to teach, but He was so moved by the pain and suffering He saw that He performed miracle after miracle.

My friends, if you are feeling alone in your current season, I want you to know that the God of the universe has great compassion and mercy for you. His Word promises that we never walk alone in our circumstances. He is with us and it is His desire to see us restored and to be blessed. He loves you with an everlasting love and that is why He sent His Son Jesus Christ to die for us. He made a way to break the chains of sin, pain, and suffering so that they may no longer have a hold on us.

Father, thank you for this reminder of the compassion You have for all of Your sons and daughters. Your Word says that You and Jesus are one and that the things we see displayed in the life and ministry of Jesus are a clear representation of all You want for us. I am so thankful that I can go to Your Word when I need encouragement and strength. Jesus said that this world would always have struggles, but that we could rest in His promise that He overcame the world. I declare that this truth will resound in the hearts of Your children that need a fresh revelation of this in their lives. All glory and honor are Yours! Amen.

HE KNOWS YOUR SUFFERING

Then Pilate ordered Jesus to be brutally beaten with a whip of leather straps embedded with metal. And the soldiers also wove thornbranches into a crown and set it on his head and placed a purple robe over his shoulders. (John 19:1–2 TPT)

Recently, I watched The Passion of the Christ, directed by Mel Gibson. It is not the first time I have seen the movie, but because it had been a while since I had seen it, the brutality of the way Jesus was treated before He was hung on the cross left me with tears streaming down my face. I cannot fathom how one person can take an object and repeatedly strike another, knowing that it will rip the flesh off their body. However, that is exactly what Roman soldiers did to Jesus. Then they forced a crown of thorns on His head, pushing it down and embedding the thorns into His flesh. The cruelty of it still wrenches my heart. I cannot imagine the amount of pain this caused for Jesus.

So maybe, like me, you are in a season where you have been going through trial or pain. In this season, maybe you have had people say something timely or encouraging that you needed to hear. Or perhaps you have had those well-meaning people say things that have left you feeling more alone in your suffering than ever. God, our Father, wants you to know that you are not alone. Jesus Christ understands the depth of pain and suffering that you are experiencing in every circumstance. Broken relationships, infertility, death of a child, or addictions. He understands and wants you to know that you are not too far that He can't reach you in whatever situation you are facing. The beatings, the ridicule, the death on the cross were not the end of the story. Jesus' resurrection gives the promise of new life. A hope for the future. So cry out on the name of Jesus! He is our ransom, our Savior, and our friend! He loved you so much that He gave up every right, suffered every injustice, so that you do not have to go through the tough things in this life alone.

Jesus, we cry out to the one name that can save! We need You! This life can be full of sadness and pain, but You promise a life of hope and joy. I lay down my will and surrender to the one who gave it all for me. I need You to guide me in this life and show me the way in each and every moment. You are my Savior, You are my brother, You are my friend. I cannot thank You enough for all You endured for me on the cross. I receive Your promise of abundant life, and the indwelling of the Holy Spirit. I hold onto the hope I see in Your resurrection. Be glorified in my life. Amen.

RESOLUTIONS THAT IMPACT MY SPIRIT

Therefore if any person is [ingrafted] in Christ (the Messiah) he is a new creation (a new creature altogether); the old [previous moral and spiritual condition] has passed away. Behold, the fresh and new has come! (2 Corinthians 5:17 AMP)

When the new year begins, many people make a resolution to change something in their lives. Most often, it relates to our overall health and fitness in some way. There is nothing wrong with that, but for me personally, I have always struggled with maintaining some exercise plan I devise at the beginning of the year. The statistics about the number of people who make gym memberships at the beginning of the year and then drops off in thirty-to-ninety days say I am not alone in my inability to stick to an exercise regimen. So several years ago, I decided to stop making resolutions in the new year relating to physical health and exercise and work on who I am in Christ.

I am not saying we shouldn't maintain a healthy lifestyle, or eat nutritiously, or exercise. All of those things are important for our physical bodies, but I know that when I focus on the flesh, it will not sustain me. The spirit is what needs to be exercised to stay strong, to grow and develop in spiritual muscle. As much as we become new creatures in Christ, the world will continue on in the same patterns. Darkness in the world continues to grow, as sin will exist until the Second Coming of Christ. I want to be working on keeping my inner spirit in condition to stand strong in any spiritual battle. If any of you have been a Christian for any length of time, the battles will come because we live in the world. Jesus even told His disciples that living in this world equates to having troubles (John 16:33). We have to stay connected to the One who has overcome the world!

As I look ahead into the new year, I want to lay aside the things of the past, my mistakes, my selfish pride, and my inability to surrender every area of my life. I want to dig deeper into the Word of God. He declares He will provide fresh revelation that we need in each moment. I want to experience all that He has for me. I see His mighty hand and the way He has sustained me from former trials. He has been faithful. I owe Him the very best of me. The first offering of anything I have to give. I challenge you to look at the past year, and see how God has been working in your life. How could you step closer to Him this year? What is your offering to the Lord for this new year, this new season? The beautiful thing about our Father is when we step out for Him, He is willing to meet us, and walk with us and sustain us.

PURSUING THE KINGDOM

But seek (aim at and strive after) first of all His kingdom and His righteousness (His way of doing and being right), and then all these things taken together will be given you besides. (Matthew 6:33 AMP)

In this era, we have access to so much information. Technological advances have placed information at our very fingertips. There are not too many of us who have not used Google to get information on so many topics, even healthcare. Even though it can be wonderful to have access to information to help us in many aspects of our lives, it can also be dangerous as well. It becomes dangerous because we begin to rely other resources and not turning to God for all our needs. We become confident in our own ability to figure things out, and not turn to the one who supplies all our needs.

Whenever we attempt to take control and move ahead of God's leading and will in our lives, we are acting in disobedience and indicating our lack of trust in His goodness. We are in essence saying we don't believe that our Heavenly Father will keep His promises to us. When we take control, we are operating in response to fear and in direct opposition to faith.

Having information is not a bad thing, but not going to the Lord and listening for His leading in every decision and circumstance is the quickest route to stepping out of His will for your life. I have made this mistake multiple times in life, and I am working now at placing God at the forefront of every decision, every situation, in my life.

Waiting on His Word and leading will always prove to bring out God's purpose and blessing in my life.

Father, thank you for Your Word and the reminder that You ultimately have everything in hand for my life. There are no surprises to You. You see every moment of my life as it is about to unfold. Different seasons are always challenging for me, but Your Word says that I never walk through one moment alone. I want Your best for me because it is better than anything I could imagine. I praise You for the love You always shower over me. Even when I make mistakes, You never forsake me. You are always pouring Your love over me, calling me sweetly to Your arms. You are my source of comfort and strength. I trust You. You are a good, good Father. Amen.

MY PORTION

The Lord is my portion or share, says my living being (my inner self); therefore will I hope in Him and wait expectantly for Him. (Lamentations 3:24 AMP)

This is part of a larger scripture usually quoted in Lamentations, but I wanted to focus on this part specifically. The word portion means "the determined part that is separated for each person." As a son and daughter of God, He has set aside an abundance of all He has to provide for us. His Word tells us many times that it is God's desire to bless us and provide for us (Matthew 6:8).

This concept is in direct contrast to what the world says. Let's be honest, there aren't too many people who haven't been affected by the "great toilet tissue shortage of 2020." The news stated that paper products, including toilet tissue, may be in short supply; and, in fear, the stores were full of people buying up as much toilet paper as their carts could hold. Instead of trusting that there would be enough for everyone, people grabbed to get their share. Fear drives people to grab for anything they can get their hands on. I am going to be blunt, if you spend a great deal of time watching the news, then you have a greater chance of being instilled with world perspectives and that includes fear.

We have to grasp the most important truth and hang onto it with both hands. We have a Heavenly Father who wants us to walk in faith. That faith will build our strength in times of trials and God will be your source of provision in every area of your life. If He is the creator of all the heavens and earth, and He designed everything to work so intrinsically together, how does He not have exactly what you need at all times? I did not say what we want at all times, but what we need. Our Father knows what each of us needs and what is best for us—even if we cannot see it ourselves. Spending time connected to Him in prayer and the Word is the best way to keep our eyes centered on the One who is our portion and will provide all that we could ask or think.

Abba, thank you for Your Word and for helping us stay centered on You. There is nothing that You cannot do or work for my good. I trust in Your Word and not what I see in this world. This world did not recognize You or Your beloved son. Their eyes were shielded by darkness and fear. Thank you for peeling the scales from my eyes that I get to behold the wonder working power of Your hand. I recognize the blessing of salvation and being Your child. I trust in You. You are more than enough, Lord. I love You. Amen.

PUTTING AWAY CHILDISH THINGS

When I was a child, I spoke as a child, I understood as a child, I thought as a child; but when I became a man, I put away childish things. (1 Corinthians 13:11 NKJV)

I feel an urgency in my spirit for the people of God to grasp hold of the truths in His Word and to have a deeper recognition of His anointing and power living inside of them. It's time to let go of the things that hold you back. No longer say that you cannot be used of God, that you are not qualified. That is self-deception. Every one of us has a calling that God has placed on each of His children. Jesus Himself told the disciples that we are to go into all the world and teach of Jesus and God (Matthew 28:18–20). We often make doing the work of God about us and our qualifications; however, it has never been about us, but the glory and power of God, who is able to do all things.

I challenge you to be open to being used by God in the circle that you have been placed. There is someone that you interact or connect with that needs to see the light of hope, strength, and joy that is manifested in the hearts of those that have Christ living inside of them. I challenge you to spend less time thinking about what we need God to do in our own lives, but how we could use this life (that He sacrificed everything to save) to serve others in need. Living by the example of Jesus Christ himself who said, "The Son of Man did not come to be served, but to serve." (Matthew 20:28)

God, give me eyes to see and a heart tender with compassion to see those I interact with every day with the same heart Jesus had when He saw me in my sins, yet thought I was worthy of it all. Let me be more generous with my time and my gifts, that I could show people that there is light in this dark world. More than I ever, I see how people need to know You. I declare a new level of boldness in the sons and daughters of God. That they would recognize that the power of Christ that is inside of them through the Holy Spirit. Let us lay aside our childish thoughts and put on the armor of God so that we become skilled warriors in the army of our Lord. May the power of His Word be our greatest source of strength in every moment of our days. Glory and honor and power are Yours alone, God. Amen.

THE ONE YOU NEED

A father to the fatherless, a defender of widows, is God in His holy habitation. (Psalm 68:5 NKJV)

In our society filled with broken marriages, many children are left fatherless. Many women are in a role of single parent. Although in our generation there are more options for single mothers in the workforce, it still is a life filled with hardship and figuring out to fulfill roles in life that were meant to be shared.

I have been thinking about the word husbandry in relation to God and His relationship to us. The word husbandry in the Oxford Dictionary means, "The care, cultivation, and breeding of crops or animals." A second definition states, "The management and conservation of resources." The root of husbandry contains husband, which in its origin meant "head of the household." I think this is such a beautiful picture of God's love toward each of us. He wants to be the leader of our families. That is why the image of Him as our Father is one that we need to see when we look at Him. Many people don't have great experiences or memories of their earthly fathers, but God is nothing like man. He is loving and merciful. He is the one who wants to bless and prosper each one of His sons and daughters. He wants to fill you to overflowing (Psalm 23).

Lord, I love the way You reveal hidden treasures in the use of words connected to Your character. I am so humbled by Your desire to be my father. It's the image of Your steadfast love that first caused my heart to turn toward You. You know us each intimately, and each of us need the love of a father. Thank you for this promise, that we can always turn toward You and You will not only be our father, but also a defender. You truly are my source for all things. I give You glory and honor and praise. Amen.

CREATION EXALTS THE ALMIGHTY

And some the Pharisees called to Him from the crowd, "Teacher, rebuke your disciples." But He answered and said to them, "I tell you that if these should keep silent, the stones would immediately cry out." (Luke 19:39–40 NKJV)

In the verses 37 and 38, the disciples begin to give glory and praise to God and declare Jesus a king. I love how Jesus tells the Pharisees that the rocks would praise and give glory to the Lord if people stay silent. I find it hard to not see the way all of creation testifies to the glory of the Creator. The mountains, the seas, the skies, the sun, the moon, and the stars in all their beauty declare that the Lord is awesome in power and in His creativity. Scientists have spent thousands of years studying and understanding all that God has created.

If all of creation testifies to the power, majesty, and glory of our Heavenly Father, why is it so many people deny His very existence? The Bible tells us in Psalm 19, verses 1 to 3, that there is no speech or language that cannot hear the testimony of creation. That means that not one single person has an excuse not to recognize the works of God. The Pharisees' hearts were hardened. They knew the law, but could not see the very move of God and that Jesus was the very manifestation of God on earth. Their own perceptions and self-knowledge blinded them to the truth.

Take a minute today to look at the beauty all around you. All that the Lord has created and called into existence with His Word. Even the stillness of snowfall in a blanket over the earth has such beauty in it, we just need to quiet ourselves and see it.

Thank you, Father, for the reminder that all the earth speaks of Your power and Your glory. There is nothing that the Creator of the universe cannot accomplish. Just the way You created the earth, all the animals, the mountains, seas, and skies reveals how amazing You are! I love You, and will give You all praise for all that You have done! Amen.

INVESTING IN THE WORD

But his delight is in the law of the Lord, and in His law he meditates day and night. He shall be like a tree planted by the rivers of water, that brings forth its fruit in its season, whose leaf also shall not wither; and whatever he does shall prosper. (Psalm 1:2–3 NKJV)

Anyone who knows me knows that I love to cook and bake. I enjoy searching for new recipes to try. I enjoy the process of taking ingredients and putting them together to make something that tastes good. I don't hesitate taking a risk and trying a new recipe for dinner guests. However, this wasn't always the case. In fact, my family has many stories about how several recipes I have tried over the years were utter disappointments. The key to my success with cooking and baking now is the time I have spent over the years practicing cooking and spending time learning about cooking and baking. When I was a beginner, I knew less and the outcome had successes and failures. But I invested the time.

These verses in the first psalm of David point a clear connection to the Word of God and success. We cannot have successes in life, if we don't study God's Word and learn how to navigate the different challenges of life. It gives us a way to stand in integrity and strength in the midst of daily challenges. It shows us that love and compassion are better choices than hurt and bitterness. It teaches us that there is a spiritual battle going on to separate God's people from Him for all eternity. If I never pick up His Word, if I never spend time reading the Bible, I cannot learn these truths.

I will never be a professional chef or baker, but because cooking and baking are things I enjoy, I continue to invest the time to learn. My spirit needs the knowledge of the Lord to learn how to walk daily in strength and in faith. Otherwise, when things go wrong, like those early attempts at cooking and baking, I could lose my ability to pick myself back up and continue my journey with God. I will flounder instead of prosper. That is not what God wants for His children, and it is why He gives us His Spirit-filled Word.

KEEPING ACTIVE IN YOUR FAITH

Don't fool yourself into thinking that you are a listener when you are anything but, letting the Word go in one ear and out the other. Act on what you hear! Those who hear and don't act are like those who glance in the mirror, walk away, and two minutes later have no idea who they are, what they look like. (James 1:22–24 MSG)

In my career, part of my scope of practice is to work with people and strengthen their cognitive skills. Cognition refers to the functions of the brain, including: language, attention, memory, and the ability to solve problems. When working with memory or recall, I remind people of the strategies that we employ to learn information. There are very few people who have photographic memory, or can see something once and commit it to memory. Most of us need to employ a strategy of rehearsal. This is repeating the information either verbally or visually until it is stored in our memory. This isn't the only strategy, but it is a core strategy that most people need to utilize for retaining information.

Becoming familiar with the Word of God is a twofold process. It involves active listening—listening with the intent to learn—and putting the Word into practice in our daily lives. That involves a combination of studying the Word, praying or speaking the Word out, and engaging in worship of the One who created the Word for us. We cannot rely on anyone else to walk out our faith and our relationship with the Lord. If we expect to grow in our knowledge of the Word, we have to personally choose to study it for ourselves.

When I work with people to strengthen their cognitive skills, I give them ideas on how they can continue to strengthen their skills on their own. I often express the concept of "use it or lose it." If your brain is a muscle, then you have to exercise it to retain skills. The same principle applies to Christians. We cannot grow or maintain our faith if we are not actively engaged in keeping the Word of God in the forefront of our minds, hearts, and spirits.

GOD PLACES HIS POWER INSIDE YOU

And then, after your brief suffering, the God of all loving grace, who has called you to share in his eternal glory in Christ, will personally and powerfully restore you and make you stronger than ever. Yes, He will set you firmly in a place and build you up. (1 Peter 5:10TPT)

There are many people hurting in this world, who like me, probably do not feel as if any amount of suffering should be described as brief. It is the part of life we all like the least. But because we live in world that is covered by sin, we cannot escape this part of life. I want you to take your eyes off the word suffering in this verse and look toward the section that describes what God will do in your life through a time of trial. He will "personally and powerfully restore you and make you stronger than ever" and "He will . . . build you up."

I hear the voice of the Lord in my spirit saying: "My child, I waste nothing. I use all things for My plan and purpose. Nothing is wasted. No tear is wasted, not one minute on your knees in prayer is wasted. No heartbreak is wasted. No battle is wasted. Not one moment of wisdom and revelation is wasted. Not one moment of unbelief that turns to restored faith is wasted. Not one moment of your questioning is wasted. I am doing a work in you. It is a labor of My love. Like a farmer, I am breaking apart the ground to loosen the dirt and ensure the nutrients are spread to all parts of the field, so that not one piece of ground is wasted. So that the seed planted in the ground of your heart will grow mighty and strong. Tilling the ground is intense work, but it is necessary for the growth of any seed. The seed of My Word can only grow in a heart that is softened and pliable in My hand. You have a choice in this process. You can surrender to the process and allow Me to complete my good work and plan in your life. You can choose to keep your heart hardened and turn away from My love for you. I know that faith takes time, and it takes standing firm in the challenges that come your way. If you hold fast, and do not let go of my hand, I will guide you in the journey. Hold fast to me. I will complete all that I purposed for your life. Nothing will be wasted. I am making something beautiful out of all the pieces that you think are unusable. Choose Me. Choose to be patient in the process. Look for what I am teaching you and showing you in each moment. You are My child and you are strong enough. I will give you grace for each day. Not one moment will be wasted. I am the God who uses all things. Nothing too broken, nothing too dead, that I cannot call it back to life."

Thank you, Lord. I needed this reminder that You are in control. There are no surprises to You. You see the end from the beginning. Your plan for me is good. I will keep my heart surrendered to You. Reveal to me all that You want me to know that I may pass on the revelation of Your great love to others. In Jesus' name. Amen.

A LIFE OF WEALTH

Tell those rich in this world's wealth to quit being so full of themselves and so obsessed with money, which is here today and gone tomorrow. Tell them to go after God, who piles on all the riches we could ever manage—to do good, to be rich in helping others, to be extravagantly generous. If they do that, they'll build a treasury that will last, gaining life that is truly life. (1 Timothy 6:17–19 MSG)

This is one of those scriptures that clearly divides between the values of the kingdom of God and the values of the world. Let's face it, if you look around this world, you can clearly see that people in the world have become obsessed with wealth and lovers of money. There are people who will exploit any weakness in man to gain wealth. Exploiting our vanity, lusts, or fears are all part of the sales pitch. Believe me, I have fallen for it many times myself. I cannot begin to add up the amount of money I have thrown away on hair products that will transform my crazy locks into glorious curls or beautiful shiny, healthy hair. Every new hair gadget that tempts me never gives me the beautiful hair seen on the model in the commercial. I recently read how many major corporations are now focusing on children to sell their products. Through sites like YouTube and TikTok, children are entering into the arena as influencers and businesses want to capitalize on people who are watching these videos on these sites.

Our God and Father knows that we need things to live: food, shelter, clothing. He is not against us having things. However, we need to guard our hearts against being lovers of things, including the gaining of wealth, instead of loving the giver of all things. We live in a world where people are driven by their desires and are willing sacrifice morality to gain what they want. We need to be filling ourselves with the Word of God and the truth, so that we are not swayed by the same things that the world places value on. We need to search the desires of God's heart and long for the same things He longs for. His Word clearly tells us to look to Him and His kingdom first, and He will provide for all our needs. It is definitely more important than ever to guard our hearts and minds against the love of money, and the desires of the world.

NOT ALLOWING GOD TO LEAD

Daleth: I lie in the dust; revive me by your word. I told you my plans, and you answered. Now teach me your decrees. Help me understand the meaning of your commandments, and I will meditate on your wonderful deeds. (Psalm 119:25–27 NLT)

In Psalm 119, the recurring theme is focusing on understanding and following the Word of God. Following and obeying His direction. In the first part of this verse, we see the writer state, "I told you my plans, and you answered." The line after that leads me to question the response that God gave. My interpretation of the next line leads me to think that the writer's plans were not what God had in mind, so the author then requests guidance from the Lord.

As I think about my own life, I know that I don't go through one single day without making a plan of some sort: what to wear, what to have for dinner, plans of what errands need to be accomplished on the weekend. I don't believe that God is against any of us making plans, but I believe God is concerned with out tendency towards rigidity. Consider this: Have you ever had an experience where you needed God to move, but you had already decided how that should look like? Then, when you felt like the answer God was providing didn't line up with the way you wanted it to go, you decided to take control over the situation? Unfortunately, I have done this very thing multiple times. Basically, I decided that my plans were more important than God's leading and His purpose in my life. In short, I missed out on opportunities to show my trust and faith in the One who wants to work all things for my good.

The wonderful thing about our God is that He is rich in mercy and grants new mercies every day. So, if you have made the same mistake of making your plans a priority over God's path for your life, don't give up. God is faithful to forgive us as we confess our mistakes and is always there to help us continue our journey and walk with Him. When things don't work out the way we expect, it is a fresh opportunity to turn and draw closer to the One who sees the end from the beginning. Press into Him. He is tenderly waiting for you to listen for His voice. He will give you another opportunity to hear from Him and walk in His ways.

Lord, I turn my eyes to the wonderful things You have done in my life. Forgive me for the times I have made my plans more important than Your instruction and calling in my life. I want to remove the need for rigidity and control and allow complete surrender of every area of my life to Your ways. Your ways are higher than mine, and will reveal Your glory in my life. Thank you that when I turn to You for wisdom and understanding You give it readily. I will see the wonderful working of Your hand and give You all thanks and praise. In Jesus' name. Amen.

RECOUNT YOUR BLESSINGS

Oh give thanks to the Lord; call upon his name; make know his deeds among the peoples! (Psalm 105:1 NKJV)

Bless the Lord, O my soul, and forget not all his benefits. (Psalm 103:2 NKJV)

There have been multiple research studies on positivity and the impact it has on overall health. In a study at Johns Hopkins, Lisa R Yanek, M.P.H, discovered that people with a family history of heart disease were one-third less likely to be at risk for heart-related illnesses than those with a negative outlook. There are multiple studies that look at perspective and how it impacts our overall stress levels and health.

King David wrote a lot of the Book of Psalms, and although there are times when he cries out to God about the turmoil that he is dealing with in his life, David most often points to the wonder, power, and ability of God to do great things. God created us in His image and to have a connection with Him. He created us to bring Him glory and honor. Not because He needs us to feed His ego, but because it connects us with the truth about who He is when we are faced with challenges. I recently talked about the challenges I have faced within my own body, and I have had moments where my mind, my fears, would have consumed me, if I was not constantly talking to myself about the greatness of God. If I did not take a look back on other events of my life and see the blessings of His hand on me as I walked through other difficult times.

Practice, practice, practice! Learning to talk about God's goodness and greatness and power will not come naturally at first. Our flesh wants to talk about what we see, what we hear, what we feel. It is in direct opposition to the supernatural power of God in your spirit. So, we have to practice giving God glory, honor, and praise, so that it will be what comes out of our mouths in seasons of hardship, that we might have hope and not fall short of His plan and purpose in our lives. Spend a little time today recounting the goodness of the One who formed you in your mother's womb! He is a great God!

ENCOURAGEMENT AND HOPE

The right word at the right time is like a custom-made piece of jewelry, and a wise friend's timely reprimand is like a gold ring slipped on your finger. Reliable friends who do what they say are like cool drinks in sweltering heat—refreshing! (Proverbs 25:11–14 MSG)

I just happened to discover this scripture this morning during my personal devotional time. I really don't believe in coincidences when it comes to God, but I believe that He is always confirming His Word in our lives. Yesterday, a sweet sister in Christ sent me a quick text containing scripture verses. It was a Monday, which means that there is very little time in my day at work to look at anything personal, and so I didn't have an opportunity to open it until after dinner that evening. The scripture was the perfect word of encouragement I needed to hear in regard to a desire of my heart; a desire where I was struggling to hang onto hope. Where the length of timing and the wait had begun to make me question if I really heard a particular promise from God. Maybe one of you has been in that place, too? You recognize that the all-powerful, mighty, wonder-working God can do anything, but maybe the mistake was in what you received. I am so thankful for my sweet friend being obedient to the voice of the Holy Spirit. The enemy is devious and if he can't get you to doubt the power of God, maybe he can get you to doubt the sound of God's voice or words of instruction to you. That is exactly what he did in the Garden of Eden, questioning, "Surely, God didn't say, 'You shall not eat of every tree of the garden'?" (Genesis 3:1) The enemy is always looking for a way to become a barrier between us and the power of God's Word in our lives. He will even manipulate the words God says, twisting them and making them into the opposite of what God intended. We need to be actively encouraging one another. Listening for the leading of the Holy Spirit and coming alongside our brethren to lift them up with the truth. We all have times of doubt, God is aware of our strengths and weaknesses, and He is faithful to provide timely encouragement to each of us.

If you are that person in need of an encouraging word to rekindle hope, ask the Lord to reveal a word of discernment to you. If you are that person who God is speaking to share a word with someone, I encourage you to be bold and courageous! God is allowing you to be a source of blessing to them. Be obedient to His leading. We need to be mindful of each other and demonstrate loving-kindness towards one another. This life can be difficult, but we can support one another and help one another overcome adversity. Christ's power is in us! We can silence the enemy when he attempts to speak against the Word in our lives. We need one another! I challenge you to be an encourager to someone today!

WALKING THE LIFE OF CHRIST

But whoever keeps His Word, truly the love of God is perfected in him. By this we know that we are in Him. He who says he abides in Him ought himself also to walk just as He walked. (1 John 2:5–6 NKJV)

This Scripture verse is truly a great description of self-examination. Looking at our lives and the choices we make and seeing if they align with the Word of God. Seeing if our actions look like the actions of Jesus Christ. It reminds me of the coined phrase that became so popular a few decades ago: What would Jesus do?

If we look back at the verse 4 in this chapter, it states: He who says, "I know Him," and does not keep His commandments, is a liar, and the truth is not in him. There is nothing wishy-washy about this verse. It gives a clear picture of what we should be doing as followers of Christ, and if we are not, then we cannot claim to have Christ in us. Now, I am not saying we don't all miss it sometimes, but this is referring to the constant disobedience of a person. One who is caught up in religion, but not really surrendering their heart and lives to the Lord. This is the person who maybe wants salvation, but doesn't want to change the way they are living and live a life sold out to Christ. These verses link us to the scripture in Matthew 6:24 that states: "No one can serve two masters; for either he will hate the one, and love the other; or else he will hold to the one, and despise the other." I remember being a young person, not fully in love with the Lord and looking at God through the lenses of religion. God was full of rules, and it meant that

I couldn't do things my friends were doing. I resented what I saw as rules and regulations instead of what, years later, I recognize as my Father lovingly trying to protect me from making decisions that led me far from Him and through multiple painful experiences.

As Christians we need to be constantly pursuing the knowledge and truth of God. Seeking to spend time in His presence and in His Word. Feeding our spirits, so that our flesh cannot rule our lives. Our flesh is linked to the things of the world and it will rule us if we don't purposefully keep it surrendered to our spirit.

God, Your Word is truly like life-giving bread to my spirit. It feeds me so that I am satisfied and strengthened to resist the calling of my flesh. Thank you for teaching us of the main battle within ourselves and how to pursue things of righteousness and how to hear Your leading. I am strengthened when I am connected to You. I am protected and guided when I listen to Your Word. Thank you for promising to be my Shepherd and teaching me to listen for Your voice. I am whole when I follow after You and hold fast to the One who promises to keep me grafted into Himself. Thank you for the faithfulness of Your mercy and grace over my life. I am healed and restored because of Your love. I give You all thanks and praise for the gift of forgiveness that I can never earn. Thank you, Abba! I love You, but You will always have loved me first!

THE HEART OF FRIENDSHIP

The heart knows its own bitterness, and stranger does not share its joy. (Proverbs 14:10 NKJV)

We are all carrying something inside that has caused us some sort of heartbreak or pain. It is part of this life. I was reminded again recently that many of us are good at putting our best foot forward. Sundays we get up, we get dressed up, and put on our best smile. We go in the doors of the church and we greet one another, sing worship songs, hear the Word preached, say goodbye, and leave the building. All the while, we have masked the hurt, the heartbreak or trials, we are going through. We feel isolated and alone, but we don't dare let anyone in for fear or shame that we don't have the perfect cookie-cutter lives that every Christian family is supposed to have. When are we going to stop buying into the lie that we have to have it all together one-hundred-percent of the time? When are we going to realize that the enemy wants to keep us bound up in pain and shame and fear? Satan's plan is to keep us alone and isolated and not building each other up in the spirit or praying for one another.

I don't need one thousand friends on Facebook who think I have it all together. I need a handful of friends, who know who I really am, and have come alongside of me in my joys and heartbreaks in this life. I need a handful of friends who will remind me of God's love and goodness, even if the day-to-day struggle doesn't seem good. I need a handful of friends who will challenge me to press in, when I really want to throw in the towel and give up the fight. But guess what?

That also means I have to invest in finding those handful of friends. They don't have the ability to break down any walls I erect to keep them out. I have to bold and brave and reveal that sometimes I am a mess. That every part of my life isn't perfect and that I am a work in progress. I am blessed that I have that handful of friends. Sometimes, I am still good at putting up the walls and staying isolated in my pride, but the moment I reach out—they have always responded with love.

We have to realize that we don't have to have a perfect life as a Christian. That we will all need the body of Christ to stand with us so that we can rise up from the pain, the storms, and the trials of this life. We need to be real with each other. Not only will it benefit each of us as we stand united in love and compassion for one another, my mess might just be the source of encouragement or testimony to help someone through the valley experiences of life.

God, thank you for the reminder that we all need one another. That perfection is not what You are after and we shouldn't be either. Forgive me for the times I allow my fear or pride get in the way of being real with people. Thank you for demonstrating a heart of compassion and that You are always working to heal and restore the brokenhearted. Help me have eyes to see people and needs. Love and compassion are needed more than ever in this world. Amen.

LAST DAYS

But mark this: There will be terrible times in the last day. People will be lovers of themselves, lovers of money, boastful, proud, abusive, disobedient to their parents, ungrateful, unholy, without love, unforgiving, slanderous, without self-control, brutal, not lovers of good, treacherous, rash, conceited, lovers of pleasure rather than lovers of God—having a form of godliness but denying its power. (2 Timothy 3:1–5 NIV)

Lord, I fall to my knees as I read this scripture and recognize that many of these things are here in this present age and time. It makes me recognize that time is growing short for the hearts of men and women to be changed and the bonds of sin to be broken in lives.

I proclaim that Your people, the Church, would awaken to the desperate situation of the time and hour that is near. That, with hearts full of love and compassion, would use their anointing and power as part of the royal priesthood of Christ, to boldly tell the world of Your goodness, Your mercy, and Your love. That the Church would no longer be a barrier to the hurting world, locked in religiosity and regulations, but would yield to the power of the Holy Spirit. That they would recognize their spiritual giftings and use them to bring hope to those needing refuge and restoration from the brokenness of this world. I declare that Your sons and daughters would rise up and prophesy life in the face of death, healing in the face of sickness, restoration in the face of what is broken, salvation to the prodigals, forgiveness in the face of shame, and hope in the face of fear.

I declare that Your people will humble themselves and intercede for the souls of this world., We, Your Church, are the remnant that is holding back the enemy and the darkness that wants to envelope this world. May we each put down our phones, put down our agendas, put down our own self-righteousness, and see the desperate needs of those around us. May we be obedient to Your voice and calling to serve with compassion. We once were all in a place of great desperate need. For all fall short of the glory of God except through the sacrifice of Your only Son, Jesus Christ. Let us remember the mercies and kindness made new in our lives every day and chose to surrender our plans to Yours that not one soul will have to be separated from You. We will be the people who glorify Your name, Your power, and Your might in opposition to things of this world. Amen.

THE ART OF DISCERNMENT

You are of God, little children, and have overcome them, because He who is in you is greater than he who is in the world. They are of the world. Therefore they speak as of the world, and the world hears them. We are of God. He who knows God hears us; he who is not of God does not hear us. By this we know the spirit of truth and the spirit of error. (1 John 4:4–6 NKJV)

This scripture is filled with so many little pieces of wisdom. First, the encouragement that when we are connected with God we will overcome, because He is greater than all things. Nothing is impossible for God. I don't know about you, but when constantly in among the world and subjected to worldly talk, I definitely need this truth to resound in my mind. I think I have mentioned before that I limit my time watching the news, because I believe that it is a great source of fear and making things of this world greater than our God.

The second great piece of information is how to discern people and if they are walking with God and the spirit of truth or if they are under the sway of the enemy and this world. John is giving us a clear picture of true Christians. They are able to hear things of God and have understanding of them. We saw in the books of Matthew, Mark, Luke, and John that the Pharisees and Sadducees knew the law of Moses, but they did not understand who Christ was and were unable to discern the truth He shared from His Father. They could only hear the world and the way they had manipulated the law to suit their own religious bigotries. They were so rigid in their own beliefs that when

Jesus performed miracles, instead of celebrating, they wanted Him put in prison. People who don't know God are threatened by what He wants to do in their lives, and have hardened their hearts to hear His truth. We see this in our every day. Have you ever heard someone say, "Well, I believe God is a God of love and, therefore, everyone can be saved." Or, perhaps someone has said, " I believe some of the things in the Bible, but not all of it applies to us today." Unfortunately, that is not true; the Scriptures are clear that there is only one way to salvation, and that is believing in Jesus Christ as the Son of God, and in His death and resurrection. We must proclaim that with our words and believe it in our hearts for our salvation (John 3:5). The Word and God cannot be separated, so it is either all true or none of it is true (John 1:1).

We have to be great discerners of the people we are interacting and spending time with, and become aware of what their mouths are declaring they have aligned their hearts with. Not to sit in judgment, but to be interceding for the Holy Spirit to provide a tender heart, open to hear the truth when the time is right. If they are speaking of the world and you try to give them God's Word, it will be like a seed planted among weeds and it will get choked out. Make sure you are discerning the leading of the Holy Spirit in your interactions. Sharing God, when they are closed to hearing, leads to disappointment and frustration for the believer. Wait on God, He will make a way in His perfect timing.

DECLARING STRENGTH

Be strong and of a good courage for to this people you shall divide as an inheritance the land which I swore to their fathers to give them. (Joshua 1:6 NKJV)

The words "be strong" are written in the King James Version of the Bible thirty-six times. It is one of those phrases that bears repeating, because the Lord realizes that we need reminding that we will have to stand strong in the face of many battles during our lifetimes.

Maybe today, like me, you woke up and felt overwhelmed that the situations you are facing having not begun to change. That the waiting has been an act of enduring, and it takes every ounce of strength to put one foot in front of the other to make it through the day. Our battles are not identical, and I cannot say that I understand your specific struggle, or know the breakthrough you are waiting on God to make happen, but you are not alone. God the Father wants you to hear this today: BE STRONG! God is not slow in working on your behalf to bring about the breakthrough you have been praying about. God is always right on time. Looking back at other battles and times when we have needed the hand of God to move on our behalf demonstrates that He is good, and He never fails us. He is faithful, generous, and kind. He is the God who promises to complete the work in your life, that it might be a beautiful testimony to bring Him glory and honor. It will be a beautiful work to display to others that need to see the evidence of hope, faith, and an enduring love. If God sent His Son to the cross to die so that you might live, is He not big enough to gain the victory in every battle you face?

Brothers and sisters, the time to be strong and of good courage is right now. Declare the wonder-working power of God. Praise His name for your salvation, for victory over the grave, and for the countless blessings He has poured over each of us daily. For every good gift from our Heavenly Father. He is like no one else. He will never leave you or forsake you. He cannot go against the very nature of who He is: righteous, holy, powerful, loving, filled with mercy and grace. He loves you with an everlasting love. It might not look like things are changing, but God's Word never fails. BE STRONG! Hold fast to His Word. Do not forget the good things He has already done. He is not finished yet!

WATCHING OUR WORDS

You are the Lord who reigns over your never-ending kingdom through all the ages of time and eternity! You are faithful to fulfill every promise you've made. You manifest yourself as kindness in all you do. (Psalm 145:13TPT)

In time spent with the Lord in prayer lately, I keep feeling the Holy Spirit reminding me to keep confessing the promises of God and hold fast to them. That I need to keep a tight guard over everything else that comes out of my mouth. I am reminded that the enemy wants us to deny the power of God in our lives, and doubt that God will be victorious in our lives over every circumstance. Our words are so powerful! Time and again Scripture tells us that the tongue is like a weapon and difficult to tame (James 3:8). In the Book of Proverbs, we are reminded that the tongue can speak life and death (Proverbs 18:21).

We need to take this very seriously. Every day, as I enter the world and am surrounded by people who do not walk with the Lord, I hear death come from their very lips. I hear confessions of fear, anxiety, sickness, of remaining in brokenness. I hear confessions of generational curses. It breaks my heart to watch people, who do not understand the power that could be living inside of them, profess their own death. We do know the truth, and we do recognize the power and anointing living in us as the temple of the Holy Spirit. This was gifted to us through the death and resurrection of Christ Jesus. This power was made available to us when we confessed Christ as Lord in our lives. We need to be steadfast and self-controlled in the words we speak as His sons and daughters. There is power in what we profess.

Thank you, Abba, for the reminder that I need to guard what I allow to be spoken. That I need to ensure that I am filling myself with the truth of Your Word. Your Word is life and it can bring life into dead places. You allowed us to be part of Your royal priesthood so that we may bring our anointing into situations that need to be filled with life and hope and Your power. Help me to boldly proclaim Your faithfulness and Your promises in all situations. Help me to keep guard over my tongue and my emotions, so that I am not ever out of alignment with Your plans and purpose. Forgive me for the times when I have fallen short and allowed myself to speak death instead of life into situations around me. I want to do all You have called me to do as Your child and disciple. Thank you for Your love and faithfulness. Your kindness is like nothing I have ever known before. You are a good, good Father! Amen.

GENERATIONAL PROMISES

But the mercy of the Lord is from everlasting to everlasting on those who fear Him, and His righteousness to children's children, to such as keep His covenant and those who remember His commandments to do them. (Psalm 103:17–18 NKJV)

But Lord, your endless love stretches from one eternity to the other, unbroken and unrelenting toward those who fear you and those who bow face down in awe before you. Your faithfulness to keep every gracious promise you've made passes from parents, to children, to grandchildren, and beyond. You are faithful to all those who follow your ways and keep your word. (Psalm 103:17–18 TPT)

I love this scripture in The Passion Bible. God's love is unbroken and unrelenting. His is a love that pursues us beyond our brokenness, beyond our sin, beyond the things that we believe no one can reach or restore. God is the God of doing the IMPOSSIBLE. He made a shepherd boy a slayer of giants and later made him a king. He gave Abraham and Sarah a child well beyond their childbearing years. He used Moses, who was by his own words: slow to speech and a murderer, to lead the Israelites to freedom. He used Esther, a Jewish woman, to ensure the safety of the Jewish people. God is in the habit of using people who don't have extraordinary power or capabilities in their own right, but grants them an anointing through the Holy Spirit to do great things for the glory of His kingdom. A kingdom that is in direct opposition to what this world values.

God sees you as a treasure. He loves you with an endless love. He wants you to see yourself through His eyes. He, who is able to do more than we could ask or think, is doing a work in you. Transforming you in the image of Christ. You are not held back by any perceived shortcomings, but a new creation in Christ. Filled with the Holy Spirit, and anointed with the power as a son and daughter of the living God, you are becoming all God has called you to be. And, when you see the amazing hand of God in your life, and keep His ways, He is faithful to keep every promise He has made to you, to your children, and their children. There are no generational curses in the family of God, for they are destroyed and His Word says they are replaced by His covenant (Jesus) and we have access to every promise He has spoken. What a powerful and amazing thing it is to be a child of our everlasting God!

YOUR NEEDS WILL BE MET

I am convinced that my God will fully satisfy every need you have, for I have seen the abundant riches of glory revealed to me through the Anointed One, Jesus Christ! (Philippians 4:19 TPT)

God is able and willing to supply exactly what you need. Let me say that again: God is able and willing to supply exactly what you need. What you need and what you have been praying or asking God for, in this season, may not be the same thing. I have been praying for certain things. I believe the things I have been praying about align with the will of God: prayers for salvation, for healing, for growth, for a family. These prayers are not in opposition to the will of God for my life or in anyone else's. I was thinking about the fact that I haven't been able to see God move in these areas that I have been praying about, but what I have seen God doing is giving me more time. Time to spend in His Word. Time to hear from the Holy Spirit. Time to get down the words on His heart that He has me putting down in this devotional and every devotional I have been writing. I have been sensing His urgency lately. He has been giving me what I need to fulfill His plan and purpose right now.

Listen, because this is hard for most of us to grasp and hold onto. Don't mistakenly think that God is inactive on your behalf. Just because He seems slow to answer in our minds, doesn't mean He isn't working things out to arrive in perfect timing. I don't have the ability to understand the complete workings and mind of our God, but from how He has operated in my life in previous seasons and trials, I know that He is good. He is faithful to His Word and His promises to His children. For me, right now, He is moving and working on granting me the time I need to complete this calling He placed on my heart. The enemy had been stealing my time through various attacks, but God in His abundant grace is granting me the time needed to press in and complete the assignment. Where I felt like I was failing, God is showing me that the victory is always found in Him. It may not be exactly what I have been looking for, but God is not absent in my life, and He is not absent in yours. He is always working and moving on our behalf, we just have to keep our eyes open to see it. When the timing is right, God will be answering our prayers. That is what good fathers do! Be open to Him, He wants your heart, He wants time with you, and He will always supply every need you have! Even when we don't understand what it is that we may be needing in this very season we are standing in.

Father, thank you for this precious gift of time. I had been struggling with the task You laid before me. My own strength was not sufficient to work it all out, but You, Lord, knew exactly how to grant what I needed. Forgive me for the way I narrow my vision and constantly question the way You work and move. I am more like the Israelites than I could ever imagine, constantly losing sight of the miracle-working God and the way You have always fought for me. There has never been a single battle that I faced alone. Forgive me for allowing the circumstances to be bigger than the mighty God and Father I know You to be! Thank you for once again granting mercy and grace over me, and giving me new opportunities to see Your goodness at every turn. I worship You, Father. Help me to have the scales completely removed from my eyes. I want to see You clearly in every circumstance. I love You, Lord. Amen.

CASTING DOWN THE PAST

Then I heard a loud voice saying in heaven, "Now salvation, and strength, and the kingdom of our God and the power of His Christ have come, for the accuser of our brethren, who accused them before our God day and night, has been cast down. (Revelation 12:10 NKJV)

Stop looking in the rearview mirror of your life and thinking you are the same person before your received the Spirit of God inside of you! You are born again, all things about you were made new and whole again! When the thoughts of your past come creeping in and you hear the voice of the accuser say, "Remember what you have done, how could a righteous God possibly love you?" I want you to claim the blood of Jesus! You say out loud, "I am redeemed by the blood shed for me on the cross. I am made new. The old parts of me, the ones that left me chained in my sins, are broken! Christ has set me free!"

Remember the example of how Jesus handled the temptations of Satan in the desert? He spoke the Word of God. We need to become practiced at the same thing. Satan wants to keep us from believing in the power of God and the power of God's Word. We have to become knowledgeable about how Satan attacks and be equipped with the Word of God to stop him in his tracks.

Jesus described Satan as the father of lies (John 8:44). We are of God, and we contain the indwelling of the Holy Spirit, our guide in all truth. We have the Word of God in the Bible to study and learn. We are not left without weapons to fight. We are who God says we are:

His beloved, chosen, redeemed, restored, healed, His sons and daughters, part of a royal priesthood, anointed, filled with power, filled with life-giving water, set free from death and sin. There are so many scriptures that show us the reckless love and wonderful promises of our Heavenly Father toward each of us. But, to become equipped, we need to start becoming acquainted with His Word.

Heavenly Father, I thank You for the reminder that You are not my accuser, but the lover of my soul. You made a plan to rescue me and redeem me from my own sins. You only desire for me to have the best life and to recognize the bounty of Your love poured out for me. I will keep looking at Your Word, remembering the power I have, because Your spirit is alive in me. I am strong, and I am Your chosen daughter. I will reveal Your glory. The enemy is defeated in my life and the lives of all who come to know Jesus Christ as their savior. I proclaim revelation knowledge to each of them, holding fast to the truth that Your power is alive inside of them, and, by the Word of God spoken in truth, they can shut the mouth of the enemy. They will remember they are new creations, created in the image of Christ. All the old, all our past sins, are swept away and forgotten because You are God and Your Word is true! Praise be to the creator of heaven and earth, who transforms those trapped in death to new life! Amen.

THE PLACE OF WANT

And not many days after, the younger son gathered all together, journeyed to a far country, and there wasted his possessions with prodigal living. But when he had spent all, there arose a severe in famine in the land, and he began to be in want. (Luke 15:13–14 NKJV)

We all know how the story of the prodigal son ends. And although that is the part of the scripture we all like the most, I don't want to focus on the end of this parable told by Jesus. I want to focus on the beginning, because I believe we need to remember that God sometimes allows us to be in want, so that we will recognize our need for Him. Let me say it this way, sometimes we have to let certain things die so that God can help us be resurrected from the inside. Many of us are waiting for salvation to come to our family members, but sometimes that means we will have to watch them face the consequences of their prodigal living, consequences for their actions. They might have to suffer through their own personal "famine" to be in a place where they can open their eyes and recognize their need for a God who is their salvation.

The problem is that many of us don't want to watch the people we love go through the very thing that could lead them to the Lord. We want to fix it ourselves, or worse, we become angry at God for the situation that is causing our loved ones hurt. First, God didn't cause the situation, but He uses all things to turn hearts towards His own. Second, many of us want an instant fix, but God is in the business of bringing about rebirth and restoration. Those processes take time.

Most of us are still growing in our own walk with the Lord, and most of us have much more growing to do. Our faith is not instant, it is borne out of daily perseverance and daily connection with the One who sees the end from the beginning.

I understand that it is hard to watch the people you love go through heartache and pain, but I encourage you to trust our Heavenly Father. He loves them with an everlasting love (Jeremiah 31:3). He is drawing them to Himself. Just as He did with each of us in our own journey to a relationship with Him. I encourage you to declare the Word of God over their lives. We have the benefit of knowing the end of the story: the prodigal son comes home and the Father celebrates his return!

Father, I thank You for pointing out that we can't always rush through to the end of the story. That each life, each soul, may have to come to a place to be in complete and desperate need for what only You can give them. That was definitely true for me; I had to recognize that nothing else could fill the emptiness inside of me except for the love You have for me. That I could have everlasting life and redemption through the saving work of Your Son, Jesus Christ. I declare that my brothers and sisters will stand strong and declare the promises of Your Word and salvation over the people in their lives who need it. I declare that they will recognize that You alone, Lord, see how that resurrection process needs to occur, so that it will be complete. You alone are faithful to complete a good work in all of us. Your Word never fails. Thank you, Abba, I love You so much. Amen.

A MERE CHILD

Here's what I want: Give me a God-listening heart so I can lead your people well, discerning the difference between good and evil. For who on their own is capable of leading your glorious people? (1 Kings 3:9 MSG)

Solomon, son of King David, becomes King of Israel. He recognizes that leading a nation is an impossible job by himself. In verses 7–8, Solomon describes himself as a "mere child," not equipped on his own to know all the requirements of leading a nation.

If we are honest with ourselves, there are many moments when we are not capable of handling situations on our own. There are moments that tear us down, break our hearts, and knock the wind out of us. We need to remember that we don't have to stand in our own strength or rely on our own wisdom. We have the help of our Heavenly Father in any situation. We just need only ask. The Lord was pleased with Solomon's recognition that he could not be a good leader without the hand of God in his life. God gave Solomon the wisdom to lead Israel and also things he did not ask for. That is the heart of a father's love for his child. To help him acquire all that he needs, but also to bless him with an abundance of what he did not expect. Ephesians 3:20 reminds us that "God is able to do exceedingly abundantly above all we ask of think."

Lord, give me the heart of a child, to be humble and recognize my need of You. It is only through the anointing and gifting that You pour into me that allows me to stand in strength in all circumstances. I want to discern well so that I may always point to the love and life that flows from Your hand. Let my words and actions be a reflection of Your love, always. I am just a child, and without You, Abba Father, I am powerless. Thank you that Your Word promises to equip us for every season. That when we recognize Your sovereignty, You will pour out Your blessing on us. Keep revealing Your truth to my heart, God. I want to know You more. Amen.

TEST THE LORD WITH YOUR RESOURCES

Bring all the tithes (the whole tenth of your income) into the storehouse, that there may be food in My house, and prove Me now by it, says the Lord of hosts, if I will not open the windows of heaven for you and pour out a blessing, that there shall not be room enough to receive it. (Malachi 3:10 AMP)

I will be honest, for many years, I was a Christian who didn't tithe. I didn't trust God to provide for me. I had this concept that I had a right to keep what I thought I earned. I worked hard for it. Then, about seven years ago, I came to a place in life where I didn't know if I was going to make ends meet. I didn't know how I could stretch my resources any further, and I heard in my spirit a challenge to tithe and test the Lord God in this promise. I began tithing that very month, and God has always been abundantly generous with me. Not only supplying all I need but, at times, giving me enough to have things that I don't necessarily need.

See, my mindset was in complete opposition to the Word of God about money. I don't own anything I have—it is all a gift from my God. He is the only one who could have created the heaven and the earth and all that is within it. He is my creator, and all that I am and gifted with that I use to make a living, belongs to Him. Any other preconceived thought that I have earned my income is not recognizing the hand of

God in my life. Not tithing was an act of faithlessness, and an act of disobedience.

I don't know where you are in your journey of faith with God, but this scripture is a reminder that we can test God in this promise. Moreover, it is an act of thankfulness for all that we have in this life. A gesture of love to a Heavenly Father who wants to demonstrate that He can multiply all that we have, so that we can be blessed and have enough to bless others.

Father God, I pray for my brothers and sisters, who might be struggling with trusting You with their finances. Lord, unveil their eyes to the powerful love You have for them. Give them boldness in this area, that they may receive the blessings You have been saving up to pour over them when they respond in obedience to Your Word. Help them discern in their spirit that they share in all You created and all You have gifted them with in this life. You are the one who possesses it all. You want us to have a heart that shares in love and compassion, as You have demonstrated that same spirit of compassion and sharing all that You have with each one of us. Help them to receive this knowledge like never before. I know that Your faithfulness will be revealed in their lives. Amen.

STEADFAST LOVE OVER SACRIFICE

For I desire steadfast love and not sacrifice, the knowledge of God rather than burnt offerings. (Hosea 6:6 ESV)

Enter his gates with thanksgiving, and his courts with praise! Give thanks to him; bless his name! (Psalm 100:4 ESV)

We have many different areas in our lives where we may express our preferences: what we eat, what we wear, or what activities we enjoy doing on our time off. I believe it grieves God in His spirit when we begin to expect church and worship to meet our desired preferences. Please understand, I am not stating that we don't have choices about the type of church we attend. We should be mindful that we gather together at church to hear the anointed Word of God. We need to be discerning that the church we attend is filled with the Spirit of God. However, we have made going to church about our own needs. Do they play the type of music I enjoy? What type of message does the pastor bring? Does the pastor talk about things I don't like to hear about? Does the worship music get played too loudly? Am I asked to serve too often?

We have become our own idols and barriers to obtaining all God has for us, when we have this mindset about church! The tabernacle was a place where the Holy and Almighty God came to dwell among the people. It was so holy a place that people could not enter all the way into the innermost chamber with the exception of the priests. Churches today may be built with human hands, and earth-made materials, but they are a representation of a place where the body of Christ can gather and worship the Lord. It is a place that we should look at as holy, where we bring our best acts of worship and adoration for the One who made us. Our hearts are supposed to be focused on Him completely, and not on the service perfectly meeting our expectations.

If you have begun to find yourself in this place of expectation, requiring the church to fulfill your needs in order to attend, it is time to examine your heart. It is time to get back to a place where when you enter church, you view it as the House of God, a holy place. It is time to bring your best offering of worship without expectation. The wonderful thing about our Heavenly Father is that He is so merciful and kind, and He wants most of all to draw you close. Church is about growing and drawing close to Him. You can choose your preferred praise music when you spend time with the Lord alone.

THE SHEPHERD OF YOUR LIFE

What do you think? If a man has a hundred sheep, and one of them has gone astray and gets lost, will he not leave the ninety-nine on the mountain and go in search of the one that is lost? And if it should be that he finds it, truly I say to you, he rejoices more over it than over the ninety-nine that did not get lost. Just so it is not the will of My Father Who is in heaven that one of these little ones should be lost and perish. (Matthew 18:12–14 AMP)

When I was a child, those teaching me about God pointed more toward characteristics about a God waiting to sit in judgment and punish me for every mistake I made. It really wasn't until I was an adult that I learned about God as a Father or a Shepherd. One who looks after the ones placed under His care. It really is transforming to recognize that the One who created all things, has such tender love toward each of us personally. To come to the deep understanding that if I was the only one who needed the saving grace and the atoning sacrifice of Christ on the cross, God would still have sent Jesus to die for me. It grips me and stuns me to my innermost being still after all this time. It brings me to a place of such gratitude.

Maybe, like me, you were taught or had a different image of God in your mind. It certainly wasn't of someone willing to rescue you. Now, I want you to stop, close your eyes, and see God as the champion you have been waiting for to change your story. To rescue you from the darkness and place His light and love inside your spirit. I want you to see the things that have risen up against you—bitterness, heartbreak, pain, addiction, fear—like an enemy of soldiers surrounding you and trying to defeat you. And now, suddenly, they flee before your Mighty God! He is both the lion and the lamb. God will fiercely pursue you and work to destroy the things that are barriers to your heart connecting to His. As the lamb, He represents his tender love for us, such a deep love that He would lay down His life for ours.

Lord, I thank You for this description of Your love toward each one of us. You love us like a father loves their own child. It is a love like no other, a sacrificial love, where You gave it all so that I may live a life full of abundance. It breaks me. It brings me to a place of surrender, and to a place where, in adoration, I want to serve You. Thank you for searching for me when I was lost and didn't understand that You wanted to rescue me. For so long, I couldn't see beyond what others had spoken about You, until You opened my eyes to Your Word in a new way. I experienced the beautiful expression of Your love through reading about who You are and all You have done for each of us. You are my champion. You alone fight for me. I love You and trust You. You are so, so good. Amen.

REVEAL THE HIDDEN THINGS

God, I invite your searching gaze into my heart. Examine me through and through; find out everything that may be hidden within me. Put me to the test and sift through all my anxious cares. See if there is any path of pain I'm walking on, and lead me back to your glorious, everlasting ways—the path that brings me back to you (Psalm 139:23–24TPT)

I confess, Father, I have so far to go in becoming more like Your Son. I don't want to become complacent in examining my daily walk with You. There are days that go well, and days my flesh gets the better of me. Forgive me for my capacity to be prideful and to cast my own judgment on others. Help me keep my eyes firmly fixed on You and my journey. I should not be looking at any path, but the one You are guiding me on. I know that I am not where I used to be, but I don't want to stop getting to know You more. This love, Your love for me and the way You take time for me, is so precious. I don't know how I would go from one day to the next without You. The only time my faith falters is when I take my eyes off You. How long will it take me to learn? I am so thankful for Your Spirit inside of me. I know that each day that I stop to listen to Your voice, I grow stronger in recognizing Your spirit and the way You are placing Your will in my life. Forgive me for lacking contentment in the growing seasons. I truly become like such a child—anxious for the next thing. You cannot be pushed, because You alone know how long my journey and growth will take. I thank You for revealing Your wisdom and knowledge to me in the seasons of growing. I offer You my whole heart, Abba, purify me. Purify me. Purify me. Amen.

TEACH YOUR CHILDREN

"Therefore you shall lay up these words of mine in your heart and in your soul, and bind them as a sign on your hand, and they shall be as frontlet between your eyes. You shall teach them to your children, speaking of them when you sit in your house, when you walk by the way, when you lie down, and when you rise up. (Deuteronomy 11:18–19 NKJV)

In this passage, Moses is reminding the Israelites of the commandments of the Lord and of the Lord's great promises. He charges the elders and the parents to teach their children the ways of the Lord. I must have read this passage several times before, but today the verse regarding our responsibilities towards teaching our children the ways of God really jumps off the page.

When you think about the amount of time we have to invest in our children's future, eighteen years is really not a lot of time in the course of an eighty-to-ninety-year life span. If we are not putting the love of God into their hearts from the very beginning, the world will fill them with its ways. There are lots of things in this world shouting to get our children's attention. Social media is designed to grab your child's attention and tell them what to think, what to buy, and what to value. Do we really want that for our children? If we are not investing in them and teaching them the vast love of God for them and how they were created and purposed for a Spirit-filled life, is it any wonder that they end up filled with hate, envy, and a sense of emptiness that they try to fill with worldly things?

If the Word of God discusses what parents need to be teaching their children at home, shouldn't we open our hearts and ears to hear it? Could we not possibly see the value in the direction and leading of our Heavenly Father? We cannot leave it in the hands of the Sunday school teacher, or our family members, or leave it up to them to learn when they are of age—we need to be speaking the Word of God into their spirits now. Think about how long it has taken some of the truths of our Lord God to permeate our hearts and minds. If we do not plant seeds in the lives of our children, the next generation grows barren, and the generation after that even more so. Soon, we have a world so dark and a people so far from recognizing our God. Unfortunately, I believe that some of this has already begun to be evident. We have people teaching our children that there are many ways to get to heaven. That we can be intimate with multiple people without consequences. Teaching our children to call life an embryo, to try to minimize the choice of destruction of an unborn child.

I see this scripture today, and I am grieved in my heart. We have to go back to teaching our children about who God is right now. We cannot wait. Moses warns the Israelites that to break the commands brings a curse. I recognize now that Moses isn't saying God will curse them, but that the disconnection from God brings its own curse—a life without the Spirit of God living inside of us, granting us power, anointing, and wholeness. It is not what I want for our children.

CHRIST-LIKE BEHAVIOR

Tell the older women to behave as those who love the Lord should. They must not gossip about others or be slaves of wine. They must teach what is proper, so the younger women will be loving wives and mothers. (Titus 2:3–4 CEV)

I remember, as a young woman, I discovered that a close friend was discussing my financial struggles with other coworkers. She was boasting about how she had gifted me with her cast-off clothing, so that I would have business attire to wear to work. It was so hurtful to discover that someone who I thought I could trust, really only cared about looking great in the eyes of others. Her assistance was not really formed out of generosity, but out of her own need to inflate herself. She had no difficulty belittling my hardships to do just that.

Gossip between women is not found in this generation alone, as Paul was instructing Titus about the need to teach on the subject over 2,000 years ago. This tendency to talk about one another does nothing to build up the body of Christ. It in fact, puts those who partake in a position where they are acting as a judge over others. The Bible is clear that only God is Holy and only He is in a position to judge (1 Peter 1:17). It also reminds us that not one of us is righteous on our own, but only through the outpouring of Christ's blood on the cross for each of us who had been trapped by sin.

The only time we should be discussing others is in an act of building each other up. In 1 Thessalonians 5:11, it is written, "Therefore encourage one another and build each other up, just as in fact you are doing." Isn't life hard enough, without men and women tearing each other down? Aren't we supposed to look different from the world as followers of Christ?

I challenge you, the next time you approach someone to talk about someone who is not present in your group, ask yourself these questions:

Why do I need to share this information? Will this draw my sister or brother closer to Christ? Will this information be encouraging them or will it tear them down? If Jesus was present in this group, would I still be talking about this?

SAME WEAPONRY—STILL DEFEATED

The snake was sneakier than any of the other wild animals that the Lord God had made. One day it came to the woman and asked, "Did God tell you not to eat fruit from any tree in the garden?" (Genesis 3:1 CEV)

Now Jesus, full of the Holy Spirit, left the Jordan and was led by the Spirit into the wild. For forty wilderness days and nights he was tested by the Devil. (Luke 4:1–2 MSG)

The other day, my husband's father was in an accident and needed to be hospitalized for treatment. The particular hospital that he went to was still restricting access to family members. The procedure that he underwent, like many, wasn't without risk. I found myself thinking about these past two years and how the enemy has skillfully used his same tactics to drive fear into the hearts of man.

These two Scriptures reveal Satan's first tactic: separation and isolation. He is a coward, so he will make sure he attacks when you are alone and tries to keep you feeling isolated. His second tactic is to get you to question what God has said. If the Devil is successful in these two strategies, then he can begin to cause fear where faith once lived. Then that fear drives us to disobedience and to acting as if we do not have a God who has promised to fight for us. We believe man over the power and miraculous work of our Heavenly Father. We trust in man-made weapons and science, instead of the life-giving, eternal Word of the Lord.

I am talking about the enemy and his weapons of warfare so that we may be aware and be able to stand against his attacks. Jesus tells us we will be attacked or "have trouble," but that He is already victorious. He has overcome the plans of the enemy to keep us eternally separated from the Lord. Nothing can take you from the mighty hand of God once you are His child. Not only is the enemy's plans to destroy you defeated, but our Mighty God promises to restore and multiply that which was stolen from us. What a good and faithful Father we have in Him.

Don't allow the enemy to make you feel isolated and alone. You have the power to call on Christ, the One who is the Savior of every soul. And you can reach out to others that can stand in agreement with you in whatever battle you are facing. Reach out to those who can help you in finding the truth and promises of God in your life. He will never leave you or forsake you. The only way the enemy can win is if we take our eyes off the One who is Faithful and True.

LOVING IN TIMES OF OPPOSITION

"You're familiar with the old written law, 'Love your friend,' and its unwritten companion, 'Hate your enemy.' I'm challenging that. I'm telling you to love your enemies. Let them bring out the best in you, not the worst. When someone gives you a hard time, respond with the energies of prayer, for then you are working out of your true selves, your God-created selves." (Matthew 5:43–45 MSG)

This morning, after reading this verse as part of my devotional time, I realize that God is speaking to me about missed opportunities just this week. It has been a conflict-filled week. Dealing with people in the world can be trying at the very least. It's not in my direct response to these people in the moment that God is speaking about, but about my responses afterwards. I vented about the experience and then, when I was done venting, I vented some more. I stewed over the situation, playing the exchange and words spoken again and again in my head. I decided that the whole experience would be a great reason to give up on trying to show the love of Christ to the people of the world. I had a completely selfish, immature response.

What didn't I do? I didn't talk to God about it. I allowed the situation and the experience full control over my emotions, and I allowed my flesh to rule over me. I did not have peace, and I did not have a restful night of sleep. I woke up this morning dreading the fact that I was going to have to deal with these same people again today. Then

I read this scripture. It is definitely an "Ouch!" moment. Praying for these people is the last thing I feel like doing. But I am not supposed to walk by my feelings. I am supposed to walk by the Word of God. So, after missing the mark so completely yesterday, I heard the voice of the Lord clearly and prayed for those who are trying to bring out the worst in me. I can't say it doesn't feel plastic at first, but God will continue to help me turn it over to Him. In response to my obedience, God gives that peace that surpasses all understanding. That peace and the hope that follows that I can go out into the world and maybe, just maybe, shine for Jesus.

GUARDED IN ALL SEASONS

I have told you these things, so that in Me you may have [perfect] peace and confidence. In the world you have tribulation and trials and distress and frustration, but be of good cheer [take courage, be confident, certain, undaunted]! For I have overcome the world. [I have deprived it of power to harm it and have conquered it for you.] (John 16:33 AMP)

Maybe like me, when trials come at you, you tend to react before remembering to be still. You try to operate in your own strength before stopping in the moment and praying. It is something that I have been actively trying to do better in my personal journey with Jesus. This scripture came to mind during a time of prayer recently. I felt the Lord say to me, "I didn't tell you that you would overcome trials, but that I have already overcome them." Our constant striving to fix the problems in our lives, instead of releasing them to our Heavenly Father, can result in delaying His working it all out.

I love this version of John 16:33 because at the end it points out that God has conquered the world and all the attacks the enemy could ever plot and plan against us are defeated. The realization that I get to celebrate the victory my God has provided makes me want to jump and shout with joy. I want to hold onto this knowledge in the day-to-day and in the life-changing storms that happen as long as we live on this side of eternity.

Ultimately, I believe that God will not allow me to be a hindrance to His purpose and will. However, I realize that I often am allowing my own will and actions to steal the peace that comes when recognizing that with God nothing is impossible. It is just another reason I am thankful for the mercy and grace of our good, good Father. He allows me another opportunity to grow my faith and obedience in His Word and in His awesome power.

Lord, how I love Your Word. This is just the most amazing journey I have been on and, although I may not get everything right, You keep helping me get up and take the next step. Thank you for pointing to Your Word for the wisdom I need when battles come. I love the Holy Spirit pointing out the beautiful intricacies of Your Word and placing them in my heart. I declare that this Word would penetrate deep in my heart and deep in the hearts of all who see these words. That we would recognize that You have already overcome the world and any trial that comes against us. That we would remember that we can celebrate the victory that You have already secured for each of us. I declare that I will surrender all the battles to You and not operate in my own abilities. I will listen for Your voice and move at Your direction. Amen.

TRUE LOVE

Love never gives up. Love cares more for others than for self. Love doesn't want what it doesn't have. Love doesn't strut, doesn't have a swelled head, doesn't force itself on others, isn't always "me first," doesn't fly off the handle, doesn't keep score of the sins of others, doesn't revel when others grovel, takes pleasure in the flowering of the truth, puts up with anything, trusts God always, always looks for the best, never looks back, but keeps going to the end. Love never dies. (1 Corinthians 13:4–8 MSG)

Growing up, I struggled to see God as the ultimate source of love. For many of my formative years I equated Him with the God of the Old Testament stories, full of wrath and ready to punish those who stepped out of line. Even though I was taught that Christ died on a cross for me, there was disconnect with the teachings about his love and grace. It wasn't really talked about that it was a free gift and so, for many years, I focused on trying to earn His love. The lack of understanding about the truest love I have ever known led to misunderstanding on how to give and receive love in my all of my relationships. Because I didn't understand the most complete source of love, I failed at so many relationships. They were filled with things like distrust, envy, and selfishness and I certainly kept a record of all their wrongs. In short, I really didn't know how to love at all.

I would like to tell you that one day I just woke up and figured it all out and everything moved perfectly from there. But the truth is, it took some time for me to recognize God's unrelenting love for me. I tried to make human love the most important source to fill my heart time and again, and always came up short. Other people in this world cannot fill the space that God designed for Himself inside of your spirit. It is only in connecting with Him first that we truly begin to understand what love looks like. His love was so profound that He allowed Christ to die for us while we were sinners (Romans 5:7–8). We weren't even interested in His heart or His love, and many of us rejected the very thought of Him as Lord and Savior, but He still went to the cross for us. Verse 7 points out worldly love as: "Very rarely will anyone die for a righteous man, though for a good man someone might possibly dare to die." Without God, human love falls short of the mark! We would all still be knocking each other down and grabbing at anything to get our next fix or thrill, or something that made us feel good for the briefest of moments. But God's love is a never-ending well that will never run dry. We simply reach out to Him and He is ready to spend time with us, and speak words into us like: beloved, worthy, anointed one, my child, precious, priceless, restored, redeemed, and wholly loved.

Look first to the most fulfilling source of love you could ever receive. You need it first before any other relationship. You need to understand what His love for you looks and feels like. Having His love inside of you will help you love others so much better.

OUR HEARTS' DESIRES

God can do anything, you know—far more than you could ever imagine or guess or request in your wildest dreams! He does it not by pushing us around but by working within us, his Spirit deeply and gently within us. (Ephesians 3:20–21 MSG)

When I was a young girl, I wanted to be so many different things as I grew up: one of Charlie's Angels, a singer, a veterinarian, a zoologist, a journalist, or an author. These ideas of who I would become changed over time. They changed as I grew and changed and learned more about who I was and the desires that I had in my heart. I believe we all have a portion of a dreamer and a portion of a pragmatist living inside of us. We have hopes and dreams and a sense of creativity, but oftentimes the need to make a more reasonable choice pushes our innermost desires to the background. I am referring to a healthy desire to use our talents and creativity for good and a purpose.

Now, imagine twenty years after having a profession in healthcare, the Lord begins to take me back to my dream of becoming a writer. It is not exactly as I would have expected it, but God is not a man, and often does things in unexpected ways. I will say, I am having a wonderful time writing for the Lord. It is such a blessing to watch Him use me and grow me that I might be able to use the giftings and desires He placed inside of me.

Maybe you are struggling with waiting for a chance to see the desires of your heart come forth. God is never slow in His timing. I would never have had the ability to write about the Word all those years ago because I hadn't been spending any time with the Word or God. Other things were more important. He had to wait for His spirit to be leading me to the right time and place in order to see this part of my heart's desires fulfilled. Don't quit. He hasn't given up on making your dreams come true. He is just working in you to bring you to a place of readiness.

Father God, You are so wonderful! Thank you for this Word about how You make us ready to receive the good things You want for us in life. You are more concerned about our hearts and spirits. You see that sometimes we are not ready yet for the plans You have in store for us. But You do not place desires in us that You cannot see fulfilled. For You alone are a wonder-working God. I give You all honor and praise. I see Your goodness and Your hand in every moment of the journey. It is so very beautiful. Thank you, Father. I love You. Amen.

A CALLOUSED HEART

'Keep on hearing, but do not understand; keep on seeing, but do not perceive.' "Make the heart of this people dull, and their ears heavy, and shut their eyes; Lest they see with their eyes, and hear with their ears, and understand with their heart, and return and be healed." (Isaiah 6:9–10 NKJV)

Over the course of this winter, the cold air, the low humidity, and the constant washing of my hands (soap and water and/or hand sanitizers) have left my hands very dry. As I look at my hands, some areas are tender and raw but, in other areas, the skin has thickened. It is my skin's attempt at protecting itself from the lack of moisture that it usually has, trying to protect areas prone to crack and split apart. This is a scripture from the Old Testament, and God is instructing Isaiah to tell the people that their sin will result in separation from the Lord. That because of their continual disobedience, God is closing to them the door to healing and deliverance for a season.

The calloused skin does not occur overnight and neither does a calloused heart. The condition of your heart is in your hands. You can choose to make it a priority to go after the things of God, and His Word, or you can go through the motions. Eventually, over time, if you are not putting God's best into your heart, your heart will be filled with the things of the world. Your senses become dull and your flesh becomes the thing you will be attempting to satisfy. Your heart and spirit will take a back seat. Matthew 6:24 states that we cannot have both the world and the spirit. The flesh and our spirit are in constant battle against each other. That is what the Bible means when it talks about us needing to conquer our flesh.

We have all seen what man does to one another in the flesh: jealousies, hatred, stealing, and killing each other. When we don't have the love of God growing in our heart and spirit, then the opportunities for hatred and fear become the things that fill us. The urgency to press in, to look for the goodness of God and the wisdom and guidance He has for us in His Word, resounds inside of me. I may be able to combat calloused hands with some store-bought lotion, but only the powerful Word of God can keep my heart soft and full of love and compassion.

ETERNAL IMPORTANCE

Don't love the world's ways. Don't love the world's goods. Love of the world squeezes out love for the Father. Practically everything that goes on the world—wanting your own way, wanting everything for yourself, wanting to appear important—has nothing to do with the Father. It just isolates you from him. The world and all its wanting, wanting, wanting is on the way out—but whoever does what God wants is set for eternity. (1 John 2:15–17 MSG)

I must confess, I love a pretty dress! Any of the other ladies out there with me? There is nothing quite like that one dress that you slip into with the perfect shoes—and all of a sudden, you feel a little like Cinderella at the ball. Am I right? However, I have to be careful with the desire I have for that feeling. It really isn't something that is going to fulfill me. And like anything else in this world, the moment is fleeting. Plus, I might have a really unhappy husband when I take over both sides of the closet with all my clothes. Not to mention how that need could affect our financial resources. Oh, don't get me wrong, I can shop at a thrift store like nobody's business, but it is still pursuing something that will not sustain me long-term.

Let's face it, we are in a consuming society. Everything we want is at our fingertips. Just a click of a button and it is on its way. Our cell phones have become our shopping centers. Somehow the things we discuss that we may have need for suddenly pop up in advertisements on whatever email or social media sites we frequent. And what was just an idea in our head is now even more tantalizing, because every advertisement seems to agree with how much we "need" it. Before we know it, we have closets that are packed full and garages with no spaces for our vehicles. But we just can't seem to stop purchasing the next new thing. Sometimes it's easy to forget that all this life will pass by like a vapor. Sure, we need clothes and food and things, but they are temporary. They are just a means to assist us in the day-to-day. The important things are the moments with God. Feeling His presence and seeing His hand in our lives: healing, restoring, breaking down strongholds, growing us in wisdom. Growing in Him so that we can see those living in the darkness of this world, with all of its broken promises, brought into an eternal life with all the hope and promise that God has to offer.

Forgive me, Father, when I take my eyes off You and trust in the things of the world. When I struggle in my own flesh and forget about the power of Your spirit dwelling in me. You are the giver of all good things. And Your utmost desire is to see all that I need provided for me. Help me to chase after You first, because I have faith in the Father that wants to give His children a hope and a blessed future. You are not against prospering Your sons and daughters, but You desire them to love You more than what they are in need of. I see You. I love You. I desire more of You. Amen.

NOTHING HIDDEN

For we have the living Word of God, which is full of energy, and pierces more sharply than a two-edged sword. It will even penetrate to the very core of our being where soul and spirit, bone and marrow meet! It interprets and reveals true thoughts and secret motives of our hearts. There is not one person who hide their thoughts from God, for nothing that we do remains a secret, and nothing created is concealed, but everything is exposed and defenseless before his eyes, to whom we must render and account. (Hebrews 4:12–13 TPT)

This is such a powerful pair of verses in the Book of Hebrews! First, thinking of the Word of God as active in our lives. Recognizing its power to change things. The power to save, to heal, to restore, to redeem, to provide! The description of God's Word as a "two-edged sword" is powerful because it reinforces that Gods Word is absolute. Nothing can stop the Word and God who are one from doing what He purposed it to do!

I also love how it says that nothing about us remains secret. It means that I can be my complete self with my Heavenly Father because He already knows everything about me. Every thought I have, whether I speak it out loud or keep it to myself. And let's be honest, most of us have only a handful of people who see us in clear detail. Usually, it is our spouse or family or a childhood friend. How wonderful that the God who created me knows everything about me. I don't have to feel like I need to hide anything from Him! It just allows for this openness in my relationship and communication with Him. He loves me and knows me, and understands my joys, sorrows, successes, and failures. It offers such freedom from fear of being imperfect, that I am so completely loved and known. I don't have to wait to have it all together to come before Him. I can come to Him anyway I am, and He will forgive my mistakes, and work on healing me from the inside out!

Father, I just thank You for this beautiful reminder that I am fully known by You! I don't have to pretend to be perfect or to have all the answers. You offer me love freely in my imperfections and in all the highs and lows of life. If I spend time with You and Your Word, it will become alive in me and infuse me with the power that You said was mine as Your child. I declare boldly that Your power and anointing is in me and will be manifested in the opportunities You set before me. I don't have to worry about protecting myself from You for Your love is like none other I have ever experienced. It is fierce and wide and it is always working to see all that I was created to be revealed, so that others may see the goodness of Your hand! Lord, thank you for this freedom that I find in You. Sometimes, it is still so difficult to understand such a wonderful love—a love given so freely. This relationship with You is what I desire most. Keep revealing my heart, so that nothing has to remain secret. For there is such freedom found in being known by You. I love You and am so thankful that You first loved me! Amen.

POWERFUL WORDS

And He said to me, "It is done! I am the Alpha and the Omega, the Beginning and the End. I will give of the fountain of water of life freely to him who thirsts." (Revelation 21:6 NKJV)

God said to Moses, "I Am Who I Am." And he said, "Say this to the people of Israel: 'I AM has sent me to you.'" (Genesis 3:14 ESV)

I believe that our God and Father has always emphasized the importance of words. It is an integral part of who He is. There is no mistake that in the beginning God spoke and created the heavens and the earth. It was by the power of His Word that everything was given life and existence. Time and again, we are told how we become part of God through receiving salvation through Jesus Christ. That we become united or one with both Jesus and the Father. Jesus also reveals to the disciples that through His Spirit we will have the same power and authority. That we will be able to use our words to make changes in the lives of others. Jesus gave us so many examples, in His time on earth, of how words could set people free, heal, restore, and even resurrect the dead. The disciples were able to do all that Jesus called them to do, because they were filled with the power of the Holy Spirit and understood the power of the spoken Word.

We need to get back to the place where we recognize the power and life in God's words. We have the benefit of having the Word of God placed before our very eyes. Of the understanding of all that transpired during Jesus' death and resurrection. We have the promises of

God for us to see and read, but we lack the spiritual discernment to operate in the power and authority that He has given us. We have allowed the Word of God to be weakened by man's understanding and interpretations. Instead of asking for the Holy Spirit to keep our eyes pure to see the Word of God revealed to us in all truth, we have set ourselves up as judges to determine which words in the Bible are true and which are not. If God and His Word are one, then every word written and inspired by the Spirit of God is true—even if we don't like what it has to say.

MAN OF SORROW

He was despised and rejected and forsaken by men, a Man of sorrows and pains, and acquainted with grief and sickness; and like One from Whom men hide their faces He was despised, and we did not appreciate His work or have any esteem for Him. (Isaiah 53:3 AMP)

This passage in Isaiah has been on replay in my mind lately, particularly the phrase used to describe Christ as the "Man of sorrows and pains." I have spoken before how the enemy's plan is for us to feel isolated, rejected, and unloved. We look around at people going about their everyday lives while we may be in a season of trials and think, "No one can possibly understand what I am going through."

There is One who understands every pain, every sorrow, and every tear you will ever shed. God placed all of the world's sin, sickness, and grief on His shoulders. If that wasn't enough on its own, God also placed the rejection of all mankind, He felt the loneliness of those who are separated from God. Jesus was the ultimate sacrificial lamb, spotless, and without sin or blemish, but still He was despised and made to carry all our sin and anguish to the cross. Jesus has firsthand experience with whatever personal heartache and pain you are going through. It is His sacrifice of love and His intercession for us that allow us to receive the love of our Heavenly Father and the hope of all the promises that His Word brings into our lives.

There is a reason we are encouraged to cry out to Jesus in our time of despair. Because He who was beaten, broken, pierced, and rejected—

He chose to take all the things that came with going to the cross—He chose to die so that you could live.

His compassion for you is never-failing. His love for you is undeniable. His salvation is unshakeable. His restoration over your life is incomprehensible. His plan for you is to prosper you and give you a hope and a future. Even in the trials of this world, He never leaves you. He knows sorrow and He knows your pain. He is waiting for you to call out to Him. His arms are open wide. He will give your spirit a place to rest, to find peace, to be renewed again.

THE SEEN CREATED BY THE UNSEEN

By faith we see the world called into existence by God's word, what we see created by what we don't see. (Hebrews 11:3 MSG)

By faith we understand that the worlds [during the successive ages] were framed (fashioned, put in order, and equipped for their intended purpose) by the word of God, so that what we see was not made out of things which are visible. (Hebrews 11:3 AMPC)

Through the ages, man's curiosity about the way things were designed and work have led to all sorts of discoveries. Through research, we know that the life cycle of a butterfly begins with a pupa that turns into a caterpillar which cocoons itself to become a butterfly. Science was borne out of a desire for revelation knowledge about how all that was created, all that we see, works. It still surprises me that so many people look at the intricacies of all of creation, and still suggest that we are a cosmic probability. That by chance it all worked out and here is all of creation just happening, just being.

They are trying to make something so wonderfully complex and so well-conceived fit into human wisdom and conceptions. That is the opposite of faith. Even with all our research and current understanding about the world, there are still so many mysteries and so much that we will not understand this side of heaven. Faith is understanding that not everything will be revealed to us, but believing that the God who formed it all is more than capable of handling everything that comes our way. Scriptures say that it is the very creation that we see with our eyes, that prophesies the existence of our great and awesome God. It states that no one will have an excuse to suggest that they could not know Him (Romans 1:20).

As we transition from winter to spring this year, I am reminded again about the vast creativity and amazing power of our God. That after a time of rest the earth gives birth to new life. But we cannot have springtime without winter. They do not exist separately from one another. They have a relationship where both are required for the earth to act as it was intended and purposed by God. Without faith, we cannot fulfill our intended purpose. In our own wisdom and power, we will not be fully equipped to become all that God has called us to be. It is through acknowledging Him and seeing His hand in us and the same ability to work through us, in His anointing, that enables us to be all that He has called us and purposed us to be. We were fashioned by His hand, and when we recognize His handiwork in our lives, we become enabled to testify His name, His power, and His glory!

REMEMBER THE MIRACLES

Only take heed, and guard your life diligently, lest you forget the things which your eyes have seen and lest the depart from your [mind and] heart all the days of your life. Teach them to your children and your children's children— (Deuteronomy 4:9 AMP)

There are several places in Scripture where we are reminded to guard our hearts and minds and to focus on the things that God has done. Just like the Israelites, we often can lose focus on how big God really is when we enter one battle after the next. The enemy often uses the tactic of attacking God's people in multiple areas of their lives. He is always trying to steal our focus away from who God is and what He is capable of doing.

The same God who ransomed you, who rescued and redeemed you, is fighting for you! The same God who put His very breath into your lungs, and spoke His plan and purpose into your life before you were born, is working in you today. Don't let the battles overshadow all the victories God has already purposed in your life!

In a brief conversation with an acquaintance last week, miracles became part of the topic. In such sweet and timely wisdom, this person stated, "We have tiny little miracles occurring all the time, we just have our eyes focused on looking for the large miracles and oftentimes miss the little ones." I know that has been true for myself. Looking for the big miracle, I wonder how often I have missed those precious little miracle moments God has placed before me? I am grateful for the way the Holy Spirit reminds me of the importance of recalling who God is and of how important keeping my perspective in the proper place helps me see the miracle-working God in the little details.

Father God, I thank You for Your wonder-working power. In You, I have received so many precious gifts and miracles. They are more than I could possibly grasp or count. Forgive me when I lose perspective during the battles. I declare that I will have eyes that see You in the midst of any storm, and I will have recall through the Holy Spirit of Your power and might. Fear and anxiety will have no place in me because I see the One before me who holds every victory in His hand. Lord, I declare that my brothers and sisters in Christ see You clearly as well. That they remember that You are the God who parts seas, that resurrects the dead, that heals and restores, and that You are the One who already made a way to free all those who are held captive. Give us boldness to declare Your power in our lives to all who have ears to hear. From generation to generation, that You may always be glorified. I love You, Father; and, thank you for Your countless blessings in my life. Your goodness is beyond words. Amen.

NEVER TOO LATE

And there was a woman who had had a flow of blood for twelve years. And who had endured much suffering under [the hands of] many physicians and had spent all that she had, and was no better but instead grew worse. She had heard the reports concerning Jesus, and she came up behind Him in the throng and touched His garment. For she kept saying, "If I only touch His garments, I shall be restored to health." And immediately her flow of blood was dried up at the source, and [suddenly] she felt in her body that she was healed of her [distressing] ailment. (Mark 5:25–29 AMP)

This is a well-known scripture in the New Testament and, in fact, is retold in the chapters of Matthew and Luke as well. There are so many wonderful things to point out and discuss in this scripture. If you have never read it, or it has been awhile, I encourage you to go back and read it again. Today, for the sake of time, I want to point out two details: first, the woman had suffered with her infirmity for a very long time and had exhausted all her options and money. She had nothing left. No one had been able to help her and she, in fact, was worse than before. Second, when she pursued Jesus and placed her hope and faith in Him, she was made well. I particularly want to point out that Jesus didn't make her beg or ask for forgiveness first, and He certainly was aware that she had drawn her healing from Him. He simply told her that her faith had made her well (verse 34).

Simply, I believe that is the message of God's heart for anyone who is suffering with any affliction today. He doesn't care if you spent your last penny on treatments elsewhere, and if you are worse off than when you began looking for help—He just wants you to come to Him for all you need. He loves you, and is waiting for you to draw close to Him. He is still the God of miracles. He is still the God that can resurrect the dead. He is still the God that draws us out of despair and puts peace and restoration in our lives. For each one of us, that journey to healing will look and be different, but the God who created you is willing and able to do all things for your good.

Thank you, Lord, for the hope Your Word brings to the hearts of so many sons and daughters. It is a bold thought that, by the power of Your Holy Spirit and indwelling of Your Spirit inside each one of us, we can have access to all Your promises including healing. I declare that You will pour out Your wisdom over each person specifically and give them clear understanding of what that healing walk looks like for them. That they will recognize that ultimately, no matter if it comes from the hands of a physician, You, God, will equip everyone who touches and interacts with them in their walk towards wholeness. Thank you that even when we struggle and at times may be suffering due to our natural bodies, You never leave us or forsake us. You are pouring out strength and mercies afresh every day. Help us to be strong in the periods of waiting. Help us to keep our eyes on You. I love You, Father. Even when I don't feel good, it doesn't change that You are always good. Amen.

THE TABLE IS SET

You become my delicious feast even when my enemies dare to fight. You anoint me with the fragrance of your Holy Spirit; you give all I can drink of you until my heart overflows. So why would I fear the future? For your goodness and love pursue me all the days of my life. Then afterward, when my life is through, I'll return to your glorious presence to be forever with you! (Psalm 23:5–6 TPT)

This scripture makes me want to leap for joy with loud shouts of praise and dancing! Only our mighty God would think of preparing a banquet table full of all we would ever need in the midst of any battle. He gives us all of Himself through the outpouring of the Holy Spirit. That means we have access to His power, His strength, His love, His grace, His mercy, His protection, His provision. He already knows He has secured the victory, so He wants to start the celebration early!

I am reminded of the image of Jesus at the Passover meal with the disciples. He knew what would take place in the days to come, but He recognized the importance of coming together with those He loved and fellowshipping together. The relationships and faith that had been built during His ministry was about to undergo a tremendous battle. I imagine that the disciples would recall the dinner shared during Jesus' trial, sentencing, and execution. They would remember His words that His body would be broken for them and that the spilling of His blood would be the beginning of a new covenant, a sacrifice for not just them but all mankind (Mark 14:22–24). This meal, this sharing of who Jesus was meant to be for all mankind, would give them strength in the beginning of their own battles and their own steps into carrying on the ministry of Jesus Christ.

It reminds me that today, no matter what battle I am facing, I have the opportunity to enjoy a banquet with my God. I can rest in the knowledge of His Word. I have the victory won over everything that would try to separate me from the love of Christ. It has been conquered through His sacrifice. I have everything I have ever needed to have victory in every area of my life, and I did nothing to earn it. It was given as a beautiful gift, out of a Father's love. I will shout, I will praise, and I will dance! For my God is good and He deserves all the glory!

NEVER GIVE UP

Here's what I've learned through it all: Don't give up; don't be impatient; be entwined as one with the Lord. Be brave and courageous, and never lose hope. Yes, keep on waiting—for he will never disappoint you! (Psalm 27:14 TPT)

Have you ever been on a hike and seen two tree trunks that have literally wrapped around each other as they have grown? It really is quite beautiful and amazing that two separate trees could be entwined and grow together and thrive. Entwine simply means "to wrap around another, to embrace." But this scripture takes the concept of entwining even deeper and suggests that we become "as one" with our Heavenly Father.

This isn't as impossible as we Christians sometimes think. We have the spirit of the living God already inside of us. We were given this gift when we accepted Christ as our Savior. In John 17:22, Jesus prays that all believers would be made perfect in one, in unity with both Jesus and the Father.

As we connect with God through His Word, in worship and prayer, we begin to change. The parts of us that were like the world diminish and our spirits that are connected with the Lord grow stronger. We begin to demonstrate the characteristics of Jesus and the Father. Their characteristics are identical because they are one (John 17:21). When we have Christ in us, we become infused with His strength, His love, and His compassion. We become bold and courageous because we want others to have what we have. We recognize the faithfulness of God and His ability to take everything that transpires in this life and work it for good.

Lord, I love how Your Word gives such a beautiful picture of how You want to be one with me. That You never want us to be separated. I want You to have Your way in my life. I want to do something that gives You glory and honor. Let there be less of me and more of You. You have so much love for Your children. And, when we see how we are entwined, we can recognize that we have every reason to hold onto hope. I declare that my brothers and sisters in Christ would see that You are always faithful and never will disappoint them. I love You, Lord! Keep changing me to be the masterpiece You intended. Amen.

ACCESS TO THE HOLY ONE

Yes, down to this [very] day whenever Moses is read, a veil lies upon their minds and hearts. But whenever a person turns [in repentance] to the Lord, the veil is stripped off and taken away. (2 Corinthians 3:15–16 AMP)

The veil of the tabernacle was to separate the Ark of the Covenant and the mercy seat from the rest of the tabernacle. It was to be set apart because the Lord would appear in a cloud in this part of the tabernacle. It was a holy place, and only the High Priest could enter this area once a year. He would enter this area to offer blood sacrifices and burnt offerings for the sins of all the Israelites (Leviticus 16).

In the New Testament, in the Gospels of Matthew, Mark, Luke, and John, we are told that when Jesus died on the cross, the veil in the temple was torn in two from top to bottom. This demonstrates how there is no longer a separation between individual people and our Heavenly Father. Every person, when they repent of their sins and confess their belief in Jesus Christ as their personal savior, gains direct access to the Lord. We do not have to go through religious rituals and perform sacrifices to the Lord. Jesus Himself was the ultimate sacrifice.

The veil has been torn. We, as the sons and daughters of the Living God, have access to Him. That access, through the blood covering us from Jesus' death, gives us the promise of the inheritance that Jesus has as the Son of God. We are now part of the royal priesthood and are equipped with every promise of God. As we spend time with Him, in worship and prayer, the veil that covers our eyes and minds about the Lord is stripped away. We become built up in our faith and wisdom. Our minds become open to the things that God has for us.

Father God, once again I am so grateful that we each have direct access to You through the sacrifice of Jesus. We were created to have a relationship with You and, until that happens, many are left with an emptiness that cannot be filled with anything else. Thank you for coming and residing inside my heart and providing me with Your spirit. I thank You that I have access to all You have for me. Every promise, all the anointing that Jesus had in His ministry, is for every son and daughter. Lord, I want to make a difference in this world for You. That everyone would know the beautiful love that You have for each one of us. Help others to see how accessible You are to them. I cannot wait to see all the lives You will change for the glory of Your name! Amen.

BLESSING UPON BLESSING

Blessing after blessing comes to those who love and trust the Lord. They will not fall away, for they refuse to listen to the lies of the proud. O Lord, our God, no one can compare with you. Such wonderful words and miracles are all found within you! And you think of us all the time with your countless expressions of love—far exceeding our expectations! (Psalm 40:4–5 TPT)

The Bible is filled with images of real people with real-life difficulties. They had many of the same hopes, dreams, and challenges that we do today. King David was no different. He was overlooked by his own family, hunted by his father-in-law, and he made his own mistakes along the way. He desired another man's wife, took her, and then had her husband killed while he was in battle in David's army. King David understood his need to stay close to the Lord. He recognized the destructive things that can happen when we fall away. These verses are a reminder of the goodness that comes from staying close to the Lord at all times.

This world seems to go from crisis to crisis, but those who keep their eyes on the One who created them and who loves them with an everlasting love will be able to stand in every season. They will see the goodness flowing from the hand of God over their lives. They will see how God will exceed all that they could ask or think!

Lord, I thank You for Your Word. It helps guide me and teach me every day about who You are! Still, I cannot begin to understand Your great love for us. You love like no one else. Thank you for displaying in Your Word that You recognize our imperfections in this human body, but You want our hearts to change and mirror Your image. Thank you for the day You took out my heart of stone and gave me a tender heart. Thank you for Your forgiveness and tender mercies toward me. Search me, and continue to change anything that is not pleasing in Your eyes. I want to love like You, Lord. You show compassion like no one else. I praise You and give You thanks. In Jesus' name.

SATISFIED SOULS

The righteous eats to the satisfying of his soul, but the stomach of the wicked shall be in want. (Proverbs 13:25 NKJV)

This scripture really provides great imagery of the battle between our flesh and our spirit. Our flesh is never satisfied. It is filled with pride, envy, selfishness, arrogance, and self-righteousness. Our spirit, when aligned with the Word and will of God, contains faith, love, kindness, perseverance, humbleness, and a servant's heart. Both the flesh and spirit talk about being fed, but only one leaves a person in even greater need. There is something very basic, but so vital, for every human to find fulfillment in their lives. To recognize their purpose and to search for peace and joy. Only God can satisfy those needs. God, our creator, designed us to be complete when we are connected to His spirit dwelling within us. We cannot be fulfilled with anything this world has to offer. It will not provide any long-term satisfaction. Our flesh is temporary, just like the things that fill our flesh: food, water, and all the material items we seem to need in one moment, but discard the next. Our eternal spirits need the eternal presence of our God.

I enjoy a delicious meal just as much as the next person, but I recognize that once my body processes what it needs and uses that energy—it will demand more. I also recognize that what we put into our bodies affects our overall health and well-being. When we put junk into our body, we tend to feel drained and less energetic. When we try to keep our diets balanced, our bodies respond better and our energy and strength can increase. We should also be hungry for the Word of

God, to digest it and use it to transform into all He has created us to be. When we stay in close proximity to God, we are satisfied with all that He has provided. We recognize the profound goodness He has poured over us and honor Him with our love and service.

Father God, I thank You for speaking to me in language that makes sense. Just like I need to watch what goes into my physical body for a healthy life, I need to watch what I am putting into my spirit. Only Your Word and Your presence can fully satisfy my soul and what I need to make my spirit whole. I declare that I will always have a desire to learn and grow in Your Word and in my relationship with You. That I may be all that You called me to be as Your daughter and as Your disciple. That hunger will grow my spirit and keep me equipped to boldly proclaim Your greatness and the wonderful God and Father You are. Amen.

REMAINING MYSTERIES

The secret things belong to the Lord, our God, but the things revealed belong to us and to our sons forever, that we may observe the words of this law. (Deuteronomy 29:29 NIV)

Being in the healthcare industry for the past twenty years, I have had the opportunity to see miraculous recoveries from all sorts of medical diagnoses. However, I have also seen those who have not been as fortunate to recover from various diseases. In my area of profession, attempting to use all the knowledge I have been given to aid in any recovery or restoration of function means improvement in quality of life for those I treat. It is often heartbreaking for a patient and family when recovery is limited.

It is difficult for me to accept that I cannot always help everyone in a way that will bring the recovery they desire. There are times, in providing treatment to these patients, that I have been give opportunities to talk of God's infinite power and to pray for their healing. In others, their hearts do not appear to be open to talking about the Lord. I recognize that it God's desire that all would know Him and have access to His promises, including healing, but that not everyone will choose to know God. Therefore, the promises are shut down to them because they do not recognize or have knowledge of all He is able to do.

Above all, I have grown to recognize that I am not meant to have complete understanding of all things. That God will continue to have some mysteries that I cannot understand during my life in this world.

They are for revealing during my entering the kingdom of heaven. I have to focus on all that I do know about God. He is loving and good. His heart's desire is for us to know Him, but He will not force us to choose Him. He is always on time, and always faithful to His Word.

Abba Father, I recognize that there are things that You reveal and things You keep hidden because I cannot begin to understand them at this time. I see how medical technologies can save lives, but sometimes result in impacting quality of life. In the end, we are not the miracle worker—only You are. The Creator, the one who can make the dead rise and restore health and wholeness to Your children. You enable men and women to be part of the process but, ultimately, it comes from You. Grant me peace when all my attempts to help someone appear to fail. Allow the Holy Spirit to guide me in sharing You to the hearts that are open that they might be encouraged by Your great love for them. Keep my heart tender and full of compassion for those that come across my path for that is why You have placed me here—to be a light and represent the love of Christ. Thank you for the opportunities to make a difference in someone's quality of life, but also in their spirit, their faith, and in the hope they may need in the day-to-day. Amen.

CALLED TO USE OUR GIFTS

We have different gifts, according to the grace given to each of us. If your gift is prophesying, the prophesy in accordance with your faith; if it is serving serve; if it is teaching, then teach; if it is to encourage, then give encouragement; if it is giving, then give generously; if it is to lead do it diligently; if it is to show mercy, do it cheerfully. (Romans 12:6–8 NIV)

I am horrible at giving gifts. I tend to think too practically and pragmatically to ever come up with something that will "wow" my husband on his birthday or at Christmas. I think I have only really "wowed" him once with a gift, when I took him out to go zip-lining for his birthday a few years ago. However, most often, my husband realizes that if he doesn't give me a good idea for a gift, he is most likely going to end up with something very practical that he needs.

We are all created with innate skills or gifts from our Heavenly Father. He designed each specifically for a divine purpose. A way that our life will bring glory to Him. I cannot remember where I heard it, but I know that someone once suggested that your gifting often corresponds to something you feel passionately about. My husband has a heart for serving. He has an adept way of looking at problems and figuring out ways to fix them, and he loves to use those skills to help others. I believe that my gift is one of encouragement. I want to build others up to point them to the promises of God and remind them of where their hope and future lie. If you are a son or daughter, then you are gifted to be part of the church body and to fulfill a need in that body. Although I serve at church, I don't have specialized skills and it is not my natural gifting. I have to work hard at finding a way to serve in the body. Even if it is just helping in the nursery. My natural gifting to encourage others comes more readily to me.

Don't think that you have to be great at every role that needs to be filled at church. It's not how the church is supposed to operate. The people are supposed to come together like pieces of a puzzle; fitting together to make the body of Christ effective. I encourage you to get involved, and if you aren't sure what your gifting is yet, ask God to open a door for you at church that leads to you edifying the body and using that specialized gifting He has given you. God grants wisdom to those who ask for it.

Father, I thank You that we are all each wonderfully and fearfully made and called to fulfill a specific purpose in Your kingdom. Lord, help me to operate fully in my gifting that I may bring glory to You. I declare that my brothers and sisters in Christ will have knowledge and wisdom in relation to the gifts You have given to them in their spirit, and that with boldness they would operate in those gifting for the body of Your Church and to win the souls of the lost. Thank you for the wonderful way You made us to each work together. None of us is meant to do it all on our own. We need one another to reach out into all the world. May we with fear and awe always use our gifts for Your glory alone and not ours. Amen.

SPIRITUAL KNOWING

And they said to one another, "Were not our hearts greatly moved and burning within us while He was talking with us on the road and as He opened and explained to us [the sense of] the Scriptures?" (Luke 24:32 AMP)

This scripture in Luke is after the crucifixion and burial of Jesus and when the ladies have been to the tomb to find that Jesus' body is no longer there. The followers of Jesus have watched as Jesus suffered, died, and was buried. Even though his body has been found missing from the tomb, they do not really have complete understanding of what it signifies. Jesus begins revealing Himself to the disciples at various times in attempt to help them understand His resurrection from an eternal perspective and not an earthly one. Remember that the disciples really thought that Jesus had come to deliver the Israelites from the oppression of Roman rule.

This scripture reminds me of how Jesus promised that He would not leave us without guidance but would provide the Holy Spirit to lead us in truth (John 16:13). When faced with doubts or uncertainty in time of hardship or struggle we have to rely on our spirits and its direct connect with the Holy Spirit. We all have the ability to recognize His leading. Ever have something or someone come to mind, and it just grips your heart and won't let go, until you complete the task set before you? Maybe it is a phone call, or to send a card or email, but you just can't seem to feel at peace until you have done that one thing? That is the communication of the Holy Spirit. Or maybe you experienced the opposite, you had made a decision about something: a new job, purchasing a new home, or some other life-changing event. It made no sense, but you had this overwhelming peace the whole time; revealing that God through the Holy Spirit was guiding you and helping you know you were doing the right thing.

It is so important in the noisiness of this world to be able to be quiet and hear the Holy Spirit within us. We always have a choice to either listen or to suppress that leading within us. Doubt or fear are usually the two largest barriers to us opening up to the leading of the Holy Spirit. I know I have personally missed many opportunities to follow after Him because of those two things. I am so thankful that God is the God of second chances!

Lord, let my heart leap and burn within me at the presence of Your spirit. That I may be useful to You. That I would not miss what truth and purpose You have for me because of fear and doubt. Your Word promises that I will recognize Your voice and I proclaim that I will have ears to hear You and Your Word clearly. You will provide wisdom and knowledge and discernment in all the directions You take me on in our journey together. I thank You for the wonderful gift of Your Word, through the Scriptures, that I may learn of who You are and grow in my connection with You. Thank you for being the God of multiple chances. I want to be obedient in Your calling and leading. Keep my eyes open for the presence and direction of Your Holy Spirit. Amen.

A PRIESTHOOD

But you are a chosen race, a royal priesthood, a dedicated nation, [God's] own purchased, special people, that you may set forth the wonderful deeds and display the virtues and perfections of Him who Called you out of darkness into His marvelous light. (1 Peter 2:9 AMP)

At our small group this past week, we spent some time in prayer together. During this time, I had an image of the sons and daughter of God. In this image, I saw row upon row of men and women in priestly robes. I heard in my spirit that we as children of God cast off our filthy rags, or sackcloth, and receive priestly robes of righteousness. (Isaiah 61:10, 64:6)

I feel the Spirit of the Lord is calling His Church to put on their priestly garments. To become the nation of people He has called us to be. This world is showing more and more darkness, but we are the light. We are the ones who are supposed to take the power and the anointing of God the Father and reveal it to those who need to see it. We need to be the ones who will go and answer the call of the Lord. We have become too complacent and, instead of recognizing we have all been given a part in the Great Commission, we put the job off on our pastors, their wives, and the spiritual leaders in our churches. Each one of us is a member of the body, and we each are called as His own.

Lord God, I declare over Your sons and daughters reading this now that they will see themselves clothed in the robes of righteousness

You have placed upon them. They no longer have rags or sackcloth because they are washed in the blood of Jesus Christ and are new! I declare that they will feel the Spirit burning within them and will, with boldness, declare the powerful Word of the Gospels to those they meet. I thank You, Lord, that You have equipped us each to be part of Your family, Your priesthood. We have all that we need to become disciples and to reveal Your glory. Amen.

RELATIONSHIP, NOT RELIGION

Therefore the law was our tutor to bring us to Christ, that we might be justified by faith. But after faith has come, we are no longer under a tutor. (Galatians 3:24–25 NKJV)

Have you ever had someone start a conversation with you using the words: "You are religious, what do you think about—?" These are people who don't understand that being born again means that we are not holding fast to religion but to our faith and relationship with God. I try to remember that, at one time, I, myself, had limited understanding and believed that following God meant following a bunch of rules. A list of dos and don'ts.

As believers, we can often see the difference in someone who doesn't quite recognize that the covenant through Christ supersedes the covenant with the children of Israel in the Old Testament. We cannot earn our Heavenly Father's love, we can never be good enough in our own selves. That is why Christ came to earth, to become the spotless lamb to be slain once and for all. He was the ultimate sacrifice as required by the law of the old covenant. Once Christ was crucified, died, and resurrected, the barriers of sin were broken. We can go to the Father because we have received the atonement of Christ.

In Galatians, the apostle Paul was writing to the church at Galatia to remind many of them of this very same thing. It hadn't been very long since Jesus had come to walk among them, and then died and rose again; however, people found it difficult to navigate this new road of faith. Some people believed that this freedom from religious rules would result in people becoming lawless. Paul wanted to demonstrate that freedom from extreme rules and religion and focusing on relationship would result in people being changed from the inside. This change would be demonstrated in lifestyles that would please our God and Father. Later in this letter, he even discusses "the fruits" of living in righteousness through faith (Galatians 5:22).

Father God, I thank You for making a way that we could focus on growing our relationship with You and letting go of religiosity. That we have an opportunity to walk in faith, and grow our righteousness, to display the fruits of the Spirit. It is having a right spirit and a heart full of compassion that truly demonstrates the power of a wonder-working God in our lives. We could never have done any of it through trying to be obedient to laws. It is by knowing how great the cost of our freedom, through Christ, that makes me want to live a life that pleases You. I am so thankful that You have been so faithful and full of mercy and kindness. There is nothing so precious as knowing that You want to have a relationship, a friendship, with me. Thank you for removing my heart of stone and replacing it with the one that is filled with Your love. Keep working and molding me into all You have purposed me to be in Your kingdom. I love You. Amen.

A CROWN OF GLORY

At that time, God of the Angel Armies will be the beautiful crown on the head of what's left of his people: Energy and insights of justice to those who guide and decide, strength and prowess to those who guard and protect. (Isaiah 28: 5–6 MSG)

Seeing this scripture today reminds me that we have such a faithful God. He promises to provide us with all we need in the midst of every challenge, every trial, and every heartbreaking circumstance. I believe that we need this reminder more than ever. We might not be the Israelites under attack from an Assyrian army, as in the time this scripture was written, but we still live in a world that seeks to please itself and seems to constantly manifest and grow fear and hatred. We still live in world where there is injustice and the weak are taken advantage of.

Not only does our God command an army of angels, but He is the one who will give knowledge and wisdom. He promises to renew our strength and abilities to fight and stand in the middle of life's daily battles. Whatever is on your heart today, whatever you are going through, bring it to the God of the Angel Armies. He is not slow in His moving on behalf of those who cry out to Him. He will do exactly what He said He will do. Every battle belongs to the Lord and He will always have the victory. When He turns your trial into a testimony, He will be glorified.

Lord God, I pray for those in this world, in every corner of the earth, who are in the midst of a battle. Lord God, You are the one who raises up a standard against the attacks of the enemy. Jesus came and defeated sin and death once and for all. I declare that You will move and provide according to Your Word. That You will place resources and people in place that will work to provide assistance and healing and point hearts toward the God who sees, the God who provides, and the God who never fails. Lord, I thank You for the anointing in Your church that we can bind the plans of the enemy and his plans and purposes will always fail. Lord, I also proclaim that the Holy Spirit is softening hearts and opening eyes to see You. Without You, we will remain lost, but in You we have hope, we have salvation, and we have eternal life. I give You all the glory. In Christ, Amen.

CHRIST-LIKE COMPASSION

He always comes alongside us to comfort us in every suffering so that we can come alongside those who are in any painful trial. We can bring them this same comfort that God has poured out upon us. (2 Corinthians 1:4TPT)

Two years ago, after only being in our home for six months, we had our house damaged in a fire. The damage was so great that we were out of our home for a year during the restoration process. This scripture reminds me of all the ways God sent His love upon us. He used so many people from our church. We had people house and feed us for the first week as we worked with the insurance company and figured out a temporary housing situation. We had meals brought to us and donations of items that we would need. We had church family just hug us and pray with us and remind us that everything was going to be all right. Then, there was God. Speaking to our hearts and reminding us that all that is taken from us will be restored. That He is always working things out for our good. He was so very faithful. A little over a year later, we were back in our home. Everything was brand-new and we couldn't have felt more blessed.

Six months later, a friend was displaced from their home. My husband and I were now in a position to provide comfort and assistance to someone else. We had received such love and compassion from others it was the least we could do for someone else. We didn't do anything grand, but we showed up and offered what support we could. We answered questions about the restoration process when there is damage to a home. It doesn't always make every moment of a painful situation go away, especially when it comes to damage or destruction of a home or other such tragedies. However, to be able to ease someone's hurt for a moment, or to help be a source of comfort, is a blessing. I believe that compassion doesn't always come naturally to people, it is something learned. When we receive the compassion of God, then we learn how to display it to others. Looking back, I see God using this situation to equip me to be what He called all of us to be.

God, I definitely don't think like You, but You have such wonderful ways of demonstrating Your goodness. Part of that goodness is teaching us how to be more like You. How to demonstrate the love of Christ to one another. In this world, there are so many times that the tender love of Christ is needed. It ultimately comes from You, but what an honor to be able to used to support our friends, family, and brothers and sisters in Christ when we are needed. Compassion and loving-kindness are something that have to be grown and nurtured in our spirits. Thank you for teaching me these priceless gifts. I have been so passionately loved by You, and I want to do a better job of loving others. In Jesus' name. Amen.

ALL IN

He who loves father or mother more than Me is not worthy of Me. And he who loves son or daughter more than Me is not worthy of Me. And he who does not take up his cross and follow after Me is not worthy of Me. He who finds his life will lose it, and he who loses his life for My sake will find it. (Matthew 10:37–39 NKJV)

We all have choices to make. We can choose to live our lives according to the way that we believe pleases man or we can live our lives to please the One who gave it all for each one of us. Sometimes that means making a decision for Christ that goes against your upbringing or heritage. Let me assure you that you will never regret your decision to follow Christ. Everyday won't be easy. You will no longer conform to the old you. The person who you used to be will now be brand-new. The image your family and friends had of you will have to change as they see the manifested change in you. Maybe they won't understand it and maybe they won't like it. You may have to hear things like, "You think you are so much better than us now" or "You are one of those crazy holy rollers." Remember that it doesn't matter what they say about you. Think about what God says about you: beloved, wanted, chosen, set apart, restored, redeemed, renewed, reborn, and free.

So, be ready to be all in. God knows that sometimes that means leaving past relationships behind. He will always replace what is lost. The alternative is losing out on being with God forever. Enjoying the perfect peace, joy, and rest that await us. Enjoying the freedom to worship and praise and dance and sing before the Lord. It is a homecoming I cannot wait to be a part of and I don't want to give it up. Not for one single person on this earth. My relationship with God is my choice. You have a choice to make, too.

GIFT OF THE SPIRIT

Don't grieve God. Don't break his heart. His Holy Spirit, moving and breathing in you, is the most intimate part of your life, making you fit for himself. Don't take such a gift for granted. (Ephesians 4:30 MSG)

We all have the ability to hear from God once we have surrendered our hearts and lives to Him. Sometimes we get a word of knowledge through reading the Bible. There are times when the feeling of peace or unrest guides us in our daily decisions. Still, other times, we will hear a voice inside of our spirit. That is the Holy Spirit. The Lord God living inside of us and communicating with us. The Holy Spirit is one with God and is God. It is difficult for us in our human minds to fully grasp the complexity of the Triune God. Jesus told the disciples to wait in Jerusalem until they Holy Spirit came to fill them (Acts 1:4).

Our Heavenly Father wants each of us to be connected to Him through the Holy Spirit. I believe that helps us to be equipped with all God has promised for us in His Word. Without it, our spirits are dry and weakened and we find it difficult to stand in times of battle. I remember a time when I didn't understand this part of God. I didn't understand that if I am both flesh and spirit, then my spirit needs to connect to God through his Holy Spirit. My flesh cannot connect with God. Not really. Galatians 5:17 states that the flesh and the spirit are in opposition to one another. We need to build up our spirit and keep it filled with the things of God. This assists us to walk with God and not walk in the world. It assists us with maintaining righteousness and not returning to sinful lives. The Holy Spirit is a wonderful gift that helps us tap into the supernatural things of God. Things our earthly bodies and mind cannot grasp. But, when connected with God through the spirit, our spirits leap within us.

Holy Spirit, come. We want You to move and fill us. Keep the fires of our spirits burning bright and hot for the righteousness of God. You are the one that gives us supernatural wisdom and sight. To see what our earthly eyes cannot see and to hear beyond what our earthly ears can hear. I am so thankful for the gift of the Your Spirit, God. Thank you for the promise to fill me up to overflowing. I will have living water flowing through me. Holy Spirit, I am listening. Fill me with the truth and guide me according to the will of the Father. I surrender my spirit to You, God. I am Yours. Amen.

EXTRAVAGANT LOVE

"She has been forgiven of all her many sins. This is why she has shown me such extravagant love. But those who assume they have very little to be forgiven will love me very little." (Luke 7:47 TPT)

This is part of the Scriptures in Luke where a woman, believed to have been a prostitute, comes into the home of a Pharisee and washes Jesus' feet with her tears, dries them with her hair, and then anoints his feet with an expensive perfume. A man named Simon, who is hosting the dinner, is of course appalled that Jesus is letting such a sinful person touch him.

It reminds me of how little understanding we have of our own sinful nature. We believe we have the right to sit in judgment of others and to condemn them for their mistakes, but all sin brings only death (Romans 6:23). Not a single one of us enters into this world without being covered and marked by sin. It is only in recognizing that without the mercy and forgiveness of Christ and His sacrifice on the cross that we are made worthy to be called a child of God (1 John 1:7).

If we, then, are all equal in our flesh and sinful nature, and only found righteous through the outpouring of Christ's blood on the cross, should we not be so humbled ourselves? Should we not be so devoted to love and serve others? The Bible tells us to love God and to love and serve one another.

Are you looking at people in your life who have caused you hurt or pain, and holding onto bitterness and unforgiveness? If you are, then you are placing yourself in the judgment seat of the Lord. You cannot sit there because you, in your own power, are not clean enough. We are called to forgive others, as we have been forgiven ourselves. Read the Scriptures again about Christ's journey to Calvary. He suffered. He was broken. He was ridiculed. He was pierced. He took on all our sin and shame so we could have freedom. He took on all our sin and infirmities so that we could be in the presence of God. Don't forget all that has been done for you when you didn't deserve it. Don't throw away the gift of extravagant love to walk in bitterness. Forgive and love, because you have been forgiven and you have been loved at great cost.

Father God, examine my heart. Show me where I am holding onto bitterness or lack of forgiveness against another. I surrender every bit of it into Your hands. I forgive because You have shown me such tender love and mercy. I will always fall short in my own strength, but You, oh God, help me to look more like Your Son Jesus every day. I will keep my eyes on You, and not what anyone else is doing. I will keep my heart and mind on the tender mercies showered upon me. I will rejoice in my freedom and follow Your example of love and compassion. Your love is so extravagant. Thank you, Father, You are good! Amen.

ABIDE AND FIND REST

So He Himself often withdrew into the wilderness and prayed. (Luke 5:16 NKJV)

"Are you weary, carrying a heavy burden? Then come to me. I will refresh your life, for I am your oasis. Simply join your life with mine. Learn my ways and you'll discover that I'm gentle, humble, easy to please. You will find refreshment and rest in me." (Matthew 11:28–29 TPT)

Honestly, we can all get to the point where we just feel worn out. Usually, it's not just one thing, but a multitude of things that have been pulling us in many directions. Maintaining work, family, and health is definitely challenging at times. These past two weeks I have been feeling exhausted. I have doggedly been just pushing myself to keep going. One foot in front of the other, just keep marching and plastering the very fake "I'm alright" smile on my face. Anyone else done this same thing?

Getting ready for work one morning this week, I had a change in my schedule and I heard the voice of the Lord in my spirit, calling me to use that time for a deeper moment with Him. It reminded me of all the powerful works Jesus had done. It had to be physically taxing to be in crowds and crowds of people all coming to Him to have their needs met. To have sight restored, to have arms and legs healed, to have their sins removed, or to have demons cast out. I cannot begin to imagine that Jesus in His physical body didn't feel tired. Jesus refreshed and refilled His spirit and His body by spending time with the Lord. He didn't rush it. He understood that to be used by God would mean He would need to be refilled by God and God's Holy Spirit. That extra twenty minutes in prayer helped me refill my spirit. I need to become earnestly aware that I cannot complete the works I am called to do, if I am not staying connected and filled by the One who has called me to the task. I cannot have knowledge or anointing, or the equipping required to walk in His purpose, if I don't stay connected to Him. It isn't wrong for me to have a desire to do the work, but I can't take my eyes off the One who has purposed it in my spirit. I have to make sure that I am abiding in Him first and ensuring that I am relying on Him to work out His purpose through me and not in my own strength. Trying to operate in my own strength, I will find myself quickly exhausted and spent. I will quickly become unable to be useful, until I turn to Him again and find rest. My heart was in the right place. I believe in serving God and working to fulfill His purpose in my life, but I need to stay full of Him. Maybe you need this reminder, too. If you are feeling weary, used up, or dry in the day-to-day—withdraw—find your secret and quiet place to spend time with God. The beautiful thing is that He is waiting there for you.

Thank you, Lord, for always showing up when I need You. For the promise of filling me until I overflow. I am called to Your purpose, but most of all I am called to You. To talk with You and spend time drawing close. I want that, I want You, Lord, above all else. Amen.

LOVING GOD IN EVERY MOMENT

A time to weep and a time to laugh, a time to mourn and a time to dance (Ecclesiastes 3:4 AMPC)

"In this godless world you will continue to experience difficulties. But take heart! I've conquered the world." (John 16:33 MSG partial)

Life sometimes can seem a lot like a roller-coaster ride. You get strapped into a car for the ride and off you go on the track up a steep incline. The ascent is slow, you get to the top hesitating only for a second, when suddenly you are practically free-falling through a rapid descent. These moments on the ride can sometimes truly be mirror images of our walk through this life. God doesn't want us to be unprepared. He gives us Scriptures to remind us that life is full of highs and lows and, during our time here, we will experience both. I love that He doesn't just end it there though, but reminds us that nothing we face will overcome us completely, because He has already overcome the things of this world. We have an eternal victory.

Life lately has been a bit like a roller-coaster ride for me. In the beginning of a conversation with a friend, who was checking in on me, I said, "I am looking for the beauty and the good. Sometimes I cry in the bittersweet moments. But I am loving God through it all." I would like to think my Heavenly Father smiled at that heartfelt honesty in the moment. God is all right with our tears and moments of heartache.

He is prepared to hold us when we are sad or feel lost. He is not surprised at our great need for Him; He purposed and designed us that way. So, why do we resist it? Why do we feel like in our weaknesses we are less in His eyes? We have a way of transforming God into our image of Him and making Him less than He truly is. We place our trust in tangible things. We become self-reliant. We become our own barriers to the One who has all the answers, the wisdom, and is the best source of help and hope. God doesn't need us to have it all figured out. He just needs us to be willing to come to Him. To see Him and to hunger to know Him. To love Him because of the great love He has showered on us before we recognized our need of Him.

Don't wait until you have it all together. Call on God now. In the moment where you are at. No matter what it looks like. God knows that there are things in this life that will bring us to our knees. He didn't cause it to happen; He wants to help you stand back up in the midst of the weight of the world heavy on your shoulders. He has overcome the world. He will take your brokenness and replace it with a peace and begin to heal you. Don't listen to the lies of the enemy that God doesn't want you. Our God is the restorer, the redeemer. He brings dead things to life!

WEAPONS OF WARFARE

In every battle, take faith as your wrap-around shield, for it is able to extinguish the blazing arrows coming at you from the Evil One! Embrace the power of salvation's full deliverance, like a helmet to protect your thoughts from lies. And take the mighty razor-sharp Spirit-sword of the spoken Word of God. (Ephesians 6:16–18 TPT)

Our God and Father is so very good. He wants His sons and daughters to be always prepared for anything and everything that comes our way. Not only does His Word remind us that, as followers of Jesus, we will be in direct opposition to the world and, therefore, in a spiritual battle. He tells us how to best be protected and armed for the battles we have to face. Even if we have been in many spiritual battles before, and used the weaponry provided to us by God, there may always be that one battle that knocks us down for a short time. We all need a reminder at times on what to do when it seems like the enemy is getting the upper hand in our lives.

We have the Word of God which is sharper than any two-edged sword. We need to stand and speak against the mountains and giants in our lives. Sickness, be gone! Broken relationships, be healed! Physical healing, manifest yourself in our bodies! Provisions, come! Opportunities, come! Favor of the Lord, pour out! No weapon fashioned against me or my family will prosper because I am protected. I am hemmed in before and behind. My God goes before me and, every weapon the enemy will attempt to use against me, my God will raise up a standard against it. No evil will befall me. God is my fortress and

I am never in a more secure place than when I am in His presence. Thank you, Father! I trust You. Your Word says that I am victorious through Christ Jesus. I have all that I need when I have the promises of God for they never fail.

If you are in a battle right now, I want to remind you to use the Word of God. It doesn't have to be elaborate. It doesn't have to be long. It can be direct. It just needs to be spoken out loud. You need to hear yourself speak the Word of God out loud. So, whenever you have a moment—getting ready for work, in the shower, on your commute—start declaring victory over that situation and battle you are facing today. Be reminded that God is working for you.

Thank you, Lord, for the way You help us remember that we are equipped with Your Word which is so very powerful. I pray that my brothers and sisters would learn to use the armor You have provided. That they would become proficient in using the powerful Word You gave us during the spiritual battles that come. I believe in You, God. I trust in You and Your Word. You have never failed me. Let Your Word be the first thing that comes to me in every circumstance. That I am always fully prepared, and in full confidence stand in every battle, because I know that the ultimate victory is Yours. I thank You for providing me with all I need. Amen.

KEEP A THANKFUL HEART

Make a careful exploration of who you are and the work you have been given, and then sink yourself into that. Don't be impressed with yourself. Don't compare yourself with others. Each of you must take responsibility for doing the creative best you can with your own life. (Galatians 6:4–5 MSG)

Imagine working for months to earn enough money to surprise your child with a special gift that you know that they have been dreaming about for some time. Imagine your excitement as you make the plans for the perfect time to give them the gift, and as you watch them unwrap that gift. Then imagine how it would feel if, once they had the gift in their hands, they said, "Oh, I was hoping to have the same one my friends all have. I guess I can use this until something better comes along." Wouldn't that really hurt?

As I read this scripture this morning, I began to think about how many times I must have grieved the heart of God when He poured out His blessing in my life but, because it didn't look like what I expected—or, it wasn't exactly the same as someone else's blessing—I didn't appreciate it. The Holy Spirit is at work in my thoughts, pointing out areas I need to clean up in my life. Making sure that I am not looking around at what the Lord is doing in others' lives, and desiring what God has not purposed for me and missing out on all that He has given me. If God created us each for a unique purpose and plan, then it makes sense that the way He pours out His blessings in our lives would look different. But the world tells us we should all want the same things. That we are somehow less if we don't conform to what everyone else has or desires. How many times have we each fallen into that trap? I know I have in many times. There is a reason the Word of God tells us to fix our eyes on Him. He understands that the eyes long for things it looks at and that can be dangerous to each and every one of us. The enemy is always lying to us, telling us God isn't giving us His very best. Today, as I read this scripture, I repent for all the times I have lost sight of the countless blessings of God because my eyes were not on Him.

Father God, please forgive me for the times I have not been grateful for the way You pour out Your blessings in my life. Forgive me for comparing my life and my gifting with others and thinking I need more or just something different. I recognize that You have the very best in mind for me and that it is specific for the life You created for me. No one else can serve my purpose. Holy Spirit, keep my eyes open to see the wonder-workings of God in my life and the countless ways He is ministering and blessing me. I am so thankful for Your guidance and use of the Word to show me where I need to change. I am so thankful for Your tender love and mercy. I am thankful for the way You made me. I trust You to complete a good work in me. Amen.

REMOVE THE SCALES FROM OUR EYES

Where there is no vision [no redemptive revelation of God], the people perish; but he who keeps the law [of God, which includes the law of man]—blessed (happy, fortunate, and enviable) is he. (Proverbs 29:18 AMPC)

If people can't see what God is doing, they stumble all over themselves; but when they attend to what he reveals, they are most blessed. (Proverbs 29:18 MSG)

Over and over again, in the Word of God we are instructed to seek the wisdom and knowledge of the Lord. We are told that no one is like Him and, therefore, it is difficult to discern His ways. However, that doesn't mean that God wants to keep Himself hidden from us. In fact, the Bible, the written Word of God, shows us that He wants us to know who He is. In James 1:5, we are told that we can ask for knowledge and it will be given to us. Solomon asked the Lord for knowledge to lead the people of Israel and God was so pleased with his request that He not only gave Solomon knowledge, but blessed him in abundance.

The Amplified version of this verse talks about the redemptive revelation of God. I believe that means that we need an understanding of what Christ's death and resurrection really means to each believer. Not only did He conquer death so that each believer may have eternal life, but His death brought forth the Holy Spirit. The Holy Spirit is something available to each born-again believer. When we receive the Holy Spirit, then the power and presence of the mighty God, our Creator, lives and dwells within us. We have direct access to Him and every promise that He has made to His children. That means that when He says we will do greater works than Christ during His ministry on earth (John 14:12), it is not just fancy words. We are no different from the disciples. We can heal, restore, cast out, and tell the whole world about the redeeming pouring of Jesus Christ.

Each one of us has a choice. We can make excuses and keep our eyes closed to what the Word of God reveals to us, about who we are in Him, or we can throw off the excuses, the fear, and the things that we have let bind us—to fully become the Church of the Living God.

Lord, I declare that You will clear our eyes, that we may see Your power clearly, and that power that You endued into every son and daughter. I feel the pressing of time, as the world turns darker and the enemy intensifies his plans to keep souls from knowing You. I call forth the workers for the harvest. That the Church will recognize that they must be the laborers in this time and season. That each son and daughter would have vision of who they are as Your beloved children and would fully embrace with boldness the gifts You have granted to each of them. That lost souls would be saved and lives would be restored. Through the power of the blood of Jesus Christ and in His mighty name! Amen.

THE CHANGE IN US

Turning his head, Peter noticed the disciple Jesus loved following right behind. When Peter noticed him, he asked Jesus, "Master, what's going to happen to him?" Jesus said, "If I want him to live until I come again, what's that to you? You—follow me." (John 21:20–22 MSG)

The term external locus is a term that means "a belief that what happen in life is the result of forces outside a person's control." They often feel as if they have little control over the events in their life. Sometimes they believe that what happens to them is often the result of others, and do not see their own choices as a factor.

In this scripture, we see Peter looking and wondering about the events of another disciple's life. Jesus quickly instructs Peter that his own purpose has nothing to do with anyone else's. That, as a follower of Jesus, his eyes and heart need to remain steadfast on following Him no matter what anyone else is doing.

I believe that is something all of us need to be reminded of at times. That our walk, our faith, our salvation—are ours alone. No one but God the Father travels the entire journey with us. It is a lot like a hiking trail. Just as there are several interconnecting points that lead in and go out along a central path, people will journey alongside us for portions of our walk, but maybe not remain until the end. We cannot divert our destination to follow them; it means we are no longer following Jesus. Our first obligation is to ensure that we are serving the will of God.

We often look at situations and believe that God needs to change others to make things better, but God often changes us first. I really struggled with writing this devotional because I recognize that, sometimes, bad things happen to good people. People have been hurt by others and there is nothing I can do to change those situations. But God ultimately can. God wants you to give the hurt, the pain, the feelings of bitterness, the unforgiveness, the brokenness to Him. Your choice is to live in the bondage of all of these things that hold you back—or give them to the One who can set you free. You don't have to worry about that other person, God sees, knows, all things. His Word says that one day everyone will stand before Him, and He will call every word and deed into account. He wants you to fix your eyes on Him. He wants you to follow Him. He wants to change you, set you free, and place your feet on a path that leads to hope, joy, and peace. He wants to restore you now. If you are in a place of hurting, I know this can be hard. Letting go is hard for us. Letting God change us first is scary and difficult at times. But having gone through some refining in my own life, and learning to let go of the bitterness and unforgiveness over past situations, has been the best choice I could ever have made. It set my heart free. To have joy, to have peace, to have a love with God that is like no other kind of love.

You can have that too today. Just start asking God to change you. He is faithful.

TO A THOUSAND GENERATIONS

Know, recognize and understand therefore that the Lord your god, He is God, the faithful God, Who keeps covenant and steadfast love and mercy with those who love Him and keep His commandments to a thousand generations, (Deuteronomy 7:9 AMPC)

But if the Spirit of Him who raised Jesus from the dead dwells in you, He who raised Christ from the dead will also give life to your mortal bodies through His Spirit who dwells in you. (Romans 8:11 NKJV)

A covenant is an agreement or promise between two or more parties or people. In this scripture, the reference is reminding the people of Israel of the covenant the Lord God made with Abraham and Moses. There are actually two covenants that the Lord made with man: The old covenant with the people of Israel and, then, a new covenant through the death and resurrection of Jesus Christ. The new covenant allows us to live in freedom of living under the law of Moses, because Jesus was the once and for all sacrifice for our sins. It was through His death and resurrection that we were given eternal life. The gift doesn't stop there because Jesus' death also granted us access to the Holy Spirit, which is the Lord God Himself dwelling within us.

We are so quick to believe in the science of genetic predisposition. That if a relative had this or that illness, then, we will likely get it too. That is in direct opposition to the Word of God. The Lord God came to bless those who love Him. To bless and not to curse them. He is the one who sent His Son to take on our infirmities, sickness, and diseases, that we may be healed. How can we see the image of Jesus healing those who were sick and in desperate need for healing and not believe that is the image of our Heavenly Father as well. We need to look again at the Word of God with fresh eyes and see the act of the crucifixion as a release from the bondage of sickness and death. We need to start prophesying and praising God for our wholeness and well-being. Jesus told us that we would have the same power that He himself demonstrated during His ministry on earth.

Jesus, I thank You for Your sacrifice on the cross, that not only grants eternal life, but gave me the opportunity to be filled with Your Spirit. I command anything that comes against my family in the form of sickness and disease to be gone in the name of Jesus. We have Your promise of wholeness. To be free from sickness and disease, to operate in the authority granted in Your name to heal, to restore, and to call back to life. Not in my power, but in Yours. In the name that every other thing in the heavens and the earth must yield to. I am so thankful that Your Word confirms Your promises and reminds us of how faithful and true our You always are. You are the God who keeps His Word to a thousand generations. You are good, and You are always working for the good of those who love You. I thank You and praise You. You are mighty, and holy, and worthy of all praise. Amen.

TO CONQUER THE THINGS OF THE WORLD

Every God-begotten person conquers the world's ways. The conquering power that brings the world to its knees is our faith. The person who wins out over the world's ways is simply the one who believes Jesus is the Son of God. (1 John 5:4–5 MSG)

Oftentimes, people speak of faith like it's linear, always moving in a straight line, always constant. However, faith isn't a constant, but has to be grown or built up. It is built up through growing our knowledge about who God is and by spending time with Him in His Word and in prayer. It is by watching and recognizing His hand and how He changes things in our lives along our daily walk with Him.

Think of a vast field of wheat. Before it was ripe and ready for harvest, it was empty. Seeds were placed in the soil. It was cultivated. Someone made sure it had water and protected it from weeds and insects—things that could interrupt or destroy its growth. We don't just wake up in full maturity of our faith after giving our hearts to Christ. We have to nurture our relationship. We have to guard it against attack. We have to establish truths and knowledge that we will be able to use as resources as we work to grow our faith. To keep it established. Jesus uses the very analogy about seeds and the Word of God and its importance in people's lives (Matthew 13:3–9). He describes several ways that the seed (Word) can be sown, but not grow. Our faith requires action to keep it growing, to keep it building, to maintain its strength. We can look back at events in our lives and identify the instances where we operated in faith. Other times, we allowed the Word of God to be plucked up out of our minds and hearts and our faith faltered. We became unable to stand during particular battles in our lives. But God, in His awesome love for us, gives us grace upon grace and mercy upon mercy. We will face other opportunities to cultivate our faith. We must pursue our faith, which means we must pursue God and the things of God. It is active. It is an exercise. It is like cultivating a garden. It is precious and must be tended to on a daily basis. Our faith is what enables us to live in victory over the things of this world. It is an essential part of our weaponry.

Lord, You continually reveal new things in Your Word. Things that grow our understanding of this daily walk with You. Thank you for helping us to understand the basic steps to build up our faith. For placing it so readily in our hands through Your powerful Word. Thank you for making Yourself available to each of us. That You made a way for us to draw close to You. To walk beside You every day. So that we would be able to be conquerors of the world. Help me see the world through Your eyes. To recognize that our desires should align with the things of eternity and not the things that will pass away. I thank You for the way You have enabled me to have opportunities to build my faith and given me many second chances when I have failed. There really is no one like You, God. You alone are worthy of all my love and all I have to give. Amen.

ROLLED BACK THE STONE

And behold, there was a great earthquake, for an angel of the Lord descended from heaven and came and rolled the boulder back and sat upon it. (Matthew 28:2 AMPC)

Have you ever watched time-lapse photography reveal the lifecycle of a plant? We see it buried beneath the earth; rain and sun are poured upon it and then, miraculously, there is life as the seed bursts forth. Now, we can see a sprout of vibrant green that stretches past the dark soil and stretches itself upward towards the sun. There is such beauty in the season of spring, and it is a wonderful parallel to the celebration of the resurrection of Jesus Christ.

The women had gone to the tomb to anoint his body with oil and spices because there had not been time to do that before the Sabbath (Mark 16:1). When they reach the tomb, the angel of the Lord is there to greet them and to reveal the news that Jesus Christ has, in fact, risen from the dead to fulfill all that He had prophesied.

Our Heavenly Father, who rolled back the stone to reveal that His Son was in fact resurrected after His crucifixion, is the same God who works miracles today. He never changes. He has been loving us, and making a way for each of us from the very beginning. His plan for us has always been about redemption and restoration.

This is a perfect season to return to the Lord if you have wandered away. He is risen! He promised that all who call on the name of Jesus will be saved! There is nothing you have done that cannot be forgiven. There is no sin that Jesus did not take with Him to the cross. You don't have to wait to have it all figured out on your own. Let the One who attained our victory at Calvary be the hand that restores you! He is mighty to save!

Thank you for the mighty wonders of Your hand of God. The way You reveal Your power and the capabilities that reveal a miracle-working God are so amazing! You rolled back the stone to reveal that Your plan was accomplished. Men and women could come into Your presence through the sacrifice of Jesus. Covered by the blood of the spotless lamb! What a victory! Death defeated! Eternal life restored. A way to have our sins forgiven! What an amazing Father You are! I love You, Lord. Thank you for there really is no love like Your love. I am undone by the extravagance You shower over me. I praise Your name, Abba Father! Glory and honor are Yours. Amen!

BUT GOD

For we ourselves were also once foolish, disobedient, deceived, serving various lusts and pleasures, living in malice and envy, hateful and hating one another. But when the kindness and the love of God our Savior toward man appeared, not by works of righteousness which we have done, but according to His mercy He saved us, (Titus 3:3–5 NKJV)

Ever have a situation arise with a person that leaves you extremely upset? Maybe you have a history of tension or strife with that person, and interactions always leave you feeling unsettled and, maybe, even a little bitter. I had a similar situation happen to me recently. As I sat, thinking about the situation, and putting myself in a position to judge them and their actions—God started talking to me.

I don't know about you, but God isn't subtle with me. He doesn't beat around the bush. He gets right to the point and keeps it simple. I heard in my spirit, "How many times have I offered you My mercy and grace? Isn't everyone in need of the same thing given to you?" It really is a "But God—" moment for most of us when we come to salvation.

I was lost—But God found me.
I was broken—But God restored me.
I was full of shame—But God cleaned me up and clothed me in His righteousness.
I was foolish—But God gave me His wisdom.

I was full of hate and bitterness—But God filled me with love and His peace.
I was sick—But God healed me.
I had nothing - But God has provided for my every need.
I was weak—But God filled me with His Spirit and power.

It is good to remember who we were without God, so that we can have compassion on those who still have not recognized their own need for a Savior. It is a lesson that I am grateful for, because in my flesh I am not full of compassion—and that is definitely what this world needs more than anything.

Father, thank you for Your loving reminder that I too was lost once—But, God, You showed up. You loved me, and called me Your child. All I needed to do was call on the name of Jesus and in an instant I was saved. Not because I earned it or did anything to deserve it, but because of the love You have for me. Help me keep that tenderhearted compassion toward all those who need to know You. Even if they hurt me, remind me of the gift freely given—that I may in turn give it away to others. This is Your desire for us—to love one another. You are such a faithful Father. I am in awe of Your love. Thank you! Thank you! Thank you! Amen.

THE ONLY ONE

But God so loved the world that He gave His only begotten Son, that whoever believes in Him should not perish but have everlasting life. For God did not send His Son into the world to condemn the world, but that the world through Him might be saved. (John 3:16–17 NKJV)

When you think that no one could possibly understand what you are going through, I want you to remember:

Jesus was betrayed. Jesus was abandoned. Jesus was falsely accused. Jesus was falsely imprisoned. Jesus was stripped and beaten. Jesus was essentially tortured as they mocked Him and placed a crown of thorns on His head. They placed a cross upon His shoulders and publicly put Him on display to be ridiculed. The forced Him to carry that cross to Calvary with blood-soaked clothes and blood running down His face into His eyes. They nailed Him to a cross between two criminals and continued to mock Him. He died a criminal's death on that cross so that all could be set free.

You have someone who understands everything you could be going through in this life. He is your best friend. He laid down His life for you. He would have done it all if you were the only one who needed saving. This Easter season, no matter what is happening in this world or in your life, remember: "You are so very loved, by a kind, merciful, and compassionate God. He wants you to have a life full of peace and joy and many, many blessings. Call on the name of Jesus. He will always be there for those who need a savior and call out His name."

AT THE DOOR

"Ask, and the gift is yours. Seek, and you'll discover. Knock, and the door will be opened for you. For every persistent one will get what he asks for. Every persistent seeker will discover what he longs for. And everyone who knocks persistently will one day find an open door. (Matthew 7:7–8TPT)

We just finished celebrating the Resurrection of Jesus Christ. How the tomb was empty and He triumphed over the grave. We celebrate what that means for each and every person who believes that Jesus died and rose again. Eternal life. No longer held by the chains of sin. Freedom.

As I read this verse this morning, I wonder how many people woke up this morning thinking of the struggles they are going through and trying to figure out on their own how to fix it. I wonder how grieved the Father feels this morning, as we put our Sunday best away, and take out Monday's work clothes. We lay the power of the cross aside for our own self-control, our own self-worth, our own self-sufficiency. All of it negating the wonder- working power of our God. I wonder how it breaks our Father's heart that His children don't believe in all of His Word and all of His promises, but only some—limiting Him, because of our own unbelief or our incomplete surrender.

The God of Sunday remains the God of the rest of the week, too. He wants us to know He is in the mundane, the daily grind, the little nuances of our daily lives—however simple or messy they may be. It is my fervent desire for each of us to recognize the power of God's

Word in our day-to-day lives. That we begin to see that all of His promises are true. He didn't just come to save us from our sins, but that we could live the fullest, most abundant life possible. That starts with staying connected to Him. That starts with asking for a deeper understanding of who He is and a deeper revelation of His Word. It begins with us wanting to live a life that means something from an eternal, godly perspective. Full of love and compassion for anyone who does not completely understand the power of that empty grave. Don't put away the power of Resurrection Sunday with your Easter suits and dresses. Keep that Word alive and active in your daily life. Keep searching for how God can reveal more of who He is—and the power He has for you as His glory is revealed in you and through you! He has so much more for each of us than just our personal Salvation, because He is a good, good Father. He is at the door, invite Him in and allow Him to stay and work a complete work in your daily life.

STEADFAST AND TRUE

I will recount the steadfast love of the Lord, the praises of the Lord, according to all that the Lord has granted us, and the great goodness to the house of Israel that he has granted them according to his compassion, according to the abundance of his steadfast love. (Isaiah 63:7 ESV)

Springtime is a season that is unpredictable. The weather can be warm and mild one moment and then quickly change to cold and blustery. We have been having several of those types of weeks here in our hometown throughout this spring month. It can leave a person feeling a little unsettled because of the rapid temperature changes associated with the early part of this season.

Our God is nothing like the changeable conditions of springtime weather. His love is steady. His desire is always to draw you close to him. He doesn't try to hide who He is or hold himself back from you. He loved you so much, He gave everything of Himself for you. In sending His Son to earth, to become a living sacrifice for you, He demonstrated the greatest love one can ever come to know.

There are many reasons we have difficulty understanding this great love at first. We recognize our own lack of worth. We see human love fall short. We don't have a real knowledge of who God is and we have formed Him to meet an image we created.

It is vital that we understand this great love of our Father. It enables us to begin to trust Him and His plans for our lives. It allows us to recognize that we have someone who is always interceding for us and working things out for our good. It assists us in beginning our lifelong journey to become transformed into the image of Christ and to facilitate our use of the gifts granted to us as members of God's own family. Spend time with the Father in prayer and in His Word. It is the best way to build that relationship. It is the best love you will ever know. It will be the most fulfilling choice you will ever make.

Faithful Father, You alone have given every part of You, so that I may come into Your presence and be a part of Your family. To be called Your child is the most precious gift I have ever received. I declare that those who are looking to understand who You are and need a deeper revelation of Your intimate love for them, will have their eyes opened and their hearts softened to receive Your Word. You are always looking for ways to bless Your children and to show them that You are their provider. I declare that they will grow in operation of the power and anointing granted through the indwelling of Your Spirit. Their faith in Your Word will be as steadfast as Your love for them. In Jesus' name, Amen.

SERVING OVER SUPERIORITY

Let each of you esteem and look upon and be concerned for not [merely] his own interests, but also each for the interests of other. Let this same attitude and purpose and [humble] mind be in you which was in Christ Jesus: [Let Him be your example in humility:] (Philippians 2:4–5 AMPC)

The disciples, the Pharisees, the Sadducees, and the Roman officials did not understand Jesus' purpose or plan. They all thought that He came to take something, to establish Himself as a king over and above everyone. Jesus is rightly named King of kings and Lord of lords, but He did not use His authority to oppress anyone. The example we see in His every action shows His compassion. He displayed a heart for serving and, in such a great display of love, allowed Himself to be humbled unto death on the cross.

The Church is in a precarious place regarding the winning of lost souls in the world. We will give the enemy victory if we continue to hold ourselves in spiritual superiority over those who are lost in sin. They do not need our judgment and condemnation, but they need us to emulate the love of Christ through compassion, mercy, and forgiveness. They need us to declare the love of Christ in the middle of the mess. Most of us forget that we did not come to Christ all cleaned up and shiny like a new penny, but our sin made us unholy and unrighteous before Him. Praise God for the gift of Jesus Christ, and allowing us as advocates to provide a way to be made new and clothed in the righteous robes of salvation. It is not anything we earned or could accomplish on our own. So why do we expect the people of the world to have it all together?

We need to look to the interests of others; that doesn't mean placing ourselves in a position of authority, but determining the best way to serve them. We have to look like Jesus and not like the world system and its values. We have to love one another more than we love ourselves. That is definitely in direct contrast to everything the world is shouting at the top of its lungs. The world's strongest message to everyone who will listen: "Look out for number one!" God's message is to look out for others' needs before you look to your own. We need to come to greater understanding of this message. There have been many zealous Christians who forced change upon people in the name of Christ, but that was not His way. He transformed people with love. He loved first and that was so radical, people wanted to change.

Lord, help me to love in a radical way. To give love away so freely that hearts would be changed, that souls would be found and won in the kingdom of heaven. Let me love and serve openly and not in expectation of a return. Let me see Your example and remember all that was given to me so freely is the very same thing You do for all Your children. Every man, woman, and child is worthy of Your love. You long for them to be part of Your family. It is Your promise and Your perfect plan. I am blessed to be a part of it. I glorify You and give You all honor and praise.

EQUALLY LOVED

My dear friends, don't let public opinion influence how you live out our glorious, Christ-originated faith. If a man enters your church wearing an expensive suit, and a street person comes in wearing rags right after him, and you say to the man in the suit, "Sit here, sir; this is the best seat in the house!" and either ignore the street person or say, "Better sit here in the back row," haven't you segregated God's children and proved that you are judges who can't be trusted? (James 2:1–4 NIV)

God's Word clearly states that we should not judge people by their outward appearances. Jesus was a wonderful example of this as He spent time with the sinners, the broken, and the outcasts of society.

The enemy uses media to influence how we should think:
What we ought to buy.
How we should dress.
What we ought to watch or read.
What we should spend our time doing.
What love looks like.
That we have to look out for ourselves if we want to get ahead.

God wants to remind us that He loves us through our imperfections. He doesn't care what we look like on the outside. He examines our hearts. He is concerned with transforming us from the inside. Earthly things will one day be gone forever, and we will have a new home—

an eternal home—and all the trivial things that we look at and judge from a worldly perspective will not matter.

We need to make sure that we are looking at people with love and compassion, and wanting to change them from the inside—so that they may enjoy an eternal life with our God and Father. Piercings, tattoos, the right clothes—they do not matter and are not a reflection of a heart touched by the Father. We are called to love one another as members of the body of Christ. We cannot be a body without every individual part. Our hands and feet do not look alike, but they belong to the same body. Our body cannot function well without either part. Stop listening to how the world thinks and start listening to your Father's heart. We are equally loved and should reflect that in everyone we interact with.

KEEPING YOUR PEACE

My dear brothers and sisters, take note of this: Everyone should be quick to listen, slow to speak and slow to become angry, because human anger does not produce the righteousness God desires. (James 1:19–20 NIV)

Do not be quickly provoked in your spirit, for anger resides in the lap of fools. (Ecclesiastes 7:9 NIV)

These Scriptures bring me back to a situation many years ago. In a situation that I allowed my emotions and anger to rule over me, and I spoke harshly to a family member. Not only was it wrong, but I did this in front of everyone present at a family function. It doesn't matter what happened to provoke it, it was wrong of me to allow myself to be overcome with anger to the point of little self-control. I spoke to be hurtful and the regret afterward was instantaneous and deep. I caused a lot of pain to everyone present. I am thankful for their forgiveness, but it took time and God's tender mercy to heal wounds on all sides.

I wish I could honestly say that is the only time I have spoken words in haste and anger, but that just isn't true. It has taken me a long time to grow in wisdom and self-control. I don't have it mastered yet; I am still a work in progress.

I have often regretted the times I have spoken in haste, ruled by my emotions of the moment. I have never regretted using wisdom to remain silent, waiting on the leading of the Lord for what I should or should not say in my conversations. There are a couple of practical things we can do when we are ready to speak during moments of high emotions. Pause and pray in the Spirit. There is power to pull you out of the natural when you start to pray in tongues. Walk away and ask the Holy Spirit for wisdom over what words you should speak. The Word of God states we will have wisdom when we ask for it. Sometimes, regardless if we believe we are right at that moment, we may just be instructed to remain silent and allow God to handle the situation. This is probably the most difficult one for me, especially if someone has said something deeply hurtful or I feel like I am being unfairly treated. However, angrily speaking out in my own defense has never deescalated situations, but always intensified them. If the Bible describes our words as life and death, then we should be careful at all times how we use our words. We have no excuses when we use our words to cut people down and hurt them regardless of the situation, because we know God's heart in the matter. He always wants us to have the peace that surpasses our human understanding.

Father, I am thankful for the instruction in Your words, even when it's hard. Even when the situation makes me want to react in my emotions. I declare that the voice of the Holy Spirit which lives in me will guide me in my words in every aspect of life. That I will remain silent until I hear directly from You what is good and righteous to say. I will allow You to fight my battles and be the defender of my name. For I am who You say I am above any other words spoken about me by anyone else. Thank you for the wisdom needed to navigate this life. I have to be in the world, but You call me to not be of it. I will watch You and grow in my ability to accomplish this, and demonstrate the love of Christ in every situation. Glory to God. All Glory and honor are Yours alone. Amen.

HEALING FROM ANXIETY AND FEAR

The Spirit you received does not make you slaves, so that you live in fear again; rather, the Spirit you received brought about your adoption to sonship. And by him we cry, "Abba, Father." (Romans 8:15 NIV)

Then the Lord said to him, "Peace be with you; do not fear, you shall not die." So Gideon built an altar there to the Lord, and called it Jehovah Shalom [The Lord is Peace] (Judges 6:23–24 NKJV)

Healing for each person is an individual process. There is no set pattern for everyone, because each person is unique. Pain, hurt, or emotional trauma impacts everyone differently. It takes a varied amount of time for each person. Some people need professional assistance to work through the process of healing and others may not.

Recently, I had an interaction with someone that triggered some residual stress and anxiety related to past hardship. It manifested itself in several nights of bad dreams that had me waking up feeling fatigued, unsettled, and with increased amounts of stress and anxiety. Although I had previously believed that I was healed from the events of my past, my present situation revealed that, under the right circumstances, I could be negatively impacted by events of my past.

The important thing to understand is that God doesn't resent us in the process. He doesn't set time constraints or schedules on our healing. He isn't frustrated when we struggle with fear and anxiety in our healing process. He just simply wants us to come to Him. He doesn't want us to isolate ourselves or feel like we can only talk to Him when we have it altogether. God is Jehovah Shalom—our God of Peace. If we draw close to Him, He is faithful to provide comfort and peace during our healing process. He helps us transform our mind and let go of the pain and the past. It is okay if that also includes professional counseling, but just don't keep God out of the journey. He wants to provide you with His peace which surpasses understanding.

Lord, my God, I cry out to You today. I recognize that healing from emotional trauma is not something that happens for everyone the same way. Sometimes, there are events which may result in my emotional state being triggered to react, due to my past. I just continue to come to You, just as I am, and surrender all my fear and anxieties as they manifest to You. I know that I am not alone, and You are always good, loving, and kind. I declare that You are renewing my mind and helping me release the chains of past pain and hurt. I declare that Jehovah Shalom will be my source of peace in all circumstances. Thank you for showing me that I can run to You in joy or in brokenness. Your arms are always open wide. I love You, Father. There is no one as wonderful as You. Amen.

HOPE IN HEALING

They shall not labor in vain or bring forth [children] for sudden terror or calamity; for they shall be descendants of the blessed of the Lord, and their offspring with them. And it shall be that before they call I will answer; and while they are yet speaking I will hear. (Isaiah 65:23–24 AMPC)

A little over a year ago, my husband and I took advantage of a beautiful day in February to go on a hike. The hike was moderately difficult with steep paths to climb to the top of the mountain peak. I had not had a pair of hiking boots in a while, and had recently purchased the pair I was wearing that day. On the descent, my feet kept sliding forward and my toes were getting bashed on the inside of the boot. By the end of the hike, the two largest toes were so bruised and painful. In reality I could have lost the toenails. It has taken over a year for the healing process from that injury to be complete. The nail literally had to grow out to release all the trapped blood from underneath the nail bed. Unless I wanted to have the nail removed, this is the process that had to take place.

When we are hurting or in the middle of a painful experience it is understandable that we want to be out of that place more than anything. Relief from pain cannot come quick enough. We can begin to lose hope in the midst of waiting for the healing to take place. If you are in a place of waiting for your healing to take place, I want you to read these Scriptures from Isaiah again. God hears you! He is aware of all that you are going through. He has already promised that You will be blessed and that He is working things out. We need to hold onto the faithful Word of God and hold onto our hope. Our healing cannot always be instantaneous. Sometimes the healing we are looking for will take time, but just because it hasn't happened yet doesn't mean God isn't moving and working!

In a conversation recently with a dear friend, talking about healing, she stated, "God doesn't waste anything." There is a beautiful truth in that statement. Wisdom and perseverance and faith are all grown during seasons of waiting. Although the Lord did not cause my hiking injury, He certainly has used the experience to demonstrate that healing will vary from person to person. Each will have different experiences and we cannot compare the way God works in one life to the next. He has a journey and a path for each of us and only He understands what each one of us needs to grow in our relationship with him.

I love You, Lord. Your love for each of us is fierce and deep and wide. But You recognize our differences and so each journey through life will look different. I love that You want each of us to have hope in the process. That Your Word reminds us of Your goodness and that You are already working on our behalf when we call out to You in our great need. I declare that my brothers and sisters will have faith and perseverance in their current season. That they will stay fixed on Your promises and Word. You are the great I Am. Nothing is impossible for You! Amen.

YOUR MISSION FIELD

"Now go in my authority and make disciples of all nations, baptizing them in the name of the Father, the Son, and the Holy Spirit." (Matthew 28:19 TPT)

"Yet who know whether you have come to the kingdom for such a time as this?" (Esther 4:14 NKJV)

Just recently, God has been ministering to me about my place of work being my personal mission field. To be quite honest, I have needed the spiritual correction. I work in a place filled with worldly people who scramble for the accolades of man and scrape for everything that they feel they are entitled to. I have seen fear and anxiety at its uttermost. Lately, I have wanted to be anywhere, but in that place. I have wanted solace from the negativity and the orphan mentality that I see prevalent there. However, I have heard the Holy Spirit telling me that I am called to be there for a purpose. I am filled with godly wisdom and power, and recognize the importance of speaking out His powerful Word into the lives of others. The people that I encounter that need hope to replace fear and peace to replace anxiety. People who need to be reminded that God the Father is the miracle maker. The One who never wavers and His Word remains true today.

I won't succeed everyday at making my place of work my mission field. There will be days that I stumble. That I don't hear the leading of the Holy Spirit. That I allow my flesh to silence the voice of the One who is sent to guide me in all truth. I will need times to refill my spirit to pour out into others. Thankfully, my God is a forgiving God. He gives me opportunity after opportunity. I may have not gotten it done perfectly yesterday, but He gives me new opportunities to shine His love, His compassion, His mercy, His grace, and His wisdom today.

Now, my perspective has changed. Now, I hear the voice of the Holy Spirit telling me, "You were called to this place and this time. You are filled to overflow into the lives of those around you. You know my voice. You have the anointing. You see the desperate needs. You will know when to speak and when to stay silent. I will always be there to guide you. You will accomplish all things through Me. Stay connected. Stay close. Stay in My Word. You are who I say you are, and are able to accomplish the word that I have declared over you."

Father, thank you for the Holy Spirit. Thank you that You have equipped Your children to have knowledge and to be able to fulfill Your instructions to minister to the world. Forgive me for growing weary in the day-to-day. I am so grateful that You provide a well that I can run to and refill my spirit. I don't have to run dry in the midst of being in the world because I have the perfect source for living water. Flow through Your sons and daughters so that souls that are longing for hope and peace can see that it is found only through You. You alone are all we need. Thank you for my mission field. I see it with fresh eyes. I see the desperation in hearts in need of a Savior. May all my actions and words point directly to You. Amen.

STRONG FOUNDATIONS

Now hope does not disappoint, because the love of God has been poured out in our hearts by the Holy Spirit who was given to us. (Romans 5:5 NKJV)

During a visit home to see my family, I had an opportunity to witness the beautiful gift of hope that God gives us through His Spirit. My husband and I attended church with my brother, something that we had not done in years. I was able to witness the way the Spirit of God transforms our hearts through worship and His Word, and see it unfold firsthand in my brother's responses during the service. Afterward, he shared that something shifted in him when he experienced me praying for him in the Spirit a few months ago. I have often prayed with my family at different times, but on this occasion I had started praying in tongues first. I knew that I needed the direct connection of the Holy Spirit to lead me in this particular prayer for him. Praying in tongues in front of my family is not something I do on a regular basis because most of them do not have the understanding of this gift from our Heavenly Father. I am so thankful that I listened to my spirit in this circumstance, because according to my brother, it turned things around in that instant.

The Holy Spirit is a vital part of what God has imparted to each born-again believer. I could not walk in this life and world without Him. He guides me daily. He keeps me focused on things eternal and not the visible things I see. The Holy Spirit is what provides us hope, truth, knowledge, and wisdom. Praying in tongues is a unique and vital part of that connection with the Holy Spirit. It is available to every believer. There is no easy way to begin and it feels weird and uncomfortable to pray in tongues for most first-timers. Just keep pressing in and practicing whenever you have an opportunity. It is prayer language for your spirit. Not your flesh, not your mind, just your spirit. It is a link to our Eternal Father and we each need more of Him no matter how long we have walked with Him.

Father, I pray that my brothers and sisters reading this and who do not have the Holy Spirit would be baptized with the indwelling of Your Spirit right now. Lord, that they would be filled with the gifts of the Spirit, all that You have promised, including the gift of tongues. May each one be connected directly to the power of Your Spirit dwelling inside of them and come to a greater revelation of Your everlasting hope. That You alone, Lord, would be high and lifted up, receiving all glory and honor. Amen.

WORTHY OF OUR TRUST

To all the rich of this world, I command you not to be wrapped in thoughts of pride over your prosperity, or rely on your wealth, for your riches are unreliable and nothing compared to the living God. Trust instead in the one who has lavished upon us all good things, fulfilling our every need. (1 Timothy 6:17 TPT)

A few weeks ago, returning from a trip home to visit family, my husband and I found ourselves with a flat tire on the interstate still several hundred miles from home. With the help of GPS, we found a tire station about twenty miles from where we were. Several weeks ago, my husband had been talking about replacing the two front tires on the car, because they were beginning to show signs of wear. The tire that ended up going flat was a rear tire. There was some discussion about what to do in this situation, because we knew that we would need to replace the other tires soon as well. I suggested that we just go ahead and get all the tires replaced now at the same time, because we were in a position to be able to afford it and it would be peace of mind to have them all done.

Later, as we were safely back on the road with our new tires on the car, it sparked a discussion about seasons when we did not have the financial resources to meet our needs. We spent time giving our God and Father thanks and praise as the true source of our provision. He is the one who supplies our provisions. Nothing compares. We can see the way people scramble around in this generation, attempting to grab up the next and newest phone, video system, or gadget that will entertain them. Even I have an affinity for new things: mostly dresses! These things do not provide lasting security. Just like the tire on the car gave way when it became worn or something hit a weak spot, wealth is something that can come and go.

Maybe you are in season where you feel stretched financially. Go to the Father. He wants you to see Him as your source of need. Go to Him not just for how He can provide, but because He is the source of all goodness Himself. He wants to fill you with more than earthly things. He wants to nourish your soul. To provide hope, peace, love, healing, restoration, wisdom, a sound mind. He simply wants to know you and be known by you. It is a rich relationship and He is worthy of our trust. It will be steadfast, long after everything else fade away. His love will stand.

Father, thank you for the reminder that You are my source for everything. I trust in You alone and see how You have never once failed me. I love how You call my attention to You and things that will not fade away and go the way of all the earth. You alone are always good. You alone are the One that loves like no other. I am delighted to sit with You and draw close to You. Thank you for the way Your Spirit speaks to my heart and mind, reminding me of who You are in all seasons—plentiful or barren. Amen.

FIX YOUR GAZE

I look up to the mountains and hills, longing for God's help. But then I realize that our true help and protection come only from the Lord, our Creator who made the heavens and the earth. He will guard and guide me, never letting me stumble or fall. God is my keeper; he will never forget nor ignore me. (Psalm 121:1–3 TPT)

It often surprises me how many people like scary movies. They enjoy the suspense, that "on the edge of your seat" feeling until the moment that makes them jump and scream. I learned early in life that I don't enjoy scary movies, or haunted houses, or even the thrill of a roller coaster or an amusement park ride. It makes me feel completely unsettled. Additionally, after watching a scary movie, I often have difficulties getting certain images out of my mind. Scary scenes have flashed in my mind for weeks or months and left me feeling on edge and even fearful.

Fear is in direct opposition to our faith. It is what happens to people when they take their eyes off God. There are some recounts of the disciples taking their eyes off Jesus and being filled with fear at the circumstances surrounding them. Jesus fell asleep in the boat and a storm arose (Matthew 8:23–27). Peter took his eyes off Jesus when he was walking on the water to him and began to sink (Matthew 14:28–32). It reminds me that when we allow our minds to be filled with all that we see and hear going on around us, we can be blinded by fear and doubt. It is the enemy's most common weapon, to make believers lose faith or question the goodness, the power, and the abilities of our God and Father.

Fix your eyes firmly on the Great I Am, the creator of all of heaven and earth. Fix your eyes on the one who purposefully crafted you in your mother's womb. Fix your eyes on the one who sent His Son to be a living sacrifice so that you could stand in His presence. Fix your eyes on the one who promises to draw close when the world is crashing down around you. Fix your eyes on the one who loves you with an everlasting love. Fix your eyes. Fix your eyes and be filled with faith, peace, and hope.

WISDOM AND HOPE ENTWINED

My son, eat honey because it is good, and the honeycomb which is sweet to your taste; So shall the knowledge of wisdom be to your soul; if you have found it, there is a prospect, and your hope will not be cut off. (Proverbs 24:13–14 NKJV)

Shortly after turning old enough to drive, I was gifted a brown Plymouth. It was an ugly, big beast of a car, the kind where the front seat was a bench seat and it guzzled gasoline like nobody's business. I remember needing to change the battery in the car on a spring day. I wanted to do the job myself, I wanted to take care of the car that I was so happy to have to get around on my own. I was just about ready to crank the engine over when my father came out of the house and saw that I had the battery in backwards. It would have definitely been a pricey mistake and cost me more money if he had not come to check on my work. I was grateful for his knowledge and assistance that day.

The Heavenly Father wants to give us His wisdom and guidance. We often believe that He is only interested in the big things in our lives, but He cares about the smallest details. He has so much wisdom to pour into us, so that we may see the hope in each moment of the day. Without Him, our daily lives often turn into bleak monotony. We plod through the day, placing one foot in front of the other; can't wait for the day to end to just wake up and do it all over. But God can bring so much more in our daily routines and lives, if we start out seeking Him first. Open the door to Him. Invite Him into your day. It's as simple as saying, "God, I need you every second in this day, apart from You, I cannot accomplish anything. Show me what You want me to see today. Give me wisdom to seek You in every decision and every action. You promised that as Your child I would hear You clearly. I want to go where You lead me. Amen."

Just like my father recognized that although I had the desire to be responsible for what I had been gifted with, I may not have all the knowledge I needed to complete the task—Our Heavenly Father has called each one of us to a specific role in His kingdom. Since His kingdom is not like anything we have experienced on this earth, how can we know how to best walk in His purpose, if we don't include Him in the process? We need His guidance and His hand on our lives daily guiding us along our paths. I am grateful for our Sovereign God's loving hand, guiding me and helping me grow. His wisdom and my hope are bound together. I cannot have hope for a future if I do not recognize the One who holds my future in His Hands. He has the knowledge I need to complete my purpose. I look forward to Him teaching me something new until He calls me home.

MISSING THE MIRACLE

And his servants came near and said to him, "My father, if the prophet had bid you to do some great thing, would you not have done it? How much rather, then when he says to you, 'Wash and be clean?'" Then he went down and dipped himself seven times in the Jordan, as the man of God had said, and his flesh was restored like that of a little child, and he was clean. (2 Kings 5:13–14 AMPC)

Most of us, at one time or another, need to see God do something miraculous in our lives. Maybe it's salvation, restoration, provision, or healing. It is abundantly clear that we have a deep need of what our loving Father willingly provides. I must confess that I have probably missed God's hand moving in these areas of my life because I was looking for Him to move in a big way. I was looking for the seas to dry up and the land to become clear so that I could cross from my need to the place of my fulfillment.

For me, I am realizing that in my need for instantaneous fix, I am missing what God has for me in the journey. Ever wonder if it wasn't really the Promised Land that was the true miracle of God for the Israelites, but the wandering in the wilderness? Learning how powerful and perfect their God and provider really was? That the real miracle was the birth of faith and trust in the One who is willing and able to do all things? Are we missing the miracle? The miracle of this perfect relationship borne of walking out of some difficulties and surviving the storms of life. Looking back at past events, I see myself growing stronger in faith and a steadfast assurance of where I can find everlasting hope. I see the way God arrives, always, right on time.

I confess that I often, in my desperation for comfort and ease, revert back to wanting that immediate move of God. I want that instantaneous fix to pull me out of the mire and clean up my mess. I want to look like I have it altogether instead of recognizing how God will use my trials as a testimony. How my faith and my words that align correctly with His Word can bring revelation to someone else. Someone who is watching me walk through difficulties. Maybe the miracle is someone gaining revelation from watching how God moves in response to our patient perseverance and adoration of Him regardless of the outcomes.

Lord, thank you always for the way Your Spirit reveals new ideas and thoughts to grow me deeper in understanding all that You are calling me to. Deep calls unto deep. More of You and seeing things from an eternal perspective and less of me and my earthly view. Help me to see Your miraculous hand in new ways. Not in my cookie-cutter concept of how You should move, but doing Your will. You are so good, and so patient with us as we fumble to understand that Your way is vastly different from our own. Thank you for Your tender mercies. Thank you for forgiving my narrow sight in the way You are working all things for my good. Amen.

HOLD ONTO ME

You will show me the path of life; in Your presence is fullness of joy, at Your right hand there are pleasures forevermore. (Psalm 16:11 AMPC)

Working in healthcare, I have seen many types of illnesses and different backgrounds and life experiences in the patients I interact with. It still surprises me at times when people choose not to receive all the help and expertise available in the inpatient therapy program at our hospital. They had a choice to come to the floor and decided to come for therapy, but somehow decided that they should decide what specific type of help they need. I recently had a patient refuse to complete the assessment process because, instead of facing their difficulties, they chose to be offended. They decided that the process that is designed to enable me to put together treatment options that could benefit them in their healing process was purposefully degrading to them. No amount of explanation was helpful in providing this patient with understanding about this critical process.

As I continued to think about this recent experience, and feel a little frustrated by it, I felt the Holy Spirit saying, "This is how God feels when you choose to ignore all the wisdom and truth He has for you." Can I honestly say, "OUCH!" Not quite the message any of us would like to hear from the Spirit of God, but it was truth. I need to receive it. We as a society have gotten so good at pointing the finger at others, instead of accepting responsibilities for our own choices. We only want what makes us feel good and, oftentimes, we will push others down to get it. Eternal truth tells us that earthly pleasures are temporary and that real joy is in becoming one with our Heavenly Father. Real wisdom comes from understanding that His kingdom and ways are opposite our own. To be lifted up is to serve. To be blessed is to give of ourselves. To be at peace in the midst of any situation is to look to the unseen things.

God keeps telling us to look to Him, hold tightly to His hand. He doesn't let go of us, but often we let go of His hand. We let go and wander off like a child in the mall delighted by all the visual images and sounds and smells that delight us but never fulfill us. Then those same things that delighted us suddenly become our own prison and we feel lost because we let go of the steadying hand of our Father. We have to be willing to hold onto God, to listen to His voice, and to accept the correction we need in our lives. If we keep our spirits unteachable, we will never grow. We will never attain all that God has for us. Fullness. He has fullness of life promised for us; not just once we enter heaven, but in the here and now.

EVERLASTING FORGIVENESS

Higher than the highest heavens—that's how high your tender mercy extends! Greater than the grandeur of heaven above is the greatness of your loyal love, towering over all who fear you and bow down before you! Farther than from a sunrise to a sunset—that's how far you have removed our guilt from us. (Psalm 103:11–12 TPT)

I believe the Bible lets us look at the lives of people that God changed and used for His purpose so that we may recognize that His love is unstoppable. We can't be too dirty, too broken, or too lost for Him. Many of the books in the New Testament of the Bible were written by Paul, a man who knew sin. Who, before Jesus changed his heart, had been responsible for persecuting and killing Christians. If God has this great and everlasting love for us even before we ever realize our need for Him, why do we ever categorize ourselves or anyone else as too far gone for God to redeem?

Grace supersedes the law. Laws cannot overcome our nature to sin, but grace can. Grace is gift and cannot be earned. Even with our greatest intentions, our very nature makes the most righteous man or woman unable to stand before the holy throne of God without having received the gift of the blood of Jesus Christ poured out for each of us.

God wants each of us to know that His love is never-ending. It is His desire that we know Him and have the gift of everlasting life. There is no sin that cannot be forgiven, if we truly desire forgiveness and ask for it. Stop looking at God as the one who wants to punish you— you have one enemy in this life and it is Satan. He wants to keep you separated from the love of God. He wants you to believe that God can't love you, but the Bible shows us, over and over again, that God does love us—even when we feel unlovable.

Invite Him in today. Silence the lies of the enemy. Run to the safest place you can ever be. The arms of your loving Heavenly Father.

OPPOSITE ORDER

"Blessed are you poor, for yours is the kingdom of God. Blessed are you who hunger now, for you shall be filled. Blessed are you who weep now, for you shall laugh. Blessed are you when men hate you, and when they exclude you, and revile you, and cast out your name as evil, for the Son of Man's sake. Rejoice in that day and leap for joy! For indeed your reward is great in heaven, for in like manner their fathers did to the prophets." (Luke 6:20–23 NKJV)

Jesus had this incredible way of describing God's view of things as directly opposite to what the world placed emphasis on. That in heaven those who seemed to have it all would have nothing and those with nothing would gain it all. He told the people that God's heart was for the oppressed, the broken, the infirm, and the ones everyone else seemed to have forgotten. It was a clear message of hope to the Jewish people.

This idea of opposite order has been running through my mind lately. This idea that often our concepts, our knowledge, our way of thinking is opposite of how God thinks. I have been thinking of the different people that were in need of healing that came across Jesus' path during His ministry. The woman with the issue of blood (Matthew 9:20–22); Bartimus, the blind beggar (Mark 10:46–48); and, the weeping widow in the funeral procession (Luke 7:11–17). So many, many others. We often think of the compassion of Jesus in these stories. We think of his great love and mercy, and the power in His life manifested to proclaim who He was and how God was with Him and in Him. I want to focus on those who were healed for a moment. I want to look at their need, but point out that it was not just their desperation, but also their boldness that made them pursue Christ. I see boldness in them because they were in a society that reviled them and had placed rules upon them that would keep them suppressed and marginalized, and made them feel unworthy of anything more than pity laced with a bit of contempt. I see that great need in their life giving them a desperate hunger for the hope that Jesus had to offer. Not just the benefit of healing their physical bodies, but the power of His Words, what He was teaching that made a difference in their hearts and minds. That love was the most powerful weapon.

Love of the Father and being united with Him would breakdown all the old religious concepts of who was worthy. No one was worthy, but everyone could receive. No one should set himself apart, but desire to serve one another in love. If someone desired strength, then rejoice in his own weakness, because the God of all comfort and all power would fill the weak with His own strength.

Thank you, Holy Spirit, for the birthing in my mind for this concept of opposite order. I know right now I am only seeing part of all You have to reveal to me, but I wait in anticipation for all the wisdom You will impart. I rejoice in the promise of You revealing all truth from the Heavenly Father to His children. Thank you for showing me that desperation and boldness are not mutually exclusive of one another. That people who desired a physical restoration from Jesus also recognized their spiritual need for hope and faith to be restored to them as well. I look to You to grow my faith. I anticipate all the work You promised You would fulfill in my life to be complete. I simply come and surrender all my own ideas at Your feet. In Jesus' name. Amen.

SIMPLE RELATIONSHIP

When the hour had come, He sat down, and the twelve apostles with Him. Then He said to them, "With fervent desire I have desired to eat this Passover with you before I suffer; for I say to you, I will no longer eat of it until it is fulfilled in the kingdom of God." (Luke 22:14–16 NKJV)

The word fervent comes from the Latin word fervor or fervere, which means "to boil." Jesus was telling the disciples that His longing to share the Passover meal with them was of utmost importance. We, of course, know that Jesus was about to face His accusers and be sent to the cross to die. Jesus wanted to impart things of importance to the men he called "disciples and brothers." He recognized the need to spend time face-to-face, to stay connected, and to build memories in the minds of the men who would go onto serve in the ministry.

Jesus has this same fervent desire to spend time with each of us. We cannot stay connected and grow without spending time with Him. When we make excuses about how busy we are, we are simply saying that we choose to not put God first in our lives.

It's easy to allow our schedules to be so filled that we don't have daily time to spend with the Lord. It just means that our desire for other things has grown greater than our desire to walk with the Father. We have all done it. Placed our relationship with God in a lower priority until the emptiness, the burnout, the sheer exhaustion of life makes us realize we have our priorities wrong. There He waits at the table.

He is relaxed and at ease. The table is prepared. He points to the seat next to Him. He has been waiting for you. His fervent desire to have this time with you has not ceased. He just waited for you to recognize your need.

Abba Father, thank you for the time You spend with me. You are always there when I need You. I don't deserve a love like Yours. Help me to seek the time with You every day in this life. Apart from You, I grow weary, empty, and disconnected from the source of life and fulfillment I need more than the air I breathe. Thank you for Your pursuit of this relationship. I am always secure in Your household and always have a seat at Your table. What a beautiful revelation. I love You more and more. Amen.

CONFESSION IS CONVERSATION

O God, you know my foolishness; and my sins are not hidden from you. (Psalm 69:4 NKJV)

O Lord, you have searched me and known me. (Psalm 139:1 NKJV)

Shortly after I turned eighteen, I moved out of my parents' house. I was arrogant and prideful and difficult. I decided that I didn't need to respect my parents and had no need for their rules. Several months later and several bad decisions later, my mother knew that I was in need. She called me and asked if I wanted to come home. She didn't make me beg. She simply called and offered to help bring me home. Parents have this wonderful sense of their children. Who they are and the times in which they may need help, but not always know how to ask. Years later I think about this event. I don't know if I would have gotten to the point of desperation and called to ask for help. Pride and foolishness make for very poor companions and lead to even poorer decisions. I am so grateful that my mother's love and her ability to forgive me and offer the help I needed.

Just like parents know their children and can recognize their needs, our Heavenly Father is the same. We need to recognize that the creator knows us thoroughly. We cannot hide from Him. We need to let go of our sense of pride and foolishness. If He already knows every thought and sees every mistake, there is no need to be afraid to talk to

Him about our sin and failures. We need to stop thinking of confession as anything more than a conversation. I believe it is a chance for us to talk about our struggles and the realization that we need the help of our Father in every aspect of our lives. We have become very adept at deceiving ourselves into believing that we are in control, a deception that leads us to self-worship and destruction.

This confession, or better yet, conversation, opens our hearts and spirits to the knowledge that with God's help we can overcome and we can grow and change into people who look like Jesus. I don't want to be a better version of myself, I want to emanate God through my words and actions. I want His presence to be so powerful in my life that it permeates every moment of my day. That my will, every aspect of my life, is connected to His will, His purpose, His plan.

Every day, Lord, You are changing me from the inside. I love that I can open up Your Word and have new insights and revelations to this relationship we have. Lord, I love that You already know me, every aspect of my character is revealed to You. Forgive me my selfishness, my pride, and my moments of doubt. I trust You. I want every part of me to walk completely in Your will and plan. It is better when my Father guides my feet along the path. This journey would be treacherous without Your guidance. Forgive me when I have decided to control my own life and foolishly decided I could do it better. We both know how wrong I really was in my thinking. You alone are good and You love me like no other. Thank you, Lord! Amen.

OUR NEED OF A SAVIOR REVEALED

Bring forth fruit that is consistent with repentance [let your lives prove your change of heart]; And do not presume to say to yourselves, We have Abraham for our forefather; for I tell you, God is able to raise up descendants for Abraham from these stones! (Matthew 3:8–9 AMPC)

The Bible is such a wonderful roadmap for life. It makes me wish that I had recognized the value of God's Word so much earlier in my life. Maybe I would have had less battles and trials, because my spirit would have been open and teachable? In this scripture, we have a very clear equation between repentance and the results in our lives. When we are repentant, we are humble and we start to change the way we are living to line up with God's Word. It demonstrates our recognizing that we have a need for a Savior, for a Father that wants to be in every area of our lives. Pride demonstrates the exact opposite. It is self-serving and reveals that we believe that we are our own god. That we know better, and can do it better, without anyone else's help.

Another mistake that we often make as Christians is measuring sin. We compare our lives to others, and attempt to equate our behaviors as better or superior to someone else's life choices. The Bible clearly states that every single person on earth (except Christ) falls short of the glory of God. We are not good enough to enter His presence without the atoning sacrifice of His Son. God sees jealousy, lack of forgiveness, gossiping, and discord in the same manner as He sees sexual immorality, stealing, and murder. There is no distinction in His eyes. We need to recognize that our flesh is full of things that are opposite the Spirit of God. We need repentance as a reminder that we recognize our need for God's Spirit and power in our lives. This is what takes out our heart of stone and changes it into one that is soft and pliable in the potter's hand.

Today, I am reminded that I need to repent daily because I need more of God in me—than myself. I need the power of the Savior. He has all that I will ever need.

FREE FROM ALL FEAR

Listen to my testimony: I cried to God in my distress and he answered me. He freed me from all my fears! (Psalm 34:4 TPT)

Let's just be honest, we all have situations that come up that may cause us to feel fear. An untimely report from a doctor or something happening with a loved one or child. We feel fear because we cannot see what the outcome will be. It is unknown to us. I don't believe that God thinks that we will never feel fear, but that He doesn't want us to stay trapped in our fears. Staying trapped means "we cannot move forward." We feel frozen in place. Our fear becomes like a prison for us; the door is locked and we don't have the keys to open it. The wonderful thing about God is that He has given us access to the key to open the door. We make it so complicated, but it is very simple. When we spend time with God, in His Word, in prayer, and in praising Him—we will be able to be freed from fear. Jesus promised His disciples that He would leave them with His peace (John 14:27). As children of God, we have the same access to God's peace.

I cannot fix whatever is going on in your life today that is filling you with fear and doubt, but God can! He wants to display His love and power in your life. He always shows up in our time of need. He can give you the peace you need in every situation. Let Him use the power of His Word in your heart and mind to replace the anxious thoughts that keep swirling around.

Thank you, God, that You always show up in the darkest night to calm me in my fears and doubt. You and Your Word are one and so very powerful. I love that word You always plant in my mind when I tell You I need encouragement or comfort. You never fail me. I declare over the person reading this right now that feels gripped in fear. I declare that they are freed from the stronghold of fear in their lives and feel the supernatural peace that can only come from You. I declare that You will give them a word to stand on—that they may not falter. They will not be overcome. In the name of Jesus! Amen.

STRONG FOUNDATIONS

When the whirlwind passes by, the wicked is no more, but the righteous has an everlasting foundation. (Proverbs 10:25 NKJV)

This weekend we had several severe thunderstorms pass through our area. I watched as the blue sky was replaced by dark grey clouds. The wind picked up and the trees around our home which always seem so strong and powerful begin to sway. The rumble of thunder precedes the flashing of lightning in the sky. You feel the temperature fall rapidly. Then that first anticipated patter of rain hits, and then suddenly the rain is coming down furiously. Everything that was dry is now wet. During one storm we even had some hail, with small little bits of ice on the patio table and chairs. Then it's a matter of minutes, the storm is over —blown by those fierce winds to the next area.

The attacks of the enemy can seem like these spring storms that happen this time of year. There is peace and a wonderful flow in our lives until, all of a sudden, the ground beneath our very feet can be shaking. The enemy attacks areas in our lives that result in fear, stress, and worry. It could be at your work, or in your family, or in the area of finances or health. It doesn't matter to Satan—his purpose is to steal, kill, and destroy.

Maybe you are in one of those storms right now. I want you to know that Satan cannot win if you have God in your life. Satan has already been defeated. The chains of hell are broken. The Word of God declares that God always hears the cries of His children and does not leave us defenseless in the midst of our battles. Get that. God didn't say we wouldn't have battles. He said He would never leave us or forsake us. Not ever.

Get your foundation under you. Get the Word of God in your heart. This life has bumps and twists and turns along the road, but God is always faithful and always there. He is our everlasting hope. Amen.

UNDIVIDED

Angry, they kept insisting that he answer their question, so Jesus stood up and looked at them and said, "Let's have the man who has never had a sinful desire throw the first stone at her." (John 8:7 TPT)

Upon hearing that, her accusers slowly left the crowd one at a time, beginning with the oldest to the youngest, with a convicted conscience. (John 8:9 TPT)

During a recent conversation with a friend, they stated that they had held off coming to me with a personal need while at church. They were concerned about what other people in the church would think and say if she came to me with her need and asked for prayer. This really grieves me that we feel unable to seek the assistance we need in our churches. That we feel exposed and that we feel that we will be judged by others in the body of Christ. And yet, I know that it is something that still happens, and I have experienced it myself on occasions.

The Word of God tells us that we all fall short of the glory of God. No one but Jesus was in a position to judge this woman caught in adultery. When you read the next few verses in the Book of John, it tells us that Jesus did not condemn this woman, yet demonstrated compassion and forgiveness for her mistakes. We have to get to a place in the body of the church where we are united in love and compassion for one another. That when one person stumbles, we lift them up, and not use them to place ourselves a little closer to the throne room.

God does not demonstrate favoritism. He has the same love for each man, woman, and child. He wants all to be reconciled to Himself—not just some, but every single one, borne in sin, but worthy of suffering and dying for—the undivided church. He does not glory when we start to be filled with pride and believe we have the right to sit on the judgment seat. We did not earn that position. We could not attain heaven on our own merits.

Gossip, envy, and strife are the things that keep those suffering from coming to the body of Christ for healing. We need to be steadfast in asking God to look at our own hearts and show us the things we are hiding in the darkest recesses—we need to have the last bit of our flesh subject to the sovereignty of God. We need to lay any illusions aside that one of us is more worthy of salvation than another. We need to become undivided in the sole purpose of healing the lost and broken of the world. Not through judgment, but through compassion and love.

Lord, this truth is powerful. I declare that Your Church would lay aside any pride any lofty thought that tries to exalt itself above Your Word. I declare that we purify our hearts and minds in Your Word, staying close to the One who is full of compassion and love, and that it would permeate to the marrow of our bones. That we may be all You desire in Your Church. A beacon of hope for those who need You. Amen.

CAREFUL LISTENING

"But I say to you that for every idle word men may speak, they will give account of it in the day of judgment. For by your words you will be justified, and by your words you will be condemned." (Matthew 12:36–37 NKJV)

While I realize that this passage refers to what people speak, I want to suggest that if God says He is taking into account what people are saying, then so should we. The Bible tells us to carefully look at the fruit of peoples' lives as an indicator of their relationship with God. I believe this is valid in determining who we allow to speak into our lives. In short, whose words we will value and whose words we will not take to heart.

Recently, during a conversation with an acquaintance, after finding out I did not have any children, they stated, "Well, you better just admit that you made your work a priority in your life over having a family." Let's be blunt, I was deeply offended. It was just another experience of people casting their judgments on situations in someone else's life, when they have no idea of what they have walked through. It has been an area of personal pain in my life. Later, as I took time to think about this experience, the Holy Spirit whispered to me, "You allow people power in your life that have no business wielding any. Do you care about the judgment of man or do you care about what your Father says about you?" This stopped me in my tracks.

There was no real spiritual fruit in this person's life. I have the power to let them speak into me or to recognize that they do not have anything that will benefit the growth of my spirit and I can close off my spirit from the things they attempt to impart. Each of us has that ability. God wants us to be discerning with what we speak and what we listen to.

Remember that God and His Spirit speak life not death, they speak conviction not condemnation. We do not have to allow another person to bring any type of shame or condemnation into our hearts, minds, and spirits. We need to be vigilant and watch who and what we allow to have power in our lives. We need to tune our ears to listen for the voice of God through the power of His Spirit. Don't give power to those who do not demonstrate the fruit of the Spirit in their lives—it doesn't matter if they are a stranger or your closest family member—if they are not walking connected to God and His Spirit, they do not have anything but worldly wisdom to offer. Worldly wisdom is like dust. It will pass away in the gentlest breeze, and you will be left stagnant. Your growth and wisdom will be stifled without the power of God's Word, which brings forth new life.

IN PURSUIT OF HIM

But as for you, O man of God, flee from all these things; aim at and pursue righteousness (right standing with God and true goodness), godliness (which is the loving fear of God and being Christlike), faith, love, steadfastness (patience), and gentleness of heart. (1 Timothy 6:11 AMPC)

In the earlier years of my walk with the Lord, I often felt confused about His purpose for me and how I could become the godly woman He desired me to be. In all honesty, I wasn't spending time in the Word. Other than reading the Gospels of Matthew, Mark, Luke, and John, and knowing some of the stories in the Old Testament, I really didn't have a devotional or prayer life. I prayed because I had a need for God to fill. I knew enough to run to Him for help, but I certainly wasn't living up to my purpose.

It took being planted in a good church with a Spirit-filled pastor, who spoke with the anointing of God, to begin to deepen my understanding. We have the greatest resource at our fingertips in the Bible. It is the inspired Word of God. He reveals Himself in the pages and the words penned on the paper. He provides direction and instruction on how He wants us to live and serve Him. We have an option of just using God as our crisis center operator, or understanding how we can be equipped to face battles with His leading. We can decide to be lukewarm Christians, tossed about by every change, or rooted and grounded in the foundation that cannot be shaken. We can choose to do nothing about our personal relationship with God, or we can pursue Him and the things that are pleasing to Him. When you understand the great love He has for you and the cost to bring salvation to all of us, the very basic response should be gratitude, humbling of our heart, and a desire to glorify Him. You will either pursue God or pursue the things of the world. The things of the world will not fulfill you because you were designed by your Creator to have a relationship with Him. Everything else remains a distraction to that deep calling. Everything else is a barrier to all the beauty God has in store for your life.

I look back and wish I could make up for lost time. I know that my journey and the way I had to grow are no surprise to God, but with the wisdom I have now is a sense of longing. A wondering of what I could have accomplished in my life through His power, blessing, and anointing if I had understood it all sooner. If I had laid aside the distractions of the world sooner. But God is faithful and He will always accomplish His completed work in our lives as we yield to Him and lay our own plans aside. Don't wait. Be in pursuit of Him now. He will change your life in radical ways and you will be all the beautiful for it. Amen.

MY FUEL SOURCE

Bless the Lord, O my soul, And forget not all His benefits: Who forgives all your iniquities, Who heals all your diseases, Who redeems your life from destructions, Who crowns you with lovingkindness and tender mercies, Who satisfies your mouth with good things, so that your youth is renewed like the eagle's. (Psalm 103:2–5 NKJV)

The beginning of summer is upon us now and I, like many others, am looking forward to cookouts and campfires. As I was thinking about some of the delights of summertime, and campfires in particular, I was reminded that fire requires a fuel source. Excessive heat is applied to some type of item that will burn, but in the absence of that source of fuel, it will die out. When we want the fire to die down at the end of our evening, my husband simply stops applying more wood to the fire. Without something to feed it, the fire eventually burns itself out.

In Psalm 103, King David is reminding himself of who the source of all the good things in his life really is: our Heavenly Father. He created us to know Him and then provided His Word through the Bible so that we could learn all about His character. God is our redeemer, our healer, our provider, the very one who takes and blots out all our sin and binds up our sorrows. He is my source of strength. He provide me with peace when all around me seems in chaos. He takes away my sorrows and replaces it with joy.

Maybe you have been searching for something to be your fuel source in your life. You have tried to fill that space inside with many things, but nothing really keeps you filled up. Nothing keeps your heart on fire. God can and will be your source of fuel. He promises that He can be your ultimate source and, if you run after Him with all your heart, mind, and strength, He is faithful to be your ultimate source of provision in every circumstance. Tell the Lord that you need Him, that you need a savior and that you recognize that Jesus Christ died for you that you could be cleaned from all your sin and past mistakes. God wants to shower you with His tender mercies and fill you up until you overflow. His love is an all-consuming love that always burns. Its source of energy is limitless.

All glory and honor and praise to His name. Jesus, I love You. Amen.

THE STORY OF YOUR TAPESTRY

You formed my innermost being, shaping my delicate inside and my intricate outside, and wove them all together in my mother's womb. (Psalm 139:13 TPT)

You saw who you created me to be before I ever became me! Before I'd ever seen the light of day, the number of days you planned for me were already recorded in your book. (Psalm 139:16 TPT)

A tapestry is designed by taking fabric and weaving it back and forth in and through other fibers that are vertical and make a type of grid. Tapestry work is an extremely detailed and can take months or years to complete. Now, think of how the psalmist describes the handiwork of God in your creation. How much thought and time and purpose were placed on how you were formed? For each one of us is more precious than any type of tapestry that could be created. Each one of us is uniquely designed and formed. With special gifts, and every day already detailed in God's book.

The Holy Spirit keeps whispering to me today: "Not one thing is wasted." It is easy to look at our lives, our past, our mistakes, our pain, and believe that we have missed the opportunity that God has for us. Here, what the Spirit of God is saying: "Not one thing is wasted." The God who created you is walking with you as you walk out your story. Not one tear, one heartache, one shout for joy, is wasted. They are all delicately woven into your story. These experiences, the good times and the challenging times in life, are all purposeful in molding you into the disciple that you are meant to be. We have to stop comparing our story and our journey with anyone else's. You will not follow the exact path of anyone else because you are created to be unique unto yourself. Your mountaintop experiences will be different; your journeys through the valleys will be different. Your breakthrough will look different.

A couple of weeks ago, we had visiting pastors speak at our church and pray for many people for healing. There were several people who testified to immediate healing. Not everyone's healing will be the same. I am receiving my healing from an injury ten months ago. It isn't looking like everyone else's healing, but that is perfectly okay. It is meant for me alone. It is my breakthrough. It is the way God has purposed it in my life. And nothing has been wasted. This time of waiting has not been wasted. God has been using it to build up my faith, to demonstrate that I have a need for Him that is beyond my personal daily needs in this world. It has demonstrated that apart from Him, every aspect of my life is empty and without purpose. All my hope, all my strength, all my ability for love and compassion comes from knowing Him. I am lost and desolate and desperate without Him.

Not one thing in your life is wasted. Don't look around to see the path of anyone else's life. Your walk with God is as unique as you are—God took time to prepare a place for you. It is yours and yours alone. You are a beautiful tapestry being woven together every day and God is not done writing your story.

I love You, Lord. Thank you for the beautiful reminder that You are not done writing my story and that my story will look completely different than anyone else's. How amazing that You designed this journey for just the two of us and that it is like no one else's. Help me to love like You love. To keep my eyes fixed on the center of Your heart and keep shaping me into exactly all You called me to be. I want to look exactly like You imagined me as You began Your perfect plan for my life. Amen.

HEARTFELT THANKSGIVING

Therefore by Him let us continually offer the sacrifice of praise to God, that is, the fruit of our lips, giving thanks to His name. (Hebrews 13:15 NKJV)

Most of us have experienced meticulously planning a gift of surprise for someone we love. Maybe it was your spouse, a child, or a parent. We are both excited and apprehensive as we watch the ribbon and wrapping paper being torn off the package. We try to catch a glimpse of the person's facial expression as they open the box and we are both relieved and happy when we see the smile upon the person's face. Perhaps some of us have experienced the opposite—the gift giving did not delight the intended person. I have personally experienced this misfortune when I have listened to my siblings and purchased clothing for their children instead of toys! It is feeling of dejection and lack of appreciation that can hurt the gift giver.

I imagine that is how our Heavenly Father feels when we are provided with such provision, grace, and mercy daily, but do not pause to give Him thanks. We are like that child surrounded by a pile of boxes wrapped in an array of assorted colors and ribbons, and we open one box to toss it aside to quickly move onto the next.

First, I should express that the greatest gift we have ever received is the ability to have a direct relationship with our Creator. That we have access to Him through His Spirit is a treasure that I don't want to take for granted, but I know that at times I have. It is very easy in this present age, where we have direct access to so many things, to be less aware of how our loving God is working to provide for us in our day-to-day lives. We gloss over the small, seemingly insignificant gifts and only remember to be thankful for the miracles we are longing to see manifested. Your God is in the day-to-day, the minute-to-minute, the smallest detail in your life. He wants you to see Him in the green grass blowing in the fields, or the song of birds filling the air, or the drops of summer rain plunking on the umbrella as you race into work.

I know that this verse spoke to me this morning, and I humbly pause to say: "Thank you, Father, for the day-to-day, the things we just allow to be absorbed into what we view as our routine, when every aspect of how You touch our lives is extraordinary. Forgive me, when in my haste, I forget to acknowledge You first in my day. Every day from You is a beautiful gift waiting to be unwrapped. I am blessed by Your loving-kindness and I will offer the fruit of my lips to You now in all glory and adoration. You alone are worthy of all my love and all my praise. Amen."

CALLED TO BE MORE

Keep reminding God's people of these things. Warn them before God against quarreling about words; it is of no value and only ruins those who listen. Do your best to present yourself to God as one approved, a worker who does not need to be ashamed and correctly handles the word of truth. Avoid godless chatter, because those who indulge in it will become more and more ungodly. (2 Timothy 2:14–16 NIV)

Have you ever had a day that went horribly wrong and you were angry with events that took place, and decided to go home to vent to your spouse and/or family? Instead of the release of emotion and stress that had built up during the course of the day, it just allowed the emotions to be churned up and boil to the surface again. After listening quietly to me for several minutes, my husband will often place his hand on my arm and say, "Take a breath, and try to calm down." It is advice that has varied results, but when the situation has passed and my emotions are in check, his advice is for my benefit.

We are not supposed to allow ourselves to stay angry. The Bible talks in Ephesians 4:26 about not allowing ourselves to sin in our anger and not allowing ourselves to stay angry for more than a day. Our Heavenly Father knows that our emotions going unchecked can lead to sin. I know that I have spoken in anger and often have regretted it later.

Just before Paul warns Timothy about godless chatter, he gives him direction on how to avoid discord: Become a worker who handles the word of truth correctly. We need to become filled with the Word of God. It needs to be a source of knowledge and information to us that we can use in any given situation. It is the one way that leads to better decision-making and choices regardless of our emotions in any daily event. We have to learn to push down our emotions and check in with the Word of God to determine our talk and our actions. It isn't instantaneous, but takes practice.

Thank you, Lord, for Your Word. It gives wisdom and direction. It always leads back to You. Apart from You we cannot accomplish anything, but with You all things become possible. Examine me, Lord, and help my words and actions to align themselves with Your heart. I do not want to be the cause of others falling away from You. Allow my life to be a reflection of Your love. Help me with Your Spirit to keep tight hold of my emotions. They should not be how I regulate my thoughts or talk. I love You, Lord. I continue to choose to surrender daily to Your leading. Amen.

OPPORTUNE TIMES

And the Lord said to Satan, "From where do you come?" So Satan answered the Lord and said, "From going to and fro on the earth, and from walking back and forth on it." (Job 1:7 NKJV)

From the moment that Adam and Eve sinned against God in the Garden of Eden, Satan has continued his attempts to keep people from recognizing the goodness of God. Satan's plan is to attempt to keep people from seeing the love of God that has conquered death and separation from Him. This scripture clearly tells us that Satan is operating on earth. In Luke 4:13, at the end of Jesus' temptation by Satan in the desert, it states that "he left him until an opportune time." This indicates that Satan was watchful for other opportunities to separate Jesus from His Heavenly Father.

This is the very reason we, as sons and daughters of the living God, need to recognize the power and authority that we have inside of us. If Satan was not shy in his pursuit of the Son of God, why do we think he will not continually try to keep us isolated, separated, and under attack? He will, but that is not the end of the story. We are equipped to know that the battle is here and real, but that we already operate from a position of victory. Victory won by Jesus Christ Himself. Death is defeated. Sin is defeated. We have access to the Mighty One. The Alpha and the Omega, Jehovah, King of kings! We have the powerful Word of God to use as our shield, and also as our sword. We speak it against any lies that try to bring themselves above the Word of God. We can cast down strongholds. We can have peace and joy unspeakable. We need to be aware of the enemy, but we don't have to live in fear. We don't have to be the character in a scary movie, crouched down in the corner waiting for the attack. We stand in boldness because our God is bigger, our God is stronger, and our God has already won every battle!

THE LIGHT WITHIN YOU

Jesus said, "For a brief time still, the light is among you. Walk by the light you have so darkness doesn't destroy you. If you walk in darkness, you don't know where you're going. As you have the light, believe in the light. Then the light will be within you, and shining through your lives. You will be children of light." (John 12:35–36 MSG)

Perhaps some of us have experienced walking somewhere down a well-lit hallway only to have the power go out and be submerged in total darkness. Without the light, which is necessary for our sense of sight, we can easily lose our sense of direction and sometimes our sense of balance. In the medical field, it is well known that most falls happen to people at night because there wasn't enough light and it impacts our ability to balance ourselves during movement.

Jesus during this time was trying to prepare His disciples for the future when He would not be with them. We know from reading the Bible that the disciples still did not understand that Jesus would be crucified. As I read this scripture this morning, I am very aware of how important the light of Jesus is to this world. The past several years have been filled with more hatred, more division, more fear; and, if I didn't have the light of Christ within me—I too would be subject to despair. I find myself, again and again, going back into God's Word, and purposefully spending time in the things that bring forth hope and peace in these seasons. As Christians we all know the truth that this world will pass away and we will be entering a new heaven and a new earth prepared for us. In that place there will never be darkness for God's glory itself will illuminate everything. However, we are not celebrating in eternity yet, and we need to be purposeful to keep the light burning inside of us. The light will be what draws others from their darkness and guide them safely into the arms of a loving Father.

Father God, although I am familiar with this scripture, I find myself in need of the comfort of the promise again today. I do not have to be consumed by the darkness and dark things of the world. I have the light and life of Christ that dwells in me. I have the promise that the Spirit of God will keep me filled up and overflowing with life—an abundant life. You have been so faithful and true. I am so amazed by Your love for me. Although I look forward to a new home without the tragedies of this world, I know that You delay Your return to give everyone an opportunity to repent and call out to You for redemption. You are so tender and compassionate that You do not want one person to miss out on all You have for them in heaven. Lord, I call forth the revival of this nation and declare that pride would be broken and hearts be softened. That men and women would have their eyes opened to the wonders of Your love. They would be healed of their sin and their brokenness be healed. You alone are worthy, for only You can save! Amen.

FERTILE GROUND

"Now these are the ones sown among the thorns; they are the ones who hear the word, and the cares of this world, the deceitfulness of riches, and the desires for other things entering in choke the word, and it becomes unfruitful. But these are those sown on good ground, those who hear the word accept it, and bear fruit: some thirtyfold, some sixty, and a hundred." (Mark 4:18–20 NKJV)

This is such a great parable that Jesus used to teach his disciples about the value of planting God's Word in your heart. It starts in Mark 4:1–20. I believe that this portion of the Scripture is really important for so many of us in the United States today. We have access to so much more than any generation before us and I don't believe it is necessarily a good thing. In most of our hands is a minicomputer, giving us access to food, services, news, and entertainment. We never have to look up to engage in human interaction if we don't choose to. How many hours have each of us wasted on our phones shopping or playing a game or searching for ideas on Pinterest? I know for me, personally, it is probably more than I really want to recognize.

We have to keep evaluating our daily lives and what we are investing our time and attention in. We need to make sure that we are keeping the ground of our heart and spirit fertile and soft. Ready to receive and hear from our God. If you are feeling like God has been distant, you need to check first with what you are doing daily. God never leaves us, we are more likely to wander away from Him.

Several years ago, I use to wait until the end of my day to spend time with God. I was so tired and had used up all my energy. Most of the time when I attempted to read the Word or a devotional at bedtime I couldn't concentrate or fell asleep. I felt so empty on the inside. I made a commitment to get up thirty minutes earlier in the morning so that I could start my day in the Word of God. I won't say that every day is perfect, but there is definitely a difference when I set my eyes on my God before anything else in my day. I have more joy, more peace, and more strength to face the cares of the daily world. Even on a day off from work, I stick to this routine because it grows me from the inside. I want to be fruitful. I don't want to allow all that God has done in my life to be choked out. Everything I have and everything I am is because of the wondrous love He has poured out over me. I want to do whatever I can to remain in Him, to stay close to Him. He is the good in me.

REVIVAL NOT RHETORIC

He knew it was a trick question, and said, "Why are you playing these games with me? Bring me a coin and let me look at it." They handed him one. "This engraving—who does it look like? And whose name is on it?" "Caesar," they said. Jesus said, "Give Caesar what is his and give God what is his." Their mouths hung open, speechless. (Mark 12:15–17 MSG)

True freedom is not found based on enrollment in a particular political party. It is not granted through the process of forming laws and in the way a particular government works. True freedom is found in following the living God, in recognizing the salvation gifted to you via the cross.

The political rhetoric over the past few decades has just intensified. Even when I purposefully try to minimize my exposure to the media, it trickles in because of technology being literally everywhere. I had never really thought much about this exchange between Jesus and the Pharisees with exception that they were trying to incriminate Him in some way. But now, I am realizing that Jesus was letting people know that faith in God and a man-made system, such as governments, are separate. A man-made system is inferior to any design that God intended. A man-made system will be tainted by the world—which means "linked with the flesh and sin." That is just as it has been since the Garden of Eden. It will be the way of things are until the return of Christ and a new heaven and earth are formed.

We don't need more political rhetoric, more man-made promises, and more world systems seeking to serve themselves. We all need more of Jesus. We need a strong and mighty God, who is also full of love, mercy, and compassion. We need to grasp hold of His wisdom and truth and operate in the power and authority to cast down everything that would exalt itself against Him. We need revival. This world system is broken and so many are lost and hurting.

Father God, thank you for Your Word. Thank you for reminding Your children that things of this world are part of a broken existence. Only in You and through You can we be made whole. Father, I declare that men and world systems that attempt to exalt themselves above You will be brought low and fall at Your feet. I prophesy a spirit of repentance in this place. That mankind would hear and see that You are calling them to a better more righteous walk. Your Word declares that You alone are the light of the world—may Your Church shine brightly in this world and break through the darkness attempting to dampen the hope that is from You. I glory in the knowledge that the enemy is defeated and in You there will always remain victory and freedom. I declare that revival is coming. Breakthrough is coming! Help us to see rhetoric for what it is and Your Word alone as truth. Amen.

WAITING YOUR RETURN

And the Lord said, "Simon, Simon! Indeed, Satan has asked for you, that he may sift you as wheat. But I have prayed for you, that your faith should not fail; and when you have returned to Me, strengthen your brethren." (Luke 22:31–32 NKJV)

Jesus Himself has prayed for you. In John 17:20–26, Jesus prays to the Heavenly Father for every single person who comes to believe in Him and confess Him as Savior. You have the power of Christ in you and also advocating for you. We will fall short, we will make mistakes, but we don't have to live from a position of defeat. The One who obtained the victory on the cross, the One who made way for the Holy Spirit to be poured out on all who are born again, is always interceding for us. We have a champion in our corner.

We act as if our Heavenly Father is just waiting to catch us making a mistake so he can reign down a little hellfire on us. That we are so worthless and messed up that He just looks at us and shakes His head. That is a lie that Satan wants you to believe. The first part of this verse states that the enemy wants to separate us from God. His tactics never change. But we have a God that is stronger, mightier, and has the ultimate power and victory in our lives. Look at what Jesus says to Peter at the end of the verse: "when you have returned to me." I love that it's not a question about whether Christ will stay with us or abandon us—it is a question of when will we return to Him. How quickly we see our need to return to the truth, the light, the only source of freedom that matters.

This is a call to get over ourselves. Quit acting like children. Every child falls down, but learns quickly they can get back up and keep moving. We need to recognize that we will have challenges, we might get it wrong, but if we get back up and quickly return to God, He will be waiting with open arms. It isn't about us, but about strengthening those around us. Pointing the way to truth. Pointing the way to hope. Pointing the way to the greatest love we have ever known.

You have the greatest power living inside of you. It is time that we tap into that knowledge and hold fast to our faith and strengthen those around us.

HONOR THROUGH SURRENDER

Even them I will bring to My holy mountain, and make them joyful in My house of prayer. Their burnt offerings and their sacrifices Will be accepted on My altar; For My house shall be called a house of prayer for all nations." (Isaiah 56:7 NKJV)

In chapter 56 of the Book of Isaiah, the Lord is proclaiming that all people will have an opportunity to be connected to Him and be part of His Church family. I love that God is a God for the marginalized. He is for the brokenhearted, the ones that are forgotten, the ones that no one seems to be fighting for. God is fighting for each and every one of them! His Word says that He gathers the outcasts.

What a beautiful image, that anyone who surrenders their heart and life to God through Jesus Christ can have a place of honor in heaven. That every person who remains faithful to the Lord will receive the crown of life. We make this relationship with God the Father so complicated. God again and again reveals that a relationship with Him simply means surrender, and relying on His Word.

It has always been God's plan that every soul should be saved. That no one should be lost. The choice is truly ours alone. He displayed such elaborate love for us and sent His Son to die as a final sacrifice for our sins. Our sin can no longer hold claim to us, when we lay it at the feet of Jesus. We have the ability to live out our lives as sons and daughter of the Living God, no matter where we come from or how broken we believe ourselves to be.

Come to the House of the Lord, find a church that is filled with the Spirit of God. It will be a place where there is love and the anointed Word of God is spoken. Every tongue, every tribe, and every nation is welcome in God's house. Come to the Holy Mountain, and rejoice at the love and tender mercy poured out over all who are lost. The Father will lead you to a place of safety. He will guide you in all truth through His Word and His Spirit. God is so, so good and He has a place for you. Amen.

GRACE THAT IS SUFFICIENT

And He said to me, "My grace is sufficient for you, My strength is made perfect in weakness." (2 Corinthians 12:9 NKJV)

This year, with the help of my husband, I am trying to grow some vegetables on our deck. We chose to grow things there because everything growing on the ground in our area is considered a great source of food for the many deer that wander around. As I have watched some of my plants die and others start to grow, I recognize the frailty of things. Each seed, each plant that could bring forth food is also subject to attack from weather, insects, and other things that could hinder its growth. I have also watched some seedlings that I thought were too weak to make it begin to flourish. I recognize that just because something looks weak or frail doesn't mean it won't make it.

In his letter to the church at Corinth, Paul has been addressing the issue of the church wandering away from their teaching of Jesus Christ. The church has been flooded with many visitors that are sharing words in direct opposition to the Gospel. In this part of the passage, Paul is talking about how he has been inflicted with an infirmity. In his request for healing the response was what we see in verse 9, above.

Americans have a strong sense of national pride, a deep longing for independence and freedom, and many have fought and died for the values many of us get to enjoy. This sense of being weak to exhibit strength is so foreign to us. I believe that, once again, we are being pointed to first seeking God for His wisdom in all things. Waiting on

His leading and timing in the day-to-day. That we become stronger when we rely on His truth and stay close to Him. I am not saying that it is easy, but it is what is required to stay strong in the middle of fierce battles. It is how Jesus had the strength to fulfill God's plan and go to the cross for each of us. He stayed connected to God through His Spirit. When we are facing trials, heartache, and pain that bring us to our knees—God calls to us, "Come to me, my grace is enough to sustain you." Life can be fragile. Just like my seedlings, things attack us and try to devour us, but the God of the universe is with us. He is ministering to you, and will speak strength into your spirit if you will stop trying to fight in your own strength. If you will be still and listen. He will give you supernatural strength and supernatural peace. He really is the only one who can help you stand.

LIVE ABUNDANTLY TODAY

Do not boast about tomorrow, for you do not know what a day may bring forth. (Proverbs 27:1 NKJV)

My husband has a family member who has been critically ill. There has been medical treatments in the way of surgeries and medications provided. The doctors have given their prognosis. We have been interceding in prayer, speaking life, strength, and peace into the situation; it is all we can do from so many miles away.

We all have the certainty of leaving this earthly body at some point. For many people, it is a terrifying thought and they avoid thinking about how quickly time passes here on earth. I used to be one of those people myself. The unknown of death was so frightening to me. Now I understand that to leave this world means to be united with my God for eternity. I have given my heart to Him and understand that it is the death and resurrection of Jesus on the cross that enables me to have eternal life. If you are not sure where you will spend eternity, call out on the name of Jesus at this moment. All who call on the name of Jesus for salvation will be saved.

I also want to challenge you to live abundantly today. I am not saying to spend money like crazy doing whatever pleases you at the moment. I am saying look at each day as a gift. Focus on the blessings that you have right now. Look around you at your family and friends. They are precious and should be treasured. That we have the opportunity to love and be loved is a blessing. Keep your eyes open and your heart tender. People are hurting and feel lost and alone. You may be crossing their path for a divine purpose. Speak hope, speak joy, speak peace, speak compassionately into the lives of those around you. Don't let the day-to-day be mundane. Ask God to reveal to you the miraculous things in each day. Stop taking so much in this life for granted. We have this expectation that life will go smoothly and then crumble when the challenges come. But, if we have this eternal hope and recognize that our strength comes from our Creator, then we can look beyond what we see and feel in the moment of crisis. We can have faith that no matter the outcome, our God is good. His overall plan for each of us is good. It is to unite us with Him in a home that we will never have to leave. It is an eternal life without pain, without sorrow, and without loss. God is good, and His mercy will endure forever and ever. Amen.

KEEPING IT SIMPLE

"Truly I say to you, whoever does not accept and receive and welcome the kingdom of God like a little child [does] shall not in any way enter it [at all]." (Luke 18:17 AMPC)

Driving home from church last night, looking out the passenger window, I saw lots of flashes of lights. Fireflies! Along the edge of the road in the fields and tall grasses were hundreds and hundreds of twinkling little lights. Now, typically, I am not a big fan of insects. I recognize they have a job to do in the world, but I prefer them to stay outside and not come inside near me. However, something inside my spirit is delighted every summer when I see fireflies in the evenings. It brings images of laughter and racing around the yard with a glass jar to catch them and watch them light up the jar before letting them go again. It leads to thoughts of summertime play and times when life was less complicated. I believe the feeling of joy and the memories linked to watching fireflies in the summer nights are a great lesson from God about returning to a simpler time.

There are Scriptures that remind us over and over that God wants to be our complete source and that we can trust Him to be everything we need. Just like a child has faith in their mother and father to help pick them up when they fall down. In 1 Peter 5:7, we are reminded to "cast our cares on him because he cares for us." Jesus told the disciples that "my yoke is easy and my burden is light" (Matthew 11:28–30). We are not meant to try to do everything on our own. That just demonstrates how little trust we have in our Heavenly Father and how little we have come to know Him.

We really do make it complicated. If you are struggling today, and you don't know how you can resolve situations in your life, simply present them to God. It really is as simple as praying: "God, I recognize that I need You to be my source. I don't know where to go from here. I cannot fix or change anything without Your help and Your leading. I need wisdom. Your Word says that I can ask for wisdom, strength, joy, peace, provision, and healing. When we draw close to You and return to You with a surrendered heart, You remain with us. I bring my anxieties, my cares, my needs and lay them at your feet. Help me to not try to pick it all up and take control again. I thank You for the promise that I will clearly hear your voice, your leading and have understanding of where you are guiding me. I thank You for your love and patience as I struggle with keeping it simple. Help me to always have child-like faith. Amen."

ALWAYS SATISFIED

All may drink of the anointing from the abundance of your house. All may drink their fill from the delightful springs of Eden. To know you is to experience a flowing fountain, drinking in your life, springing up to satisfy. In the light of your holiness we receive the light of revelation. (Psalm 36:8–9 TPT)

The oceans of the earth, full of water, will do the opposite of quenching your thirst. The salt content in the water dehydrates the human body. In the middle of the ocean, with all that water surrounding you, you might as well be in the desert. You could drink and drink the water but become thirstier and thirstier.

In this psalm, King David talks of God as a flowing fountain, that to spend time with the Lord is to be satisfied. It makes me envision sitting next to a brook and hearing the gentle flow of the water through the rocks and over the earth. The ground around it is lush and green. Everything that wanders to the bank of the brook finds fresh water to drink. There is that sense of peace and comfort that envelops you and you find yourself at rest.

I love that our God wants us to always be filled with His peace and be at rest. He doesn't want us to experience spiritual dryness. That generally results in each of us trying to overcome obstacles in our own power and we become even more weary and more dry. We allow our flesh and our emotions to rule unchecked. Instead of peace and nourishment, we find ourselves wandering in a dry and barren place.

Each day we have to choose to enter into the Lord's presence, to look to His Word. To fill ourselves up. Everything living is drawn to water to help it survive. Wild animals will search for water to drink. Trees will grow roots that reach towards sources of water. They don't wait for someone to bring water to them or they will die. They search for it on their own. We have to seek the presence of God. We have to go to the source that sustains us. In His Word we have the promise of having our souls satisfied.

Thank you, Lord, Your Word is truly the nourishment my body, my mind, and my spirit need. You are the one who restores my soul. I love that You promise to fill us up to overflowing. I declare that Your Holy Spirit continues to fill up all Your sons and daughters. That we then, being full, can pour out into the world, into the dry places. That we reveal Your goodness and glory in the middle of barren spaces. That we may be a source of life because we carry Your Spirit inside us and are equipped by Your mighty hand to bring the truth to all who are thirsty. Amen.

FIRMLY ESTABLISHED

But the Lord is faithful who will establish you and guard you from the evil one. (2 Thessalonians 3:3 NKJV)

When my husband and I traveled to the West Coast of Florida last year, we saw many new homes under construction. These homes were completely built from concrete blocks and reinforced with steel rods. Then the blocks were filled with more concrete. These buildings are designed to withstand the potential hurricanes and the force of winds that threaten the coast every year. I love that this scripture states that God establishes His people. The word establish means to be "set on a firm or permanent basis."

Think about this promise. Your salvation in Christ cannot be shaken or broken. The promise of the Lord to be your source is permanent. The promise of grace, love, and mercy is yours forever. There is nothing more permanent than the Word of God. It was there in the beginning of all things and it will continue to be long after this world ends. God has declared that His people will live with Him in a new kingdom for all eternity. No plan of the enemy can change what God has established with you through His Word.

Lord God, as always, Your Word just opens my eyes to see how good You are and that I am made strong in my connection to You. I love the picture of You coming alongside of me like a mighty lion in the midst of any battle. Fierce and bold, You will protect me in every storm that comes my way. Stronger than any man-made shelter. Your arms surround and protect me when I need it most. Thank you for Your promises. Thank you for Your Word. Thank you for Your love. You are an amazing Father. You are an awesome God. Amen.

POWER FROM ABOVE

God said to me once and for all, "All the strength and power you need flows from me!" And again I heard it clearly said, "All the love you need is found in me!" (Psalm 62: 11–12 TPT)

Technology has made things so easy to obtain and so readily available. Most of us are basically carrying a minicomputer around with us in our cell phones. We can access anyone we want, anywhere, and at any time. We can order food and have it delivered. We can access news and information from anywhere. We can even entertain ourselves via music, videos, and games on our phones. The very ease of all these things can lead to a false sense of self-sufficiency. They are also the very things that keep us distracted and literally drain all our extra time. Each generation spends more and more time looking at a screen and less time engaged in real interactions.

King David was especially good at staying connected to God. His formative years in the fields watching his father sheep gave him time to learn to draw close to God. He became acquainted with God's power and nature by spending time with Him. That is how David was so clearly able to state the characteristics of God, because he took time to get know Him. We have to purposefully draw close to God. To realize despite all our access to so much in this world, it all comes from His hand. If He created the universe and everything in it, including man, then all we have created He has granted. He gives knowledge and wisdom. He is the source of all things. When we have our focus on the One who created all things, we become less inclined to worship things or ourselves. We recognize that without connecting to Him we will be powerless. We will have less ability to demonstrate love and compassion. We will not be able to impact the world in an eternal way.

Lord, let me never lose sight of You. Interrupt my comfort if You need to get my attention. Interrupt my idleness if You need me to move. Interrupt my complacency if I am not spreading Your truth to the world. You have equipped us to reach further than ever, but we distort the gift and become idle in the work that we were called to accomplish. Forgive me when I lose the vision and restore to me the calling. In Jesus' name. Amen.

EXPOSURE

There is not one person who can hide their thoughts from God, for nothing we do remains a secret, and nothing created is concealed, but everything is exposed and defenseless before his eyes, to whom we must render an account. (Hebrews 4:13 TPT)

I am reminded that when Adam and Eve ate of the tree of knowledge of good and evil, they became aware of their nakedness and tried to hide themselves from God (Genesis 3:7–10). This was the beginning of all mankind being exposed in their mistakes and sin and trying to hide them from God. In Genesis 3:11, God asks, "Who told you that you were naked? Have you eaten from the tree of which I commanded you that you should not eat?" I don't believe that God asked Adam this question because He didn't already know the answer, but to drive home to Adam and Eve that their choice is what changed them and the relationship of trust and obedience with the Lord.

We also recognize the part that the enemy played in the separation of man from God. He created a barrier of sin that was designed to make us feel ashamed and unworthy of God's love. It is still his weapon of choice to attack God's people. We believe the whispered lie that God cannot love us, that we have made too many mistakes and we have fallen too far to receive His forgiveness. Satan is a liar. He is the father of all deception. God so loved you and every man, woman, and child He created, that He sent His own son to die as an atoning sacrifice for our sin. He made a way for all that separation to end. He wants us to go to Him and bring all our mistakes, all our strivings, all our pain, and all our triumphs to Him. He wants us to know that we can be vulnerable to Him. We don't have to feel like we need to defend our mistakes. Just turn from them and run back to our Father's arms. This scripture in Hebrews reminds us that there are no secrets from our Heavenly Father because He is all-seeing and all-knowing. He wants us to go to Him because it is good for us to recognize we never have to face anything, even our mistakes, alone. He wants us to be released from our shame and our need to hide and receive the sweet balm of His forgiveness, His love, and His grace. He wants us to draw closer to Him, learning to lean on Him and look to Him for wisdom and truth in every situation. He wants us to know that we can trust Him to love us even when we fall short, even when we mess everything up. We just have to have a heart ready to return to Him and understand that we recognize we are defenseless without all that He gives to equip us in this life.

Thank you, Lord, that You see me and know me. That I don't have to be ashamed to run back to You when I make mistakes. You made a way for me to receive mercy and grace, again and again. You understood that I would make mistakes as I work to build my faith and knowledge of who You are. I don't have to be afraid of being completely exposed and defenseless with You, because You alone are good and working for my benefit, to bless and prosper me—according to Your Word. I love You and praise You with all thanksgiving! Amen.

DIVORCED OF DISTRACTIONS

Overcome every form of evil as a victorious soldier of Jesus the Anointed One. For every soldier called to active duty must divorce himself from the distractions of this world so that he may fully satisfy the one who chose him. (2 Timothy 2:3–4 TPT)

Unless you live in a remote area, devoid of any type of connection to the world, there is always something going on to foster petitions and protests. People standing up for things they feel need to change. It could be about human rights, environmental issues, or political ideals. In itself, the ability to speak up for the things that matter to us is a valuable freedom that we as US citizens enjoy. However, in this scripture, Paul is writing to Timothy that the distractions of this world may become a source of division to the purposes of God.

In Matthew 6:33, Jesus instructed us to, "Seek first the kingdom of God, and all these things shall be added to you." Our primary calling is to the eternal kingdom of God. We must be careful to not allow the situations of this world to cause division in the Church. Jesus didn't come to earth to support any worldly established system. He came to show us that we have the promise of a new heaven and new earth (Revelation 21:1), and that this world will one day pass away. There will be injustice in this world, and the righteous should always stand for righteousness, but our primary mission is to demonstrate the love of God. Our primary call to arms and our orders are to save the lost. Our duty is to walk in the anointing and speak the things of heaven to come to pass on the earth until we are called home. Any other ideal or cause will become an obstacle to the primary purpose of the Church. We are called to become the royal priesthood (Peter 2:9), and that means laying aside our self- interests and focusing on the eternal things of God's kingdom.

God's children can clearly see the darkness of the world. I do believe we are called to stand and be the light. However, we just need to make sure that our purposes, our use of our voices, truly align with the will and purpose of our God.

Lord, I see the enemy attacking the world on so many sides. I recognize that we are to be stewards of all that You have gifted us with in this world, but I don't want it to overwhelm my voice for the things of the kingdom of God. I don't want it to become a point of division between my brothers and sisters in Christ. You need Your body to be unified and to represent the love and compassion of Jesus Christ in the world. Our purpose needs to be a place where the lost can find You. In the end, only Your kingdom matters because this world will eventually pass away. I am thankful to know that I will be called to a new home and that You have made a place specifically for me. My mission, the calling You have given every son and daughter, is to tell everyone of an eternal home waiting for them. Help me to be that voice, that beacon of hope, above all other things I am passionate about. In Jesus' name. Amen.

WORLDLY TOLERANCE

You have become spiritual adulterers who are having an affair, an unholy relationship with the world. Don't you know that flirting with the world's values places you at odds with God? Whoever chooses to be the world's friend makes himself God's enemy! (James 4:4 TPT)

James was passionate about faith being demonstrated by our actions. Here, he is unequivocally stating that aligning or going along with the values of the world is in direct disobedience to God.

I think this is very powerful message, even more important today. The world is shouting from every corner about tolerance. We should be tolerant of every single person's personal idea of love. We should be tolerant of every person's right to kill their unborn child. We should be tolerant of every person's personal right to speak their mind, regardless of how offensive it might be. We should be tolerant of children's disrespectful behaviors towards adults. We should be tolerant of people manipulating morality to fit their situations. We should be tolerant of mainstream media posting suggestive or blatant sexual content in our living rooms.

The world is shouting, "Tolerance, tolerance!" However, they do not demonstrate any tolerance towards those who are standing for Christian principles as highlighted in God's Word. We cannot change the Word of God. Every man, woman, and child without repentance and salvation is locked in their sin. Romans 3:23 tells us, "For all have sinned and fall short of the glory of God."

In Galatians 5:19, the works of the flesh are pointed out to us and include: "sexual immorality, impurity, sensuality, idolatry, sorcery, enmity, strife, jealousy fits of anger, rivalries, dissensions, division, envy, drunkenness, orgies." We cannot change what God sees as sinful behavior. The Bible is the inspired, life-breathed Word of God, written as His Spirit poured out on those writing it. If we call His Word into question and say that any part of it is false, we are calling all of God's character into question. We cannot have both values that align with the world—what the world cherishes—and the values of a righteous and holy God. Even Jesus told his followers, "No one is good, except the Father" (Mark 10:8). We have to remain connected with God and His Word to understand and follow after His righteousness. We each have to personally examine ourselves and our choices and measure them against the Word of God. We will make mistakes and get it wrong sometimes. But if we continue to press in and to seek forgiveness when we are wrong and we sin against God, He is faithful to forgive and to give us guidance for the future. We cannot become tolerant as the world is demanding. We cannot let our guard down and allow our eyes to be shielded from the truth in God's Word. If the world loves it, it should be a sign to us to check in on what God says about it. He does not vary of shift like a shadow.

SWEET SONGS FOR OUR SOULS

I will sing my song to the Lord as long as I live! Every day I will sing my praises to God. May you be pleased with every sweet thought I have about you, for you are the source of my joy and gladness. (Psalm 104:33–34 TPT)

Working in a hospital, I am reminded every day about what can be taken away from people. I provide therapy to people who have had life-altering illnesses. They are often overwhelmed with fear, depression, or grief at the change and loss, and even angered by their experience. All of these things are perfectly understandable in the multitude of these situations and conditions. However, I don't believe it is healthy to stay in this cycle of emotions. If we don't find something to be thankful about, these very valid feelings in the moment can turn into a root of bitterness. Maybe some of you can recall a friend or loved one where this has happened. They are angry at what has happened and the loss of independence and sense of well-being they had, and they talk about it all the time. In fact, it is all they can talk about. Even if you point out something good, they quickly tell you everything that is not good about their lives.

I am not trying to minimize how hard it must be for them. I believe that many of these situations are very difficult. That is why I am so grateful to have a Heavenly Father to turn to. It is so important when we walk through difficult times to be able to see that God is for us and working for our good. It is important to recall how blessed we really are. Keeping a song of worship in our hearts and minds is not only providing glory to God, but it is fuel for our souls so that we can be strong in difficult situations. In times when I feel overwhelmed, I put worship music on. If I am having a difficult time thinking of how to align my voice and my words with God's Word, worship music is a perfect solution. So many lyrics in Christian music come directly from the Bible.

This world is hard and we will have adversity for as long as we remain here. But that is not the end of the story. Our God has not just overcome the world, but He has also provided us a source of strength in His Word and through the power of His Spirit inside of us. When we sing praises to His name, it fills us and strengthens our spirit. It provides breakthrough and freedom from the things in this world that try to keep us chained. Sing to Him in every season, for He will be your source of joy and gladness! Amen.

REMEMBERING THE GOD OF MIRACLES

Yet I could never forget all your miracles, my God, as I remember all your wonders of old. I ponder all you've done, Lord, musing on all your miracles. It's here in your presence, in your sanctuary, where I learn more of your ways, for holiness is revealed in everything you do. Lord, you're the one and only, the great and glorious God! (Psalm 77:11–13 TPT)

In the verses that came before this, King David is in a situation where he is calling out for God to help him. In verse 3, he states, "As I thought of you I moaned, 'God where are you?'" David clearly felt turmoil in waiting for God in whatever situation he was facing. God recognizes that sometimes the events of our life will make us feel lost and alone. It might make us cry out in despair. I believe talking to God about however we are feeling is perfectly okay. He is a father and wants His children to come to Him. He wants our burdens, the things that lay heavy on our hearts.

It is important to understand that King David does not remain in despair and distress as in these verses above, he begins to remind himself of who God really is. David had witnessed the glory of God in his life several times before becoming king. God was with him as he was a shepherd watching his father's flocks. He was with David as he faced a Philistine giant and defeated him. David also recounted the deliverance of the Israelites out of the hands of slavery in Egypt. He knew that his God was mighty and had worked many wonders and miracles. He recognized that God is faithful and never-changing. That the love of God for the children of Israel was unbreakable.

Maybe you are going through a difficult time in your life right now. Maybe you are feeling like King David at the beginning of the psalm and are wondering where God is. That is perfectly okay, but you cannot stay in the valley of despair. You need to remember the God of miracles in your life. You need to be purposeful in recounting the blessings you have. The prior storms He has silenced and the seas He has parted for your favor. You have to call up the blessings and the promises. The Holy Spirit will help guide you when you don't know what to say, or you can simply start with, "God, I know You are good and You want good things for my life. I have seen the blessings come from Your outstretched hand. You have always been faithful. When I had nothing, You clothed me and gave me food to eat. When I felt lost, You took my hand and led me. When I felt hopeless, You spoke Your love for me into my heart, my mind, and my spirit. You never forsake Your children. The enemy wants me to believe You are finished with me, but You will never leave me. You walk with us until You call us home. You alone are good, and You always show up on time. I will not forget Your miracles in my life. Amen."

BE STRENGTHENED

So be made strong even in your weakness by lifting up your tired hands in prayer and worship. And strengthen your weak knees, for as you keep walking forward on God's paths all your stumbling ways will be divinely healed! (Hebrews 12:12–13 TPT)

So, the alarm clock rings on Monday morning and I think to myself, "I just don't want to get up today, I am not ready, I am too tired." I reluctantly roll out of bed and begin the morning routine. Anyone else out there who can sympathize with my moment?

We all feel tired at times, worn out, and lacking strength. I love this verse because it directly points to how we can be strengthened from the inside out. This morning I talked to my Father. I told Him that I am feeling worn by my daily interactions with the world, but in His Word and in His presence I will be renewed. His Word tells us that His mercies are new every morning, and that He gives a daily supply of grace. We all have heard these two verses, but do we turn to Him in our weakness? Or do we hide in shame? I don't believe it surprises our Heavenly Father that we have a desperate need for His supply. That is the way He designed us, that we would recognize our need for His divine strength and power to walk daily in this life. That we would stay connected to our source for everything we would ever need.

Thank you, Father, that you are greatly aware of all my needs. That You understand that, unless I remain connected to You, the life-giving power that flows from Your Spirit will run dry. I don't want to be empty and dry. I want the source of living water that keeps my cup overflowing. So I run to You. I say that I am weak, but with You I am made strong. I say that I can stand up and run and not grow weary. You will keep my feet secure on the path as I climb to new destinations. You take me by the hand and hold me steady, keeping me on a solid foundation. I love Your tender mercies that are available to me each morning. Forgive me when I forget to look to You first and try to rely on my own strength. It quickly is depleted because it is just not the way You designed us to operate. I will stay connected to the vine so that I can grow and yield the spiritual fruit needed for Your Church and those that desperately need You. Thank you for the Word that always turns me back to You. Without it I would be lost. I glorify You and give You endless praise. You, my Father, are worthy of it all. Amen.

CONSTANT AND ENDLESS LOVE

By your mighty power I can walk through any devastation and you will keep me alive, reviving me. Your power set me free from the hatred of my enemies. You keep every promise you've ever made to me! Since your love for me is constant and endless, I ask you, Lord, to finish every good thing that you've begun in me! (Psalm 138:7–8 TPT)

I don't know where you are right now or what you are going through. My God and Father, He knows. I want you to pull this into your spirit right now and hold onto it tightly with both hands. If God was not going to be faithful and finish what He started in you, then He never would have watched His only son beaten, cursed, and crucified for you. If your current situation is too big for God to handle, then how did He manage the salvation for every soul who needs it? How did He make a way for every burden, every chain, every sin to be washed away and to be forgotten for each of us? If He can't handle your financial need, or your medical need, or your family need?

Stop making the God who created all things, who spoke the galaxy into motion, and who lovingly formed you in the womb too small to fix what's happening in your life this very instant! Take your eyes off the situation and start looking at the power and might of your God and Father! Take a minute to reflect on other situations He was able to turn around in your life. We all have stories about how God pulled us through. We have to stop coming up to the next mountain in life and thinking, "It's too big, it's never going to move." Instead, look behind you at the last mountain that has been laid low to the valley, and the one before that, and the one before that one! Stand up! Remember who your God is! He is the beginning and the end and in Him there is no turning. If He said He will do it, then just BELIEVE.

You, Father God, are mighty and powerful. My mind cannot fully understand the way You always arrive right on time. How with just one word you can calm the most powerful storm or how You can make the largest mountains become small. I have seen Your wonder-working hand in my life time and again. Forgive me when I fix my eyes on the problem, instead of the God who promises to supply for me in every single circumstance. You are so faithful, even when I am not. Even when I forget to recount the millions of blessings, the countless miracles, I have seen come to pass in my life. I trust You to finish the work Your hands have set in motion. I can only sing praise to Your name. You are a good, good Father. I love You, Lord. Thank you for Your grace and mercies that appear to me every day. Amen.

REFRESHED BY THE WATER OF LIFE

The [Holy] Spirit and the bride (the church, the true Christians) say, Come! And let him who is listening say, Come! And let everyone come who is thirsty [who is painfully conscious of his need of those things by which the soul is refreshed, supported, and strengthened]; and whoever [earnestly] desires to do it, let him come, take, appropriate, and drink the water of Life without cost. (Revelation 22:17 AMPC)

We have the beauty of the Blue Ridge Mountains that surround us where we live. A few years ago, my husband and I took a day in early spring and went for a hike in an area along the Blue Ridge called Apple Orchard Falls. True to its name, there were beautiful paths that wound us around a stream that turned into some pretty impressive falls. The steady sound of the flow of the rushing water over the rocks and the spray of the water in the sunlight is a mesmerizing sight. The flow of this water is constant, it never dries up, and it never stops.

This is the same with what the Holy Spirit has for each believer. The Spirit will fill you with the water of Life. This is the power, the anointing, that God has for each of us to not just sustain us, but to fill us to overflowing. He wants us to have an abundance of Him and every gift that comes along with being the body, the temple, of the Living God. That means fullness of health, fullness of joy, fullness of peace, fullness of provision, fullness of faith, fullness of compassion, fullness of patience, fullness of gentleness, fullness of love, and fullness of wisdom. Our God promises that we can access all that He has for us and not just be filled, but to be abundantly overflowing with all of these things! Like a mighty, roaring waterfall that cannot stop!

If we feel like we are lacking these things, it is not because God has pulled away. He is steady and constant. I believe it is because we are not going to the source, the Holy Spirit, to fill up. This scripture states that we become "painfully conscious of our need." If you feel dry today, maybe you just need this reminder to DRINK! Go to the Holy Spirit and be "refreshed, supported and strengthened." We are never without God's resources, we just forget that we need to renew our supply!

Thank you, Father! Each day, as I turn to Your Word, I am shown wisdom and Your great provision for my life. I confess that I have been feeling empty, but I understand that it is that I have not tapped into Your life-giving water. You have been speaking to me, but I haven't stopped to listen. Thank you for Your patience with me as I continue to stumble and fall. You are always ready to pick me up and, with tender mercy, guide me to Your wisdom and truth. Right now, God, I am stilling my constant motion and I am saying I am thirsty. I will sit at Your feet and drink the cup You have poured out for me. I want all that You have for me. I desperately need it. You are the only thing that truly satisfies. Thank you, Lord! Amen.

SEEKING A REMEDY

Why should you be stricken and punished any more [since it brings no correction]? You will revolt more and more. The whole head is sick, and the whole heart is faint (feeble, sick and nauseated). From the sole of the foot even to the head there is no soundness or health in [the nation's body]—but wounds and bruised and fresh and bleeding stripes; they have not been pressed out and closed up or bound up or softened with oil. [No one has troubled to seek a remedy]. (Isaiah 1:5–6 AMPC)

This scripture reminds me of very young children at a family gathering. There are lots of loud noise and activity and the children play and play and play. They get to a point of tiredness and begin to get fussy and upset, but won't be comforted. They struggle against their parents trying to swaddle them and provide the sweet solace they need. They cry and become even more agitated, just not willing to give in to the much-needed rest their tired little bodies need. The parents know that the child just needs sleep, but until the child can settle down, the remedy (sleep) cannot take place.

I believe this scripture is a picture of our nation in these days. We are full of wounds caused by our own sinful nature. There is a cure, but we have not chosen to seek a remedy. Instead, like that young child, we just fight against the One who wants to bring us comfort. The One who took on stripes and was wounded so that we can be healed. We reject the comfort and the solution for our own sin. We wonder why we have become so weak, so fragile. I see that rebellious spirit more and more all around me. People angrily shouting about their personal rights and liberties, people shouting in hatred at one another. People living in fear and despair.

God is speaking to each of us. He says, "Come, I have the balm for your wounds. I am the One who can bind up the brokenhearted. I am the One who heals, and I am the One who can save you. Nothing else offered in this world will do it. All you have to do is seek Me. Seek Me and I can be found. I Am the Remedy. I am the solution to your sin problem. It is a problem. It is a poison that you continue to drink like milk. All the while you become more sick, for sin over time poisons the whole body and leads to death. I will bring soundness of mind and health to your weary souls. I am the Only way, there is no other way for complete freedom, complete healing, and complete restoration. Come seeking the Remedy, for I have it."

Amen.

LIBERTY IN OBEDIENCE

I will keep Your law continually, forever and ever [hearing, receiving, loving, and obeying it]. And I will walk at liberty and at ease, for I have sought and inquired for [and desperately required] Your precepts. (Psalm 119:44–45 AMPC)

Often, when speaking of freedom, we think of battles fought, valor, and sacrifice. We think of liberty in our own human and earthly perspective. Freedom to choose for ourselves what is right and wrong. We deceive ourselves into thinking we know best for ourselves. That our independence is our own. That it wasn't bought with the blood and sacrifice of Jesus Christ. This scripture is pointing to a greater type of freedom. It is the freedom from the sin that binds our spirits.

Why does obedience to God have such a negative connotation? The Pharisees and Sadducees used the law to fulfill their own personal agendas. To increase their own personal power and control. They took what God created to point the children of Israel to walk in obedience and trust of the great I Am and distorted it for personal gain. Legalism could never really make a way for all mankind to have access to God. In itself, it was part of a covenant between God and the Jewish people, leaving the Gentiles with no real hope. It was only in the sacrifice of God's only son that our separation from a Holy God could be resolved for all eternity. Our obedience comes as an act of receiving and being thankful for what we have received. Look at the first verse in this psalm. I love the Amplified translation because it walks us through the process of following God's Word. First, hearing it. Getting into the Word every day. Next, receiving it. Having a teachable spirit and allowing God, who so lovingly formed you, transform you into all He created you to be. Then, loving it. We have to get to that place that we love God's Word and His ways more than anything else. Finally, obeying it. I really believe loving God's Word and obeying it flow together in unison. If we love God's Word and recognize that He has designed everything to transform us into the likeness of Christ, we will want to be obedient. We will want to go to God first for our answers in life. We will want the peace and freedom of having His wisdom in every area.

In this world system, liberty and obedience appear to be in direct opposition to each other. That is just like God to take two concepts that seem unrelated and bind them together. I have been disobedient to God on many occasions. I can speak from experience that what ruled me in those situations was selfishness and then stress. Most often, instead of the results I wanted, my choices only led to brokenness and shame. The wonderful thing about God and His offer of liberty through obedience is that He doesn't limit our opportunities to choose His way first. If we fall short, we can ask for forgiveness and He helps us back up and gives us opportunities to walk in obedience with Him.

THE COST OF UNBELIEF

And they took offense at Him [they were repelled and hindered from acknowledging His authority, and caused to stumble]. But Jesus said to them, "A prophet is not without honor except in his own country and in his own house." And He did not do many works of power there, because of their unbelief (their lack of faith in the divine mission of Jesus). (Matthew 13:57–58 AMPC)

Ever experienced a family situation where you were praying for a family member for a particular outcome, but it didn't come to pass? It wasn't your faith that was weak, but perhaps it was that particular person's unbelief. We, as God's children, often want our family and friends to have the blessings and promises of God in their lives. We want them to be provided for, and healed, and restored. We want to see them free from the chains of addictions, mental illnesses, and broken relationships. Those are things we know that as children of God we have access to. However, if the family you are praying for does not believe in the salvation and power of Jesus, then our prayers may be ineffective. This scripture states that Jesus, God's only son, full of power and the anointing of God, was unable to do many works in His hometown of Nazareth because of the unbelief there.

Of course we want our families and friends to have their needs met, and our hearts break with compassion at the challenges they are facing. However, maybe instead of just praying for their current situation, we should be declaring boldly that their hearts of stone would become flesh that they may see their desperate need for the God that could provide for all their needs. Maybe we should be praying for their spirit to be filled with repentance, and for their eyes to be opened to their own brokenness, because of the sin of man that keeps us separate from a Holy God. Maybe we should be praying for their unbelief to be washed away through the redeeming power of the blood of Christ and replaced with a new found faith. Maybe we should be praying for them to acknowledge the authority and power of our awesome God.

Oftentimes, I know I am praying for one outcome for my family, but I hear them speaking words in direct opposition to what I am praying to God. That is because without understanding and faith, they will speak what the world speaks. They will speak without hope and without faith. If I want to see a move of God in their lives, then perhaps I need to redirect my prayers regarding their hearts, minds, and spirits—not just their current need.

Thank you, Lord, for this reminder about how costly unbelief can be. You want everyone to know You, but You do not force them to believe. If only they recognized that You are for them and not against them. Forgive me for my limited understanding of how to pray for the needs of my family and thank You for this fresh revelation. I declare that their hearts will be changed and their eyes will be opened to who You are. I declare that they will have an experience that will bring them to their knees before the One that can offer salvation. Through Your redeeming, their lives will be made whole again. In the name of Jesus! Amen.

SHOWERING IN HIS WORD

Jesus said, "If you've had a bath in the morning, you only need your feet washed now and then you're clean from head to toe. My concern, you understand, is holiness, not hygiene. So now you're clean. But not every one of you." (John 13:10 MSG)

This is the passage in John 13, where Jesus washes the disciples feet before they share a meal together. There is so much knowledge in this passage, but today I just want to focus on this one verse. I love the way the Message Bible points out that Jesus wants His friends to be aware that His primary concern for them is the condition of their spirit. He is concerned about the inside of them, not their outward cleanliness.

We all recognize the need to take a shower, and most of us in America, consumed with our appearance, take at least one shower a day. We have an understanding that just being up and moving around in the world, we end up with dirt on our bodies. Why do we have such a difficult time recognizing the dirt that can collect in our spirits if we don't get washed daily by the Word? In Psalm 121, the psalmist reminds himself that his hope is in the Lord. How do we get to know who God is if we don't look to the Bible to learn about Him? Every time I open the book, I find new scriptures jumping off the page at me, revealing new things that I didn't have a clear understanding of before.

I go out of my home every morning and go to a job where I am constantly in direct connection with people who have no idea who God is and the hope He has to offer them. Even when I am purposefully filling my heart and mind with God's Word, I have to be diligent to tap into what I have learned when constantly bombarded with the wisdom of the world. There are times in this life that, if I only got fed the Word of God twice a week, I would have fallen into complete despair. I would not have been prepared to stand on the truth. Psalm 119:11 states, "Your Word I have hidden in my heart, that I might not sin against you." We have to keep planting the Word of God inside ourselves. We cannot expect that if we only get the Word once or twice a week at church, that we receive enough truth to keep ourselves filled up. Imagine how dirty our body would be if we only showered one time every week. That is how our spirit gets when we think we can neglect filling it with the powerful cleansing flow of God's Word. It not only refreshes our spirit but keeps us filled up with His power and anointing, so that we are stronger than we would be on our own.

Lord, I hear You. Your children need to stay connected to Your Word. We need to jump into the Word and allow its cleansing work to wash the dirt of the world out of our spirits, our hearts, and our minds. Every day Your Word is revealing new things to me. I am blessed by Your promises to provide for every aspect of my life, but mostly that You are concerned with my holiness and not my hygiene. I can't clean up my outside enough to be worthy of Your love. It's my inside that You wash white as snow. That my soul would no longer have a spot or blemish, because I am washed clean by Your outpouring. Thank you, Jesus! Thank you, Lord! You are so good to me! Amen.

BREAKING FREE

His own iniquities entrap the wicked man, and he is caught in the cords of his sin. He shall die for lack of instruction, and in the greatness of his folly he shall go astray. (Proverbs 5:22–23 NKJV)

Ever made the same mistake over and over again? Last week, I was trying to organize my master bathroom and declutter the countertop. I looked under my sink and realized that I have fallen for every advertisement about hair products that has been created. As I dragged shampoos, conditioners, and creams out from under my sink barely used, I realized that I had made the same mistake again and again. I believed in that magic product that would instantaneously make my hair behave in all weather conditions. The unused products under my sink spoke a very different truth.

This is a very basic example of how we can deceive ourselves into making the same poor choices and decisions again and again. For many people, they deceive themselves into believing they don't have an addiction, or an anger issue, or issues with sexual immorality, or issues with lying. It doesn't matter what we deceive ourselves about, but it does matter what the end result will be. If we do not seek instruction and wisdom for our decisions in this life, we will end up making mistakes. Some mistakes might be minor, and some mistakes can be more costly. Choices about alcohol, drugs, and gambling can lead to loss of family and friends. All of a sudden we will be utterly alone and without the people in our lives that matter the most. We might not figure that out until it's too late. Maybe in attempting to find our value in the eyes of another person, we find ourselves in bad relationship after bad relationship. All of a sudden, instead of feeling loved, we believe the lie that we are worthless.

Hearing the Word of God in our lives is the way we break free from bad decisions. Understanding that God's ways and choices for us are far better than we can ever think leads us to a life that is fulfilling. We have to first open our hearts to Him and realize that without Him we will make decisions in the moment, based on the desires that feed our instant gratification. Filling our minds with His Word gives us insight to look at things from a more eternal perspective. We can be healed of our brokenness and our feelings of not being worthy if we look to the One who formed us and designed us with a plan and purpose in mind. When we feel that love that cannot be taken away from our Heavenly Father, we start to make better decisions and healthier lifestyle choices. No, it doesn't happen overnight for everyone, but it does happen. We can break free from our cycle of bad decisions. We just have to surrender to the One who died on the cross for us.

THE DANGER OF COMPLACENCY

I know all that you do, and I know that you are neither frozen in apathy nor fervent with passion. How I wish you were either one or the other! But because you are neither cold nor hot, but lukewarm, I am about to spit you from my mouth. (Revelation 3:15–16 TPT)

I am a coffee drinker. Every morning, I have one cup of coffee while I read the Word of God and another as I get ready for work. Some mornings when I am writing an entry for these devotionals, I will start my second cup of coffee. For me, coffee has to be hot. If I neglect drinking my coffee for any reason and it gets tepid I no longer want it. This scripture in Revelation was to the church at Laodicea, where the people began to value God less because they felt they were self-sufficient. They began to value material security far more than their relationship with God. It is reminiscent of the Israelites' relationship with God. During times their needs were met and they were not in need, they began to fall away from God and serve other gods and idols in the lands they were living in.

Growing complacent in your relationship with God doesn't happen overnight. It is a gradual thing, a slippery slope, where you lose footing in one area and take a step back. Then suddenly you take another and another. We allow other things to become more important than God. It is very easy to make excuses that we don't have time. We have more and more distractions every day provided by the limitless access to technology.

It's strange to think that God would rather people be cold to Him than lukewarm. I liken it to having that one friendship where the person only reaches out to you when they are in need. When everything is going fine in their life, you don't hear from them. Weeks or months could go by until that one situation where they find they need your help. That type of friendship doesn't usually last, because friendships require mutual respect from one another. They require investment and time. They require understanding that each person has needs. For God, He desires us to recognize that He is not a magician or a magic lamp. Just make a request of Him when we have an urgent need, throw up a quick prayer, and go back to what we were doing to entertain ourselves. We need to recognize that He is the source of all we need, not just that He provides for all our needs. When we tap into all He has for us we find more than someone who can provide that quick fix in one situation after another. God wants to be our one desire. Greater than any need we have, that we long to spend time with Him first.

LOSING ENDURANCE

Therefore do not cast away your confidence, which has great reward. For you need of endurance, so that after you have done the will of God, you may receive the promise: (Romans 10:35–36 NKJV)

It has been about eight months since my husband and I were off from work for our one-week vacation. I feel myself quite literally dragging myself into my days at work. We have a vacation scheduled in about a month, and I am doing all I can to hold on until then. My fatigue starts to leak out in negative ways now and again. I lose my patience with things at work a little easier than normal. I am not proud to say it, but some days I feel like I am giving less than one-hundred-percent effort. Anyone else out there ever experienced this feeling when time off has been too long ago?

The Lord understands us better than we understand ourselves sometimes. He recognizes our frailty and our need for rest. He is the creator of the Sabbath, which was a day intended to give His people rest on a weekly basis. Our Heavenly Father wanted His people to have time to rest and to spend time with Him.

This scripture is a great reminder that our spirit needs nurturing as well. We have to build and sustain our endurance and our faith. It is something that we have to put effort into or we will just run dry. We have all felt spiritually empty before. We overpromised our commitments to serve and we overplanned and committed all the other areas of our lives as well. We didn't take time to be fed or to rest. Quite quickly we lost our enjoyment for the things that we were excited to do and we lost our connection with the One who helps us maintain our spiritual strength and peace. The wonderful thing about our faith and our endurance is that we know who we can run to for the provision we need. God has all I need to restore my strength and refill my cup. In fact, He promises to renew His mercies, His grace, and give me enough for each and every day. It is my job to take inventory of what I need on a daily basis and then plan accordingly. If I am going through an extra difficult time in my life, then perhaps it requires a little extra time spent with God: in worship, in prayer, in just staying close and connected.

Thank you, Lord, that You have all I need. You encourage Your children to stay connected so that we will stay built up in faith and endurance. You realize that not every season brings the same level of testing, but You provide for each season perfectly. Thank you for this reminder that I need to press into You to maintain my confidence at all times. On my own, I become tired and I begin to lose heart because I am trying to operate in my own sufficiency which will never be enough in the spiritual battles that take place. You are the Champion in every battle. I love You, Lord, You are a faithful Provider for me. Amen.

THE PROMISE OF RESTORATION

Return to the stronghold [of security and prosperity], you prisoners of hope; even today I declare that I will restore double your former prosperity to you. (Zechariah 9:12 AMPC)

The Spirit of God is saying, "You have been waiting. You have been looking around and keeping your eyes fixed on what has been broken and lost for too long. You forget that I do not measure time the same as you. That in every situation that unfolds I am seeing the end from the beginning. My vantage point allows me to work things for your greatest growth and for your greatest blessing. Keep trusting in me to be your strong tower. The place you maintain shelter. I will give you daily strength, I will give you peace no matter the circumstances. I will be your source of provision in every moment of every day, if you allow me. In my perfect timing, just as I promised the former generations, I will multiply all that was taken from you. You just need to trust me. I am the God that never fails. I am the God who never forgets His promises to His children. I am the God who is faithful and true even when my children are not. I am the Great I Am, I was, I am, and I forever will be. I have more for you. Return to Me in hope and I will do all I have promised. You will see My restoration in your life. You will see me working for your good. Just stay close."

Thank you, Lord, for this word of encouragement through Your Spirit. It is a word that many need to hear. Keep fanning the fire of faith and hope in Your sons and daughters all over the world. Keep Your Spirit of fire burning within them that their light might grow brighter in an ever-darkening world. Thank you for always letting us hear from You when we stop and listen. We need to draw close and stay connected to You more now than ever before. I praise You that You never stop equipping us, growing us, and planting Your Word deep in our spirits that we may be strengthened in all seasons. I love You, Abba. I am so thankful for my Father's everlasting love. Amen.

NO SHADES OF GRAY

Whoever is of God listens to God. [Those who belong to God hear the words of God.] This is the reason that you do not listen [to those words, to Me]: because you are not of God or in harmony with Him. (John 8:47 AMPC)

Early this week, I was speaking to someone about their church. Their response or the things they were saying were relatively negative. This person was older and basically stated that the worship was too loud, too different, and the pastor too young. He alluded to needing to get the "pastor under control." I attempted to point out the call to raise up new generations in the faith, but quickly realized that I was not going to be able to change this person's perspective.

Earlier in this passage of scripture in the Book of John, Jesus is speaking to the Pharisees, who want to get Jesus under control because they do not like how popular He is becoming with the Jewish people. They do not understand His methods of teaching or what He is going to accomplish during His time of ministry. They only see with their eyes, and their hearts have long grown cold to the voice of their Heavenly Father. They are filled with religious rituals and very little faith. In verses 43 and 44, Jesus tells them their ears are shut and their eyes are closed to the truth and that they are one with Satan because they only believe his lies.

Jesus is not giving the Jewish people any way to negotiate. He basically states: "Believe Me and the truth which I bring from God or you belong to the world and to the devil." This truth is still the same today. We want to debate God's Word, and we set ourselves up in positions of knowledge. We give ourselves positions of honor against the One who formed all things, is all-knowing, and maintains all power and authority. We forget that we were formed from dust and will return to dust. We are all subject to the very One who created all things. His Word is truth and things that do not align with the Word of God are meant to deceive us.

We need to become so closely connected to God's Word that we no longer see shades of gray. We see God's Word as truth and all other interpretations or justifications as a lie. We need to examine ourselves daily and ensure that we align our thoughts, our actions, and our words with God's Word. All other things in us bring about division and break the anointing and power of God in the Church. We begin to believe there is only one generation. Instead, we need to see there are generations to come that will need to rise up in the Church and carry the purpose of God forward to reach the lost of this world. We need to ensure that we are not watering down the Word of God. There is no room for shadows. There is light and darkness. There is the Word of God and there are the lies of this world. Freedom in Jesus or sin and death without Him.

THE GOOD SHEPHERD

He himself carried our sins in his body on the cross so that would be dead to sin and live for righteousness. Our instant healing flowed from his wounding. You were like sheep that continually wandered away, but now you have returned to the true Shepherd of your lives—the kind Guardian who lovingly watches over your souls. (1 Peter 2:24–25 TPT)

There are so many verses in the Bible that describe God and Jesus Christ as shepherds watching over us (sheep). The only protection sheep have from predators is to stay grouped together in the flock. Predators will go after the ones that cannot keep up with the flock when attacked. The young or the old and infirm will often fall prey to a predator because they cannot keep up with the group during an attack. The shepherd was a vital part of keeping livestock from being killed off by prey. The shepherd's job was not only to keep the herd moving to where they could find food and water, but to protect them from potential attacks.

I love the picture of the Lord lovingly watching over our souls. We are told we live in a world where we will be under attack. We have an enemy that wants to basically kill and destroy us. In our own strength, we would be like sheep. Easily chased down and powerless to stop a predator. However, as children of God, we are not alone. We are connected to the Good Shepherd. Our Shepherd leads us to safety, He protects our souls. We just need to follow the sound of His voice. We need to follow His leading. He is our constant guide. My pastor is always reminding us that we need to practice listening to the Holy Spirit every day and in every day circumstances, so that we will know what to do in a time of distress. We have to practice listening for the voice of our God. If we do not understand how to do this in a daily way when things are going along as expected, we definitely will not be able to do it when fear is trying to grip us.

Practice today. Ask God to speak to you today. Listen for His voice in your spirit. You will know it is Him because He speaks and it always lines up with His Word. He speaks with tender mercy and loving-kindness. He speaks with conviction, but not condemnation. He speaks of repentance and forgiveness. He speaks promises of healing, favor, and blessings. He speaks His joy and strength into your spirit. He has so many wonderful things to say and reveal to you. Take time today to sit with Him. Amen.

YOUR VOICE MATTERS

All you lovers of God who want to please him, come and listen, and I'll tell you what he did for me. I cried aloud to him with all my heart and he answered me! Now my mouth overflows with the highest praise. (Psalm 66:16–17 TPT)

Recently, I had the sweetest message from my youngest brother, who thanked me for "being His voice for our generation." I have been praying for my family to come to know God and to recognize His saving grace, and all He is able to do in their lives. This past year, I have been so privileged to watch my youngest brother give his heart to God and begin that wonderful journey of drawing close to Him. I am so thankful to God to get to bear witness and be a part of this journey in my brother's life. I know that it will have generational impact because it will impact his children and his children's children. God's Word is faithful to a thousand generations!

Maybe you are in that place of doubt, after years of prayers for family and people you love. You are wondering how God can turn things around? You believe that all the seeds of truth you have been planting have fallen on unfertile ground. I want to remind you today that you serve a powerful and faithful God. He loves every person that has walked on this earth, and has purposed salvation for them, just as much as for you and I. All things are possible with God. I have been a born-again Christian for more than twenty years and have been praying for my family in all that time. God is never late. He still answers prayers. Don't give up. What the people in your life hear you speak is vital. Don't let them see you lose hope just because you have waited longer than you expected. Don't give up on God. He didn't give up on you. He sent His Son and gave Him up to die on the cross for you and every single person you know and love. You never know what word you may speak to cause that Holy Spirit fire to ignite in the heart of another. Your voice matters. God is listening and He is always working.

Heavenly Father, I lift my voice in adoration and exalt Your name! You are faithful even when I am not. Thank you for the way You show up on time. I am blessed to get to see the work of Your hands in my brother's life and cannot wait to see the ripple effect that will manifest for generations to come! I know that he will get an opportunity to praise and glorify You and that others will hear of all You have done! I will not be silent about what You have done in my life. How You took a lost child, searching for a place to be safe and provided shelter. How You took the destruction and ashes that I created in my own life, from my own sinful mistakes, and forgave me, redeemed me, and restored my life. I have joy that can never be stolen from me. I have everlasting peace in any trial. I have the Holy Spirit guiding me in all truth. I am chosen and I am loved. You are such an amazing Father! My praise will never be enough for all You have done for me. I love You, Lord! I love You. Amen.

A CALL TO BE CHRIST-LIKE

Therefore you shall be perfect, just as your Father in heaven is perfect. (Matthew 5:48 NKJV)

You, therefore, must be perfect [growing into complete maturity of godliness in mind and character, having reached the proper height of virtue and integrity], as your Heavenly Father is perfect. (Matthew 5:48 AMP)

This is the last verse in the fifth chapter of the Book of Matthew. Jesus has been teaching that His desire for people is to love and this is beyond what they had been taught by the law. That loving means even loving enemies and those that persecuted them. Returning love for hatred. Returning blessings for curses. Seeing beyond the sin into the brokenness of mankind, a people who desperately need a Savior.

As I meditate on this verse today, I am reminded how often I fail at being Christlike. If we examine our hearts, I think we all will see a need to love deeper, to judge less, and to pray for the lost even more. I wonder how many times, instead of encouragement, my family has felt my condemnation for not receiving the Word of God or accepting His gift of salvation? I wonder if my own personal agenda has been a barrier to what God purposed for each of them? I wonder if my actions, words, and foolishness have been the ocean that separates them from the love of God? I want to be better. I want to do better. I want people to recognize that I am filled to the uttermost with the love and compassion of Christ. This world needs repentance and salvation, but we cannot shout damnation at them to get them to change. Fear of eternal separation from God doesn't mean anything to someone who hasn't first discovered the Lord. Jesus demonstrated to us through His ministry that love is the greatest weapon we have against sin. That people need to understand that His love has no boundaries. It is absolute once we come to Him seeking forgiveness and salvation.

Lord, as I examine my heart today, I ask for forgiveness where my own agenda and emotions have been a barrier to others in reaching You. I know that my own judgments have resulted in those seeing You differently than who You really are. You are love. You are boundless, everlasting love. You offer grace upon grace to anyone who runs to Your open arms. Let my arms be open wide as well. That all those who need You see Your Church as a place of refuge and safety when seeking to find You. A place of hope, peace, and joy. A place where they can find the change they have been longing for in their lives. Remind us of our own journeys to keep our own walk to salvation fresh in our spirits. That we might live each day as the wonderful gift it really is. Take out anything that displeases You and transform me into the image of Your Son, Jesus Christ. Amen.

SPIRITUAL DEPOSIT

These tents we now live in are like a heavy burden, and we groan. But we don't do this just because we want to leave these bodies that will die. It is because we want to change them for bodies that will never die. God is the one who makes all this possible. He has given us his Spirit to make us certain he will do it. So always be cheerful. (2 Corinthians 5:4–6 CEV)

Working in a hospital, I see people whose tents are in various states. I see the effects of time on their bodies. I see how sickness and disease are always attacking our earthly vessels. Many voice their feelings of fear. Many voice their frustrations at the changes it makes in their lives. They went from feeling independent to feeling like a burden. They went from feeling like they could accomplish anything, but now feel like they need assistance to maintain their basic care. Some of these people are Christians and some are not. There are instances where I can declare the Word of God over their situations and times where the Spirit keeps me silent.

Today, as I read this scripture, I take hold of this beautiful promise from the Lord. That we who have received the promise of sonship and to be joint heirs with Christ in eternal glory will one day to trade these bodies for ones that will never know pain, suffering, or death. God has given each of us His own spirit as a deposit of this promise. He will faithfully complete all that He has spoken.

Maybe you are reading this today, and have been suffering with illness in your body. You have been wondering why you carry this heavy burden. You are clinging desperately to your last bit of hope. I do not have all the answers. I walk out my faith and journey with God every day. He gives me exactly what I need in each day. But I feel Him reminding His sons and daughters that there is an eternal promise to be fulfilled. We cannot escape that one day these earthly bodies will fade, because in our sin nature we were not able to be with the most Holy God. We receive the right to live with Him in eternity through the blood Jesus Christ shed on the cross. If you have accepted Jesus Christ and have received the gift of the Holy Spirit, then you have the promise of God in you. The promise for new beginnings, for a glorious homecoming, and a body that will never die. It is something to rejoice in. The way God has made a way for each of us. He restores all things. Amen.

HE IS COMING

So be patient, brethren, [as you wait] till the coming of the Lord. See how the farmer waits expectantly for the precious harvest from the land. [See how] he keeps up his patient [vigil] over it until it receives the early and late rains. So you also must be patient. Establish your hearts [strengthen and confirm them in the final certainty], for the coming of the Lord is very near. (James 5:7–8 AMPC)

This year, as prices go up in the grocery stores for many of the fresh vegetables and fruits, I decided to plant a patio garden. I have tried this a number of years ago and wasn't very successful. From insect infestation to poor soil nutrition causing fruit rot, I don't believe that year I ended up with one viable piece of fruit. This season, I am watching everything very closely. I question my husband, who used to have a landscaping business, almost daily to make sure that I am caring for the growing vegetables in the correct manner. I have again been battling a bit of fruit rot, but finally have a couple healthy looking vegetables growing on a few plants. As I tend my little patio garden, I believe that it is teaching me about being patient in the waiting, but also being expectant for the growth, and the harvest.

I imagine this is a little how God wants us to look at people. He wants to see them nurtured and growing. To multiply, bear fruit (kindness, love, gentleness, compassion), and to become mature in His knowledge and gifting. He wants us to help with this process. To see ourselves as gardeners of a more important harvest. One that changes everything for a person. It changes their eternity, because He is coming.

Jesus will be returning and it will be in a blink of an eye. The Bible tells us that there will be signs that will point to His return. I believe we have begun to see those signs in the world around us. God has been patient and has been merciful because He does not want a single person to perish.

Maybe you have been planting seeds of God's Word in the lives of others for many years and have had many seasons of patiently waiting for growth. Maybe the growth from seeds planted in your own spirit are beginning to spring forth. Wherever you are in your walk, keep looking, keep watching. He is coming. Press in. Hold on. Get ready. Know that He is faithful and He will return just as He has declared from the beginning. Amen.

DIFFERENT FROM THE WORLD

Above all we must be those who never need to verify our speech as truthful by swearing by the heavens or the earth or any other oath. But instead we must be so full of integrity that our "yes" or "no" is convincing enough that we do not stumble into hypocrisy. (James 5:12 TPT)

Have you ever taken time from your busy schedule to make plans with someone, and then at the last minute they have canceled? Maybe it was a valid reason such as a sick child or another type of emergency. I had one friend, years ago, that unfortunately would cancel last minute on a regular basis. Sometimes it was for something unexpected, but other times there really didn't seem to be a reason. I learned quickly that I couldn't rely on her to do what she committed to.

The word integrity means "being honest and having actions guided by moral principles," but it also means "to be unified or undivided." That means that we do and act without oscillation. We are firm and unwavering in our thoughts and actions.

When people look at us, do they see someone different from the rest of the world? Do they recognize us by our words and actions that we have a heavenly standard that we adhere to? That our choices and decisions are not just about what we seek in the moment, but how they will impact our spirit, our eternity? Do they recognize that we are not just trying to gratify ourselves in the here and now, but to leave a lasting legacy that will reflect our God and Father and reach a thousand generations?

Honestly, in my earlier years, I sought God for my own needs and my family and friends' needs. Now, He keeps working on my heart to see beyond my inner circle. He wants me to see from a global perspective. The world is full of people who make empty promises. They say lots of things, but their actions indicate they are about looking out for their own best interests. I am called to be different and live differently than that. It is a daily choice. Sometimes I fail at it completely. The next morning, with breath in my lungs, God gives me a new opportunity to choose to serve Him and the people He places in my path for the day. God didn't call us to perfection, but is faithful to complete His work in us that we would be made in a more perfect image of His Beloved Son, Jesus Christ. Every morning, I need to wake up and think as I step out into the world, I need to clothe myself in the anointing and sonship of Jesus Christ, that I might reflect His glory. Amen.

AN INVITATION

For this reason, beloved ones, be eager to confirm and validate that God has invited you to salvation and claimed you as his own. If you do these things you will never stumble. As a result, the kingdom's gates will open wide to you as God choreographs your triumphant entrance into the eternal kingdom of our Lord and Savior, Jesus the Messiah. (2 Peter 1:10–11TPT)

You collect your mail from your mailbox. You are sifting through it, sorting out the junk mail from items that will need your attention. Suddenly an envelope that is different from all the others catches your eye. It is larger and the paper is thicker. Clearly something important and unique awaits beyond the seal. Intrigued you slide your finger along the sealed edge to open it and solve the mystery of what it could be.

You pull out the enclosed card. It is embossed with gold lettering. The calligraphy of the letters is beautifully scripted as you read the words: You Are Invited. You feel a rush of excitement as you read the invitation further to determine what event you have been selected to join in and celebrate.

The invitation says: "Come join Me in celebrating My selection of you. I have chosen you as My child, My sons and daughters, of My Kingdom that has no end. This is an open invitation. Come as you are and I will provide all you need. I will give you food and drink to nourish your spirit. I will clothe you in garments that demonstrate the exquisite love and extraordinary honor I have placed upon you. I will seat you at the elaborate table I have set for you. We will eat this meal together, you and I. We will talk of all the plans I have to lead you to a victorious life. There will be music and dancing, because this is a celebration of our unity. I cannot wait to celebrate with you. I have been preparing this moment since before you were born. The celebration starts now, the minute you say yes to me. Your loving Father."

This is the most important invitation you will ever receive. Will you accept it? Will you finally recognize that God loves you so much that He gave His only son, Jesus Christ, as a sacrifice to save you from eternal death and separation from Him? He made a place for you in His Kingdom, but you have to accept the invitation to enter. Saying yes to an invitation from God is so simple. Just repeat this from your heart: "Yes, God, I need You. I need Your Son Jesus Christ and I accept Him as my Savior. Come into my heart and change me. I want to live a life filled with all You have for me. I accept an invitation to come sit at Your table. I can't wait to begin this celebration. Thank you, God, for choosing me. Your love fills me to overflowing. Amen."

AN ANCHOR OF HOPE

And now we have run into his heart to hide ourselves in his faithfulness. This is where we find his strength and comfort, for he empowers us to seize what has already been established ahead of time—an unshakeable hope! We have this certain hope like a strong, unbreakable anchor holding our souls to God himself. Our anchor of hope is fastened to the mercy seat which sits in the heavenly realm beyond the sacred threshold, and where Jesus, our forerunner, has gone in before us. He is now and forever our royal Priest like Melchizedek. (Hebrews 6:18–20 TPT)

Picture a large cruise ship. When it pulls into the port to disembark its passengers, it needs to ensure that it stays in place. The massive anchor is dropped to the ocean floor. The anchor itself is connected to a heavy linked chain. It would take a massive force to separate them from each other. That is the image of us connected to God. We are the chain connected to the anchor and are held fast. There is undeniable power and strength in His hold on those who trust in Him. The Bible declares that nothing can separate us from His love and nothing can pull us from His hands.

What have you been hoping for in your life? How will you bring about that desire for health in your body, or mending broken relationships, or the finances needed in certain situations in your life? Have you been trying to do it all in your own power? Spinning your wheels, feeling frustrated at the lack of progress toward that one thing you have been waiting expectantly to come to pass? The Oxford

Dictionary describes hope as "the feeling of expectation and desire for a certain thing to happen." We were created to have desires and longings, a hope deep in our souls. Yes, God created us with desires that would use our gifts, and fulfill our lives, but that hope has to be tied to something deeper. If our hope is centered only on things of this world, it is empty. For anything that we gain in this life we will eventually lose in the time of our passing. We do not take anything with us. God wants our hope to be connected with His eternal plan for our lives. To be connected to the true source of all power, all joy, all peace, and a love like no other. When we allow ourselves to be joined to the living God, all our needs fall into place as we begin to seek His eternal plan. Placing our hope in this world is empty. God reminds us that this earth will pass away. It will give way to a new heaven and earth, the one that is filled with all those who placed their lives in the hands of a Savior and found eternal freedom.

PEACE AND JUSTICE

But the wisdom that comes from above leads us to be pure, friendly, gentle, sensible, kind, helpful, genuine, and sincere. When peacemakers plant seeds of peace, they will harvest justice. (James 3:17–18 CEV)

There are many moments in life when we think or hear the statement, "That's not fair." We see in the world that when people are shouting for justice it is in a situation that it is often filled with anger. Those "peaceful" protests often tend to provoke or end in violence. It is the very opposite image we have when we look at Jesus Christ.

A group of religious leaders brought a woman caught in the act of adultery to Jesus (John 8:1–11). They were outraged and also looking for ways to trap Jesus, because they did not understand His ministry. They were afraid of the radical love He displayed to all those around Him and they did not like the popularity He gained within the Jewish community. They believed that Jesus would be as outraged at this woman's sin as they were. Jesus' actions in this passage are so important. He became silent, and stooped down to write in the sand. He took time to make sure that His emotions did not rule the situation. He knew that the law for this woman's behavior could result in punishment by stoning. His unwillingness to jump to a quick judgment angered the religious men. When they pushed further, Jesus said, "All right, but let the one who has never sinned throw the first stone." Jesus goes back to writing in the dirt. The religious leaders are suddenly exposed, for not one of them can judge her, because each of them has sinned. Jesus took an angry mob and with wisdom and kindness dissolved it. He then tells the woman that He will not condemn her. He gives mercy. He shows kindness. He demonstrates genuine love. He sought to bring the woman peace from her accusers and from her past mistakes. He chose to give her a true path to freedom from all her pain and all her sin.

There is a lot going on in this world that is wrong, that is dark. I remind you that we are not of this world. We are not staying here. This is not going to be our eternal home. You are called to be a light. Not join in the angry mobs of people shouting for justice. This world will always have injustice, because it is cast under the sin of man. We gave our authority to our enemy when Adam disobeyed God in the Garden of Eden. We recognize that God has a different plan. A new kingdom where we will reign with the Lamb of God who takes away all sin in the world for those who choose Him. Until that day, be a peacemaker. Be the image of the living God, bear the mark of Christ for all the world to see. Not just in claiming to be a born-again believer, but manifested in your actions. Choose peace. We are not called to judge the world for we are not without sin.

BE A SERVANT

But none of you should be called a teacher. You have only one teacher, and all of you are like brothers and sisters. Don't call anyone on earth your father. All of you have the same Father in heaven. None of you should be called the leader. The Messiah is your only leader. Whoever is the greatest should the servant of others. (Matthew 23:8–11 CEV)

In this passage of scripture, Jesus is instructing His disciples. He is preparing them for a time when He will no longer be with them. This chapter points out the difference between religion and walking out a life that represents the heart of God and Jesus. In other verses, He points out the things that religious leaders are doing that are not a representation of God the Father.

Jesus always had a heart for the lost, the hurting. The people that the religious leaders decided to ostracize and cause to feel shame. Jesus tells us that we are called to serve one another. We need to be looking at ways to build each other up. To come alongside our brothers and sisters and help them to keep persevering in their walk.

Serving others doesn't have to be complicated. We all are equipped with gifts. Maybe you have time to give to help a neighbor who can no longer do their own yard work. Maybe you know someone has been ill and could use a couple of meals. Maybe you are great at organizing things and can plan and put together the church family helping out someone or a local charity in need. The important part is, you were called to serve. As part of Christ's family, we all need to work together, serving one another to grow and demonstrate the love of Christ in the world.

DISCERNMENT

And they shall be Mine, says the Lord of hosts, in that day when I publicly recognize and openly declare them to be My jewels (My special possession, My peculiar treasure). And I will spare them, as a man spares his own son who serves him. Then shall you return and discern between the righteous and the wicked, between him who serves God and him who does not serve Him. (Malachi 3:17–18 AMPC)

In the United States, where we have so many freedoms and access to readily available resources, we really benefit from the ability to act from a position of discernment. God recognized that we would need His Word and had men filled with the Spirit write down God's plan for our salvation in a book. The Bible has been estimated to have five billion copies sold. My pastor often refers to the Bible as God's love letter to His children.

Earlier in this chapter of Malachi, there is a prophecy of a messenger sent to refine and purify the hearts of men. The Lord often sent prophets to call the tribe of Israel back into covenant with Him. The Israelite people would lose sight of being God's chosen people and follow the gods of the land they were living in. Their sin and disobedience often resulted in God leaving them to their own resources and eventually they would be oppressed by the stronger nations around them.

We need to be careful to not believe that we could be that different from the Israelites. Just look at the last few decades. We have separation of church from state. The Ten Commandments have been taken down from any school or public building. We have men setting themselves up in positions of power and attempting to tell people that what God calls sin really isn't sin. They justify sin with the excuse of seeking personal happiness. They justify murder with science. We are equipped to look at what is happening around us and discern for ourselves what is righteous and what is wicked in the eyes of God. We cannot trust in our own man-made values. We need to make sure that what we call "righteous" meets the heart and standards of our God and Father. Everything else is just a slippery slope into the darkness the world offers.

Lord, I want to be servant of You and to follow after the things of God. I want to clearly discern what is righteousness and what is wicked according to Your Word. I will keep reading Your Word and trusting that You will open my eyes to see areas that I need to apply it more diligently. Examine me, Lord. Show me where I am allowing the world's influence to be a barrier in my life. I will repent and choose You. You are my God, my source of strength and You are gracious and good. I want to see things the way You do, God. Open my eyes and keep my heart tender to receive all You have for me through Your Spirit. Amen.

THE VALUE OF THE WORD

The revelation of God is whole and pulls our lives together. The signposts of God are clear and point out the right road. The life-maps of God are right, showing the way to joy. The directions of God are plain and easy on the eyes. God's reputation is twenty-four-carat gold, with a lifetime guarantee. The decisions of God are accurate to the nth degree. (Psalm 19:7–10 MSG)

I enjoy being creative, whether it is refinishing furniture or crocheting or painting; I love trying to make things. I recently decided that I would try watercolor painting. I read information about budget-friendly paints and paint brushes that would still give good results for beginners online before I purchased my items. I looked at tutorials to see what techniques I will need to learn to create landscapes versus painting flowers.

We have the same possibilities to look for guidance as we walk out our Christian lives. We won't become better Christians on our own. We allow our emotions, our personal desires, and own self-interests to often rule in our lives. I think about how many of my earlier years were wasted not seeing the Word of God and its true value in my life. I look back at certain situations in my life and realize I was not prepared for some of the battles that came my way simply because I had never learned the Scriptures and who I was in Christ Jesus. I realize I could have had many more days filled with peace instead of stress. I could have been secure in who I was instead of trying to find my worth in the acceptance of those around me. I was striving for freedom, but bound in the chains of all the things I never brought to God. Maybe my broken relationships would have been restored? Or maybe I would have been a better steward with my finances earlier in life and not struggled with having my needs met? I could have understood the power of the Word of God differently and how to use it as a weapon against the attacks of the enemy.

I cannot change the past, and God doesn't want me to stay in the midst of my past mistakes, but wants me to use them to grow. He wants my experiences and eventual victories over different situations to be a testimony to others. I overcome by the blood of the Lamb and by the Word of God that preceded all things. I may not have known the Word in my earlier years, but I am learning and receiving new knowledge through God's Word every day. I encourage you, find a version of the Bible that you can understand and begin to read it. You don't have to read it from cover to cover. You can follow a reading plan. You can start in the New Testament. You get to choose, but just start somewhere. There is more God wants to show you and reveal to you. He wants to equip you for every circumstance. You would take the time to gain information that would help you invest in your financial future—why not the future of your soul?

EYES UP!

But my eyes are toward You, O God the Lord; in You do I trust and take refuge; pour not out my life nor leave it destitute and bare. (Psalm 141:8 AMPC)

It is often very hot and humid in July where my husband and I live. We do not have a pool, but we have access to a couple of lakes that are not too far away. This weekend, my husband and I went paddleboarding at the lake for the first time. We packed up the car with our inflatable paddleboards and reached the lake shortly before lunchtime. It was sunny and hot, a perfect day to be out on the water. We placed our paddleboards in at a docking area, got on, and paddled out to a calm area where we would attempt to get from a kneeling position to standing up the board. After several attempts, I made it. We paddled around in a quiet cove area getting used to the board and trying to maintain our balance. There were boaters, kayakers, and swimmers out on the lake. At one point, there was someone in a kayak coming around the cove to fish as a boat was passing through to another area. When I heard the noise of the boat and began to turn my head, I began to lose my balance on the board. Instructors encourage you to keep your head up and eyes on the horizon to help maintain your balance when standing on the board. I quickly corrected my gaze back in front of me and managed to escape falling off the board.

My paddleboard experience reminds me of how quickly we can lose our sure footing in the midst of daily life when we take our eyes off Jesus. We quickly forget how faithful He is and how He has already won every battle. We allow our gaze to be on the circumstances. We hear the voices of others and their opinions. We begin to allow our own thoughts to be laced with doubt instead of belief. Just like when on a paddleboard, in life we need to know where to look to maintain our steadfast faith and hope. We need to practice keeping our eyes fixed on the Lord at all times, in every moment of the day. This ensures us that we will know how to stand when the waves become choppy and the events of life try to throw us off balance. Keep your eyes up! Keep them on your Heavenly Father, who loves you with an everlasting love. He promises to be working for your good in the midst of every circumstance. His plan for you is perfect. He is always good, even when the circumstances don't look or feel good. The One who calms the seas can speak to your emotions and give you peace during difficult times. Keep your eyes up! Keep looking at the Lion of the Tribe of Judah! He is an awesome God! Amen.

IN THE DARKNESS

But in the day that I'm afraid, I lay all my fears before you and trust in you with all my heart. What harm could a man bring to me? With God on my side I will not be afraid of what comes. The roaring praises of God fill my heart, and I will always triumph as I trust his promises. (Psalm 56:3–4 TPT)

Working in a hospital, I see people in the midst of critical illnesses. I see fear grip the patient and families alike. They ask questions, wanting to know answers that most men do not really have in times like these. We have our experiences and the educational information that has been accumulated over the years. We have our best practices, but we don't have what these families and patients are asking for: We don't have guarantees. We don't have the absolute certainty that everything will be all right. There are so many unseen variables within each person and their medical needs. The same condition affects each person differently and their responses to treatments also vary. In times like these, I fully realize how much we need the promises of God.

I am powerless without Him. He is the One who created all things and understands the innermost workings of our bodies and spirits. He sees the end from the beginning. I have a limited view of the infinite possibilities and outcomes in any given situation. The only surety I have is in knowing through the Word of God, that our God is strong and mighty, and He is always working for the good of those who love Him. We all understand, especially after the last few years, that our human bodies are not created to last forever. God's purpose is for us to be transformed into the image of Jesus and shed this earthly body for one that will be whole and cannot be destroyed. It doesn't make the moment by moment part of a health crisis any less frightening at times. King David had a deep understanding of how to keep his inner strength and spirit built up in times of crisis. He recognized the need to praise God and remind himself of the power of God and that He had never failed in keeping His promises. In any battle, whether against our health, our relationships, or our faith, we need to do the same thing. We need to declare God's faithfulness. We need to remind ourselves of His promise to never leave us or forsake us. We need to declare the victory He has already secured. Let the praises of God fill your heart today and give you hope. Amen.

HE IS GRACIOUS

"But this is the covenant that I will make the with the house of Israel after those days, says the Lord: I will put My law in their minds, and write it one their hearts; and I will be their God, and they shall be My people. No more shall every man teach his neighbor, and every man his brother, saying, 'Know the Lord,' for they all shall know Me, from the least of them to the greatest of them, says the Lord. For I will forgive their iniquity, and their sin I will remember no more." (Jeremiah 31:33–34 NKJV)

The Bible is a beautiful description of the graciousness and lovingkindness of our God and Father on His children. He understands our very nature and all our imperfections. He chooses to love us anyway. He doesn't like it when I doubt or allow fear to win over my faith. He doesn't like it when I allow my ambitions or pride to hurt others. He doesn't like when I allow my emotions to get in the way of pursuing His wisdom and path for my life. However, our Father doesn't abandon us in our own mistakes and sin. He is always waiting for us to turn back toward Him. To have a contrite heart and an earnest desire to come back to Him. Time and again, He made a way for Israel to return to Him. To recognize His power, His goodness, and His favor pouring over them. He does the same for each one of us. Not only does God promise to forgive us, but He promises to never remember our sin. He chooses to not recount our mistakes to us. He chooses to not shame us for our poor choices. That is what love is. A heart full of compassion and ready to let go of every mistake I have ever made. It is a kind of love I don't deserve. It is a kind of love that brings me to my knees.

Father, I am undone by Your goodness and the gracious love and mercy You pour over me. I know I don't deserve it. I know that nothing I do could ever earn this kind of love. A perfect love. One that chooses to no longer see me from the lenses of all my sins. You choose to see my redeemed spirit. The one that is covered with the blood of Your Son, my Savior Jesus Christ. He saved me. Now I am walking in the power of that awesome love, mercy, and grace. I thank You. I know that, at times, I don't operate in the truth of who I am and allow my sinful nature to gain control. Thank you for the promise that I can return to You and not be rejected, but will find forgiveness and Your everlasting love. Help me each day to do better than the day before, full of the knowledge and power that I am no longer bound to the things of this world, but can reign from the heavens with You. I am full of the power of the wonder-working God and can be transformed every day. I love You and cannot praise You enough. Thank you. Thank you, Abba! Amen.

WHEN YOUR DREAMS ARE DYING

He heals the wounds of every shattered heart. (Psalm 147:3 TPT)

Even when bad things happen to good and godly ones, the Lord will save them and not let them be defeated by what they face. (Psalm 34:19 TPT)

There are so many instances in this world where we see the evidence of pain and loss. Unless you live in the remotest area and in complete isolation, the stories of wars, famines, fires, floods, riots, and illnesses seem to be always in the forefront of what is shared by mainstream media. Maybe for you the loss hits closer to home. Maybe you are in the midst of grief due to loss of a loved one, or some type of tragedy or personal trauma. Maybe you are looking at the remnants of the life you imagined for yourself and it is in pieces at your feet. You believe that the dreams you had for your life are dying. Personally, I have my own dreams that I haven't seen fulfilled. I had certain pictures and plans of what my life would look like. I feel a loss and grief for things that have not come to pass.

I believe God wants each of us to know that He understands our pain and our sorrows. Feeling them does not mean we don't have faith in Him. He always knew there would be circumstances that would require us to lean on Him. That as long as we live in this world tainted by sin we would have loss. I don't have the concrete answers for your specific situation. I cannot see God's plan in its entirety for my life or yours. I just know deep in my soul that He has loved me deeply and He blessed me and brought me through countless difficulties. I have an understanding that no matter what I am facing, God is with me and His very nature is good. I know that our God is the God who resurrects the dead. He is the one that speaks a word and things come into existence.

Don't hold onto your grief so long that it becomes the chains that keep you from moving forward into what God wants to do in your life. It is okay to grieve, but God doesn't want you to be unable to receive all that He has for you, because you won't let go of it. If your grief has caused you to become bitter, then you have held onto it for too long. Lay down those broken dreams, and come to the arms of a Father who offers you peace beyond your understanding.

Lord, I thank You for the way You speak to my heart. You understand my pain and grief at seeing some areas in my life, some of my plans, unfulfilled. I don't have to understand why to know that You love me and are good. I have seen Your hand of protection and provision in my life countless times. I will not allow my grief and loss to become so bound to my spirit that it becomes dull and lifeless. You will revive me. Your breath, Your voice, calling me to rise and renew myself in Your presence—I will come to the shelter of the Most High. I will stay in Your presence and allow You to fill me with Your joy and Your strength. You don't mind when I come and bring my sorrows and my pain. As my Father, you want to be the One I run to. Amen.

GOD THINKS OF YOU

Many, O Lord my God, are Your wonderful works which You have done; and Your thoughts toward us cannot be recounted to You in order; if I would declare and speak of them, they are more than can be numbered. (Psalm 40:5 NKJV)

Father God, this scripture verse fills my mind and spirit with awe. Not only do You think of me, but Your thoughts towards me are too numerous to count! I am on Your mind continually. I don't have to earn Your love, I already have it. It doesn't matter what people think of me. Their thoughts do not equal my worth in Your eyes. You are my Father and You love me fiercely, deeply, and unconditionally. I have always been worthy in Your eyes. It is not a big promotion that will sustain me or if people recognize me for my talents or abilities. It is Your love that gives me strength. You love me when I am at my worst or at my very best. In Psalm 139, the psalmist asks, "Where can I hide from your presence?" There is nowhere that I go that You are not with me, Lord. I love that Your greatest desire is to remain close to me. I declare that my sisters and brothers would recognize the depth of Your love for each of them. That You created them with a purpose, a calling. I pray that they would see that they are treasured in Your eyes. That Your love is freely given to each of them. A sacrificial love that doesn't have to be earned, just received and accepted. I speak that they would recognize their worth, because of that loving sacrifice of Your Son, Jesus, on the cross. That they would never believe the lie of rejection again. That the truth of how often they are on Your mind would fill them to overflowing and conquer any doubts, fears, or depression. Lord, there is no limit to Your love. There is no stopping the power of Your hand in the lives of those who have received You as a Father and Lord. Amen.

GUARDED IN ALL SEASONS

You will guard him and keep him in perfect and constant peace whose mind [both its inclination and its character] is stayed on You, because he commits himself to You, leans on You, and hopes confidently in You. (Isaiah 26:3 AMPC)

If you look at the life of Jesus, there is this evidence of constant peace about Him in the testimonies shared in the Gospels. From the time Joseph and Mary were frantically looking for Him as a boy and located Him in the temple to the time Jesus is standing before Pilate to be condemned, Jesus has this steadiness and incredible display of peace. Look at His responses to His accusers at the time before the crucifixion. In John 18:37, Pilate questions Jesus, "Pilate therefore said to Him, 'Are you a king then?' Jesus answered, 'You say rightly that I am a king. For this cause I was born, and for this cause I have come into the world, that I should bear witness to the truth. Everyone who is of the truth hears My voice.'" How was Jesus able to stay in such a place of confidence and peace, not just throughout His ministry, His trial, but through all His suffering and until his death? I believe Jesus knew where His every source of supply came from. It was found in His Heavenly Father. In many scriptures, we see Jesus going off by Himself to spend time with God. He knew that He needed to stay close and connected to the Lord. He recognized that He would have to be filled with the power of the Holy Spirit, God's Spirit, to walk through the Father's plan for his life. Jesus told the disciples, "Follow me." This wasn't just a command to go with Him in the physical sense, but to model His habits. To stay connected to the Lord God Almighty, be filled by the Holy Spirit, and stay in the power and presence of God. This equipping is what would allow men to guide others in faith to Jesus and eternal salvation even in the midst of persecution.

The same applies to our daily walk. Without staying connected to our Heavenly Father and filling up our spirit with the Holy Spirit, how can we expect to remain in perfect peace in this world? We have a life line. We are given an example, a road map, as it were through the Bible. Through the detailed encounters of how Jesus maintained His strength and His spirit. Take time today to lean on the Lord, your God. He wants to provide you with everything you need. Including the peace that surpasses all understanding.

BLESSINGS POURED OUT

"Bring all the tithes into the storehouse, that there may be food in My house, and try Me now in this," says the Lord of hosts, "If I will not open for you the windows of heaven and pour out for you such a blessing that there will not be room enough to receive it." (Malachi 3:10 NKJV)

We were driving to church a few Sundays ago, our usual route, which is never too busy on Sunday mornings at eight in the morning. About halfway through our trip, we come through a relatively quiet town, except that morning there was heavy traffic in this area. I looked around and saw a "Grand Opening" sign for a prepping store. It was packed. I was quickly reminded how short the distance between faith and fear can really be. These past few years there has been more and more talk about "doomsday prepping" than I remember hearing even after 9/11. The media is constantly stirring up various versions of how we should live in fear of the future and all the horrible things that could happen because of supply shortages or issues of access to items of necessity. We all experienced the toilet paper shortage. It is so important to look to God's Word and for His plan for our lives. If not, fear can consume us and, instead of using what God has given us in trust, we will become hoarders. Holding tightly with closed fists to all that has been a gift in the first place.

God wants us to know that He is capable of providing for us. We tend to look at the Old Testament stories as if they are just fictional tales and not evidence of what our mighty God can do. His Word says that we can test Him in the area of our resources. That if we are generous givers to Him He will take care of us. I love the way our God thinks towards us, His Words here don't state that we will be satisfied, but that we will not have enough room to receive all that He will bless us with! That is an amazing picture of His abundance and how He generously wants to pour out over our lives. We need to stop hearing from the world that we won't have enough, that we will be in want, because that is a lie straight from the enemy. Our God, who turned bitter waters into sweet waters and brought forth manna into the hands of the Israelites daily, can also supply your needs. We need to start looking expectantly at our loving Father. He will always do what He says He can do. He will not leave His children, but He will care for them and provide for their needs. He is the Creator of all things, and we have not even begun to see or hear all that His powerful hand is capable of.

Father, thank you for reminding us in times that the world is claiming uncertainty that we have Your steadfast word. We do not have to hold tightly to everything we have fearfully. You are the one who provides for us in all ways. We declare that as we trust in You and are faithful in our giving, that Your Word will come to pass and you will open up your heavenly storehouses on Your sons and daughters. We will not have just what we need but will have an abundance that we can then share with others. You will be glorified and all will know that You alone are God. I thank You for Your faithfulness to generation after generation. I love You, Lord. Amen.

GOD IS YOUR LIGHT

Arise [from the depression and prostration in which circumstances have kept you—rise to a new life]! Shine (be radiant with the glory for the Lord), for your light has come, and the glory of the Lord has risen upon you! (Isaiah 60:1 AMPC)

Imagine being in the woods at night, no moonlight or stars above you, and your flashlight goes out. You can no longer see the path in front of you. You lose your sense of direction. You try to listen and see if any sound might benefit you to guide your steps, but there are too many sounds coming from all directions. You feel frozen, unable to discern how to find your way. There are so many times in this life that you will feel under attack and, like the darkness of the situation, this world is trying to overcome you. The Lord your God wants you to know that Jesus Christ is the light. In Him is no darkness at all. When you have Jesus in your heart and life, then His glory is upon you. You will not be overcome by darkness. We have the promise of a new day coming.

The world will always proclaim darkness, brokenness, despair, and fear. It is all the world system knows because it is a fallen place. It is the place where the devil roams and looks for people to devour. I know that sounds very dramatic, but the Bible tells us that very plainly. Our home is not here on this earth. We have a new home and an eternal life waiting for us. However, God doesn't tell us this so that we walk around here and now with defeat and depression in our spirits, but so that we may operate from a place of victory. We have all the power, the strength, and the authority of the glory of the Lord as it manifests in our spirits today. We are to shine that light, like the beam of a flashlight, in this dark place. We are to shine brightly like a city on a hill, so that others may find their way to a kingdom without end. We are to use our new life, our eternal life, and born-again spirits to shout in triumph and rejoice at the love, mercy, and grace the Lord has poured out upon His people.

Father, I will shout, I will dance, and I will sing of Your greatness. Of the light of Your glory which has been poured out on me and for me to live a life that is victorious. I will shine brightly that others who are bound in darkness might see a place of refuge and hope. That they too may break free from the circumstances of this world and see that they belong in Your kingdom that has no end. That they will receive a new life and will be filled with living water. I will pierce through the darkness for Your glory surrounds me and is in me. Praise be to Your name always and forever! Amen.

WHERE IS YOUR FAITH?

Thus says the Lord: "Cursed is the man who trusts in man and makes flesh his strength, whose heart turns away from the Lord." (Jeremiah 17:5 ESV)

Now that there is twenty-four-hour access to news, everyone has something to say and an opinion to offer. News has gone from a fact-based institution designed to keep people informed with current events to a ratings-driven organization intent on keeping their broadcasting station on the leader board. The hosts demand solutions to life's situations and often point the blame at a person, political party, or organization. They believe that these man-made problems require man-made solutions. They could not be more wrong. Man left to his own will, his own knowledge and power, will not result in making things better. Only by aligning ourselves with the Holy One will we find truth, peace, and unity. We only have to look at human history to see what man-made solutions look like: abortion, cloning, addictions, sexual immorality, greed, and lawlessness. Man-made solutions work to convince people that there is no right or wrong, but only what man decides is good for himself in the moment.

If you want to remain disappointed, keep placing your hope and trust in man. If you want to know peace, joy, and freedom in a world that is growing darker every day, then turn your eyes to our Heavenly Father and His truth. It does not change like the shifting sands. It is the same yesterday, today, and forever. God's Word will guide you into all truth and wisdom. He is nothing like man. What He said were sinful a thousand years ago—murder, greed, envy, jealousies, sexual immorality, idolatry—are still sinful today. We are the ones who have watered down His Word. We have made the life-breathing Word of God conform to our selfish desires and plans. We have a way of making ourselves equal to God; no one can be equal to the one who created them. There is a season of sifting coming. God's people need to go back to the basics; go back to the Word of God and decide if it is the truth you will believe in. Anything else is self-deception.

TRUE WORSHIPPERS ARE NOT ASHAMED

"Therefore I will play music before the Lord. And I will be even more undignified than this, and will be humble in my own sight." (2 Samuel 6:21–22 NKJV partial)

He answered, "Love the Lord your God with all your heart, with all your soul, with all your strength, and with all your mind," (Luke 10:27 CSB partial)

We have experienced many visitors to our new sanctuary over the past few months. Recently, after a service, I had someone I had never met before say, "I come from a more traditional church, I found your style of worship interesting to watch." At that moment, I admit, I really did not know what to say back to this person. However, just like most interactions with people, it has given me something to think over the past week. I am reminded of the message my pastor preached several months ago that talked about how people of the world will see Christians as foolish. They will not understand why we rejoice, why we shout, why we dance, and why we sing mightily to the Lord. They cannot understand the mercy, the grace, the love, and the compassion that have resulted in our need to praise and give glory, because they have not received it. They cannot see or understand (that which we have full knowledge of) that we are going to an eternity with a God that gave everything He had to rescue us from sin and a permanent death.

I was reminded of the scripture in 2 Samuel where David's wife Mical despised David and his abandoned worship before the Lord. She attempted to shame him about his display of worship. David's response is the one every believer should have: I have been chosen by God, and in my everlasting thankfulness and love for Him, I will not be silent. I will worship the Lord God Almighty with wild abandon. I will not be ashamed of Him, because He was not ashamed of me when I was at my worst. Instead, He chose to pick me up out of the dirty pit, clean me up, and put His robe of righteousness on me. How can any believer be silent in the presence of a love like that? We are called to love Him with all we have and that requires physical action that includes worship. So I will keep on singing, shouting, dancing and giving God all my praise, because He is worthy and there is no other like Him!

REMEMBERING THE COVENANT

And He took a cup, and when He had given thanks, He gave it to them, saying, "Drink of it, all of you, for this is My blood of the New Covenant, which [ratifies the agreement and] is being poured out for many for the forgiveness of sins." (Matthew 26:27–28 AMP)

The invention of the camera gave us a way to capture memories in a unique way. We had pictures to go along with the stories that we recall at family gatherings. It is often fun to go back and look at family vacations and other important events. It enhances the memories in our minds and hearts. Jesus devised a way that the disciples could do the same thing and remember the times they had spent with Him. By having a meal with them and describing the way the bread and the wine were representations of Him, Jesus was explaining that regardless of what would happen, the promise of the new covenant was permanent.

Taking Communion is really designed to point us to Jesus, and the promise of living under the forgiveness of His blood poured out for us. We have this beautiful promise of the forgiveness of all our sins so that we do not have to be separated from God. We now have the promise of spending eternity with Him in a kingdom that will have no end. We will be renewed and have bodies that will not be subject to the cost of sin. I love that Jesus recognized that we would need a way to remember the promise of His sacrifice as we wait for His return. Having a meal with others is the perfect way to talk about the greatness of the Lord and all He has done. This is the purpose of Communion. We don't have to have the whole church present to take Communion; we are able to take part in this simple meal whenever we need to strengthen ourselves in our spirits. If the attitude of our hearts and spirits is in alignment with honoring Jesus and recalling all He has done, then we can take Communion with our own family members. It is good to recall the promises of the Lord. It is good to recall the victory secured for us on the cross. It is good to recall that we live in a time of exceptional mercy and grace. It is good that we see the sacrifice of His love and that it allows us to be adopted into a kingdom where we are seen as sons and daughters of the Most High. It is good.

Thank you, Lord, that You understand our every need, and that You always create ways to recall Your goodness and to emphasis that we have an eternal promise. This promise cannot be taken away from anyone who has called on the name of Jesus Christ to be saved. Let us join together in taking Communion as often as we need to remember the great cost of your love for us. We are so blessed to have Your Word and a greater understanding of Your plan and purpose in the day-to-day of our lives. We continue to look to things eternal and not trust in the temporary, but trust in the power of Your everlasting Word. We give You all glory, and thanks and praise. Amen.

EMBRACING THE TRUTH

"For the one who is from the earth belongs to the earth and speaks from the natural realm. But the One who comes from above is above everything and speaks of the highest realm of all! His message is about what he has seen and experienced, even though people don't accept it. Yet those who embrace his message know in their hearts that it's the truth." (John 3:31–33 TPT)

Remember the game Telephone, where several people line up and whisper a message from one person to the next until the last person speaks out what the message was to see if it matches up with the first person's message? Oftentimes, it was not the same message at all. Words were dropped or changed and the meaning of the original message ended up quite different from what was spoken at the end.

I love this scripture because it supports Jesus' other statements that He does not operate on His own authority but on the authority of the Most High God. He continues to demonstrate that He is directly connected to the Father and that His authority comes from Him and the Holy Spirit.

As we walk with the Lord, there will be times when we need to hear from Him. We will need knowledge and wisdom. We will need peace and strength to stand amidst challenging times. We practice staying connected to Him so that we can hear Him in quiet moments in our lives. We learn to lean and trust on His Word because we have the evidence of His Word fulfilled in our lives. We practice this in daily moments so that we will know what to do in times that earth is shouting at us loudly. In these times, we need to have the experience of embracing the truth in our hearts so that there will be no doubt as to whom we can trust. I wish this was a practice that I had understood much earlier in my Christian walk with God, but honestly, I did not commit to spending much time with Him outside of Sunday church. It was evidenced in how easily I could falter into believing the lies of the enemy and in the weakness of my faith. I am thankful that God is the God of second chances and third chances and on and on.

Father, thank you for Your merciful nature. Thank you that You know how to demonstrate the truth of Your Word in ways that reach deep into my spirit. I am grateful for the opportunities to grow in faith and love. I am thankful for the ability to turn to Your Word and see truth and gain strength. I love You, Lord. May Your words jump off the page at me guiding my every step. May I always hunger and thirst for more of You. You alone are what I need and my every provision. Amen.

EXCHANGING DEATH FOR LIFE

For we will discard our mortal "clothes" and slip into a body that is imperishable. What is mortal now will be exchanged for immortality. And when that which is mortal puts on immortality, and what now decays is exchanged for what will never decay, then the Scripture will be fulfilled that says: Death is swallowed up by a triumphant victory! (1 Corinthians 15:53–54 TPT)

Yesterday, I saw a beautiful red-spotted purple butterfly, which is a common black-and-blue butterfly in the Eastern United States, land on my basil plant on the back deck. The butterfly, as most of us know, have a unique life cycle. It begins as a caterpillar, then after eating enough, forms a chrysalis, and emerges later as a butterfly. Not only does the creativity of this creature speak to an amazing imagination of our heavenly Creator and Father, it also is a beautiful foreshadowing of our God doing this amazing transformation within each of us.

We are born into this world tainted by sin and placed into vessels that will eventually perish. However, we have an opportunity to be born again, to recognize that our spirits are meant to be eternal. In recognizing that our Creator gave us a spirit inside our physical bodies and surrendering our lives to the One who created us, we allow Him a way to exchange what will pass away with a new body that cannot be corrupted by time. Since many times I am still amazed by the way our natural bodies have been designed and how incredible all of creation really is, I am completely blown away to think that the Lord has prepared a body for me that will live forever!

As each year passes by and I begin to see the subtle changes of time in my physical body, I am thankful that I don't have to fear death. I have a beautiful promise of an eternal life living in a kingdom with God the Father and Jesus Christ His beloved Son forever and ever! I will have a new form that will never know pain, suffering, or sorrow because Jesus took all of that upon Himself so that I would not have to face these things on my own. Yes, I believe that we have access to healing while on the earth, now, but for this purpose we are focusing on the eternal promise. If you are unsure of your where you will be upon the death of your mortal body, then there is no time like right now to ask God into your life. Simply, from your heart, tell Jesus that you need Him in your life, that you accept Him as your Lord and Savior. The Bible promises us that those who call on the name of Jesus Christ will be saved (Romans 10:13). Once you give your heart to Jesus, don't stop there, find a church that can help you grow and learn about who God really is and how much He loves you. Your transformation has already begun. Your life has already begun to change, because God wants you to have a life full of joy, peace, and hope. You will never be alone, because He is always with you. The added bonus: You will have an eternal life and body to live with the King of kings and the Lord and lords forever!

RESPECT IN MARRIAGE

Wives, understand and support your husband in ways that show your support for Christ. The husband provides leadership to his wife the way Christ does to his church, not be domineering but by cherishing. So just as the church submits to Christ as he exercises such leadership, wives should likewise submit to their husbands. (Ephesians 5:22–24MSG)

A great marriage doesn't mean that two people will always be in agreement with one another. The very fact that we are two individuals—with different dreams and different skills—who have committed to join their lives together, basically point to times where we will have different opinions on matters. It is what we choose to do and how we choose to act in those times that will keep us connected or divided as a couple. I believe that we need to work at and guard our marriages because the enemy is looking for a way to disrupt and ruin families. Divorce rates and the number of divided families in this country indicate that Satan has become successful at destroying the family unit and separating husbands and wives.

My husband and I went to a marriage seminar held by our church earlier this year. One of the speakers discussed settling conflict within the marriage; she suggested that we bring it to God. She didn't confront her husband, she didn't try to change him, or manipulate him into seeing things her way. She simply went to God and submitted the issue to Him and asked God to change her husband's heart if it aligned where God was leading or to change hers if it was not. I thought this was a fantastic perspective and biblical, too, because she was bringing the matter before God and submitting it to Him for help.

I know, in the past, I have been too focused on the word submit in this scripture. However, we as marriage partners are supposed to have both of our lives submitted to God already. We are already supposed to be yielding ourselves to our Heavenly Father, and following His wisdom and discernment in our lives. If we are in a right relationship with the Lord, it becomes easier to be in a right relationship with our spouse because we aren't focused on ourselves, but in fulfilling the command to love each other and to put one another first. It is like everything else in life, we will have to purposefully walk this out daily. We will have to choose our responses to one another. We will have to choose love over anger, over being right. We will have to choose to surrender our issues to the one who can see the larger picture in our lives and will always be faithful with wisdom and guiding us safely through challenging times.

THE BENEFITS OF LOVE

So this is my prayer: that your love will flourish and that you will not only love much but well. Learn to love appropriately. You need to use your head and test your feeling so that your love is sincere and intelligent, not sentimental gush. Live a lover's life, circumspect and exemplary, a life Jesus will be proud of: bountiful in fruits from the soul, making Jesus Christ attractive to all, getting everyone involved in the glory and praise of God. (Philippians 1:9–11 MSG)

In Matthew, Jesus tell s us that one of the primary commandments is to love others, our neighbor, as we love ourselves (Matthew 22:39). It still is one of the most difficult commands that Christians work on fulfilling. This message of loving others is shared multiple times throughout the New Testament scriptures. If we have been even marginally awake the last few decades, we see the evidence of hatred all around us in the world. The only weapon against hatred is love.

We cannot love others if we have not accepted the power of Christ's love in our own lives. However, once having received that gift so freely, how can we choose to withhold love from anyone else? Not one of us is worthy of love and the sacrifice of atonement we received when Jesus hung on a cross for each one of us. Yet freely He gave to us, because of His great love for us—not when we are already perfect, but full of sin and the evidence of our mistakes and brokenness. We are called to share the beauty of that love with everyone else. This call to love allows us to be full of the fruits of the Spirit: patience, joy, peace, kindness, love, goodness, faithfulness, gentleness, and self-control. These are things most people long to have in their lives. They are opposite the things the world offers. There is a direct connection to these gifts and our physical well-being.

The additional benefit of loving others is glorifying the Lord God Almighty, the one who created you and all things. The one who is creating a new heaven and a new earth where one day we will spend all eternity. The one who looks upon you with such love and wants to gift you with every good thing under the heavens. He is the one who first loved us, and He is worthy of it all. The more people who see God and love our God and Father, the more light is emitted in the darkness that surrounds us while we await His return. And we need the light to force back the darkness as we draw closer to the time of His return. Amen.

FAITH TAKES DILIGENCE

Study and be eager and do your utmost to present yourself to God approved (tested by trial), a workman who has no cause to be ashamed, correctly analyzing and accurately dividing [rightly handling and skillfully teaching] the Word of Truth. (2 Timothy 2:15 AMPC)

There has been a vast amount of new knowledge that I have had to require to grow vegetables in containers this summer. First, the decision to grow vegetables in containers came from recognizing that trying to plant a garden in our yard would result in battling the vast amount of deer in our area. We were not willing to erect a nine-foot fence for our first attempt at growing some vegetables. Second, I learned that even though soil is supposed to contain nutrients for growing vegetables, during the summer season the growing plants will need to be fed. Some plants require calcium to reduce plant rot, and others require magnesium to promote growth. This past week, I discovered that container plants will still be attacked by various insects, as squash and zucchini are favorite plants for aphids to feast on. A little research into a repellent and I am working to protect the plants that will provide fresh vegetables to my family this season.

As I went to work, spraying my plants this week for the past couple of evenings, I felt in my spirit God whispering, "This is like your walk with Me. Faith takes work, and if you do not stay watchful and work at staying in the Word, your faith can be stolen away." There is definitely truth in that! Faith takes diligence. Diligence means "putting forth work and effort with persistence." I have shared before, all relationships take work. My marriage will not stay strong if I neglect my husband and our relationship. This is just as true with our relationship with God. We cannot say we love God and want to live for Him, but we never spend time building our relationship with Him. We build a relationship with Him by learning about Him through the Word and through spending time with Him in prayer.

Father God, I thank You for the reminder this week that just as we must gain knowledge for growing vegetables and keeping plants healthy, I must put forth the same perseverance in growing and building my faith. I can never just rest and not expect it to negatively impact my relationship with You. Our walk together takes commitment from me to spend time with You. You are always ready and available to me. Keep speaking to me; keep teaching me. I want to grow and to stay strong and built up so that I can overflow. The overflow of the love of God is what this world needs more than anything. I love You, Lord. Amen.

UNFATHOMABLE LOVE

"The mountains be shaken and the hills be removed, yet my unfailing love for you will not be shaken nor my covenant of peace be removed," says the Lord, who has compassion on you. (Isaiah 54:10 NIV)

Greater love has no one than this: to lay down one's life for one's friends. (John 15:13 NIV)

Every morning, my husband, who leaves for work a good hour ahead of me, brings me a cup of coffee when my alarm goes off. Then, every single day before he leaves, he comes to me and kisses me goodbye and tells me he loves me. I don't know about other women in the world, but I do not look my best first thing in the morning. I have very coarse, wiry, wavy hair. Imagine someone who has teased out their hair as much as possible . . . it is probably worse than that. We often laugh and joke about "taming my hair," because I certainly don't have wash and go hair by any means.

Anyway, this morning, as I was marveling about the unconditional love of my husband at my least becoming moments, the Spirit of the Lord spoke to my heart saying, "My love for you is even deeper than that of a loving husband. There hasn't been a moment in time when I haven't loved you. I speak to you of my love all day long. It is in the sunrise, and in the gentle patter of the falling rain. It is in the dew on the grass, or in the drifting snow blanketing the earth. It is in the song of the birds singing to you daily. It is in the soft rustle of the breeze through the leaves of the trees. I array the skies with stars for you to gaze in awe and wonder. I place beaches along the vast ocean with sand to caress your steps. Every part of creation was designed to remind you of the greatness of My love for you. I love you so much, I gave everything for you, so that we will never have to be separated from one another. I nourish your soul with My own life, with My own spirit. We have a connection that can never be taken away. Just like a ring symbolizes the covenant between a husband and wife, I have placed my seal upon you that all may know that you are My beloved. We are forever connected. I will always sing of My love for you and sing songs of joy because we are joined together."

I don't know if my mind will ever comprehend the love that God pours out for each of us. Maybe you have been disappointed by love from a human perspective. God's love is supernatural. It is like nothing we can ever experience on earth. One of my pastors recently stated, "God is love, it is not a characteristic of Him . . . it is the very essence of Him and cannot be separated from who He is." I encourage you, find out about God's love for you today. He has been trying to tell you of how precious and valuable you are to Him all along. His love will never fail you. It never stops. You cannot do anything to outrun it or break it. No mistake will ever make Him stop loving you. Once you say yes to God's marriage proposal, He never breaks His vows to you. Glory to the One who loves like no other. Amen.

THE GREATEST OF ALL

Jesus answered him, "The first of all the commandments is: 'Hear, O Israel, the Lord our God, the Lord Is one. And you shall love the Lord your God with all your heart, with all your soul, with all your mind, and with all your strength.'" (Mark 12:29–30 NKJV)

One of the most difficult things for me in my Christian walk has been not being able to share my faith with all the members of my family. Sure, they all know I am a born-again Christian (or holy roller, or happy clappy, as I have been referred to before), but the deep conversations that I long to have about the goodness of God and how He has changed my life, is still one of those conversations I have not been able to have with most of my family members. After twenty years, I still get eye rolls over wanting to pray at dinnertime. I get scoffed at when I give God glory for safe travels. I get mocked for the time spent serving my church. Although it grieves me because I want my family to know how much more God has for them, I am not sorry for being a child of God. I am not ashamed of loving the Lord. I am not ashamed of choosing to follow Him.

At some point, we all have to decide what is important in our lives. The scripture above doesn't talk about loving family above all things. I know that sounds harsh, but it is true. It states that we need to love the Lord above all things. We need to recognize our need for Him above everything else. The power of our love flows directly from Him. When we see the love He has for us, and we join ourselves to Him, then God grows us with a capacity to love deeply and to have hearts full of compassion. He transforms us; our souls are redeemed, and this heavenly connection gives us the gifts of the Spirit, to be able to operate in a world covered in darkness and sin. It allows us to love, to forgive, and to proclaim the goodness and glory of a Heavenly Father who knows how to do the impossible.

I will never regret being sold out for God. I see the grace and mercy that He has poured over my life daily, and I am so thankful. He loved me when I was at my worst. He took all that was inside of me that was broken, and made something better out it. Until my family can recognize His goodness and the power of His love in their lives, I will continue to pray that their eyes and hearts will be open to receive Him and all that He has for them. I will continue to stand for what I believe. I will love the Lord with all my heart, all my soul, all my mind, and all my strength. It is the least I can do for all that He has given to me. Amen.

WITHOUT FEAR

She is clothed with strength and dignity, and she laughs without fear of the future. (Proverbs 31:25 NLT)

We are surrounded by a world that is blanketed by fear all the time. With news that is reported twenty-four hours daily, seven days a week, we have access to how the world is growing darker by the day. As women, we could be prone to worry and stay fearful over the conditions of the world and how it will impact our families, but that is not what the women of God are called to do. In Proverbs 31, we see that godly women equip their household; they are prepared for situations to come. We may not be able to see every circumstance that will come our way, but we know the God who sees all things. We may not be able to take every heartache away from our family and friends, but we have a Father that wipes away every tear. We may not be able to predict every change that impacts the lives of others, but we have a mighty God that has all wisdom. He lights the way in the darkness that surrounds us. We do not have to be afraid of the future. We just have to hold onto the One who is always working for our good.

Father God, I thank You that today, You used Your Word to remind me that I don't have to live in fear of the future. You hold my future in Your hands. In You, I have strength and peace. In You, I find the wisdom and equipping I need to face the circumstances and the changes that may occur in my life and the lives of my family and friends. You simply ask that I trust in Your goodness and, Father God, I do. I have seen time and again how You have taken the broken pieces of my life and used it all to create something new and something even better than I could have imagined or hoped for, because that is who You are. I will keep my eyes fixed on You and the powerful wisdom in Your Word. I will trust that You will guide my every step. I will not focus on the darkness, but on Your glorious light. I will stand firmly on the rock of my foundation. I do not have to be shaken and I do not have to be subject to my emotions. I have the strength of the Living God inside me and I can live without fear. Amen.

TRUSTING GOD MORE THAN YOUR HEART

The heart is deceitful above all things, and desperately wicked; who can know it? (Jeremiah 17:9 NKJV)

He who trusts in his own heart is a fool, but whoever walks wisely will be delivered. (Proverbs 28:26 NKJV)

Recently, at church I was approached by a friend to provide advice regarding a situation she was facing. This is a conversation that we have had multiple times and a conversation that I know she has had with other friends as well. I listened to the situation and asked, "Have you prayed about this? Have you asked God what He wants you to do?" Her response was, "No, but I don't 'feel' this is what God has planned for me."

We have all had this same response in various situations in our lives. We have our own ideas and preconceived notions of what God's purpose and plans are for our lives. We can see it clearly in our mind. We make determinations and steer our own path with our own wisdom and feelings. Philippians 4:6 encourages us to bring all things before the Lord. If we don't bring things to Him and talk to Him about choices and decisions we face, how can we possibly know what He really has for us? Isn't it possible that at one time God instructed us to wait on a situation, but if we brought it to Him at a later time, it could be the time He feels we are ready to step into a new season? That our time of waiting could be complete as we have learned what God was attempting to reveal to us in the season of waiting? We will not know if we do not ask. We are supposed to keep coming to God. He doesn't get tired of talking to us about decisions we need to make in our lives. He wants us to come to Him, to rely on Him, to recognize that He will help us be bold, be brave, and to step out and live abundant lives. We are called to seek Him first in all things. Proverbs 3:5–6 instructs us to not rely on our own understanding of things. That we should trust and follow God's leading.

Lord, there are so many lessons and wonderful moments of wisdom and knowledge that You share with us each and every day. Keep my heart open to Your truth, Your wisdom. Help me to not lean on my own understanding or feelings in situations. Help me to understand that there is no moment that You are not available to me. You do not grow weary of me checking to see when my season of waiting is over. How can I know which open door to walk through if I do not ask You first? I need to have direction from You daily, and that is a purposeful and daily choice that I have to make. Seasons change, and opportunities that were not present once may appear, and You want me to come to You for wisdom in all areas of my life. Thank you for Your patience with me. Thank you for the wisdom You give so freely. I will keep choosing to surrender to You, Lord. I want what You want for my life. To go deeper, to love more, to demonstrate the indwelling and power of Your presence as a testimony to the world. Amen.

A BETTER INHERITANCE

In Him we also were made [God's] heritage (portion) and we obtained an inheritance; for we had been foreordained (chosen and appointed beforehand) in accordance with His purpose, Who works out everything in agreement with the counsel and design of His [own] will, (Ephesians 1:11 AMPC)

Part of our journey in our relationship with our Heavenly Father is to learn and understand all that He has given us as His sons and daughters. Another word for inheritance is birthright. When we become born-again Christians, receiving salvation and our spirit comes alive in Christ Jesus, we are gifted a birthright. So many of us leave that gift unopened. It sits on the table and we walk by it daily. We leave it unopened for many reasons: some are satisfied with just salvation, some do not believe they are worthy of all God has for them, or some do not understand the extent of the inheritance we have through Christ Jesus.

It is difficult to grasp at times that we have the same exact spirit of the living God inside of us—the same one that inhabited Jesus Christ. The Scriptures say that we have the same anointing and power as Christ. That we can do exactly the same things He did during His time on earth. We can heal the sick and raise the dead. We can bind things and loose things. We have this whole supernatural life to live, but many of us allow doubt and fear to hold us down. I wonder how much it hurts the Father to see so many of us not have an understanding of our destiny as His royal priesthood? We look at the move of God in other people and in various ministries and we think God is holding back on us, but it is the opposite. We hold out on God. When we do not trust in His power, then His power cannot be demonstrated in us or through us.

Lord, my God, I fall to my knees today and ask for forgiveness. Continue to peel back the layers of unbelief in my life and give me revelation knowledge of all You are and all You have done for Your people. I see clearly how my spirit is willing but my flesh remains weak. I bind my flesh and declare that my spirit, the house of the living God, will be the one who leads me. The Holy Spirit, in direct connection to my spirit, will continue to grow me and reveal a deeper understanding of the birthright and responsibilities I have to the eternal kingdom of God. I want to go deeper, I want to live sold out for You, God. Nothing less. Forgive me. I thank You that Your mercies are new every morning. You are so faithful to me even when I lack faith. I love You, Lord. Amen.

NO TRUER LOVE

Close your heart to every love but mine; hold no one in your arms but me. Love is as powerful as death; passion is as strong as death itself. It bursts into flame and burns like a raging fire. (Song of Solomon 8:6 GNT)

God is calling for His sons and daughters to love Him more than anything else. To love Him with wanton abandon. To run and not walk to the place where you find Him. He wants us to desire to spend time in His presence. To not be in a hurry and make Him part of our daily checklist.

We as a generation have become used to compartmentalizing things, combining things, making plans and schedules to fit the business of our lives. God is always available to us, but He doesn't want to be just a moment in your busy schedule. The next thing to check off on your list. He wants to be incorporated in every moment of your day. We have the spirit of the living God inside of us and yet we act as if we have to travel to find and spend time with Him. We need to quiet our minds and business, and tap into the connection to the spirit in our souls. Connecting with God in every moment of the day will not happen without effort. We have to break out of old habits and create new ones. God is looking for a church to be all in. Sold out on His love, His Word, and His faithfulness. Only a church so in love with Him will be able to walk in His supernatural equipping and meet the call to reach the hurting, to heal the sick, and point lost souls to the one who can save them.

Lord, I see the reckless abandon which You have poured over me, and I can't help but want more of You. You are the one that sees me, that knows me, and who can show me how to cast off my old self to be more like You. I want everyone to know Your goodness, Your desire to love them and bless them. I want the fire of Your Spirit to burn within me, making me bolder, and wiser in Your Word and Your ways. Only through You will we see goodness in this place. I love You, Lord. There is no truer love than the one You have poured over me. Amen.

GATHERING TOGETHER

This is not the time to pull away and neglect meeting together, as some have formed the habit of doing, because we need each other! In fact, we should come together even more frequently, eager to encourage and urge each other onward as we anticipate that day dawning. (Hebrews 10:25 TPT)

Recently, my husband and I traveled abroad to visit with family. It was a much needed extended break from work and a much needed opportunity to connect with family that we haven't seen in person for several years. It is always exciting to visit abroad and see the different aspects of different cultures. There are different mannerisms and influences in people and in the infrastructures of the area. Although it is lovely to have different experiences, I found myself, toward the end of my visit, longing for the familiarity of my home. I kept up my devotional time each morning, and my husband and I watched our church online, but I really missed the experience of corporate worship and community that we have when we attend church in person.

We live in a time where technology has allowed us to reach around the world. Through online video applications we can watch services conveniently from our couches. Although this is a positive thing for those who are shut in, out of town, or wanting to see a church service not in our hometown, it also can be a barrier to true connection. It can lead to isolation, loneliness, and disillusionment. We are meant to come together because that is where we can grow in relationships that encourage and build one another up in our fullest sense. We need a true community of believers. Each one of us has light inside us through the indwelling light and spirit of Christ, and when we bring our individual lights together we can shine brightly in the darkness that is demonstrated by the world. Separated from one another, we are more susceptible to the attacks of the enemy; but unified, our body, the Church, remains stronger.

The Bible illustrates this with the scripture in Ecclesiastes 4:9–10: "Two are better than one, because they have a good reward for their labor. For if they fall, one will lift up his companion. But woe to him who is alone and falls, for he has none to help him up." We are meant to gather together because it strengthens us and enables us to keep each other built up in our faith in both good times and bad. We need each other in this time and season more than ever before. Gather. Do not watch from the comfort of home because it leaves you open to isolation and attack.

NO MYSTERY HE CAN'T REVEAL

He explained, "You've been given the intimate experience of insight into the hidden truths and mysteries of the realm of heaven's kingdom, but they have not. For everyone who listens with an open heart will receive more revelation until he has more than enough. But those who don't listen with an open, teachable heart, even the understanding that they think they have will be taken from them." (Matthew 13:11–12 TPT)

I wish I could say that I have spent all my years as a Christian pursuing the Word of God and His kingdom first, but sadly that is not true. Like many Christians, my journey often took the shape of "two steps forward and three steps back," because I was undisciplined in my time spent in the Word of God. I allowed distractions, excuses, and past experiences to deter me from changing myself from the inside with God's Word. God, however, is so good and faithful that, when I began to obey His calling to spend time with Him daily, He began to guide me and give me more wisdom and understanding from reading His Word than I had previously experienced. He would align the Scriptures with devotional passages I was reading, confirming the intent of the Word. In essence, God was revealing the mystery of His Word and who He was to me personally. He knew exactly how to give me insight. He would use my pastor's message to open my eyes to things I could not previously understand.

I want to encourage you today to take spending time with God through reading His Word and make it part of your routine. If you are already spending time reading God's Word, God will help you go deeper, because He longs for us to see with kingdom eyes and have kingdom hearts. God will reveal new wisdom and revelation to those who are earnestly seeking Him. He doesn't hold back from us, but it is often we who hold back from Him.

Thank you, God, that there is no mystery You cannot reveal to Your children. You are the one who grant all knowledge and wisdom to those who are seeking Your kingdom. I declare that my brothers and sisters in Christ will be purposed in their hearts to hunger and thirst after You. That they will be disciplined in their daily walk and seek the One who holds the universe in His hand before they look elsewhere. Give us all teachable hearts and place Your anointed word in the mouths of Your ministers and pastors so that Your truth is what is revealed. I thank You for Your mercy and grace and that You are faithful even when I was not. I am in awe at the newness of Your Word as I look at it each day. New ideas and concepts that You show me that I could not previously understand are now open to me. It fills my heart and my mind. I find joy in Your Word. Thank you, Father, I praise You for Your goodness. Amen.

YOUR VESSEL, YOUR CHOICE

In a well-furnished kitchen there are not only crystal goblets and silver platters, but waste cans and compost buckets—some containers used to serve fine meals, others to take out the garbage. Become the kind of container God can use to present any and every kind of gift to his guests for their blessing. (2 Timothy 2:20–21 MSG)

Imagine being at one of the national parks in the United States, you come to a spot with a beautiful lake with a vast mountain, topped with snow, reflecting off the water. You walk closer to the beautiful, picturesque image, but as you approach you see more and more litter all over the ground. Instead of your eyes drawn up to the beauty of the countryside, all you can look at is the ugliness of the trash scattered all around the base of this lake. What you once thought of as lovely and beautiful has now been changed. In this passage, Paul is writing to Timothy and reminding him that we have to work at living a transformed life. We are born again and a new creation when we receive salvation, but we also have an earthen vessel in which our spirit resides. We have to work on making sure our spirit is filled and renewed so that our flesh doesn't take over.

The first part of becoming a vessel for God to use is a desire to serve the Lord. It is a complete surrender of self. Being ready to be obedient to Him and let things go that He says are no longer healthy for our spiritual growth. One of the things in my life that God had me lay aside was the type of books I was reading. I was an avid reader growing up—books took you to imaginary places and painted pictures of places I had never been. There wasn't a type of book that I didn't enjoy reading. Mysteries, historical fiction, and, of course, romance novels. Some of the content of these books were not the best for renewing my mind. Over time, I felt convicted to be more selective of what I was reading and putting into my mind and heart. It wasn't instantly, but as I became obedient to God's leading, it was easier to lay aside things that were not healthy for my spirit. I used to read for a way to escape, but now I read to gain knowledge and wisdom. There is a blessing in choosing to become a heart open to serving the Lord. In being obedient to Him about what I was going to fill my mind and spirit with. I decided to leave the garbage out. I wanted to be all that God had called me to be and that meant being purposeful in what I allow in my heart and mind.

FOREVER FAITHFUL

"Or what man is there among you who if his son asks for bread, gives him a stone? Or if he asks for a fish, will he give him a serpent? If you then, being evil, know how to give good gifts to your children, how much more will your Father who is in heaven give good things to those who ask Him!" (Matthew 7:9–11 NKJV)

Delight yourself also in the Lord, and He shall give you the desires of your heart. (Psalm 37:4 NKJV)

This weekend, I had the distinct privilege of witnessing the baptism of my brother and sister-in-law. I wept with great joy as I watched them profess their trust and understanding that their salvation was in the Lord. This is an answer to a prayer I have been waiting for God to answer for as long as I have been a Christian. This prayer goes beyond just the salvation for each of them, but for them to truly know God and have a relationship with Him. To have all the inheritance as a child of God. To understand our anointing, and to be filled with a faith that helps us in the most challenging of circumstances. To have a life filled with purpose and wonder in having an intimate relationship with a Father who loves us with an everlasting love.

Maybe, you have been waiting, year after year, for our Heavenly Father to answer your prayers and draw your family close to Him. Do not lose heart! God's Word states that it is His very desire that no one should perish. That every man, woman, and child would come to salvation. That is His faithful heart towards every person ever created. It is the very reason He is full of compassion, mercy, and grace towards this world that has grown so dark and cold against Him. Keep asking and keep seeking Him. He is the most faithful Father. Your desires toward the salvation of family and friends are in direct alignment with His own heart.

Abba Father, I just celebrate with You and give You praise as I experience the wonder of Your love and faithfulness. I rejoice as I see those I love see You with new eyes and with a spirit reborn. I watch in anticipation as I see You transform their lives and fill them with such joy and hope. I am filled anew with wonder at Your faithfulness and heart for all peoples. I continue to prophesy that the seed planted in the lives of so many families will bring forth a harvest of souls. I see all of heaven rejoicing. I am so full of love for You, Father. Your goodness knows no boundaries. I praise You and sing songs of worship to the only One who is worthy. The Great I Am. The Light of the World. The Mighty One. The Promise Keeper. I love You, Lord! Thank you for the way You love each of us. Amen.

PUT OUT THE FIRE

This is scary: You can tame a tiger, but you can't tame a tongue—it's never been done. The tongue runs wild, a wanton killer. With our tongues we bless God our Father; with the same tongues we curse the very men and women he made in his image. Curses and blessings out of the same mouth! (James 3:7–10 MSG)

One of the sayings I recall my father stating often when I was growing up was: "No one knows how dumb someone is until they open their mouth." Now, I recognize that this saying isn't necessarily kind, but I believe that my father was trying to impart that sometimes listening is more valuable than speaking. That when you choose to speak, it should be with consideration and careful thinking.

As a society, we have gotten so far away from listening and are so quick to speak, whether we have all the details or not. The world speaks often out of fear, bitterness, envy, and hate. It doesn't take long to listen to conversations of the worldly to hear these themes spoken frequently. In the Book of James, he is challenging Christians to do better. To make sure that they are aware of the words that they are speaking. Proverbs 18:21 states that there is life and death in the power of the tongue. James is reminding Christian men and women of that power they carry. We have such an important responsibility to ensure that what we are speaking brings forth life. We are told that what we speak should be edifying and build up believers (Romans 15:5), but I am not sure how many of us really recognize the importance of guarding what comes out of our mouths. If we truly understood the power of what we say, would we be so careless with our words? I am not saying that I have never called someone a jerk who cut me off on the road, but I am questioning whether I should have. According to this scripture, I definitely should not be blessing the Lord and cursing men.

In a time, where the world thinks less and less of using kindness or compassion with the words they speak, we as Christians need to be vigilant and guard what we allow to be spoken. We understand the power that we have, because we use that very power in our prayer lives. We want to see life, see miracles, see revival—yet we speak curses in haste. We are stopping the hand and move of God when we contradict ourselves.

James goes on in verses 17–18 stating: "Real wisdom, God's wisdom, begins with a holy life and is characterized by getting along with others. It is gentle and reasonable, overflowing with mercy and blessings, not hot one day and cold the next, not two-faced." Wow! What a challenge to Christians to develop characters that reflect the love of Christ within our hearts. I am challenged today to watch my words and to speak blessings and not things that are negative to others. Amen.

KEEPING IN TOUCH

"Many will say to Me in that day, 'Lord, Lord, have we not prophesied in Your name, cast out demons in Your name, and done many wonders in Your name?' And then I will declare to them, 'I never knew you; depart from Me, you who practice lawlessness!' (Matthew 7:22–23 NKJV)

It was the end of the workday, and I receive a request to go meet the supervisor in her office. I don't often receive requests such as this, so I am frantically trying to determine what the conversation will be about, and I am trying to determine what my responses will be to a myriad of possibilities. However, when I get to the supervisor's office, none of the items that I thought would be discussed were actually brought up at all. Instead of waiting and hearing what the conversation was actually about, I had predetermined it in my head and was completely incorrect in my summations.

In this passage of Matthew, Jesus is telling the people that there will be those who believe they are doing the work of the Lord, but they will miss it. They will be serving their own purposes and agendas. They will be seeking to please something or someone else other than God and His kingdom. We have the benefit of going to the Word of God for guidance. We are at a place in history where we see things that have caused a success in the preaching of the gospel and those things that have failed. We recognize that accepting Jesus is a choice that every individual has to make and not our will that we can impose on every man, woman, and child. We have the example of Christ

Himself, showering people with love and compassion. Still, there are moments that we may miss the mark and fall short in the moment. We can get so wrapped up in our own understanding that we miss what God is trying to show us or call us to do. We have to become practiced at both praying and then even more so at listening. Keeping in touch with God and His plans, His purposes, and His direction in our day-to-day lives. Without listening, we begin to guide ourselves based on our own understanding—we cannot trust in that alone—we have to be guided by our Heavenly Father.

Father God, this is an important message to me, because it reminds me to not expect I can interpret Your ways, but need to listen for Your clear instructions and leading. That You are always faithful in giving wisdom, and You know how to open and shut doors so I know where to go. Your command is, "Follow Me." I want to keep in touch with You constantly, in every moment and in every situation that presents itself. Keep my heart open, You promise if I am seeking You that I will know Your voice and I will not follow another. I am thankful for Your loving and tender heart toward me, and Your patience in guiding me. I love You, Lord. Amen.

BUILDING YOUR HOUSE

"But everyone who hears my teaching and does not apply it to his life can be compared to a foolish man who built his house on sand. When it rained and rained and the flood came, with wind and waves beating upon his house, it was swept away." (Matthew 7:26 TPT)

If you have ever watched the footage of a flood, you can visualize the damage that rising and rapidly flowing waters can have against anything in its path. It sweeps away everything it comes in contact with, and sometimes that has included someone's home. Jesus used this analogy to compare a life filled with God—including the knowledge and wisdom of God— and a life of sin. We cannot fool ourselves, it is literally one or the other. In another verse, Jesus tells us that we cannot serve two masters (Matthew 6:24). Sin is very much like the rising floodwater that will quickly come to a point where it destroys everything in its path. We cannot believe that we will be strong enough within ourselves to "swim out of it." We need the supernatural strength of our Lord, Jesus Christ. If there is an area in your life that has taken over and you want to break through that sin, shame, and suffering, call on the name of Jesus. Romans 10:13 clearly tells us that, "Anyone who calls on the name of the Lord shall be saved." We don't have to be swept away by sin, shame, fear, anxiety, mental illness, or anything else that comes against us. We can have the steadfast love of our Father and the strength and support of His promises found in His Word to build up our spiritual "house" or temple.

Lord, without You, I would be swept away by everything that this world brings: hatred, despair, envy, fear, depression. It is only in You and understanding who You are through the power of Your Word that I have hope and faith. I believe that You are greater than anything in this world. You will come to bring a new heaven and a new earth and I will live with You in that beautiful place forever. I thank You for the way You saved me from my sins and have changed me from the inside. Your Word promises that You can bring beauty from ashes. You, Father God, are a resurrecting God. You rebuild and restore lives that have been broken. I thank You for Your fierce and indescribable love and mercy that made You see me as something more than broken. I declare that anyone reading this right now that needs a breakthrough in their lives will be bold and call on the One who can save them. I prophesy that their lives will be changed, and they will begin to have a spirit, their house, that is built on the firm foundation of Your Word. In Jesus' name. Amen.

IS YOUR HEART SHUT?

But whoever has this world's goods, and sees his brother in need, and shuts up his heart from him, how does the love of God abide in him? My little children, let us not love in word or in tongue, but in deed and in truth. (1 John 3:17–18 NKJV)

There is rarely a time that we do not turn on the news that we are shown some sort of tragedy or someone hurting and in need. This is a broken world and Satan is out to destroy everything and everyone it. There has been a season of hardship across the world these past few years, with the pandemic, and wavering economies. Maybe you are looking at your resources and feel like you do not have enough for your own family. Maybe the day-to-day making ends meet is a struggle for you right now. We should never look at the statements of our Heavenly Father and think we have nothing to offer. Maybe you don't have financial resources to offer someone else in need, but you have time and talents.

We are called to give sacrificially. We are called to look different than the world and to share with one another so that no one will be in need (Act 2:45). Our willingness to share what God has gifted us, first demonstrates our understanding that He is the one who has provided for us. Secondly, it demonstrates our faith in God and not in our resources.

Maybe you know someone in need right now and you keep thinking that you don't have anything to give. Maybe you could make enough of your dinner to feed them for one meal. Maybe you could be the person to take them to their next doctor's appointment. Maybe you could buy extra school supplies when they are on sale and provide for someone else's children in your child's classroom. We make giving this big ordeal in our mind, but really it doesn't have to be hundreds or thousands of dollars. If we all do something, it helps. If we each take a piece, then the enormous task of helping others isn't as large as it once was...most of us have had a need of our own and can think of a time when we were blessed by someone else's gift.

Pray and ask, how will God use you today? Keep your heart open. Remember our resources may look differently than someone else's.

MORE RESOURCES THAN WE IMAGINE

God, the searcher of the heart, knows fully our longings, yet he also understands the desires of the Spirit, because the Holy Spirit passionately pleads before God for us, his holy ones, in perfect harmony with God's plan and our destiny. (Romans 8:27 TPT)

There are many people who experience things in this life that leave them without words to pray. Natural disasters, sickness of a loved one, loss of a child, broken relationships can bring each of us to a place where we have no words that express the depths of our hurt and pain. Our Heavenly Father was not unaware that these tragedies occur in our lives and put the Comforter, the Holy Spirit, within us for times such as these. Verse 26 in this chapter states, "But the Holy Spirit rises up within us to super-intercede on our behalf, pleading to God with emotional sighs too deep for words." God is not caught off guard by our circumstances, but instead placed us in the capable hands of the Holy Spirit to offer intercession for us in times we need it.

I see too many people describing God as distant, unjust, or inadequate. Their judgments are based on lack of knowledge, hardened hearts, and on their experiences of a broken world system. Those who know who God truly is can describe His overwhelming goodness even in the most difficult circumstances. It is in the understanding that we have a greater promise than the things of this life that free us from our broken hearts and loss. That there is something greater that we possess than the things that we have acquired on this earth, a spirit that connects us to the living God.

This verse encourages me that no matter how my flesh is feeling in the midst of the circumstances that surround me, and when I do not have the ability to speak from the heaviness of my broken heart, the Holy Spirit is already moving before God on my behalf. That the Spirit is not only telling the Lord of my pain, but also ensures that the prayers spoken for me align with God's perfect plan for my life.

JESUS ALWAYS KNEW

Father, I want those you gave me to be with me, right where I am, so they can see my glory, the splendor you gave me, having loved me long before there ever was a world. Righteous Father, the world has never known you, but I have known you, and these disciples know that you sent me on a mission. I have made your very being known to them—who you are and what you do—and continue to make it known, so that your love for me might be in them, exactly as I am in them. (John 17:24–26 MSG)

In this chapter of the Gospel of John, Jesus is praying prior to His betrayal and arrest at the Garden of Gethsemane. Jesus is fully aware of His Father's plan and what will take place. These verses show the depth of love that Jesus had, not just for His disciples during His ministry, but for you and me. This prayer is for every believer. Jesus went to the cross to conquer death and sin and allow for a way for each of us to be connected to God. That God's own Spirit could dwell in us. That we may have a deep and intimate knowledge of who God really is—Immanuel, "God with us."

Jesus prayed for you, knowing the trials you would face, knowing the mistakes you would make, knowing the sorrows you would have. There is nothing in your life that was hidden from him as he prayed for you. Just as nothing in your life is hidden from God. They are one, connected, and whole. To see who Jesus is and understand His ministry is to understand the purpose of God the Father. That everyone would receive salvation and have eternal life. That those that have received salvation would testify of the goodness of the Lord. That we would be of one mind and spirit, connected forever through Jesus Christ and demonstrate to a lost and dying world where freedom can be found.

Father, I am humbled again by the depth of Your love for me. To know that Jesus prayed for me before He went to the cross for me. To understand the greatness of His love and sacrifice. He understood that I would need His intercession, long before I realized my own brokenness and need for a savior. I am completely undone by the love and faithfulness shown to me when I least deserved them. I continue to declare unity of the body of Christ, and that those who have received salvation live transformed lives that all glory and honor may be given to You, the Holy One. I thank You, Lord. I praise You. You are so good. Amen.

HE SHALL BE YOUR PEACE

And He shall stand and feed His flock in the strength of the Lord, in the majesty of the name of the Lord His God; and they shall abide, for now He shall be great to the ends of the earth; and this One shall be peace. (Micah 5:4–5 NKJV)

Lately, one of the statements I have been hearing frequently from people is "I am feeling burnt out." This is just another way of saying they are weary, that the day-to-day tasks operating in their own strength has become too much for them. In this case, I work with them, I understand the demands of the job and how some weeks are just difficult. I have most likely said the same thing myself, especially when a period of six months or more has passed without taking any real time away from work for a vacation. However, if we stop and look for a moment at the day-to-day operation of our lives and examine it a bit closer, will we see that we are trying to accomplish the day-to-day tasks in our own strength? Are we not using the resource of the peace of Christ in the ordinary and everyday moments of life?

If Christ declared that He alone can give peace—different from the world giving peace—why are we still looking to find our peace in things like weekends, holidays, and vacations? Why are we still doing the day-to-day tasks in our own strength, and acting like we don't have someone who offers to carry our burdens—all of them—not just the largest ones, but even the mundane daily tasks of life? For those people who do not have a relationship with God, or an understanding of the promise of Jesus to be our peace, they really have no other choice but to turn to earthly options. However, we who are walking with Him daily recognize that we need to strengthen our spirits because "the spirit gives life; the flesh profits nothing" (John 6:63). We understand that we can have the peace we need for every single moment in our day-to-day when we stay connected with our Father. I know that, today, I needed this reminder of who will pour out peace in every area of my life. Perhaps you need the reminder as well.

Father, I thank You for the gift of Your Son Jesus Christ. In Him and through the power of the Holy Spirit, I can find supernatural peace for every moment of every day. Instead of focusing on weekends, holidays, and vacations to strengthen me—I come to You. I need You and the strength You give us when we draw close to You. I need to stay filled with the power of Your Spirit. You alone promise to give us wings to mount up like eagles and soar. You promise to give us sure footing in the steep and unsteady climb of many obstacles on our path of life. In You, I have my greatest joy, my greatest hope, my greatest faith, my greatest love, and my greatest peace. I will stay close to You and, if I stumble, I am confident You will call me back to You time and time again. Thank You, Lord, Your faithfulness surpasses all I could have imagined. Amen.

GIVING THANKS

Come on, everyone! Let's sing for joy to the Lord! Let's shout our loudest praises to our God who saved us! Everyone come meet his face with a thankful heart. Don't hold back your praises; make him great by your shouts of joy! (Psalm 95:1–2 TPT)

It can be easy to allow our circumstances to dictate whether we enter into praise and worship of our Father. We all go through challenges and sometimes our emotions do not align with an attitude of praise. This scripture is great reminder of the basic reason we should offer praise despite our emotions and circumstances. Our Mighty God, our Heavenly Father, has rescued us. If we have breath in our lungs and we have received salvation, these are enough reason to praise. Chances are, for most of us, God has done much more than these in our lives. He is the One who never leaves us or forsakes us. He keeps His promises from one generation to the next.

One of the things that is wonderful about worshipping God, no matter my circumstances, is that God meets me in my praise of Him. Praising Him reminds me of who He is and I renew the strength of my spirit. It is speaking the Word aloud and not only offering thanks for all God has done in my life, but declaring the truth over myself and in any circumstance I face.

You may feel broken now, or lost, or alone. You may be weeping from loss or pain. I encourage you to immerse yourself in worship music. Sing through your tears and in your pain. Offer the Lord thanks for His steadfast love. Offer Him praise for the gift of His Son, Jesus Christ, who died that you might live. It might not happen immediately, but as you sing words of God's promises and truth out loud, there will begin to be a change in your spirit. God always meets us whenever we come to Him and earnestly seek Him, no matter our condition. He has a way of meeting us at our lowest points and raising us up again.

Father God, I just want to spend some time today saying thank you. You saved me from myself and from sin all those years ago. You have never once abandoned me, but have pursued me with Your love. You have been faithful through every trial to stand with me. You have taken things that have been broken and You made something new and beautiful from the pieces. I couldn't do it, but You do the impossible. You take tragedy and turn it into blessing. You give peace when I need it most. You renew my joy. I thank You, Father. You are worthy of all my praise in every moment of every day. I love You. I will sing to You and shout to You with songs of joy. Amen.

HELD

And He Himself existed before all things, and in Him all things consist (cohere, are held together). (Colossians 1:17 AMPC)

When we take a closer look at the enemies' schemes they really have not changed over time. Satan is the father of all lies (John 8:44). He is always trying to get us to think that God is not good, does not keep His Word, and is not in complete control. We see this every day in people who are operating in a worldly system. They believe they have to look out for "number one." They scrape and claw for everything they have and they often will knock others down to do it. When it doesn't turn out for their benefit they blame everyone or even God instead of themselves and their poor choices.

No matter what we are seeing in the world, we can remember that there has never been a time when God didn't exist. He alone spoke the world into motion. He is the source of all life and He holds everything together. When man gave his power over to Satan in the Garden of Eden God made a plan for man's redemption through Jesus Christ. Through salvation and receiving the gift of the Holy Spirit, we receive the living power and authority that God intended us to carry. We do not have to worry about our future or our needs, because we serve a God who wants to provide for us. He always makes a way to provide for us. His very nature is good and loving. We witness this in watching the operation of Jesus in His ministry on earth. We may have trials, but we have the power to speak God's Word over any situation. We have the comfort of the Father's embrace in every season.

We are held. We don't have to fall apart. We don't have to listen to the whispers of the enemy. We can tell him to shut up. Jesus commanded demons to be silent, and each of us has been given the same authority. Fear, anxiety, worry, bitterness, envy, lack of unity, broken relationships, unforgiveness—these are not our inheritance. We have the promise of provision, healing, forgiveness, loving-kindness, tenderness, joy, and so much more!

Thank you, Lord, for this word. I am reminded of the childhood song "You've Got the Whole World in Your Hands." There has never been a time that You have not been taking care of Your children and demonstrating great love and mercy. Forgive us when we take our eyes off You and look at the temporary circumstances and events of this world. Our spirits are eternal and we have eternal promises that we are held and You are in control. We do not have to believe the fear that the enemy tries to instill in us. We have a mighty God who already has the victory. I thank You and praise You. Thank you for equipping us with the same power that lived in Jesus Christ. Help us to operate in it more completely that we may see Your goodness and see the lost won. In Jesus' name. Amen.

CORRECTION THROUGH CONVICTION

But this is what I commanded them, saying, 'Obey My voice, and I will be your God, and you shall be My people. And walk in all the ways that I have commanded you, that it may be well with you.' Yet they did not obey or incline their ear, but followed the counsels and the dictates of their evil hearts, and went backward and not forward. (Jeremiah 7:23–24 NKJV)

During a simple conversation with a friend in between church services yesterday, a simple question brought conviction to my heart. The question asked was, "We as Christians say we believe, but do we really believe and have faith?" I heard the Spirit of the Lord touch my heart about a specific area I was feeling doubtful about recently. Doubting that the Lord would do what He said He would do. Feeling like He would not fulfill the promise of His Word. My doubts will lead to me making the Word of God powerless in my life and in the situations I need the hand of God to effect change.

I want to encourage you today to listen for the voice of the Lord. Where is He convicting you in your life? His conviction, the voice calling you to align your heart and your ways with His Word, are for our own benefit. We can either trust in His Word and His ways, or go backwards. We need to recognize that moving forward means aligning our hearts, minds, and spirits with His Word and His truth and tearing down anything from our flesh. That is our plans, our ideas, and our own timing. God is always operating out of His goodness towards us. He is showing us the way to walk and to operate in His Word, but we can either listen or harden our hearts. If we choose to harden our hearts, then we create barriers to the power of God moving in our lives. We become less effective for the Kingdom because we allowed our own selfish ambitions, pride, fears, and doubts to become larger than the God we serve.

Lord, how can I praise You enough? Even when I don't recognize my own weaknesses becoming a hindrance to the plans You have set before me—You make a way to show me and lead me back to You. You strengthen me with the remembrance of who You are and how to walk in obedience to Your Word. Forgive me for my unbelief. Strengthen my faith. Keep Your Word continually on my lips that I may keep it like a fire in my spirit and it will burn up the areas that still contain any fear or doubt. You have always been faithful and have turned so many situations around for my good. I know that You will never fail me. Keep my heart, my mind, and my lips from ever saying anything different about who You are. I love You. Thank you for using conviction to show me the correction that was needed in my spirit. I love how You love me enough to help me when I fall short. You are such a wonderful Father. There is no one like You. May Your name alone be glorified in all the earth. Amen.

ENDUED WITH HIS STRENGTH

"Behold, I will make you into a new threshing sledge with sharp teeth; you shall thresh the mountains and beat them small, and make the hills like chaff. You shall winnow them, the wind shall carry them away, and the whirlwind shall scatter them; you shall rejoice in the Lord, and glory in the Holy One of Israel." (Isaiah 41:15–16 NKJV)

A threshing sledge is a large piece of flat wood with hundreds of bits of stone embedded into the wood. The edges of the stone that stuck out of the wood are carved or chiseled to a sharp point. This sledge would be placed behind cattle and dragged along the ground to cut down the crops of grain at harvest time. In this passage, God is telling Israel that they do not have to be afraid because God is with them. He uses this description of how they are strong enough to bring down mountains and beat them until the wind will just blow the dust away.

In the New Testament, Jesus tells us that we can speak to our mountains and they will have to move (Mark 11:23). We all have different situations that arise in our lives that seem impossible. We need to not look at the situation and make it larger than our God. God is the one who makes all things possible. He is the one that parts seas, who brings water forth from rocks, who heals the sick and resurrects the dead. There is nothing that is impossible for God. We can be strong in any situation because He is always with us. We have His strength living inside us through the power of His Holy Spirit.

Maybe you have been facing your mountain for a long time. You have been speaking to it and wondering when it is going to move. When will it melt like wax before you? God is reminding you today to keep obeying His voice. Keep prophesying to your mountain. His timing is perfect. He is working it out. He is not going to leave you in the valley and He is not defeated. You have the victory in Him. You will see your promised land. God cannot go against His own word!

Thank you, God, for showing us that we can make the mountains in our lives bow low and be like chaff. Soon they will be like small bits of sand and be blown away. We will see all that You have prophesied over our lives come into place. We will see Your glorious victory and rejoice with You! You never bring us to a situation or season that You have not already made a way for Your children to be victorious. Let my heart be encouraged by Your Word and let it resonate deep in my mind and spirit that I may not lose heart. Thank you, Father. You are good and You never fail! Amen.

READY TO LISTEN

I have called upon You, for You will hear me, O God; incline Your ear to me and hear my speech. (Psalm 17:6 NKJV)

Because He bends down to listen, I will pray as long as I have breath! (Psalm 116:2 NLT)

I love the image of God drawing close to each of us. I imagine a beautiful sunset and a campfire. The sound of the gentle breeze in the trees. The Lord is sitting next to me in front of the fire and we just talk about anything that comes to mind. Some subjects are light and humorous, but He doesn't turn away when the conversations get deep and full of emotion. He doesn't rush to give His opinion but just listens to all that is happening inside my heart. He doesn't look shocked or surprised, because He already knows. He just knew I needed to talk to share my heart and He wanted me to know He is always available.

God loves you. He created you and knows every detail of who you are—there isn't anything about you that is unexpected to Him. He understands that we have a need to share the things in our hearts, to talk about it, to let go of things that weigh us down. These verses remind us that we have a Heavenly Father that is always willing to listen. He isn't in a hurry, He understands that hurt and pain take time to share. He is willing to wait and He is willing to listen. He is a safe place. He has made Himself available at any hour we call upon Him. I have cried out to Him in the darkness of night when I could not sleep because my worries kept me awake. I told Him my doubts and fears, and that I needed wisdom and clear vision in the circumstances that surrounded me. The peace that flows after we lay our hearts before our Father is such a treasured gift. He wants to meet us with His perfect peace, but we have to be willing to trust in Him. We have to be open to receiving all that He has. Your Father already knows, but has the gift of peace waiting for you. He is ready to listen.

Abba Father, how wonderful You are! That You would want to sit with me and let me share my thoughts, my heart, and my burdens with You. That Your perfect peace is always waiting for me within every conversation that we may have. I love how You love me. It is perfect in every way. Thank you that You are always ready to make time for me—even in the darkness of night. There is no other love as complete as Yours. I worship You and give You thanks and praise! Amen.

EXPECTING CHANGE

Lord, I always live my life before your face, so examine me and exonerate me. Vindicate me and show the world I'm innocent. For in a visitation of the night you inspected my heart and refined my soul with fire until nothing vile was found within me. I've wanted my words and my ways to always agree. (Psalm 17:2–3 TPT)

When we read about the lives of those who followed God in the Bible, we are shown that God was able to use people despite their brokenness. No one was perfect. Even King David, who has been referred to as a "man after God's own heart," is found to make mistakes when we read about his life. It is God's grace that meets us wherever we are at, and accepts us when we call out to Him. The wonderful thing about God though is that once we surrender our lives to Him we can expect change to happen.

In 2 Corinthians 5:17, we are reminded that if we are in Christ then the old has died and we are made new. We don't have to be locked into our old beliefs, our old patterns, or our past. We can expect God to show up and refine us. He starts to change us from within. He shows us that we don't need certain habits, or even certain unhealthy friendships, in our lives. He puts His own desires in our hearts when we are seeking Him. Things in your life that you thought were beyond repair can be transformed in your loving Father's hands. You will no longer be broken but become a beautiful tapestry, woven together with the truth of God living inside your heart. The transformation takes our willingness to be open and obedient before our God. To be reaching for His knowledge and His truth. Engaged in studying His Word and changing what we allow into our minds and hearts. If you are pursuing God, you can expect change. God wants something better for all of us. He wants us to see that life, here in this broken world, can be filled with beauty. His handiwork and His design are for us to have fulfilled lives, full of purpose and hope.

Lord, I am so grateful that You accept us as we come to You—broken and a little banged up—less than perfect. You see beauty in each of us, because we are created by Your hand. Your love is all-consuming and You begin to work to bring about the changes in our lives and hearts that will give us more. You pour into us truth and love and strength. Your intricate plan and purpose for each of us is good. Thank you that we don't have to stay where we have always been, that through Your love and work on the inside of us we can break free from the things that hold us down. We can expect change—a transformation in our hearts, minds, and spirits. I worship You, Father, for there is no one like You. Thank you for changing me. I love You so much. Amen.

SELF-EXAMINATION

Dear friends, you always followed my instructions when I was with you. And now that I am away, it is even more important. Work hard to show the results of you salvation, obeying God with deep reverence and fear. For God is working in you, giving you the desire and the power to do what pleases him. (Philippians 2:12–13 NLT)

In the past twenty or thirty years, as the medical field shifted its focus to preventive medical practices, there are several ways we can take an active role in promoting our best health. One such practice in breast cancer prevention is self-examination. Women are asked to determine if there are any physical changes when they examine their breasts monthly to aid in the early detection of cancer. We can do spiritual checkups as well.

In this letter, Paul is encouraging believers to do a little spiritual self-examination. The basic questions Paul is encouraging Christians to ask are: "Do I look any different from those who are unsaved? Am I living a life that reveals Christ?" These are important ways we can examine our hearts and spirits. It is easy to allow ourselves to become complacent: to laugh at the slightly improper joke or to not walk away when gossip or negative talk about the boss begins. Maybe it is something more serious. Maybe it is an addiction that you thought was gone, but one little peek back and suddenly it grabs hold of you again. This scripture states that we need to "work hard to show the results of our salvation." It doesn't say that salvation is the answer to all our problems. We have to work at maintaining our new nature, because our flesh still remains with us until we are called home. We have to be aware of our own weaknesses and then make sure we are pursuing God, His Word, and the things that will fill us so that our flesh does not charge ahead of our born-again spirits. Our faith is an active pursuit. Like daily exercise that keeps our physical bodies healthy, our spiritual self needs exercise, too. The beginning of any exercise is a little self-examination— What area in your life need a bit of strengthening or refocus? Where do you need to change from a worldly perspective to a godly purpose? Change begins with the desire to improve and grow. We have the promise that, as a new creation, God is already changing us and will equip us to do just that! Verse 13 states that He is working in us through His spirit that dwells within us! What an amazing promise!

KEEPING UNITY AMONG THE BODY

Just as our bodies have many parts and each part has a special function, so it is with Christ's body. We are many parts of one body, and we all belong to each other. In his grace, God has given us different gifts for doing certain things well. (Romans 12:4–6 NLT)

When working with watercolor paints, one of the techniques is wetting the canvas first and then adding the colors to the water. This allows the painter to deepen one color by adding more, or blending colors together by changing or adding something different. It is important to note that the colors do not work or come together without the presence of water. If I were to open the palette of my watercolor paints and swirl a dry brush on one of the colors, I will not pick up any color on the brush. Water is what makes the whole process work.

Christ is the principal element in the body of Christ. We are each connected by our connection with Him. He is the foundation of our connection to one another as believers. He has to be the key element that brings believers together. If it is not Him, then we begin to see our individual values, personalities, and desires begin to guide and lead our attitudes with one another. These are the things that bring about disunity. If we have scriptures teaching about the body of the Church, we can believe that division and discord were issues in the beginnings of the Church. Here, in Romans, we are reminded that God has formed each of us differently, but that we all complement one another with our gifts and abilities. We need to understand that each believer is essential, and that without one another we are incomplete.

The time for unity in the body of Christ has come. We need to look different from the world. We are to esteem others more than ourselves, but oftentimes we look just as selfish as the world. We want to be comfortable and to have everything that fits our needs, our ideals, and our preferences. We allow the whisper of the enemy to plant seeds of division and strife among believers. If Satan was causing discord in the Early Church, he is still up to the same lies and tricks today. We have the power to stop him. We need to be sold out on Christ. That means allowing our flesh to die and to truly begin to live a life of service to the body of Christ. To lay aside our attitudes of individualism and begin to see the beauty of being part of something greater than ourselves. We were each selected to bring the gospel of Jesus Christ into the world. Our gift is essential in leading others to Christ. We do not need to have the same gifting as the worship leader or the pastor—in fact, we cannot all do those things because it leaves so many other needs unmet. Ask the Lord to reveal your gift and then be obedient in your calling. Without you, the body is incomplete.

NO DARKNESS IN HIM

Your eye is the lamp of your body. When your eye is healthy, your whole body is full of light, but when it is bad, your body is full of darkness. (Luke 11:34 ESV)

We rely so heavily on our sense of vision. It is what helps us maintain our sense of balance, our sense of direction, and a majority of how we take in experiences and sensations in the world.

During a prayer service at our church last night, I had a vision of eyes that had a milky film over them. They were eyes that were no longer letting in light or other sights. They were eyes that were blind. These were our eyes if we focus on the things of the world for too long. We become blind to the things that the Lord wants to show us. The greatness of His power, the miracles He does every single day. We can no longer see the love and compassion He has for every single person on the face of the earth. We see the despair, the hatred, and the bitterness, but we are so overwhelmed by the darkness that we forget to focus on the One who is the Light of the World.

The Lord is speaking to my spirit, stating, "There is no darkness in Me. My eyes will always see. There are no scales to peel back from My eyes, because there is no darkness that I cannot pierce through. It will be like the breaking of day where ever I look. Those who think they cannot be seen are seen clearly and fully. Those who think the darkness is all they will ever know will rejoice when the dawn bursts forth. Those who call out to Me will never have to walk in darkness.

I spoke and light existed. It's very form is in My hand. I pour it out upon the earth, but every person has a choice—they can walk in light or darkness. They can believe in Me or deny Me. They can be blind to the truth or they can fully see—I Am—I alone am the Beginning and the End. There is no shadow, there is no variation of Me. Look to Me for the light of revelation. Look to Me for the light of wisdom and knowledge. Look to Me for the light of freedom through grace and mercy. Look to me for the light of love and redemption. I Am all things. I alone Am God. Peel back the film from your eyes and truly see Me, the Creator of all things."

Thank you, Lord, for reminding us that if we want our body to be full of light we must use our eyes to seek Your face. We do not have to fear the darkness of the world, because You have overcome it. This world is passing away, but we have the promise of a new home that will never be filled with darkness. It will be filled with the glory of Your presence. My mind cannot grasp a place without the difference between day and night, but I cannot wait to live in Your kingdom. I know it will be like nothing I could describe or imagine. Thank you for the way You love us. How patient and kind You have been so that all may come to know You. I prophesy that many lost souls are given new life daily. That the news of Your love and the sacrifice of Jesus pierces hearts and transforms lives as only it can. In Jesus' name. Amen.

PRAISE IS BALM FOR THE WEARY

Therefore they shall come and sing in the height of Zion, streaming to the goodness of the Lord—for wheat and new wine and oil, for the young of the flock and the herd; their souls shall be like a well-watered garden, and they shall sorrow no more at all. (Jeremiah 31:12 NKJV)

The other day, my church held a special prayer service on a Monday evening. Mondays at work are extremely busy because there are paperwork requirements that have to be completed for patient care every Monday. This often makes it extremely difficult to complete work on time. As I rushed home, heated up leftovers, and my husband and I made our way to church—I felt tired. It has been a busy season lately. My mind was hardly ready to do any kind of intercessory prayer when we arrived at the church. Thankfully, our pastors are well-seasoned and we began the prayer session with some informal worship. Singing in the spirit and offering praise to the Lord changes the atmosphere.

In the Old Testament, we often see that during battles the command was often for the musicians and singers to lead and begin the battle with worship. I believe it is because the prophetic words of the Lord change the present circumstances. And just as promised in this scripture it provides healing for our souls. This verse says "like a well-watered garden." This summer just as my tomatoes were beginning to grow, we went away for a planned trip. There was no way to have the plants watered while we were gone. We had some rain during that time, but it really wasn't enough to keep the plants healthy. When we arrived home the leaves were burnt and the ends had turned brown. The leaves and fruits that had been growing were also spotted. The plant no longer looked healthy or vibrant. We know that water is essential to every living thing. Here the writer compares coming with rejoicing and singing with having a soul filled up and overflowing. A healthy spirit that is filled with joy in place of sorrow. Anyone who has really entered into worship before the Lord understands this miraculous transformation. God uses our praise to lift us up and give our eyes an opportunity to see things from an eternal perspective. It takes the focus off the present circumstances and places them on the One Who Is Faithful. Praise is the balm or the essential medicine that every believer needs in the midst of every aspect of life.

Thank you, Lord, for providing the balm for our spirits. A place to come before You and be refilled to overflowing. We can see how You take our sorrow and replace it with peace and joy and praise. You and Your presence through the Holy Spirit is the medicine I always need in every moment of every day. Thank you for the beautiful way You provide. You deserve the glory and the praise, but it is also a gift to us—to allow us to remember the power You alone contain. I exalt You and lift Your name above any other. All glory belongs to you, my father and my God. Amen.

A SERVANT'S HEART

Therefore humble yourselves under the mighty hand of God, that He may exalt you in due time, casting all your cares upon Him, for He cares for you. (1 Peter 5:6–7 NKJV)

I believe it is C. S. Lewis who stated, "True humility is not thinking less of yourself: it is thinking of yourself less." We live in a society that is in direct opposition to this concept. The world system continues to scream slogans such as "Look out for number one," or "Strive to make yourself happy," or "No one is going to give it you, so you better take it." The world is in a mad scramble to achieve, to accumulate, to look for that quick self-satisfying fix, but none of it is lasting, because it is all empty.

As Christians we understand that every good gift is from our Heavenly Father, and that this is not our permanent home. All that is here is fleeting. It began in dust and will return to dust. We don't have to fight for what we have because we have a Father who wants to provide for us. He created all that we see to sustain us and is happy to share it with us. He doesn't want us to struggle for our basic needs because He understands that they are necessary. Instead, He wants to ensure that we have all that we need so that we can focus on declaring His good works in our lives. More importantly, He wants us to have the attitude of a servant's heart. That we would share and work together for the good of every brother and sister in Christ, but also for those who have not yet found Him. We are to think of others more and ourselves less. It is a tall order, but not an impossible one. We have the beautiful example of Jesus, the very Son of God, sacrificing everything for each of us. He had everything, but He gave it all away because of His great love for us. He had compassion on the broken, those who were suffering and in need. This is the same heart, the same love, the same compassion we are called to show one another.

Lord, I confess there are times when I fall short of putting others before myself. Please forgive me. I recognize the amazing way Jesus served all of humanity and the gift of salvation that granted to each of us who choose it. I know You desire us to show love, compassion, and service to those in need. Help me to see with Your eyes Lord in this world around me. You have placed Your Spirit inside me and I will hear clearly and obey Your voice. The example of selfless love is the one that points to You and leads others to the cross of salvation. Help me share this love and the good news so that no one needs to be separated from You. Amen.

GREATER STRENGTH

If you faint in the day of adversity, your strength is small. (Proverbs 24:10 NKJV)

All throughout the Bible, we are reminded that we will need strength as we walk through this life. We will have moments of celebration and joy, but there will also be times of hardship and sorrow. We live in a world where we gave our authority to the one who wants to destroy us (Genesis 3:1–4, 13). As we surrender our lives to our Lord and Father, the enemy will attack us and always be trying to weaken our faith. We see this time and again in the writings of the Old and New Testaments. The statement "Do not be afraid" is used in the Bible 365 times. That is a daily reminder. We have a weapon greater than any hardship we face. Our God and Father is fighting for us. We can be strengthened in our belief that we never have to face any circumstance alone. That is how Paul was content even when imprisoned. He recognized that God was with Him and never left him, even in the hardest experiences.

Perhaps you are reading this today, and are going through some type of battle. Be encouraged that you are not alone. You God and Father is for you. He wants to be your strength and portion forever. How can God strengthen you? Through praying to Him: Tell God what you are facing and then thank Him for how He is the God of all possibility. He can change the circumstances. Read His Word: There is power in the words written in the Bible. There are real-life stories of how other people went through battles and how God walked with them. There is evidence of God's great love and mercy on every page! Praise your

Creator: There is power in coming before God and offering Him worship through singing or words—creating strength in your spirit.

If you are not going through a trial, that is so fantastic, but practice these things so that you will know what to do if the need ever arises.

Father God, I thank You for my brothers and sisters reading this right now. I do not know what they face daily, but You do. Your Word reminds us that we do not have to be afraid no matter what we are facing—You are with us. I prophesy that, as they draw close to You, You are working in their situations to make a breakthrough. You are also building up their faith and strength to stand. They will have greater awareness of Your presence and peace. Their faith will be a great testimony that brings You glory. I prophesy that they will have revelation knowledge as they draw closer through Your Word and spending time with You. That they will grasp the depth of Your love and who they are as a temple of the living God. I pray that no weapon fashioned against them will prosper and they will be giving shouts of victory as they see that Satan is defeated—Christ gave us victory forever and ever! Amen.

UNDERSTANDING HIS WILL

And if (since) we [positively] know that He listens to us in whatever we ask, we also know [with settled and absolute knowledge] that we have [granted us as our present possessions] the requests made of Him. (1 John 5:15 AMPC)

Growing up, I had a few friends who had the Magic 8 Ball. That toy that, after you asked a random question, you shook hoping to see the answer you wanted pop up in a little window. Many people are still living in that type of uncertainty, wondering about what they are asking and hoping for in their lives. Many people still seem uncertain about the will of God for their life. I love the Amplified version of this verse because it says that we can have "settled and absolute knowledge" that God listens to whatever we ask of Him.

I will be honest, just like many other people, I wasn't taught about understanding the will of God, or about speaking out His will over my life, until several decades into my Christian walk. It has taken me a little while to completely understand it and to walk it out in my own journey. I am thankful for pastors who want their church body to be knowledgeable and grow in spiritual authority, equipping us to become missionaries and disciples preaching the gospel wherever we are planted.

In 2 Corinthians 1:20, we are told that all God's promises have now become a "yes" through Christ Jesus. That means that through Christ's victory on the cross, breaking the curse of sin now and forever, we have everything the Father has promised us: salvation, forgiveness, healing, strength, power and anointing, provision, and the gifts of the Spirit. These are the things that are according to His will for our lives. He is a Father who loves us and wants to see us blessed, so that our lives are a testimony to others of His love and faithfulness. That His glory is displayed in our lives to those who are seeking and to those who are lost. At the end of this scripture in 2 Corinthians, it states that our response should be "Amen." The translation for this is "So be it." Effectively, we are saying we are in agreement with God's promises for our lives. That we trust that His will for us is ultimately good.

Put down that Magic 8 Ball. You don't have to wonder if God is going to answer your prayers. Instead, start thanking Him for He is the God who keeps His promises. He is always faithful. He was faithful to make a plan for the salvation of all mankind and to see it completed. He will be faithful in helping all things work for good in your life. Maybe you can't see it now, but you will. His Word cannot change.

Thank you, Abba, that Your promises in my life and the lives of all your children are "yes and amen." There is no one else like You. Your steadfast love and faithfulness cannot ever be changed. You stay the same—yesterday, today, and forever. Amen.

FINISH YOUR RACE

I don't depend on my own strength to accomplish this; however I do have one compelling focus: I forget all of the past as I fasten my heart to the future instead. I run straight for the divine invitation of reaching the heavenly goal and gaining the victory-prize through the anointing of Jesus. (Philippians 3:13–14 TPT)

Growing up in a family of seven, money was tight at times in our house. I remember begging to my parents to take violin lessons. They found the money to rent the instrument, but shortly after I started to take lessons, I didn't like it at all and wanted to quit. My father informed me that, if I quit taking my lessons for violin, they would not pay for the lessons or rental of another instrument because I didn't finish what I began. I am not sure that I as a child really had a complete understanding of what he was trying to teach me. Certainly at that age I did not have any concept of money or the cost of things. Their sacrifice to make something like that happen for me was not something I really understood then. Looking back through the eyes of an adult, I can now see that it wasn't just the financial aspect of things, but also my father trying to encourage me to finish what I started. That not everything I wanted to do would be easy, but would take work and effort. Our Heavenly Father wants the same thing for each of His children. Finish your race.

We are pulled in so many directions all at once. It is understandable that we feel weary and we can lose our focus on our purpose. Maybe we have suffered a setback and things did not turn out the way we thought they would. We are not sure that we have the strength to push forward. God is saying: "Finish your race." He who sent His only Son, Jesus Christ, to die for you, will not let you fall. Keep looking forward into the eyes of your loving Father. Keep reaching for Him. It is a pursuit that is worth it. It is the most valuable prize you can ever obtain. He who saved you promised to renew your strength, and He will. He understands our weaknesses and promises to provide what we need in each and every day. His Word declares, "His mercies are new every morning" (Lamentations 3:22–23). We all need rest, but if He has called you to a work and a purpose, He will be faithful to help you see it through. I should know, it has been two years of writing for me to almost have a 365-day devotional book completed. I have been tired at times, and at others been unsure that I could fulfill this purpose. But God. There is such power in those words. He is not me—He is the greater One in me, and I yield to Him, because without Him it is all empty. I will finish my race. I will press on. He is worthy of it all.

Thank you, Lord, what an amazing lesson in perseverance You have been showing me these past years. You are so generous in Your gifts of wisdom, supply, and tender mercies. The presence of Your Spirit never lets me run dry. I am so thankful for Your love. I declare that anyone reading this right now who feels unsure if they can complete their race, will know that You are equipping them to fulfill their purpose in You. Amen.

THE ONE WHO HOLDS ALL THE ANSWERS

Hear my cry, O God; attend to my prayer. From the end of the earth I will cry to You, when my heart is overwhelmed; lead me to the rock that is higher than I. (Psalm 61:1–2 NKJV)

When I was in elementary school, I began to struggle with math. All of a sudden, numbers turned into word problems, and I had no idea what I was supposed to figure out. Up until this point, school had gone well for me and I had good grades in all my subjects. Quickly that changed and I began to fail several tests. My teacher handed my last failed test to me and stated that I needed to get my parent's signature on the test and return it to him. I felt ashamed of my failure and scared to talk to my parents about it, so I forged my father's name on the paper. My teacher wasn't fooled by the signature, and my original situation of needing help in math had now become exponentially worse. My failure in math had now become an attempt at deception, and that lie had consequences. King David had a similar experience with taking matters into his own hands. He committed adultery with Bathsheba and then, to cover it up, plotted to have her husband placed at the front of battle, and it resulted in his death.

Although that may not be the original intent of this particular psalm, I believe that throughout his life King David had experiences that made him aware that he needed God's help and wisdom in every situation. Oftentimes we rely on our own strength, or turn to other people, or even the Internet for help and resources. None of those things are necessarily bad; however, we are told again and again that we have a God who cares for us and wants to give us help in our times of trouble. Instead of scrambling to figure it all out on our own, He wants us to come to Him. He is the One who created the universe and made all things to work together in ways that we have not figured out. He is the One who holds all the answers. When we surrender our hearts to the Lord, we are supposed to look to Him and not trust in our own understanding (Proverbs 3:5–6). Maybe you are in that place where you feel overwhelmed, and you have been waiting for the answers for a long time, but you feel that God has been silent. I want to encourage you that although you do not have the answer right this minute, God is not idle. First, He wants to give you His peace, but you have to stop striving to receive it. Is your striving to accomplish it in your own power getting in the way of God completing His work? Sometimes we are the barrier to receiving what God wants to accomplish in our present struggles. I know that unfortunately; I didn't learn my lesson after my first attempt to fix a problem on my own. There have been several times that I didn't turn to God, but trusted in my own resources, until my situation was too big and overwhelming for me to handle. In my brokenness, I then fell to my knees and saw my need for Him. Don't be like me. Turn to Him first; He is the One who holds all the answers.

TRUSTING

In peace I will both lie down and sleep, For You alone, O Lord, make me dwell in safety and confident trust. (Psalm 4:8 AMPC)

Have you ever known someone who just seems to live in an utter state of chaos, with stress and anxious words and thoughts all the time? Have you heard someone you have talked to say, "I just worry, I can't help it"? Standing on the outside of whatever their situation is, in that moment, we recognize that they do not trust in the Lord. Honestly, I have been there myself. Restless nights, not sleeping, not taking control of my own anxious thoughts about one situation or another. Our Father recognizes our tendencies to fixate and focus on our present situations. He provides us counsel in several scriptures:

Be anxious for nothing, but instead pray about everything with thanksgiving. (Philippians 4:6– 7)

Do not worry about what your will eat or drink, but see first the kingdom. (Matthew 6:25)

Do not conform to worldly patterns but be transformed by the renewing of your mind. (Romans 12:2)

Do not worry about tomorrow. (Matthew 6:34)

There are more scriptures as well; however, you can see our Father's heart for us—He wants us to be at peace. He knows that worry and anxious thoughts are unhealthy for our physical bodies and for our emotional well-being. He wants us to give everything over to Him. He wants us to trust in Him. This is not a momentary decision, but a constant and consistent decision on our part. We have to be determined that we will release challenging situations to God and then begin to actively praise Him for His help. Praying and praising in the spirit are essential to helping me remain in peace when I am facing trials and I do not know the outcome. I have found no other resource that helps quite like it. If I worship and praise, declaring the promises of God over situations, and then pray in the spirit—I help my heart and mind to be at peace. Otherwise, the fear that can enter my mind will quickly take hold and spiral out of control. I have had to practice this time and again.

I do not know what situation you are facing right now, but your Heavenly Father wants you to know that He is working for your good. He wants you to trust Him. He wants you to have a tranquil heart and see that He is always fighting for you. He loves you with an everlasting love and promises that His plans for you are full of hope and a prosperous future. He cannot lie and He cannot fail. Amen.

WELL-TIMED HELP

Let us then fearlessly and confidently and boldly draw near to the throne of grace (the throne of God's unmerited favor to us sinners), that we may receive mercy [for our failures] and find grace to help in good time for every need [appropriate help and well-timed help, coming just when we need it]. (Hebrews 4:16 AMPC)

Remember playing the game of Monopoly growing up? Rolling the dice and your token ending up on the spot labeled JAIL, or getting a card that told you to "Go to Jail." Then you impatiently waited for a card that had the statement "Get out of jail free." This game basically mirrored what God instituted for all of us when He gave His only son, Jesus, as a sacrifice for all of our sins. If we truly repent and ask for forgiveness, God is faithful to grant His mercy—again and again. This scripture states that we can boldly request this of our God, because it is His nature to give favor to His sons and daughters. It is His desire to help us in our time of need.

There are so many times in my life where I have made mistakes, and I have failed. I have failed to be obedient to God's calling and purpose in my life. I have failed to love others the way He has called me to love them and have, instead, selfishly served myself. I have closed my eyes to the truth and believed in the whispered lies of the enemy, Satan. I have been like the prodigal son, getting to the point of destitution in my soul, before the scales were peeled off my eyes. I cannot begin to express my gratitude for a Father's love that offered me forgiveness when I came to senses and realized that I needed Him. That, on my own, without Him dwelling in me—I would be dragged along to the grave, in the shackles of my own making, with all the others who follow the callings of this world. I probably didn't go boldly to His throne. I went on my knees—but our good and gracious God has a way of lifting up our head and reminding us that we are His children and He loves us. That He will always be there to provide the help whenever we need it. He is just waiting for us to call on Him. That is our Heavenly Father. Patient, loving, kind—never belittling us, never reminding us of our failures, and never remembering our sins. That is who He is and that is who He will always be.

Thank you, Father, for this beautiful reminder of the unearned favor You grant each of us who turn to You. That You never turn Your face away. That You always meet us in our needs. Your ear is always ready to listen. I cannot express the beauty in Your love. My words are too few to begin to demonstrate appropriate gratitude for the countless times You have saved me from myself and my own sinful ways. I thank You for the continued work You do inside my spirit, making me more in the image of Christ every day. Take out things that get in the way of filling me with Your Spirit. I just want You, God. More and more and more of You. Amen.

LET YOUR WORDS HAVE MEANING

And since you know that he cares, let your language show it. Don't add words like "I swear to God" to your own words. Don't show your impatience by concocting oaths to hurry up God. Just say yes or no. Just say what is true. That way, your language can't be used against you. (James 5:12 MSG)

When I was growing up, my sister who hated vegetables would always promise me to eat something I didn't like if I ate her vegetables. Oftentimes, she never fulfilled her promise. That led to bigger and bigger oaths and ending with the "pinky promise" before I would trust her word.

In the scheme of things, promises over vegetables are not really a big deal, but our words do reflect what is in our hearts. In Matthew 12:34–35, Jesus is speaking to the Pharisees and tells them that out of the abundance of the heart our mouths speak. What are we saying about what we believe? Are we talking about how the world is spinning out of control, or are we pointing to our belief that God is in control? Are we talking out of fear or hope? Are you talking negatively about your work situation, and saying negative things about your boss or supervisor? Do you sound just like every nonbeliever or do you sound different? If we are trying to show people that God changes things and can change our lives radically and for the good, then we need to ensure our words line up with that truth.

Honestly, I am convicted by this because the negativity at work can be like a vortex—sucking me into the middle of complaining. I have to confess that I am not always good at keeping a close watch over my mouth and not joining in the negative talk. I hear God reminding me that I need to be speaking life in every situation. Our mission is to encourage one another and to be a light to the lost, and that becomes ineffective when I allow negativity to overcome. It's not always easy to be called to a higher standard, but our Lord promises to equip us with strength and wisdom and power. We do not operate in our strength. My pastor often reminds us that if we are not sure what to say, or if we feel that our words may not align with God's truth, then we should remain silent. This is truly wise. We want our words to have meaning. To be a direct reflection of what we say we believe. This all requires self-evaluation and reflection, and then working on adjusting what does not demonstrate the will and calling of the Lord. Once we recognize that our words and actions are not Christlike, then our next step is to change. Let your words have meaning, and let them not be used against you.

Father, thank you for this reminder that all I do and say reflect who You are in my life. Forgive me for allowing my flesh to rule and not having a guard over my lips. I want to show others how great You really are and that You are the God of all hope, peace, and joy. That You alone have provided every good and perfect thing for Your children. Help me stay silent when I do not have the words of life to speak. I know that the Holy Spirit can intercede when I lack the words to say, but I need to silence myself and not speak against Your Word. Bring this scripture to my remembrance as often as You need, so that what I speak always reflects who You truly are. Amen.

OUTSIDE YOUR COMFORT ZONE

One day when large groups of people were walking along with him, Jesus turned and told them, "Anyone who comes to me but refuses to let go of father, mother, spouse, children, brothers, sisters—yes, even one's own self!—can't be my disciple. Anyone who won't shoulder his own cross and follow behind me can't be my disciple." (Luke 14:25–27 MSG)

Traveling abroad is always a challenge for me personally. I find the rushing through the airport, the customs lines, the baggage check, the baggage claim always keeping me on pins and needles the whole time. The several times I have been on a mission trip to Central America, even with people I adore from my church, does not really abate that sense of nervousness I get traveling. It is outside my comfort zone. Like most people, I prefer my quiet little patch of life, with my predictable routine and the security of my loved ones close by. However, as a believer, God is constantly working to grow us and transform us into the image of His Son, and that requires pushing us outside our boundaries.

This scripture alludes to the heart and attitude of a believer. Nothing we have in this life is supposed to come before the will of God. God designed each of us for a purpose and it is to serve in His kingdom and spread the news of hope—the gospel of Jesus Christ—so that lives may be transformed and people can experience salvation. Many of us won't experience all that God has for us, because we are not willing to step outside our comfort zone. We ignore the call to serve, to go to another country on a mission trip, or to give our testimony. Don't kid yourself; you are demonstrating your lack of trust in God. You give into the lie that you can't be used and make this faith, this walk, about you instead of the King of kings. Spending time in the Bible, we see God is no respecter of persons, instead, He chooses the weak to defy the strong. David was a shepherd who became king. Moses was a murderer and of slow speech, but he was sent to speak for the Israelites and secure their freedom. Gideon was hiding when God sent him out to fight. God's Word says that you are chosen and part of a royal priesthood (1 Peter 2:9). Following God means going where He calls you and that may mean you have to step outside your comfort zone, but I guarantee you that if He calls you to a place—He will equip you.

Father God, thank you for reminding me that my faith doesn't grow if I don't follow Your calling. I can't always see every step of the path You put in front of me—but Your Word says to pick up my cross and follow You. I may not have been here in this place before, but there are no surprises for You. I cannot grow if I do not risk anything. I am all in. I will serve when You call me to serve. I love You, Lord, my service is a form of worship. I can do no less, for You gave it all for me. Thank you, Jesus! Amen.

GENEROUS GOD

This most generous God who gives seed to the farmer that becomes bread for your meals is more than extravagant with you. He gives you something you can then give away, which grows into full-formed lives, robust in God, wealthy in every way, so that you can be generous in every way, producing with us great praise to God. (2 Corinthians 9:10–11 MSG)

Our generation has grown away from the concepts of sowing and reaping. These cultivating terms talk about what is planted into the ground then grows so that it can be harvested. In Leviticus, there were laws put into place for giving portions of what you grew, earned, or possessed. This portion or tithe was then given to the priests and the poor. It was a concept put into place by God to do two things: first, be a reminder that God was the provider of everything we have; and, second, provide for those called by God into ministry and also support the poor.

When we refuse to be obedient to God in giving back what He has provided for us in our lives, we essentially close the door to other blessings He has for us. The Word tells us that without faith it is impossible to please God (Hebrews 11:16). If you are holding onto everything you have tightly with a closed fist—you are demonstrating your lack of faith in your Heavenly Father. Tithing is the one area that God calls us to put Him to the test, because He wants an opportunity to show you His generous nature (Malachi 3:10). Tithing is money given directly to the church in which you attend or have membership.

Anything else you support in your church community is extra and not to be subtracted from your tithe. Many churches struggle because if the leadership has an outreach of some kind, many members take their tithe money and shift it to support the outreach, leaving the church short of funds to pay its basic operation.

So many people in the church get uptight when the pastor talks about tithing, but he is being obedient to the Lord. The pastor is responsible for teaching the children of God to trust in His ability to provide for their daily lives. If he never talks about tithing or the principle of sowing and reaping, how will we understand or grow in our faith? Early in my Christian years, I didn't tithe. Those years were filled with financial hardship and struggles. God didn't punish me. I didn't demonstrate my trust or faith in Him with what I had and, unfortunately, I sealed the doors to the heavenly storehouses that could have been open to me. The minute I began to tithe, I had more than enough for everything I needed. God has always come through for me. He wants to show all of His children His generous nature. His extravagant love for us will then shine like a beacon to those who desperately need hope. It all serves the same purpose: glorify God and reach those souls who are lost. Will you sow what has been so generously given to you or will you hold onto it tightly? Don't close the doors to God's outpouring of provision in your life.

BRINGING HIM YOUR BEST

We will show mercy to the poor and not miss an opportunity to do acts of kindness for others, for these are the true sacrifices that delight God's heart. (Hebrews 13:16 TPT)

Two years ago, when we stood and looked at the damage to our home after a house fire, we could have been consumed by the loss and the devastation to the home that we had just recently purchased. Instead, we felt strengthened and encouraged by the acts of kindness poured over us by our church family. One family opened their home to us for that first week as we made arrangements to move into some sort of rental property. They fed us and washed our clothes and just were so wonderful. Other kindnesses were in items we would need such as toiletries and kitchen items. Still others were monetary gifts. God used all these hands to support us and to demonstrate His love. The prayers and words of encouragement from our brothers and sisters in Christ were always timely. We knew that God was working for our good.

We are called to take the love and all the provision God has given us and make it available to those who are in need. It is in these times that we truly reflect the compassion of Christ. If we say we are following in His footsteps, are we not to embody His very nature? Are we not called to the same level of sacrifice—the ability to lay oneself down for another? To give of our resources, our time, our gifts? These are the things that make a difference in the lives of those we come in contact with and the things that make our Father's heart full.

This morning, as I read this scripture, I am challenged yet again to examine myself and make sure that I am looking to be used by God to bless others. To pour myself out as an offering. To not hold tightly to all that God has given me, but to open my hand. Allowing others to see that, as a follower of Christ, compassion is essential and, combined with love, it should be the primary force that flows toward all others. The Word says, "Freely, I give to you." Christ freely gave everything He had—even His life was given as an offering for you. As disciples we are called to do the same for others. Ask God to reveal to you who might need you today. There is such great need in this world. We are the embodiment of His light. Shine brightly and break through the darkness in someone else's life.

Thank you, Lord. Your Word is good and more and more is revealed to me every day. Keep bringing Your knowledge to me again and again, so that I will be reminded of what You desire to see in my life. Help me bear fruit and to be poured out in a way that glorifies Your name. You have blessed me so much, how could I not share the wonder of who You are and pour that compassion and loving-kindness back into others? Show me who needs You today. Amen.

GROWING AND ENCOURAGING

For you can all prophesy in turn and in an environment where all present can be instructed, encouraged, and strengthened. (1 Corinthians 14:31 TPT)

Years ago, during a church service with a guest speaker, a prophetic word was spoken over me. This man I had never met before during a time of praying for many members of our church congregation took my hands and stated, "These hands are the healing hands of the Lord. You will use these hands to heal many." This person had no way of knowing that I worked in a hospital. I was dressed in street clothes and did not have any identification on my person during this service. It was a word from the Holy Spirit, encouraging me in my calling and in my profession.

Just recently, our pastor taught on the gift of prophecy. It is strange how we can have this grandiose idea about the things of God, but God wants to make His gifts and resources available to all of us. He really keeps it simple for us, but we tend to make things so complicated. My pastor explained that in its basic form, prophecy is a supernatural word to provide encouragement and instruction, and is shared in love. It can be direct to one person or it can be spoken to a multitude. Think about this: The next time you tell someone that they are precious and loved by a God who gave everything to rescue them from an eternal death, you have prophesied to that person.

We all need this gift, because it is a source for each one of us to build up the other members of our body. Just the other morning, I sent a quick word of encouragement to my brother. He stated, "How awesome that God knew I needed to be encouraged today!" God has equipped us to operate in the anointing to strengthen one another so that we may be filled with His Spirit and show the world His glory. If you are uncertain about the gifts of the Holy Spirit, read chapter 14 of 1 Corinthians and talk to someone you know who understands these gifts: a pastor or other church members.

Thank you, Lord, for the gift of prophecy. For a new understanding that it is a gift that all have access to and can use to strengthen one another. It doesn't need to contain revelation or a word of wisdom, but can just be a timely word given in love to encourage my sisters and brothers. I love how You supplied everything we would need to stay connected and grow in You. Thank you for revealing more to us every day. The way You prepare us for this journey is so beautiful. I give You glory and praise! Amen.

GOD'S WAY ENDURES

I know that whatever God does, it endures forever; nothing can be added to it nor anything taken from it. And God does it so that men will [reverently] fear Him [revere and worship Him, knowing that He is]. (Ecclesiastes 3:14 AMPC)

Since Creation, when God spoke and formed heaven and earth and then created day and night, the sun has been rising and setting. Generations upon generations of men, women, and children have watched the sun rise and set in awe and wonder. They have watched the shifting of seasons: spring, summer, fall, and winter. Each season with its own type of beauty. God's creation displays the artistry of His hands. Magnificent and powerful. There isn't a detail that He didn't see or take into account.

Maybe you are in place where it is difficult to see God's handiwork around you. You see the chaos of the world, clothed in darkness and sin, and you are wondering where God is. First, understand that man is responsible for the brokenness of this world. We allowed sin to separate us from God, and we have an enemy that continues to try to separate each of us from God every single day. The darkness that you see around you has always been a part of this world, because we are meant for different world—an eternal place filled with the light and glory of our God and Father. We first have to reconcile ourselves to our God and Father. Recognize our sinful nature and surrender it to Him through the grace and gift of salvation bought by Jesus Christ. His plan for you is to spend eternity with Him. That was His plan when He created man and woman and set them in the Garden of Eden. It is still His plan today. Whatever He does will endure. His plans for His children are good. He will call us all home to a place where there will be no more sorrow or pain. Fear will flee, because it cannot be in a place so overflowing with love. They cannot coexist together. We will be filled with awe and wonder. There will be rejoicing and worship of the King of kings and Lord of lords. Every knee will bow in reverence. Not because He needs our worship, but because we were created for worship and for a relationship with Him. He is our very breath of life. In joyful adoration, we will exalt the One who made all things.

He is working out His plan for His children even today. If you struggle with what you see around you, remember that this is not your home. We gave it away to Satan; therefore, God promised to bring a new heaven and earth to His children. The corrupted world will pass away and the incorruptible world will be made available to all who believe in the Lamb. He will endure—yesterday, today, and forevermore!

HE KNOWS YOUR PAIN

Then one of the twelve, called Judas Iscariot, went to the chief priests and said, "What are you willing to give me if I deliver Him to you?" And they counted out to him thirty pieces of silver. So from that time he sought opportunity to betray Him. (Matthew 26:14–16 NKJV)

There are very few of us who live this life that will not experience being hurt or being the cause of hurt to another person. We acquire wounds and scars as we build relationships that sometimes do not last the test of time or from our own selfishness. We need to be careful that our pain does not linger long enough to turn into bitterness. We have a God who understands our pain and wants to provide us with freedom and healing.

I remember a time in my life where my pain was more familiar than anything else. I wore it like a blanket, wrapped tightly around myself. Holding onto it meant I didn't have to risk anything. It meant I could walk through each day knowing that I wouldn't have room for anything else—not joy, not peace, not hope, not love. Pain had filled my bucket to overflowing. I can't remember exactly how God reached me in those days. I know I didn't look for Him. I was too busy nurturing my own thoughts, my own emotions, but I have a God who doesn't run away when I am at my worst. I was thinking back on that experience and recalling how one of my many thoughts was that no one understood my pain. But I was so wrong. Jesus understands. He was betrayed. He was wrongly accused. He was made fun of. He was stripped. He was beaten. He was spat upon and shouted at by the crowd. He was abandoned by his closest friends. He was called a liar. He had nails pierce his hands and feet. He was hung on a cross. He felt alone. He gave the ultimate sacrifice. He died on that cross. He did it for you and for me. That we would understand that we are so very loved. That we are valued. That we do not have to be captive to anything in this world. That we can lay down our pain at the feet of Jesus and He will carry it for us. In turn, He will pour out supernatural peace, hope, love, and joy.

There came a time in my life where I desired to let go of the pain—to cast it off and break free from it. I wanted more for my life. I wanted freedom from the things in this world that keep us tangled up in the pit of despair, disappointment, and bitterness. I let go of those things and received the promises of the Father. Love, forgiveness, peace, joy, a sound mind, and grace upon grace. God moved me from darkness to light. He wants to do the same thing for each of you. He knows your pain; He understands how you got to this place, but He wants to set you free. Put it down. Let it go. Let God into your heart and He will begin to be the medicine that you need. He loves us so much and wants us to be free from our sorrows and our pain. He gave it all for us so that we would see He has such love for us and an understanding of all that we face. Jesus conquered it all for your freedom. Now, be free!

KNOWLEDGE IN KNOWING HIM

Skilled living gets its start in the Fear-of-God, insight into life from knowing a Holy God. It's through me, Lady Wisdom, that your life deepens, and the years of your life ripen. Live wisely and wisdom will permeate your life; mock life and life will mock you. (Proverbs 9:10–12 MSG)

Imagine being on the ocean in a boat. You are standing at the helm, guiding the ship toward your destination. Suddenly, someone else walks up and places their hands on the wheel and begins to steer the ship in the opposite direction. You struggle against the one that is guiding the ship in the opposite direction. In this scenario, God is attempting to turn you where He wants you to go, but you are not relinquishing control. You are not yielding to His knowledge and understanding of the larger picture you cannot see, and you are not trusting in Him to guide you. You are trying to control the outcome, but you do not have the knowledge of the landscape and you will end up adrift.

Perhaps I have mentioned it before, but I am not necessarily a great fan of change. I don't like surprises in my day. I oftentimes plan, even overplanning things, in an attempt to have order and control in my day. It isn't necessarily just organization, but an attempt to direct the events in my everyday life. Lately, I have become more aware that as I do this, I close the door to opportunities that God may have in the day-to-day events of my life. When I get upset at the delays or the sudden switches in my schedule at work, I am missing opportunities to see what God could be orchestrating in my day.

It edges in slowly, the subtle need to control the events of the day, but it means that I am not checking in with God about the details. God is not just in the big life events over the course of our lives, but in the day-to-day. He wants to meet us in the moment by moment sequences throughout our day. It is something that we have to practice, changing our habits to check in with Him frequently in our days and ask for guidance and grow in our trust. I have to surrender the need to control everything and turn my life over to God, each and every day. If I want a full life, an abundant life, I need to surrender it to the One who can fill it with supernatural power through His spirit. I have to recognize that I don't have all the answers, and by looking for God's wisdom, I cannot be led in the wrong direction. His word says that whoever asks for wisdom will receive it (James 1:5–6). That knowledge comes from knowing God. Spending time with Him, and having Him examine you and provide correction. He reveals ways that we are holding back and, in turn, blocking the blessings He wants to pour out in our lives.

God, I surrender control again. Forgive me for not recognizing sooner the ways I put up barriers to Your guiding hand. I welcome the Holy Spirit and the wisdom that comes. Keep my spirit in alignment with Your ways and not my need to have organization and order. That is the beginning of fear and not of faith. I love how You guide and teach me. You are so faithful to show me things I need to let go of in this life to receive all You have purposed for me. I love You. All thanks and praise are Yours alone. Amen.

A GOD WHO DWELLS WITH HIS PEOPLE

Behold, the virgin shall become pregnant and give birth to a Son, and they shall call His name Emmanuel—which, when translated, means, God with us. (Matthew 1:23 AMPC)

Have you ever thought about the emphasis God places in names? There are instances that He changes the names of people in the Bible, to signify the change in them, as they became His people. He did this with Abram and Sarai, who became Abraham and Sarah (Genesis 17:5). In the New Testament, God changes Saul's name to Paul after He accepts who Jesus Christ is and becomes a disciple (Acts 9:17–18).

It was no accident that God determined that Jesus Christ would be called Immanuel. He wanted us to see that He was making a way to dwell with us. He is a God who wants to live wholly connected to us. Not just be viewed as a distant God, but a God endued with power but also full of love. A God that wants to dwell in and through His people. A God that recognized that a building to house His Holy Presence was not enough. That each one of us would need a direct connection with Him in order to have eternal life. Yeshua, the Hebrew name for Jesus, is defined as "the Lord of Salvation." He came to live among us and to provide salvation for each of us. He did it so that not one of us would have to walk alone in this world. To have the promise of eternal life. At the beginning of time, God created us to live with Him forever, and our sin is what separated us from Him. He made a way with a divine gift, from Himself, to return us to a place of everlasting life.

Take time to investigate all the names of God listed in the Bible. They are a beautiful illustration of His Divine nature. One of my favorites will forever be Immanuel—"God with Us."

Thank you, Lord, for coming to rescue us. We needed You and You made a way. We divided ourselves from You through sin, but You found a way to call us home. Not only to live among us, but to live inside us through the power of Your Spirit. It is the most precious gift we could ever receive. It is an everlasting gift. One that we will celebrate and rejoice over for all eternity. I praise you, Immanuel, the God who came to dwell with His people and who came to dwell inside each of our spirits—to connect us together. I declare that Your Spirit dwells in each of Your sons and daughters richly, that they may each recognize the power of the anointing and walk according to Your plan. That all may see Your glorious nature and run to the foot of the cross. For there is one way to eternal salvation—through Yeshua, Jesus, the Lord of Salvation. Amen and amen.

www.ingramcontent.com/pod-product-compliance
Lightning Source LLC
Chambersburg PA
CBHW020937230426
43666CB00005B/63